Policing
and
Human Rights

·················

Policing
and
Human Rights

Compiled by

F Nel

J Bezuidenhout

Juta and Co, Ltd

First published 1995
Second edition 1997

© Juta & Co. Ltd.
P O Box 14373, Kenwyn 7790

ISBN 0 7021 3905 X

Cover design: The Cooperative Workshop, Cape Town
Editing: Carol Balchin, Cape Town
Book design and typesetting: C Bate, Cape Town
Printed and bound in the Republic of South Africa by
Creda Press, Eliot Avenue, Eppindust II

Foreword

SOUTH AFRICA has the newest and probably the best Bill of Rights in the world. However good it may be, it will not be of any real or lasting benefit to our people unless its aspirations are translated into a way of life. In other words, for the first time in South Africa, we have to develop a human rights culture.

The Bill of Rights relates primarily, but not exclusively, to the relationship between the state and its citizens. It is in that area that the South African Police Service has a vital role to play — a role that is consistent with respect for the rights enshrined in the Constitution and no less with the need to ensure that all citizens are able to live their lives in safety and with security.

During the apartheid era, the old South African Police were in the front line of the enforcement of many criminal laws which were devoid of morality and founded on the underlying policy of racial discrimination and the oppression of the majority of the people. Those policemen and women were seen by the majority as being the least friendly arm of the state. That perception resulted in the very negative mutual relationship between the police and the people — one of mutual fear and often hate.

In societies where human rights are constitutionally protected, the relationship between the police and the citizenry can more easily be one of cooperation and support. There is a huge burden on the SAPS having regard to the high rate of criminal violence in many parts of the country. It is crucial for our future that this unacceptable state of affairs be corrected without encroaching upon, let alone sacrificing the very heart of the Constitution — the Bill of Rights. In turn, that can only be achieved if every policeman and policewoman not only knows but also understands and appreciates what those rights are and how they relate to law enforcement.

This second edition of *Policing and Human Rights* is particularly welcome and reflects the commitment of Technikon South Africa to ensuring that our society becomes a healthy one in which the police can enjoy the trust and earn the respect and appreciation of all of our people.

Richard J. Goldstone
Justice of the Constitutional Court of South Africa

Editors and compilers

Francisca Nel
BLC(Pret) LLB(RAU)
Advocate of the Supreme Court of South Africa
Deputy Chief Lecturer, Technikon SA

Jan Bezuidenhout
LLB LLM(RAU)

Contributors

J Neveling
BA LLB H.Dip Human Rights LLM
Advocate of the Supreme Court of South Africa

JH Bezuidenhout
LLB LLM

GO Hollamby
LLB MBA
South African Law Commission

FJ Viljoen
LLB LLM
University of Pretoria

P Mtshaulane
Meester in de Rechten (Vrije Universiteit Amsterdam)
Advocate of the Supreme Court of South Africa

D Bouwer
BProc LLB LLM DIP IR(DMS) DPIR(SBL: Unisa) NAD(RAU)
South African Police Service

R Krige
LLB
College of Justice

DM Clark
LLB LLM
South African Police Service

HC Lötz
BIuris BProc
South African Police Service

J Koekemoer
BLC LLB
South African Police Service

L Johannessen
CAND.JUR (Copenhagen)
Centre for Applied Legal Studies
University of the Witwatersrand

T Cohen
BA LLB
Centre for Applied Legal Studies
University of the Witwatersrand

BJ King
Dip Iuris BProc
College of Justice

T Geldenhuys
BA(Law) LLB LLD
South African Police Service

HR Snyman
DLitt et Phil (Criminology)
University of South Africa

E Raubenheimer
BLC LLB
South African Police Service

E Venter
BA(Law) LLB LLM
South African Police Service

M Pansegrouw
BIuris LLB LLM
South African Police Service

C van Riet
BA BLC LLB
Lawyers for Human Rights

MR Rwelamira
LLB (Hons) (Dor) LLM J.S.D. (YALE)
University of the Western Cape

DJ Titus
BA LLB Drs. Juris (Leiden) LLD (Leiden)
Technikon SA

Contents

Chapter 1
A Historical Overview of Human Rights

Danfred Titus

SUMMARY

*A*LTHOUGH the term *human rights* is in effect only two centuries old, it is founded on concepts of law and justice dating from much earlier times. An overview of natural law, the Renaissance, the Reformation, the Glorious Revolution, the American Revolution and the French Revolution is therefore provided. A few precursors of the Universal Declaration of Human Rights — the fundamental international statement of the inalienable and inviolable rights of all members of the human family — are discussed, namely the Magna Carta, the Habeas Corpus Act of 1679 and the Enlightenment. Brief reference is also made to non-Western developments. On a national level, the gradual process leading to the recognition of human rights in South Africa is traced, culminating in the adoption of the 1993 and 1996 Constitutions.

1.1   INTRODUCTION

When examining the historical background to the development of human rights, it must be borne in mind that, although it was Western civilisation which first gave expression to the concept, the idea of human dignity is deeply rooted in practically all civilisations. Human rights are therefore not necessarily of Western origin. It is interesting to note that the term *human rights* does not appear in the Bible and neither does the idea of the autonomy of the individual. However, it would be difficult to deny the existence of these concepts in the biblical or Christian context.

In this chapter a broad outline of the background to the development of a human rights culture is given. The focus is on the Universal Declaration of Human Rights (UDHR) of 1948 and on the developments leading up to and following this Declaration.

The main theme of this chapter is how the concept of human rights has evolved through struggle. The first period of development is characterised by the struggles of particular sections of society, for example the barons under the Magna Carta, the guilds of the Middle Ages, the intellectuals of the Renaissance. The human rights that were subsequently recognised related only to these particular sections of society. Nevertheless, they are regarded as decisive milestones in the broader development of human rights for all. This process reached its climax in the UDHR of 1948, in which it is stated in articles 1 and 2:

> "All human beings are born free and equal in dignity and rights.
> "Everyone is entitled to all the rights and freedoms set forth in this Declaration, without distinction of any kind, such as race, colour, sex, language, religion, political or other opinion, national or social origin, property, birth or other status."

In tracing the events leading up to the UDHR, attention is given to natural law and human rights, the emancipatory processes of the Renaissance and the Reformation, political and social revolutions, particular precursors of the UDHR, and brief reference is also made to non-Western developments.

This outline does not follow a linear, chronological pattern: it attempts to explain developments at various levels in broad terms and does not cover overlapping periods.

1.2   KEY OBJECTIVES

The key objectives of this chapter are to enable students to discuss:
- the period leading up to the Universal Declaration of Human Rights;
- classical theories, Christian conceptions and modern theories of human rights;
- the Renaissance, the Reformation and three revolutions as historical moments in human rights development;
- the following precursors of the Universal Declaration of Human Rights: the Magna Carta of 1215; the Habeas Corpus Act of 1679; the Enlightenment;
- non-Western developments in the recognition of human rights;
- the periods following the adoption of the Universal Declaration of Human Rights;
- the recognition of human rights in South Africa.

1.3   HUMAN RIGHTS INSTRUMENTS

The Universal Declaration of Human Rights, 1948

The International Covenant on Economic, Social and Cultural Rights, 1966

The International Covenant on Civil and Political Rights, 1966

The International Covenant on the Elimination of All Forms of Racial Discrimination, 1965

The Convention on the Elimination of All Forms of Discrimination Against Women, 1979

The Convention Against Torture and Other Cruel, Inhuman or Degrading Treatment or Punishment, 1984

The Convention on the Rights of the Child, 1989

1.4   INTERPRETATION AND DISCUSSION

1.4.1   The period leading up to the Universal Declaration of Human Rights

The term *human rights* is in effect only two centuries old, that is, it dates from the time of the American freedom struggle and the French Revolution. This period thus also provides the historical background to the UDHR. However, earlier historical developments also gave rise to important concepts of law and justice which have formed the basis of human rights. Although there are no direct links between these developments and the universal recognition of human rights in 1948, a study of these earlier periods will provide a much broader historical background.

Human rights are those rights which human beings are perceived to have by virtue of their humanity and inherent dignity, and not by virtue of human laws or customs. Human rights may be regarded as a method of attaining the aim of human dignity.

In the more powerful early civilisations we find a long-established pattern of strong hierarchical relationships where secular as well as religious leaders determined what was good for their subjects. Instead of rights being generally applicable to all people, favours and privileges were granted by the emperor or priest, who not only determined their content and to whom they were to be extended but who also had the power unilaterally to withdraw any favours which he had previously granted. The same is true of the city states of the Middle Ages. In the latter, the privileges granted were in effect nothing more than counter-performances for allegiances to a feudal lord. These "rights" could also be obtained through the necessary payments.

In contradistinction to the positivist approach ("the law is the law") is the natural law approach. The basic premise of this approach is that there are permanent characteristics of human nature that can serve as a standard for evaluating conduct and civil laws.

1.4.1.1   Natural law and human rights

Natural law is regarded as fundamentally unchanging and universally applicable. However, the term *natural* can also be ambiguous and can lead to varied interpretations. One aspect of natural law which has been universally accepted is that it is an ideal to which humanity aspires and that it generally concerns the way human beings usually act. As indicated above, natural law can be contrasted with positive law, the enactments of civil society.

(a)   Classical theories

It appears that ancient Greek philosophy was the first to articulate a natural law doctrine.

- *Heraclitus* spoke in the sixth century BC of a common wisdom that pervades the whole universe, "for all human laws are nourished by one, the divine".
- *Aristotle* spoke of the rule of justice that is natural, has the same validity everywhere, and does not depend on our accepting or rejecting it.
- However, it was the *Stoics* who, in the third century BC, introduced a systematic theory of natural law that resembles human rights. Here the approach was that all men are equal in principle, and that man is quite capable of discovering what true justice is.
- The Roman emperor, *Marcus Aurelius*, was strongly influenced by the Stoics. He formulated the revolutionary idea of one state with one law for all people and with equal rights and freedoms for all citizens. Although this

ideal never materialised in the Roman Empire, we can observe some traces of it in early Roman legislation, for example the fact that women and slaves were granted certain rights which they had been denied in the past.

- In the first century BC the orator *Cicero* gave a famous definition of natural law in his *De Republica*: "True law is right reason in agreement with Nature; it is of universal application, unchanging and everlasting; it summons to duty by its commands, and averts from wrongdoing by its prohibitions ... There will not be different laws at Rome and at Athens, or different laws now and in the future, but one eternal and unchangeable law will be valid for all nations and for all times."
- The *Corpus Iuris Civilis,* codified Roman legal material, also refers to a natural law, the *ius naturale*. However, there is no indication that natural law was regarded as superior to positive law.

(b) Christian conceptions

Christians could quite easily reconcile the natural law doctrine of the Stoics with their beliefs.

- *St Paul* spoke of Gentiles who did not have the Mosaic law "doing by nature what the law requires" (Romans 2:14).
- The sixth century Spanish theologian *St Isidore of Seville* affirmed that natural law is observed everywhere by natural instinct; he cited as illustrations the laws ordaining marriage and the procreation of children.
- *St Thomas Aquinas* in his *Summa Theologica* (Summary Treatise of Theology) calls the rational guidance of creation by God the "Eternal Law".

(c) Modern theories

The Dutch jurist *Hugo Grotius* is regarded as the founder of the modern theory of natural law. He supported the traditional definition of natural law as that body of rules which can be discovered by the use of reason. Furthermore, he posed the hypothetical argument that this law would have validity even if there were no God or if the affairs of human beings were of no concern to God. In this way Grotius moved away from theological presuppositions and paved the way for the purely rationalistic theories of the seventeenth and eighteenth centuries.

- The German jurist *Samuel von Pufendorf* (1632–94), the first to hold a chair of natural law in a German university, developed the concept of a law of nature more fully.
- The seventeenth century English philosophers *Thomas Hobbes* and *John Locke* proposed an original state of nature from which a social contract arose and combined this theory with that of natural law. We see today how Locke's doctrine that nature has endowed human beings with certain inalienable rights which cannot be violated by any governing authority is reflected in the American Declaration of Independence and in subsequent declarations.

In the nineteenth century a much more critical approach to natural law was adopted. "How do you prove natural law?" people asked. The existence of a natural law was generally regarded as unprovable. Natural law then came to be replaced in legal theory by utilitarianism, as formulated by the English philosopher *Jeremy Bentham*. This related to "the greatest happiness of the greatest number", maximum pleasure and minimum pain. Legal positivism then became the most dominant doctrine replacing natural law. The English jurist *John Austin* (1790–1859) popularised basing the law simply on the "command of the ruler".

While legal positivism remains highly relevant today, it was the atrocities committed by *Nazi Germany* during World War II that revived interest in a higher standard than positive law. The United Nations in its Charter and Universal Declaration of Human Rights began to prepare the way for a universal standard for human rights.

1.4.1.2 The Renaissance, the Reformation and three revolutions

While the above outline of the development of the natural law doctrine provides us with a broad, historical overview of the various schools of thought which evolved, it is also important to examine the influence of certain historical events on the development of a human rights culture. We will therefore focus on the Renaissance, the Reformation and three revolutions which played a significant role in the eventual recognition of human rights for all.

A very important basis for the rise of human rights was laid during the emancipatory processes of the *late Middle Ages*. These processes had a profound influence on the histories of Europe and America. Two of the most influential movements were the *Renaissance* and the *Reformation*.

The *Renaissance* was a liberation process of massive proportions which placed strong emphasis on the creative capacity of man and on liberation from the whole system of oppressive ethical and religious bonds. Nevertheless, once again only a privileged few benefited from this process, even though they did in fact make important contributions to civilisation.

The *Reformation* constituted its own liberation movement in the sphere of church and religion. Although this is viewed today as a natural phase in church history, it was for a long period nothing but a resistance movement against the authority of the Roman Catholic Church.

The most profound influence on human rights thinking, however, derived from the great political and social revolutions of the eighteenth, nineteenth and early the twentieth centuries. Each successive revolution provided material which formed the basis of later human rights texts. These early beginnings laid the foundation for the growth of the concept of universally applicable human rights — rights no longer accorded only to a particular social or religious group, but to all people, everywhere, and at all times.

The three revolutions of particular importance were briefly the following.

- The *Glorious Revolution* of seventeenth century England. This was the culmination of several hundred years of judicial and legislative restraints which had been gradually imposed upon the monarchy. In 1689 the English Parliament adopted the Bill of Rights, and thereby established representative government in England.
- The *American Revolution* of 1776. Through the Declaration of Independence, the American revolutionists successfully achieved independence from a European colonial power, England, mirroring centuries of struggle for freedom in England. The second great charter of liberty to issue from the American Revolution was the US Constitution. In its first ten amendments, known as the Bill of Rights, the Constitution established guarantees of civil rights.
- The *French Revolution* of 1789. This revolution destroyed the feudal system in France and established representative government. Once again, we see a particular grouping of people taking the initiative to formulate their own rights — but for the first time in history, not just a small elite, but an overwhelming majority. From the well-known revolutionary triad of liberty, equality and fraternity, key concepts concerning freedom, property and security were formulated almost simultaneously.

1.4.1.3   Precursors of the Universal Declaration of Human Rights

The UDHR is the international embodiment of human rights and is regarded as a "common standard of achievement" for the nations of the world. This is the document that became the face of human rights in the world. However, our historical puzzle will be totally incomplete if we do not highlight some of the national developments that also paved the way.

(a)   The Magna Carta of 1215

Generally speaking, the Magna Carta is regarded as the oldest agreement linked to the Universal Declaration of Human Rights. As indicated above, during the Middle Ages various social groups sought to wrest certain privileges from the sovereigns in their struggle to gain power.

It was this kind of struggle that resulted in the signing of the Magna Carta, which was imposed in the thirteenth century upon John, King of England, by a group of barons. King John was under severe financial and political pressures to compensate for the heavy tax burden which he imposed upon the barons, he had to grant them certain rights and privileges. For example, none of them could be arrested without trial. However, while the document is considered to be of great significance in the progress towards human liberty, it must be noted that it did not apply to all citizens: it was an agreement between the king and the English nobility only.

(b)   The Habeas Corpus Act of 1679

It was only in 1679, when the Habeas Corpus Act was passed by the English

Parliament, that ordinary citizens were granted access to similar rights. *Habeas corpus* is a Latin phrase meaning "you may have the body". In legal terms it means a writ or order issued by a court to a person having custody of another, commanding him or her to produce the detained person in order to determine the legality of the detention. The original purpose was to liberate illegally detained persons, and it is still a protection against arbitrary imprisonment. The writ became a powerful weapon in protecting the liberty of the monarch's subjects.

It is interesting to note that the extension of these kinds of rights to ordinary citizens and not just to a particular sector of society occurred a century earlier in the Netherlands. In 1579, in terms of the *Unie van Utrecht,* all citizens of the new *Statenbond* were granted freedom of religion.

(c) The Enlightenment

In the progress towards equal rights the recognition of man's innate abilities played a very important role. The period of the Enlightenment (extending over a large part of the seventeenth and eighteenth centuries) highlighted the independence of man, philosophers such Voltaire and Kant being prominent in this regard. Liberty — a right to act without interference from any source — was defined as a natural right of man. However, voluntary submission to the necessary limitations was required in order that the benefits of organised social existence might be enjoyed. They challenged the theory of the divine right of kings to rule. The new thinking was that the source of all governmental power should be the people, and that tyranny began when the natural rights of men were violated.

These were the ideas that moulded the thinking of the leaders of the French Revolution and led to the Declaration of the Rights of Man and of the Citizen in 1789.

1.4.1.4 Other non-Western developments

The historical background outlined above generally reflects the development of Western democracies. While it is not disputed that Western democracies have indeed made invaluable contributions to the establishment of a human rights culture, the charge from other nations is that human rights still appears to be the domain of Western imperialism. In the South African context we recall a similar charge in the mid-eighties that the interest by white South Africans in a Bill of Rights amounted to little more than interest in a Bill for Whites.

The contribution made by the various world religions to the field of human rights is currently very much under discussion. Christian leaders recently admitted that Christians cannot really be proud of their involvement in the struggle for justice. The Christian contribution to the struggle for human rights has involved only a small minority.

From the newly formed United States of America the clarion call rang out that all men were born equal and were endowed by their Creator with certain inalienable rights, such as the right to life, to freedom and to strive for happiness. This provided the basis for the constitutions of many other countries after their liberation from colonial powers. Quite interesting is the fact that Vietnam used the same words in the preamble to its declaration of independence in 1945.

A freedom struggle of a different kind — the Russian Revolution of 1917 — led to a fundamental reorientation of human relations. The 1917 *Declaration of the Rights of the Workers and of the Exploited Masses*, laid the foundation for the first constitution of this new form of state. In contrast with the West with its focus on individual rights, the emphasis here was on collective rights, based on the ideas of Karl Marx. There was therefore less emphasis on civil and political rights and much more on social and economic relations. To Marx, the individual human rights of the West were nothing but glorified egotism. According to him, such rights secure private property and personal opinion but, at the same time, they turn human beings into competitors, thus impeding their social interaction.

The Russian Revolution of 1917 therefore offered a challenge to the traditional concepts of liberty. The Soviet state, which was based on Marxist theory, held that all previous codes of liberty were ideologies of the ruling classes or of classes aspiring to power, and thus did not benefit the vast majority of the population. True liberty was possible only through the elimination of class exploitation.

It is beyond the scope of this chapter to address adequately the contributions of all civilisations to human rights. It is clear, however, that the contributions made by other civilisations, societies and religions, for example Chinese, Japanese, Islamic, African, Latin American, etc to a common humanity cannot be excluded in a proper evaluation of the human rights and human dignity culture.

Our discussion thus far has highlighted the gradual progression through the ages from the granting of rights to a few privileged sections of society to general rights for all. However, at this stage even in its best form universal human rights had not yet been attained. The following shortcomings were still apparent:

- a slave could not lay claim to any of the acquired freedoms;
- Western democracies applied different standards for their own citizens and they did for the population of their respective colonies or overseas territories;
- these highly valued ideals of freedom were not enough to stop the two ensuing world wars.

It was only after the two world wars that the need for universal human rights was awakened. The immediate concern about impending worldwide destruction was a powerful influence. In this context it was President Roosevelt of the United States who gave international human rights an important impetus. A new set of rules was needed for the international community to promote and protect human rights in the world. In his classic address before the American Congress in 1941, Roosevelt delivered his "Four Freedoms Speech":

- freedom of opinion and expression;
- freedom of conscience and religion;
- freedom from want;
- freedom from fear.

It was this speech that provided the backdrop to the architects of the United Nations Organisation in 1945. In the United Nations Charter of 1945 clear reference is made to human rights both in its preamble and in a number of its articles. One of the first decisions of the UN was to establish a Human Rights Commission.

1.4.2 The Universal Declaration of Human Rights

This declaration was accepted by the UN on 10 December 1948 and is regarded as the fundamental international statement of the inalienable and inviolable rights of all members of the human family. As stated above, it is intended to serve as "a common standard of achievement for all peoples and nations" in the effort to secure universal and effective recognition and observance of all the rights and freedoms which it encompasses.

When these rights and freedoms are examined, the profound influence of liberal Western thought is clear. The authors did, however, endeavour to combine the individual civil and political rights with the more collective social and economic rights.

Being only a declaration it still had to be given legal teeth. It took eighteen years of deadlock between the then Eastern and Western blocs to finally come up with the two sister covenants of 1966, namely the International Covenant on Civil and Political Rights and the International Covenant on Economic, Social and Cultural Rights.

These developments were subsequently termed the International Bill of Rights, with the following components:

- the Universal Declaration of Human Rights (UDHR) of 1948;
- the International Covenant on Economic, Social and Cultural Rights (ICESCR) of 1996;
- the International Covenant on Civil and Political Rights (ICCPR) of 1966; and
- the First Optional Protocol to the latter covenant.

It is important to note that human rights were now placed within the orbit of internationalism: state parties to the respective international documents incur international obligations to promote and protect the rights in the documents. As an example, article 2(3) of the ICCPR states:

"Each State Party to the present Covenant undertakes:

(a) to ensure that any person whose rights or freedoms as herein recognized are violated shall have an effective remedy, notwithstanding that the violation has been committed by persons acting in an official capacity;

(b) to ensure that any person claiming such remedy shall have his right thereto determined by competent judicial authority provided for by the legal system of the State, and to develop the possibilities of judicial remedy;

(c) to ensure that the competent authorities shall enforce such remedies when granted."

The focus within the United Nations and its respective human rights bodies is on the implementation of these human rights norms. The general approach is twofold:

- the standard-setting phase where the norms and standards are set; and
- the implementation phase where the rights and freedoms are effectively implemented.

With regard to the latter phase, the UN has enacted a range of measures to assist member states with implementation. The broad range of international human rights documents that have developed are:

1 the Universal Declaration of Human Rights of 1948;
2 the International Covenant on Economic, Social and Cultural Rights of 1966;
3 the International Covenant on Civil and Political Rights of 1966;
4 the First Optional Protocol to the ICCPR;
5 the Second Optional Protocol to the ICCPR, aiming at the abolition of the death penalty (1989);
6 the International Covenant on the Elimination of All Forms of Racial Discrimination (1965);
7 the Convention on the Elimination of All Forms of Discrimination Against Women (1979);
8 the Convention against Torture and Other Cruel, Inhuman or Degrading Treatment or Punishment (1984);
9 the Convention on the Rights of the Child (1989).

Many more documents have been issued, particularly at regional (African, European and American) level; however, the above provide a sufficient overview. These instruments operate on the principle that national states cannot be entrusted with the sole responsibility of ensuring the promotion and protection of human rights. States need assistance in this daunting task hence the added protection of international human rights treaties.

It is important to note that South Africa has signed all of the above documents except the two Protocols, and has also ratified the Convention on the Rights of the Child.

1.4.3 Debate on the recognition of human rights in South Africa[1]

The first document in South Africa to contain a list of fundamental rights was the Orange Free State's constitution of 1854. In the hands of an independent judiciary, these rights were enforced in practice. However, during unification in 1910, these rights were not included in the Constitution.

The fact that only whites and a limited number of coloureds had the vote gradually led to dissatisfaction among black South Africans. In 1912 the ANC (called the African National Native Congress at the time) was established to express black resistance.

Under a system of parliamentery sovereignty, parliaments are bound to certain formal requirements (manner and form). The courts have the power to declare invalid any law made without due regard to this prescribed procedure, although a law may not be declared invalid on the basis of its content.

An illustration in the South African constitutional history of the functioning of this kind of system was the removal of the coloured voters from the common voters roll in the 1950s. Franchise for a limited group of coloureds was entrenched in the 1910 Constitution. This meant that the provision securing their franchise could only be amended if a two-thirds majority in a joint sitting of the House of Assembly and the Senate agreed to the amendment.

In 1951 the government proposed a Bill that would effectively deny all coloureds the vote. The Bill was approved by a simple majority (more than 50 per cent) in each of the two houses (House of Assembly and the Senate) separately. Voters who were removed from the common voters roll approached the judiciary for legal aid. In the Harris case,[2] the Appellate Division found that the adoption of the Bill was unconstitutional and therefore invalid. The government then attempted to sidestep the constitutional provision by adopting the High Court of Parliament Act (1952). This Act stipulated that members of the two houses would serve in a superior court and hear appeals against the constitutionality of laws. This Act was also declared unconstitutional and invalid. Thereafter the Senate Act of 1955 was adopted, which changed both the composition and size of the Senate. It was precisely the lack of support among senators that withheld the government from adhering to the constitutional provisions. After the adoption of the Senate Act, government supporters grew from approximately 29 out of 48 to 77 out of 89. The newly composed Senate then achieved a two-thirds majority at a joint sitting in a vote on a Bill which would once again attempt to remove coloureds from the common voters roll.

Aggrieved voters again initiated a judicial review of this latest attempt to disenfranchise them. This time the court of appeal found that the formal requirements had been met, and consequently the law was declared valid. The courts cannot declare any Act invalid on the basis of its content.

The amendments were presented as part of a policy of social transformation and reconstruction, which followed the National Party's victory at the polls in 1948. Various laws were adopted to further the ideology of apartheid: the Group Areas Act, the Population Registration Act, the Separate Amenities Act, and so forth. In terms of the doctrine of parliamentary sovereignty, no court of law could declare these Acts invalid, even though they treated people with the most blatant inequality and unfairness. Black dissatisfaction was expressed in the Defiance Campaign of the 1950s. The government's response to this campaign was to adopt security legislation, such as the Internal Security Act of 1950 and the Riotous Assemblies Act of 1956. By means of amendments to Acts, detention without trial was authorised for 90 and later for 180 days. After the shooting incident at Sharpeville in 1960 a state of emergency was declared.

Against this background of human rights violations, various anti-apartheid movements in South Africa (the Congress movement) sent about 3 000 representatives to the Congress of the People at Kliptown in June 1955. Here they drew up the Freedom Charter. This was the first important human rights document which found support among a large group of South Africans. The Freedom Charter was not a justiciable charter but was more in the line of a political manifesto. Rights or ideals contained in the charter were, among others: "All national groups shall have equal rights! All shall be equal before the law! All shall enjoy equal human rights! There shall be work and security!" Because of the ANC's acceptance (in 1956) of the Charter as official ANC policy, the organisation split in two. The Charterists (ANC) subscribed to the principles contained in the Charter, particularly the part of the preamble stating that "… South Africa belongs to all who live in it". A group opposed to this sentiment, the adherents of black consciousness, held that South Africa belonged to the blacks alone. They broke away from the ANC and formed the PAC (Pan-Africanist Congress).

In 1961 South Africa was proclaimed a republic outside the British Commonwealth. The principles of separate development led to the establishment of "independent" states in the 1970s. The first of these was the Transkei in 1976. This took place in the same year as the Soweto Uprising, which clearly signalled the deep frustration and resistance experienced by black youth in particular against government policy. Limited constitutional reform led to the 1983 Constitution, which established separate houses for coloureds and Indians in Parliament.

The ANC remained true to the Freedom Charter throughout. When the party published its Constitutional Guidelines for a Democratic South Africa in 1988, a justiciable human rights charter formed part of it. Later revisions contained more detailed guidelines.

In the early 1980s the Nationalist Party government was opposed to a charter of human rights. In 1986 the Minister of Justice instructed the Law Commission to draw up a report on group and human rights. The Law Commission's interim report made a strong case for a bill of human rights, clearly stating that protection of human rights, not group rights, should be considered. This finding obviously caught the government unawares.

Soon other voices began to be heard in the call for a bill of human rights. It became a central issue among the supporters of liberalism. The first international congress on human rights in South Africa was held in Cape Town in 1979, and the first conference for the promotion of a bill of human rights was held by Afrikaans academics at the University of Pretoria in 1986. In addition, the KwaZulu/Natal Indaba released its report in 1986. Although their proposals were never implemented, they presented a justiciable human rights document as recommendation.

The Interim Constitution of 1993 was a product of negotiations after the unbanning of the ANC and the release of Nelson Mandela in 1990. After a number of derailments, the negotiation process got underway. The final draft was adopted by the Multi-Party Negotiation Process at Kempton Park. A technical committee was assigned the task of drawing up a chapter on fundamental rights, which was to be included in the Constitution.

The committee had many proposals to consider. All the major parties (ANC, NP, Inkatha, Democratic Party) placed their recommendations on the table. Other recommendations were those by a group of Western Cape academics ("A Charter for Social Justice"). Foreign and African organisations offered further sources.

The technical committee's work was complicated because two opposing interests had to be reconciled. On the one hand the ANC placed a high premium on liberation. People had to be liberated, particularly from the bonds and constraints which poverty and deprivation had brought about. The value this group emphasised was equality. On the other hand there were those (in the NP, DP, business circles) who wanted freedom to take precedence. According to them, the individual should have the freedom to work out his or her own fate unhindered. An ad hoc committee, consisting of politicians, was appointed as mediator to resolve these conflicting views. They were to support the technical committee, which consisted of members of the judiciary.

After numerous proposals, the final list of fundamental rights was included in Chapter 3 of the Constitution (Act 200 of 1993).[3] These rights have now been included in the Bill of Rights contained in the 1996 Constitution. The final Constitution that was adopted earlier by the Constitutional Assembly did not stand the test and was referred back to the Constitutional Assembly. The Constitution still needed to be certified by the Constitutional Court before taking effect. The Constitution was referred back to the Constitutional Assembly to rectify the problems and the amended Constitution was adopted by the Constitutional Assembly on 11 October 1996. The Constitution was finally certified by the Constitutional Court on 4 December 1996. On 10 December 1996, International Human Rights Day, the Constitution was signed by the President of South Africa, Mr Nelson Mandela. The Constitution, Act 108 of 1996, commenced on 4 February 1997.

1.4.4 The 1996 Constitution (Bill of Rights)

From the above outline it is clear that, despite the unique formulations in our Constitution, we have only passed the standard-setting phase. The next crucial challenge is to proceed with implementation. Confusing the two phases will lead to unnecessary frustration and to disillusionment with human rights. It is important to bear in mind our history of human rights violations and to contextualise our situation within the ambit of international developments. By the same token, we must then be clear where we are heading and plan for the future in the context of the international human rights situation.

1.5   SUGGESTED READING AND SOURCES

An-Na'im, Abdullahi A, Gort, Jerald D, Jansen, Henry & Vroom, Hendrik (eds). 1995. *Human Rights and Religious Values — an Uneasy Relationship?* Michigan: Wm B Eerdmans.

Hosten, WJ, Edwards, AB, Nathan, Carman & Bosman, Francis. 1983. *Introduction to South African Law and Legal Theory.* Durban: Butterworths.

Kik, Aad. 1982. *Geloof en Mensenrechten.* Kampen, The Netherlands: JH Kok.

Nel, F & Bezuidenhout, J. 1995. *Human Rights for the Police.* Cape Town: Juta.

Titus, Danfred J. 1993. *The Applicability of International Human Rights Norms to the South African Legal System — With Specific Reference to the Role of the Judiciary.* Doctoral dissertation, Leiden, 1993.

Webb, Pauline (ed). 1994. *A Long Struggle — The Involvement of the World Council of Churches in South Africa.* Geneva: WCC Publications.

. . . .

ENDNOTES

1   Nel, F & Bezuidenhout, J. 1995. *Human Rights for the Police.* Cape Town: Juta 8–11.

2   *Harris v Minister of the Interior* 1952 (2) SA 428 (A).

3   Nel & Bezuidenhout Op cit 8–11.

Chapter 2
South African Constitutional History and Background

Patric Mtshaulana

SUMMARY

*T*HIS chapter traces the constitutional history of South Africa from the time of Union up until today. This history shows an evolution from dominion status to a fully fledged Republic retaining the basic tenets of British constitutionalism. One of the essential characteristics of this system of constitutionalism is the sovereignty of Parliament, in terms of which the will of Parliament may not be tampered with even by the courts. In a country in which the majority were excluded from the political process and were deprived of basic human and individual rights, the untrammelled powers of Parliament enabled the minority to pass laws violating human rights and granted state organs the power to do almost anything to preserve the minority's control over the country. The Interim Constitution of 1993 and the final Constitution of 1996 mark a break with the past — parliamentary sovereignty has been done away with and the supremacy of the Constitution has been upheld.

The chapter also outlines the role of the South African Police Service (SAPS) by tracing the force's organisation and functioning up to 1995 when the new South African Police Service Act [1] was passed. The new Act, unlike its predecessors, is subject to the Constitution and follows the directives laid down by the Constitution. The police as a service also have to operate within the framework of the Constitution. Under the new Constitution the office of Public Protector has been instituted. The Public Protector, whose task it is to protect people against improper conduct and the abuse of power, can play a vital role in the transformation of the Police Service.

2.1   INTRODUCTION

Constitutionally, South Africa came into being for the first time, as one political entity, in 1910 when the South Africa Act was passed. The Act was an ordinary Act of the British Parliament and could be amended or repealed like any other Act of Parliament. The Act sought to unite the various colonies into one entity, governed and run by one government under the British Crown as represented by the Governor General.

The significance of the Union of South Africa Act lay mainly in the fact that it created new constitutional institutions. It did not grant any more powers to the new Parliament than the Parliaments of the old republics and colonies had had. If anything, it was still subordinate to the British Parliament, and any Act of the Union Parliament which was in conflict with a British Act of Parliament was null and void in terms of the Colonial Laws Validity Act of 1865. Furthermore, in terms of the same Act, the British Parliament [2] reserved for itself the power to pass laws which were applicable in the Union. The Union Parliament was subordinate to the British executive. British ministers could at any stage interfere with the legislative process through the advice they gave to the Crown and to the Crown's representative, the Governor General.

In general, the South African Parliament had the power to amend the provisions of the South Africa Act. Only sections 35, 137 and 152 were entrenched, which meant that they could only be amended by a special procedure. It was only through a process of evolution[3] — including the passing of the Statute of Westminster in 1931[4] — that the Union eventually became a sovereign entity independent of the British Crown. That process culminated in the proclamation of the Republic of South Africa in 1961.[5] Despite the declaration of the Republic, South African constitutional law remained anchored in British constitutional conventions. In particular, Parliament remained sovereign and could pass any law it deemed fit. The executive had a powerful role with the State President exercising only ceremonial powers. The constitutional system was based on the active and dominant position of the ruling political party. As a result, the Nationalist Party (which had come to power in 1948) played a dominant role in the political life of South Africa. It was not only the ruling political party but all executive and security organs were dominated by its members or by people who sympathised with the party. Not only were prominent politicians and administrators members of the Nationalist Party but they also had to be members of the powerful Broederbond.

The Union was formed from the former republics and the former British colonies. In the Boer republics of the Transvaal and the Orange Free State, black people were not represented and played no role in politics. In the Cape and Natal, the former British colonies, black people who satisfied certain qualifications were allowed to vote. In the 1908 Convention it was decided as a compromise that the situation would remain as it was, that is, that black people in the former British colonies would continue to have limited voting rights, while those in the former Republics would have no voting rights at all.

African and coloured people, led by Rubusana and Abdurman, tried to persuade the British government not to pass the South Africa Act as long as it discriminated against the blacks in the former Republics. Their efforts were in vain. It was in reaction to this that in 1912 the South African Native Congress was formed to fight for the rights of the African people.

2.2 KEY OBJECTIVES

The key objectives of this chapter are to enable students to:
- understand and discuss South Africa's constitutional history from 1910 up until 1996;
- understand and discuss the origin of the Police Act;
- understand and discuss the place and role of the South African Police Service in the constitutional history;
- discuss the powers and functions of the South African Police Service;
- discuss the role and functions of the Public Protector.

2.3 APPLICABLE LAW

Colonial Validity Act 1865
Constitution 1961

Suppression of Communism Act 44 of 1950
General Law Amendment Act 37 of 1963
Criminal Procedure Act 96 of 1965
Police Act 7 of 1958
Public Protector Act 1994

2.4 INTERPRETATION AND DISCUSSION

2.4.1 Apartheid

From 1910 to 1924 the South African Party (SAP) of Louis Botha, which represented liberal Afrikaner and British interests, was in power. In 1924 this party was ousted and replaced by General Hertzog's Nasionale Party. This party, which had been formed in 1914, had come to power after the great miners' strike of 1921 in which the white, predominantly Afrikaner, workers demanded job reservation for whites. After coming to power, Hertzog had immediately passed the Industrial Conciliation Act of 1924. In 1927 he passed the Black Administration Act, in terms of which all Africans fell under the rule of the Governor General who was the Supreme Chief of all natives.

At the time of the great Depression of the 1930s, a strong government was needed to boost the country's economy. In order to solve this problem, Hertzog approached the opposition party, the SAP. The discussions that ensued culminated in the formation of the United Party, which was a fusion of the South African Party and the Nasionale Party. This step by Hertzog so angered the conservative elements of Afrikanerdom that they formed a new party, the Nationalist Party, under the leadership of Dr DF Malan. Influential leaders of the new party included Dr HF Verwoed, Dr N Diederichs, and many other Afrikaners who later played a prominent role in South African politics.

In 1948 the United Party, which at the time was led by General Smuts, was defeated by the Nationalist Party (NP) in a general election. The NP had come to power under the ticket of apartheid — Separate Development. The essence of the policy of the Nationalist Party was a future in which whites and blacks would have completely separate and distinctive lives. This would involve a complete separation of the races politically, socially and economically.

2.4.2 Apartheid laws

To achieve this grand scheme, Parliament had to pass a number of laws.

1 The Asiatic Laws Amendment Act 47 of 1948 withdrew Indian representation in Parliament.
2 The Electoral Laws Amendment Act 50 of 1948 made it more difficult for coloured people to register as voters.
3 The Prohibition of Mixed Marriages Act 55 of 1949 made marriages between blacks and whites illegal.
4 The Population Registration Act 30 of 1950 introduced separate birth registers for the different races and identity cards bearing the race of the holder.

5   The Immorality Amendment Act 21 of 1950 prohibited illicit carnal inter-course between whites and non-whites.

6   The Group Areas Act 41 of 1950 provided for the establishment of racial residential areas.

7   The Separate Representation of Voters Act 46 of 1951 provided for the removal of coloured people from the common voters roll.

8   The Black Authorities Act 68 of 1951 provided for the establishment of tribal, regional and territorial authorities.

9   The Reservation of Separate Amenities Act 49 of 1953 permitted the establishment of separate amenities for the different races.

10   The Black Education Act 47 of 1953 transferred the administration of black education from the provinces to the Department of Bantu Administration.[6]

2.4.3   Opposition to apartheid

Needless to say, the system of apartheid came under considerable opposition, especially from the black community. The African National Congress (ANC), which had been formed in 1912 as a reaction to the formation of the Union of South Africa and the exclusion of the African people in the former Boer republics from the voters roll, sought to mobilise other opposition parties for a united struggle against the apartheid regime. The nature and character of the struggle changed from a battle for the extension of existing rights to other provinces to the defence of existing rights by opposing all forms of encroach-ment on those rights. This necessarily meant fighting any law sought to dimin-ish existing rights. The ANC established close co-operation with the South African Indian Congress, the African People's Organisation, and later the South African Coloured People's Congress. These organisations held a Congress of the People in 1955 at which the Freedom Charter was drawn up. This docu-ment was a reaction to and a rejection of the policy of apartheid. It proclaimed that South Africa belonged to all its people — both black and white — and that no government could justly claim authority unless it was based on the will of the people. The struggle waged by these organisations remained peaceful and non-violent throughout the 1950s. It was only after 1960, after the Sharpville massacre, that the black political parties began to review their strate-gies and tactics. In 1961, and when all peaceful and non-violent means of opposing apartheid had been exhausted, when all avenues of peaceful struggle had been closed, the ANC decided to engage in an armed struggle. The armed struggle was not a substitute for the mass struggle. The ANC remained commit-ted to a non-violent, peaceful struggle, and whenever it was possible, violence was avoided. In 1976, the students in Soweto waged a non-violent protest against the use of Afrikaans as a medium of instruction in black schools. The government reacted with force, and the result was a massacre of children. After this event South African politics changed dramatically, as did the world's atti-tude towards apartheid.

The opposition by the ANC and other political organisations representing those who had no right to vote and who had been deprived of land was a direct challenge to the aims of the Nationalist Party. The Nationalist Party therefore also took measures to crush the opposition. One of the very first clear signs that the government was not prepared to countenance any opposition was the passing of the Suppression of Communism Act in 1950.7 This Act (now the Internal Security Act 74 of 1982) was the first in a series of laws that were aimed at crushing the opposition. Every form of opposition was eradicated and, where necessary, brute force was used. The famous incidents which took place in Sharpville, Soweto and many other areas where the police shot people down in cold blood are examples of how the government reacted to the opposition to its rule.

The use of brute force was complemented by attempts to reform the constitutional system. An example of this is the reforms which the government introduced after the Soweto uprising. The position of Prime Minister was abolished and the powers of the Prime Minister were combined with those of the State President. This was partly intended to grant the head of state the additional powers necessary to deal with threats from the opposition. In 1983 the Constitution was also amended: in terms of the new dispensation coloured and Indian people were to be co-opted to give the constitutional system some measure of legitimacy. Parliament was to consist of three houses — the House of Representatives (coloureds), the House of Delegates (Indians), and the House of Assembly (whites). The majority of the population were still excluded from the whole system. Opposition to the new reforms culminated in the formation of the United Democratic Front (UDF) and the intensification of the struggle against apartheid. The Constitutional Court characterises the period as follows:8

> "[5]   South Africa's past has been aptly described as that of 'a deeply divided society characterised by strife, conflict, untold suffering and injustice' which 'generated gross violations of human rights, the transgression of humanitarian principles in violent conflicts and a legacy of hatred, fear, guilt and revenge'.9 From the outset the country maintained a colonial heritage of racial discrimination: in most of the country the franchise was reserved for white males10 and a rigid system of economic and social segregation was enforced. The administration of African tribal territories through vassal 'traditional authorities' passed smoothly from British colonial rule to the new government, which continued its predecessor's policy.
>
> [6]   At the same time the Montesquieuan principle of a threefold separation of state power — often but an aspirational ideal — did not flourish in a South Africa which, under the banner of adherence to the Westminster system of government, actively promoted parliamentary supremacy and domination by the executive. Multi-party democracy had always been the pre-

serve of the white minority but even there it had languished since 1948. The rallying call of apartheid proved irresistible for a white electorate embattled by the spectre of decolonisation in Africa to the north.

[7]   From time to time various forms of limited participation in government were devised by the minority for the majority, most notably the 'homeland policy' which was central to the apartheid system. Fundamental to that system was a denial of socio-political and economic rights to the majority in bulk of the country, which was identified as 'white South Africa', coupled with a Balkanisation of tribal territories in which Africans would theoretically become entitled to enjoy all rights.[11] Race was the basic, all-pervading and inescapable criterion for participation by a person in all aspects of political, economic and social life.

[8]   As the apartheid system gathered momentum during the 1950s and came to be enforced with increasing rigour, resistance from the disenfranchised — and increasingly disadvantaged — majority intensified. Many (and eventually most) of them demanded non-discriminatory and wholly representative government in a non-racial unitary state, tenets diametrically opposed to those of apartheid. Although there were reappraisals and adaptations on both sides as time passed, the ideological chasm remained apparently unbridgeable until relatively recently.

[9]   The clash of ideologies not only resulted in strife and conflict but, as the confrontation intensified, the South African government of the day — and some of the self-governing and 'independent' territories spawned by apartheid — became more and more repressive. More particularly from 1976[12] onwards increasingly harsh security measures gravely eroded civil liberties. The administration of urban black residential areas and most 'homeland' administrations fell into disarray during the following decade. The South African government, backed by a powerful security apparatus operating with sweeping emergency powers, assumed strongly centralised and authoritarian control of the country.[13]

[10]   Then, remarkably and in the course of but a few years, the country's political leaders managed to avoid a cataclysm by negotiating a largely peaceful transition from the rigidly controlled minority regime to a wholly democratic constitutional dispensation. After a long history of 'deep conflict between a minority which reserved for itself all control over the political instruments of the state and a majority who sought to resist

that domination', the overwhelming majority of South Africans across the political divide realised that the country had to be urgently rescued from imminent disaster by a negotiated commitment to a fundamentally new constitutional order premised upon open and democratic government and the universal enjoyment of fundamental human rights." 14

In 1989 the government of the then State President De Klerk released from prison the leaders of the ANC and opened negotiations with all political parties. The negotiations were to culminate in the adoption of the Interim Constitution of 1993 which lays the basis for the democratic rule of the country and the observance of human rights. Chapter 3 of the Constitution contains a Bill of Rights.

2.4.4   Laws violating individual and human rights

Prior to the 1993 Constitution, Parliament and not the Constitution was sovereign. What Parliament decreed was law and no other organ of state could question the will of Parliament. Because Parliament represented the minority which sought to entrench its power, and which was faced with determined opposition to its aims, many of the laws passed by Parliament were immoral and violated the most basic human rights of individuals. In the absence of an organ which was authorised to act as watchdog over Parliament, the courts were forced to recognise all laws passed by Parliament — and this naturally included all infringements of fundamental rights which were encompassed by such laws.

There are several examples of such legislation. In 1963 Parliament passed the General Laws Amendment Act. This Act authorised the continued imprisonment of any person whose sentence had expired if the Minister of Justice was satisfied that such person was "likely to advocate, advise, defend or encourage the achievement of any of the objects of communism" on his/her release. Although the law was not permanent, it could be renewed by resolution of both Houses of Parliament. The importance of this law lies in the fact that the Minister of Justice admitted that the law was aimed in the first place at the continued detention of Robert Sobukwe, the PAC leader, who was due to be released from prison after the expiry of a three-year sentence for incitement arising from the PAC campaigns of 1960. The law was extended every year for five years until 1969 when Sobukwe was eventually released from Robben Island.

The law was bad because it empowered the Minister of Justice to extend prisoners' jail sentences without the intervention of the courts. It was also bad because, although it pretended to be a law of general application, it was in actual fact applicable only to one person, Robert Sobukwe.[15]

In the same year (1963), the 90-day detention law[16] was passed, empowering senior police officers to arrest without warrant and to detain for up to 90 days any person whom they suspected on reasonable grounds of having committed an offence of sabotage, or an act in terms of the Suppression of Communism or Unlawful Organisations Acts. The courts had no "jurisdiction to order the release from custody of any person so detained".[17] In 1965 the 90-day detention law was replaced by the 180-day detention law.[18] This law authorised the Attorney-General to order the arrest and detention of any person who it was deemed could give material evidence for the state in any criminal proceedings relating to certain political and common-law offences, if he was of the opinion that such person was likely to abscond or whenever he deemed it to be in the interests of such person or of the administration of justice. A person so detained could remain in detention without access to relatives and friends and would only be visited by state officials.

2.4.5 The place and role of the South African Police Service

Successive South African governments have relied on the security forces, especially the police, to enforce their laws. At the time of Union there were various autonomous colonial, rural and urban police forces in the different territories that had existed prior to Union. These police forces were independent of each other and there was no single national police force.[19] After Union Parliament, which had sovereign authority in and over the Union and had full powers to make laws for the peace, order and good governance of the Union, began exercising these powers. One such law passed by Parliament was the Police Act 14 of 1912.[20] This Act was passed in the main to provide for the establishment, organisation and control of the South African Police (SAP). At the time, even though the SAP had been formed, the task of policing was shared between the SAP and the SA Mounted Riflemen who were essentially military forces empowered to perform police functions in the rural areas in peacetimes. The SA Riflemen were disbanded in 1926 and their police functions were taken over by the SAP.

It is important to note that, although the South African Act empowered Parliament to make laws for peace, order and good governance, there was no provision for the formation of the SAP with its wide-ranging powers.

2.4.6 Powers, functions and duties of the South African Police Service

The Police Act did not define the duties and functions of the police force. Section 7(1) of the Act only defined the powers of a member of the force. The section provided:

> "Every member of the force shall exercise such powers and perform such duties as are by law confirmed or imposed on a police officer or constable but subject to the terms of such law, and shall obey all lawful directions in respect of the execution of his office which he may from time to time receive from his superiors."

This provision is an important factor in an understanding of the powers, functions and duties of the police up to the adoption of the 1993 Constitution.

It also serves to place in context some of the abuses that may have taken place in the past by members of the police force. The SAP operated not in a vacuum but within a certain political and constitutional framework.

This particular provision is characterised by the fact that it does not specify the duties and powers of the members of the force but only states that they have the powers which are conferred on them by law. Furthermore, the provision provides that members shall *obey lawful instructions given by superiors* (our emphasis).

The question of the functions of the police and whether or not the investigation of crime was part of their task came before the Cape Provincial Division (CPD) in 1926 in the case of *Mentor v Union Government*.[21] The case involved a claim against the police brought by a citizen of Griqua origin who had been bitten by police dogs when he was erroneously mistaken for a thief. The judge pointed out that, although the investigation of crime was not provided for in any Act, this was indeed a function of the police based on the common law:

> "I am not aware of any provision which lays it down as part of the
> duty of the police to investigate crime and pursue criminals, but it is
> in the highest interest of the community that they should do so."

In the 1950s another question that came before the courts was whether or not the function of preserving internal security was a police task in terms of the law. In the case of *Wolpe & another v O C South African Police, Johannesburg*[22] the court held that this was the function of the police on the basis of the nature of their official duties:

> "Dit is die plig van die polisie, uit die aard van hulle amp, om bin-
> nelandse veiligheid van die staat en die openbare vrede te bewaar
> en misdaad te voorkom. In die wye sin van die woord vind
> voorkoming van misdaad deur die inhegtenisneming van oortreders
> en deur bewaking plaas. Daar rus egter ook 'n plig op die polisie,
> ampshalwe, om stappe te doen om die pleeg van misdaad te
> voorkom indien daar redelik gronde bestaan vir die vermoede dat 'n
> misdaad gepleeg gaan word ... Maar my mening was dat dit nie die
> bedoeling van die Wetgewer was met genoemde artikel 7 om die
> basiese pligte van die polisie weg te neem en te vervang deur
> statutêre pligte nie. Dis 'n artikel wat duidelik maak dat die basiese
> pligte uitgebrei of meer uitvoerig omskryf kan word deur wette, iets
> wat reeds vir eeue plaasgevind het, sowel in die Romeins-Hollandse
> as in die Engelse Reg."[23]

The significance of this case in our attempt to understand the development of the powers and functions of the police is the judge's clarification of the order of importance of rights within the community. According to him, justice is important, but not as important as the rights of the offender, which are in turn not as important as the rights of the community. At page 94A he states:

"Dit ly myns insiens geen twyfel dat die polisie in die eerste plek voorkomende pligte het ten aansien van misdade wat gerig is teen die veiligheid van die Staat en die versteuring van die openbare orde. As grond hiervoor kan aangevoer word ... dat die belange van die geregtigheid heilig is, die belange van die oortreder dubbel heilig maar die belange van die gemeenskap drie maal heilig is."

When the Police Act[24] was passed in 1958 an attempt was made to define the powers of the police. Section 5 of the Act provides that the powers of the police include:

(*a*)   the preservation of the internal security of the Union;

(*b*)   the maintenance of law and order;

(*c*)   the investigation of any offence or alleged offence;

(*d*)   the prevention of crime.[25]

The significance of the Act lies in the fact that for first time the powers and functions of the police were clearly defined in a statute. Probably by some strange coincidence, the preservation of state security[26] was placed as the first task of the police. By yet another coincidence, the years that followed were to see the role of the SAP concentrated around the preservation of internal security. One possible explanation is indeed that the "belange van die gemeenskap drie maal heilig is".

To give effect to the importance of the function of the police as preservers of internal security, the special branch or security branch was created to combat terrorism and sabotage and to act as an intelligence service to detect and counter unconstitutional activities. As a further extension of this function the police got involved in military activities against so-called terrorists in Zimbabwe and later in Namibia and South Africa.

2.4.7   Wide powers of commissioned officers[27]

From its inception in 1958 the Police Act gave the police wide-ranging powers. Section 31(1), for example, exonerated a member of the force from liability if he had acted in compliance with a warrant.[28] This meant that a citizen who was a victim of such a defective warrant had no redress in law. The Police Amendment Act 43 of 1958 widened this power by providing that a member would not be liable for an act which was based upon a defective legislative Act.[29]

Originally section 9 of the Act had given commissioned officers the power to fine or sentence members of the force for breaches of the Act. Thus, members of the force could be sentenced to imprisonment without the intervention of the courts. Records of the proceedings had to be transmitted to the Deputy Commissioner. The only available redress was to appeal to the Minister who only had the power to review the sentence within the four corners of the record but had no power to rehear the matter. Against the decision of the Minister there was only the possibility of administrative review.

In 1961 the powers of police officers were further extended when the

Police Amendment Act 53 of 1961 made provision that the records were no longer to be transmitted to the Deputy Commissioner but to the Commanding Officer of the Police controlling the area in which the police member was stationed or to a lieutenant colonel of the force.

An analysis of police activities should take into account the powers enjoyed by the commissioned officers and the lack of proper control, as well as the fact that ordinary police members were at the mercy of their superiors whose orders they had by law to obey. They themselves were not protected and the protection of the courts was far removed and probably very limited.

The force itself was divided into classes.[30] The police were part of the system and since they were an arm of the executive, which was itself constitutionally bound to execute the laws passed by Parliament, they also had to execute the law. Thus, when it is said that the SAP spearheaded the gross violations of human rights under apartheid, this statement is only a restatement of what happened and not an attempt to attack those who served in the police force under the regime.[31]

Since 1994 South Africa has had a Constitution. This Constitution contains an entrenched Bill of Rights. The police are an arm of the state and are also bound to observe the rights entrenched by the Bill.[32] In 1995 Parliament passed the South African Police Service Act.[33] Section 18 of the Act provides for the establishment of Community Police Forums whose powers are:

(*a*) to establish and maintain a partnership between the community and the service;

(*b*) to promote communication between the service and the community;

(*c*) to promote co-operation between the service and the community in the fulfilment of the community's needs with regard to policing;

(*d*) to improve police services to the community at national, provincial, area and local levels;

(*e*) to improve transparency and accountability of the service; and

(*f*) to promote co-operation between the service and the community in the identification of problems and in their solution.

The aim of this provision is to attempt to close the gap that has developed over the years between the police and the general populace. The fact of the matter is that the police are seen by some as enemies rather than as helpers, working against the people rather than as their protectors.

We submit that, in order to promote the police–community relationship, the Police Act must contain a provision making it a duty of the police "to help the general public". For example, the Dutch Police Act[34] provides:

"De Politie heeft tot taak in ondergeschiktheid aan het bevoegde gezag en in overeenstemming met de geldende rechtsregels te zorgen voor de daadwerkelijke handhaving van de rechtsorde en het verlenen van hulp aan hen die deze behoeven."

(The task of the police is to ensure the maintainance of *the legal order* [our emphasis] and to give help to those who need it. They act in conformity with existing rules of law and follow instructions given by authorities legally empowered to give such instructions.) (Translation by PMM.)

Clearly, the emphasis is on the maintenance of the legal order rather than on "law and order". Furthermore, the police must act in compliance with the law;[35] they must give help. At present most members of the police in the country find it difficult to maintain law and order. However, if their task was first and foremost to protect and defend the constitutional and legal order, they would instinctively know not to use methods which would conflict with the very constitutional and legal order they want to maintain.

The duty to assist the public would enable police commanders to assign members of the service to help the elderly and other members of the community who might require their help. This could lead to the development of a relationship that would enable the public to help the police in the performance of their other duties. From such mutual assistance co-operation between the police and the public will be born.

2.4.8   The Public Protector and the police

The Public Protector is an office established under the Constitution whose powers are:

(i)   to investigate ministries, departments or the officials performing functions within such organs;

(ii) to investigate ministers at national and provincial level, police officials, police stations, clerks and/or civil servants.

The Public Protector's investigations must relate to:

(*a*) complaints about maladministration by any state organ or institution in which the state is a majority or controlling shareholder;

(*b*) abuse or unjustified exercise of power by state officials;

(*c*) unfair, capricious, discourteous or improper conduct;

(*d*) undue delay by any official performing a public function;

(*e*) improper enrichment;

(*f*) unlawful enrichment;

(*g*) receipt of improper advantage or promise thereof;

(*h*) any act or omission which results in improper prejudice;

(*i*) any act or omission which results in unlawful prejudice;

(*j*) any improper or dishonest act or omission or corruption with respect to public money.

The Act[36] does not define the persons against whom complaints can be lodged. The Constitution refers to "maladministration in connection with affairs of government", while the Act refers to "institutions in which the state is the majority or controlling shareholder" or "a person performing a function connected with his employment". It must be assumed that "person" refers also to state organs. This means, for example, that when the delay cannot be attributed to a particular official but is due to the slowness of processes within a certain state department, the complaint shall be against that department and not against a specific person. Read in this way, the Act will apply to ministers, ministries, departments and officials of departments, not only in their capacity as officials but also in their individual capacity. Consider, for example, the case of a complaint against a police officer who tightly handcuffs an old man of 70 years as if he were a young criminal likely to escape. It is at the discretion of this particular police officer (and not at the discretion of the department) whether or not to use handcuffs. Thus under certain circumstances a particular police officer's use of discretion may amount to abuse of power. However, the situation is different where, for example, the department issues orders instructing police personnel never to leave a charge office unattended. Should a citizen phone a charge office requesting assistance at the scene of a crime, only to be told that the police officer answering the phone is alone and cannot leave the charge office, any resultant complaint will have to be directed against the police service itself and not against the police officer in question. This is because such a police officer was simply acting according to the rules of the police department, and not in his/her personal capacity.

2.5   CONCLUSION

The Constitutions of 1993 and 1996 mark an important milestone in the struggle to build a democratic South Africa. Unlike their predecessors, they have secured for all, both black and white, the right to vote and to participate in the political life of the country and have guaranteed the protection of human rights for all citizens. The way has been paved for the transformation of organs such as the SAP from instruments of oppression into institutions serving to protect people's rights. This process of transformation will be aided by the active participation of offices such as that of the Public Protector, whose task it is to help eradicate old tendencies which led to abuse of power, with the assistance of a constitutional system in which the Constitution, which clearly defines the powers of state organs, is the supreme law.

2.6   SUGGESTED READING AND SOURCES

Dugard, J. 1978. *Human Rights and the South African Legal Order*. Princeton: Princeton University Press.

Matthews, Anthony S. 1986. *Freedom, State Security and the Rule of Law*. Cape Town: Juta.

Verloren van Themaat, JP. 1985. *Staatsreg*, annexure 3, edited by M Wiechers. Durban: Butterworths.

Visser, PJ. 1984. *Law of South Africa*, vol 20.

....

ENDNOTES

1   South African Police Service Act 68 of 1995.

2   Section 2 of the Colonial Validity Act of 1865 provided that any colonial law which was in any respect repugnant to the provisions of any Act of the British Parliament extending to the Colony would be absolutely void and inoperative. See Verloren van Themaat/Wiechers Annexure (Bylae) 3.

3   As a result of the pressure from, among others, Hertzog, the Imperial Conference of 1926 decided that the dominions were autonomous communities within the British Empire, equal in status and in no way subordinate to one another in any aspect of their domestic or external affairs. They were linked together by common allegiance to the Crown.

4   In terms of section 2 of the Statute, the Colonial Validity Act of 1865 would no longer apply in the dominions and therefore no law of a dominion would be void simply because it conflicted with a British Act of Parliament.

5   In terms of the 1961 Constitution, the Crown was no longer head of state: the State President assumed all powers which immediately before the Republic had been exercised by the Governor General as representative of the Crown (section 7(4) of Act 32 of 1961).

6   The list is not exhaustive.

7   Act 44 of 1950.

8   See Certification of the Constitution of the Republic of South Africa, 1996, CCT23/96, paras 5–10 (A. Historical and Political Context).

9   See the first and third paragraphs of the postscript to the Constitution of the Republic of South Africa Act 200 of 1993, headed "National Unity and Reconciliation".

10   In the Cape Province persons of certain other ethnic origins enjoyed a limited franchise and provision was made for representation of African interests in the national legislature.

11   For people who were not classified as either "European" or "Bantu", apartheid theory did not purport to offer a rationale for its discrimination.

12   When student unrest, which started in Soweto on 16 June 1976, escalated and spread to many parts of the country.

13   In *Executive Council, Western Cape Legislature & others v President of the Republic of South Africa & others* 1995 (4) SA 877 (CC); 1995 (10) BCLR 1289 (CC) at para 7, a pen-picture of the government at that time is given:
     "The Constitution itself makes provision for the complex issues involved in bringing together again in one country, areas which had been separated under apartheid, and at the same time establishing a constitutional State based on respect for fundamental human rights, with a decentralised form of government in place of what had previously been authoritarian rule enforced by a strong central government. On the day the Constitution came into force 14 structures of government ceased to exist. They were the four provincial governments, which were non-elected bodies appointed by the central government, the six governments of what were known as self-governing territories, which had extensive legislative and executive competences but were part of the Republic of South Africa, and the legislative and executive structures of Transkei, Bophuthatswana, Venda and Ciskei, which, according to South African law, had been independent States. Two of these States were controlled by military regimes, and at the time of the coming into force of the new Constitution two were being administered by administrators

appointed by the South African authorities. The legislative competences of these 14 areas were not the same. Laws differed from area to area, though there were similarities because at one time or another all had been part of South Africa. In addition the Constitution was required to make provision for certain functions which had previously been carried out by the national government to be transferred as part of the Constitution came into force, and simultaneously for functions that had previously been performed by the 14 executive structures which had ceased to exist to be transferred partly to the national government and partly to the new provincial governments which were to be established. All this was done to ensure constitutional legislative, executive, administrative and judicial continuity."

[14] See *The Azanian Peoples Organisation (AZAPO) & others v The President of the Republic of South Africa & others* (CC) Case no CCT 17/96, 25 July 1996, unreported, at paras 1 and 2.

[15] Section 33(1) of the 1993 Constitution provides that a law limiting a right must be a law of general application. See also section 36(1) of the 1996 Constitution.

[16] General Law Amendment Act 37 of 1963 (s 17).

[17] In terms of section 11 of the 1993 Constitution (section 112 of the 1996 Constitution) this would be a violation of someone's right to liberty and such a person would have a right in terms of section 7(4)(b) to apply for appropriate relief.

[18] Section 7 of the Criminal Procedure Amendment Act 96 of 1965 inserted section 215*bis*.

[19] Visser PJ. 1984. *Law of South Africa*, vol 20 para 236, at 271.

[20] The Act was adopted on 1 April 1912 and was to come into effect on 1 January 1913.

[21] 1927 CPD 11.

[22] 1955 (2) SA 87 (W).

[23] *Wolpe* case at 94B et seq.

[24] Act 7 of 1958.

[25] It must be pointed out that this law does not include helping members of the public as one of the tasks of the police. Thus, outside a state of emergency, members of the police force have no duty to help the public.

[26] It is significant that under the 1993 Constitution, section 215 provides that the powers are:

(i)   the prevention of crime;
(ii)   the investigation of any offence or alleged offence;
(iii) the maintenance of law and order;
(iv)   the preservation of the internal security of the Republic.

[27] Section 31(1) of Act 7 of 1958 : "If any legal proceedings be brought against any member of the force for any act done in obedience to a warrant purporting to be issued by a magistrate or justice of the peace or other officer authorized by law to issue warrants, that member shall not be liable for any irregularity in the issuing of the warrant or for want of jurisdiction in the person issuing the warrant containing the signature of the person reputed to be a magistrate or justice of the peace or other such officer as aforesaid and upon proof that the acts complained of were done in obedience of the warrant, judgment shall be given in favour of such member."

[28] Section 55(1) of the South African Police Service Act 68 of 1995 retains this provision. It remains to be seen whether the courts would allow the exoneration from liability in the

light of section 7(4)(*b*). If someone's right to liberty is violated by an arrest by a state organ and the act of arresting does not pass the test of section 33(1) because the arrest did not take place according to the requirements of a law of general application, how can that violation be justified? This provision is vulnerable to constitutional attack.

29   Section 31(2) inserted by Act 43 of 1958 provided that: "A member of the force who in good faith performs any act in accordance with or in the enforcement of any provision purporting to be an enactment of a competent legislative authority, shall, notwithstanding any irregularity in the enactment of or defect in such provision or want of jurisdiction on the part of such legislative authority, be exempt from liability in respect of the performance of that act to the same extent and subject to the same conditions as if such irregularity had not occurred or such defect or want of jurisdiction had not existed."

30   The Police Amendment Act 64 of 1964 provided that regulations may be made with reference to different classes or categories of members of the force (s 19(2)).

31   This should not be interpreted as meaning that the police are exonerated for their individual involvement in breaches of human rights. It means that the police as a force operated within a certain political and constitutional framework.

32   Section 7 of the 1993 Constitution provides that "This Chapter shall bind all legislative and executive organs of the state ….". See also section 8 of the 1996 Constitution: "… binds the legislature, the executive, the judiciary and all organs of the state".

33   Act 68 of 1995.

34   Artikel 2 Politiewet 1993.

35   "… in overeenstemming met de geldende rechtsregels".

36   Public Protector Act of 1994.

Chapter 3
History and Role of the Constitutional Court of South Africa

Patric Mtshaulana

SUMMARY

*T*HIS chapter discusses the origins of the Constitutional Court (CC). The process which culminated in the formation of the Court involved a long struggle for the establishment of a democratic South Africa based on freedom and the respect of human rights. The main task of the Constitutional Court is to serve as the ultimate protector of the Constitution as the supreme law of the land. The chapter shows how the jurisdiction of the Constitutional Court differs from that of the other divisions of the Supreme Court and the Appellate Division. To illustrate these differences, sections 98 and 101 of the 1993 Constitution[1] are examined in some detail. For a proper understanding of the relationship between the two courts and the system of judicial review adopted by the 1993 Constitution, a brief comparative study of the systems of judicial review is made. A distinction is made between the centralised and the decentralised systems of judicial review on the one hand, and the preventive and repressive systems on the other. The 1993 Constitution has introduced new procedures for the appointment of judges, especially those of the Constitutional Court. These procedures are dealt with in detail together with the composition of the Judicial Service Commission which is the body which plays a pivotal role in the appointment of constitutional and other judges. The chapter concludes with a brief description of the procedure to be followed in order to gain access to the Constitutional Court.

3.1 INTRODUCTION

On 14 February 1995 the new Constitutional Court of South Africa was officially inaugurated by President Nelson Mandela. The Minister of Justice, Mr Dullah Omar, said on this occasion that "[i]t was a long, long journey that brought us here, a journey full of suffering and pain. A journey that was so long and so arduous that many died in making it. But there was one thing that sustained us on that journey. Hope. The hope that, one day, in South Africa, we would win human rights for all. The belief that, one day, the cry that the people of South Africa sent out to the world in 1955 would at last be heard: 'That South Africa belongs to all who live in it, black and white, and that no government can justly claim authority unless it is based on the will of the people.' Today, forty years after the Congress of the People held at Kliptown, we come together to inaugurate an institution that will have, as its most sacred task, the guarding of the rights of all South Africans.[2]

"The Constitutional Court, as the culmination in many ways of that 'long journey' and the starting point for a fresh route towards a different future, bears a heavy responsibility: the emblem of the court depicts a group of people, black and white, sheltered under the protective branches of a tree. In the paradigm of legal theory and in the popular imagination, the court is the embodiment of the promise of 'never again'."[3]

Of course, the Court is established at present under the 1993 Constitution but the 1996 Constitution[4] also contains a Bill of Rights. It is therefore self-evident that the interpretation of this Bill (of the new Constitution) will be informed by the jurisprudence developed under the Interim Constitution. In this sense, the 1993 Constitution has established a court, the Constitutional Court, which will forever enforce the Constitution as the supreme law of the country and which will forever ensure that Parliament and other organs of state are kept in check and are prevented from violating the individual's rights as contained in the Bill of Rights.

3.2   KEY OBJECTIVES

The key objectives of this chapter are to enable students to:
- understand and discuss the process of appointing judges;
- understand and discuss the composition and role of the Judicial Service Commission;
- understand and discuss the constitutional jurisdiction and certification processes;
- understand and discuss the system of judicial review; and
- understand and discuss the procedures to be followed in order to gain access to the Court.

3.3   INTERPRETATION AND DISCUSSION
3.3.1   The Constitutional Court
3.3.1.1 The appointment of judges

The Constitutional Court consists of the President of the Court, his or her Deputy[5] and nine other judges. The President of the Court is appointed by the President of the Republic in consultation with[6] the Cabinet, after consultation with[7] the Chief Justice[8] and the Judicial Service Commission.[9] For the purposes of the appointment of the first President of the Court, which took place before the establishment of the Judicial Service Commission, the consultation with that Commission was dispensed with by the Constitution;[10] the President had only to consult the Cabinet and the Chief Justice.[11]

After appointing the President of the Court, the President of the Republic has the power to appoint four additional judges to the Court from the ranks of the judges of the Supreme Court. He appoints these judges in consultation with the Cabinet and the Chief Justice. The Judicial Service Commission has no role in this process.[12]

3.3.1.2 Composition and role of the Judicial Service Commission

Because the Judicial Service Commission plays such an important role in the appointment of the judges of the Court, it is important to note the composition and role of this body. The Commission is a body established in terms of section 105 of the 1993 Constitution. It consists of:
(i)   the Chief Justice;
(ii)   the President of the Court;

(iii) one Judge President designated by the Judges President;[13]

(iv) the Minister of Justice;

(v) two practising advocates designated by the advocates' profession;

(vi) two attorneys designated by the attorneys' profession;[14]

(vii) one professor of law designated by the deans of all the law faculties at South African universities;[15]

(viii) four senators;[16] and

(ix) four persons who should be either practising attorneys or advocates designated by the President in consultation with the Cabinet. In general, the function of the Judicial Service Commission is to make recommendations regarding the appointment, removal from office, terms of office and tenure of the Supreme Court and Constitutional Court judges.

While the Judicial Service Commission has to be consulted in the appointment of the President of the Court, it plays an even greater role with regard to the appointment of the remaining six judges of the Constitutional Court.[17] The Judicial Service Commission alone has the power to invite nominations from the general public. From the nominations, it compiles a short list of twenty-five names and interviews the short-listed candidates. The interviews are public, but cameras are not allowed. On the basis of the interviews a short list of ten names is compiled which is presented to the President.[18] The President appoints six judges from the short list of ten.[19]

Persons eligible to be nominated and appointed must be:

(i) judges of the Supreme Court; or

(ii) persons who are qualified to be admitted as advocates or attorneys, and who have practised as such for a cumulative period of ten years, or who have lectured in law at a university for that period; or

(iii) persons, who by reason of their experience or training have expertise in the field of constitutional law, provided that no more than two persons from this category are members of the Court at the same time.

The procedure adopted in the appointment of judges of the Constitutional Court is similar to that followed in the appointment of the judges of the Supreme Court. The remuneration of all judges is guaranteed in section 104(2) of the Constitution.[20] A judge may not be removed from office except by the President, on the grounds of misbehaviour, incapacity or incompetence, as established by the Judicial Service Commission; his or her removal must furthermore be requested by both the National Assembly and the Senate.[21]

The mode of appointment of judges differs from the manner in which judges were appointed under the old dispensation. Then, as is currently the case in Canada,[22] the State President, who was the head of the executive, had the power to appoint judges and had only to consult his Cabinet. The new procedure allows for greater involvement by the legal profession in the appointments and the interviews allow for some transparency in the process. All in all, the process by which judges are appointed is far more transparent: the executive retains the power to appoint, but that power is constrained by the extensive consultation requirements. Arbitrariness is minimised by the fact that the executive does not control the compilation of the list from which appointments have to be made and by the greater involvement of the legal profession.

Another significant departure from past practice is the fact that it is now possible for attorneys and academics, who are not members of the Bar, to be appointed to the Bench.[23] This is an innovation in South Africa. In the past, to be appointed a judge one had to be a Senior Counsel. Junior Counsel, attorneys and academic lawyers were completely excluded from appointment to the Bench. This new framework for the appointment of judges is likely to contribute a different perspective to the deliberations of the Court and will in all probability lead to a closing of the gap between the academic profession and legal practice, both of which stand to be enriched by the new system. Allowing attorneys right of audience in the court will undoubtedly make the court more accessible to the public.

The appointment of judges was certainly the subject of some of the most heated debates at the multiparty negotiating process at Kempton Park. There were those who advocated that Parliament should have the power to appoint judges; some wanted the Constitutional Court judges to be appointed from the ranks of existing judges; others thought that the judges of the Constitutional Court should be drawn from outside the existing judiciary entirely. The formation of the Judicial Service Commission was a delicate compromise between these extremes[24] and remains controversial: although only five of its members are politicians,[25] the President has the power to appoint the four attorneys and advocates and, although they may not necessarily be party members, the President is not constrained from appointing persons who might be sympathetic to his views. Thus, although direct political intervention in the appointment process has been minimised, the ruling political party still retains considerable influence on the appointments.

A more significant characteristic of the new procedure is its openness. The candidates are interviewed publicly by the Judicial Service Commission. This only applies to six judges, since the President of the Court and the other four judges are appointed by the President of South Africa. This procedure came under considerable attack and criticism. Kriegler J[26] found it a "bit embarrassing to have to sing for my supper";[27] O'Regan J indicated in her interview that the split process, whereby some judges were interviewed and others not, was the product of a compromise, but she felt strongly that, in future, all candidates should be subjected to the grilling process.[28] The 1996 Constitution introduces new provisions in this regard. Firstly, all judges[29] are appointed after they have been interviewed. Secondly, section 178(*b*) specifically provides that the smaller parties must be represented in the Judicial Service Commission. Thirdly, section 174(4) provides that the President must make his choice of judges after consultation with the leaders of the smaller parties represented in Parliament.

Presently, the President of the Constitutional Court is Justice Arthur Chaskalson, a distinguished jurist with a long track record as a human rights lawyer. He was a member of the defence team which defended Nelson Mandela and his colleagues in the Rivonia trial in 1964 and was a founder of the Legal Resources Centre, a human rights organisation which defended detainees and accused persons in the 1980s. The Deputy President of the Court was Justice Ismail Mahomed, Chief Justice of Namibia, Judge of the High Court of Lesotho and Swaziland and a distinguished human rights lawyer. Justice Mahomed has now been appointed as Chief Justice. The judges drawn from the Supreme Court presently serving at the court are: Justice Richard Goldstone, who was appointed to chair the Goldstone Commission which investigated the "third force" activities of the army and the police in the period before the elections and who is presently serving as prosecutor for the International Criminal Tribunal for the former Yugoslavia and Rwanda,[30] Justice Johan Kriegler who was a judge of the Appellate Division and chairman of the Independent Electoral Commission which oversaw the first democratic elections; and Justices John Didcott, Tholakele Madala and Laurie Ackermann who are judges from the Natal, Transkei and Cape Provincial Divisions respectively. All of these judges were vigorous advocates of the protection of human rights during the apartheid era. In 1987 Ackermann J resigned his post as a judge and inaugurated the Harry Oppenheimer Chair in Human Rights Law at the University of Stellenbosch, the first of its kind in South Africa; Madala J was active as an advocate in the Transkei and played an important role in establishing anti-apartheid advocates' forums, while Didcott J is renowned for several decisions protective of human rights which were ultimately overturned by the Appellate Division.[31] One such decision was one in which he proclaimed that indigent accused have a right to counsel in order to ensure a fair trial. The other four positions on the Court were filled by prominent academics and advocates. Justice Pius Langa was a Senior Counsel and noted defender of human rights who also served as President of the National Association of Democratic Lawyers; Justices Yvonne Mokgoro and Kate O'Regan are the only women and were both prominent academics with a reputation for outstanding scholarship and active involvement in human rights issues. Mokgoro J is the first black female judge in the country. After completing her studies, she worked as a public prosecutor and later became a law professor. As a researcher attached to the Centre for Constitutional Analysis of the Human Sciences Research Council, she conducted extensive research and published many articles on human rights issues. O'Regan J had a distinguished academic career and, as an attorney specialising in labour issues, she was often in contact with the problems of ordinary working people. She has published extensively on gender, equality, land redistribution and labour law. Sachs J was an advocate who left South Africa after having been detained under the 180-days detention law. He lived in exile and was the victim of a car-bomb blast orchestrated by South African security agents in Maputo. In the blast he lost his right hand and it is a miracle that he survived. He has written extensively on constitutional law and human rights and was the senior member of the ANC Constitutional Committee which assisted in the drafting of the Constitution. The term of office of judges of the Constitutional Court is seven years and is not renewable.

3.3.1.3   Constitutional jurisdiction

Under the 1996 Constitution, the Appellate Division[32] remains the highest court of the land on all non-constitutional issues,[33] while the new Constitutional Court is the highest court on constitutional issues. The Constitutional Court has jurisdiction as the court of final instance[34] over all matters relating to the interpretation, protection and enforcement of the provisions of the Constitution. In terms of section 98(2) of the 1993 Constitution, the Constitutional Court has exclusive jurisdiction over the following matters:

(i)   an inquiry into the constitutionality of an Act of Parliament, irrespective of whether such law was passed or made before or after the commencement of the Constitution;

(ii)   any dispute over the constitutionality of any Bill before Parliament;

(iii)   any dispute of a constitutional nature between organs of state at any level of government; and

(iv)   the determination of any dispute as to whether any matter falls within its jurisdiction.[35]

The Supreme Court, established in terms of section 101 of the 1993 Constitution, retains the jurisdiction, including its inherent jurisdiction, which it had before the commencement of the Constitution. While the Appellate Division has no jurisdiction to adjudicate on any matter within the jurisdiction of the Constitutional Court,[36] the provincial and local divisions of the Supreme Court have concurrent jurisdiction with respect to the following constitutional matters:

(i)   an alleged violation or threatened violation of any fundamental right entrenched in chapter 3;

(ii)   any dispute over the constitutionality of any executive act or administrative act or conduct or threatened executive or administrative act;

(iii)   any dispute of a constitutional nature between local governments or between a local and a provincial government;

(iv)   any dispute over the constitutionality of a Bill before a provincial legislature; and

(v)   the determination of disputes as to whether any matter falls within its jurisdiction.

In all these matters, the provincial or local division of the Supreme Court features as court of first instance and appeals against its decisions lie to the Constitutional Court. With regard to the issues over which the Constitutional Court has exclusive jurisdiction, the provincial or local division of the Supreme Court has no jurisdiction and, if in any matter before it an issue which falls within the exclusive jurisdiction of the Constitutional Court is raised, the local or provincial division must suspend the proceedings and refer the issue to the Constitutional Court.[37]

3.3.1.4 Certification process

In terms of section 71(2),[38] the Constitutional Court has jurisdiction to certify "that all the provisions of such a text [of the new Constitution adopted by the Constitutional Assembly] comply with the Constitutional Principles referred to in subsection (1)(*a*)". On 8 May 1996 the Constitutional Assembly adopted the new Constitution by a majority of some 86 per cent of its members.[39] In its judgment the Constitutional Court ordered [40] that:

> "National (NT) 23 [41] (section 23) failed to comply with constitutional principle (CP) XXVIII.
>
> "NT 241(1) [42] failed to comply with CP VII because it shielded a statute from constitutional attack."

3.3.2 System of judicial review

In theory two systems of judicial review are known in constitutional states: the centralised and the decentralised[43] systems. A centralised system of judicial review refers to the form of judicial review where a single court has the power to test the validity of legislative instruments. The German Constitutional Court is an example of such a system. This Court alone has the power to declare Acts of Parliament invalid on account of their inconsistency with the Constitution. In France, the *Conseil Constitutionnel* is also the only organ vested with the power, but its jurisdiction extends only to Bills which have not yet become law. Decentralised systems refer to those forms of judicial review where all the courts at all levels have the authority to test the validity of legislative instruments. The United States system of judicial review is decentralised, since lower courts also have jurisdiction to pronounce on constitutional issues if those issues are important and pertinent to the determination of the matter to be resolved. However, the Supreme Court is the court of appeal in all cases where the validity of a statute is in question. In this sense the United States Supreme Court is comparable with the Canadian Supreme Court.[44]

Another way of classifying systems of judicial review is to examine whether the courts have a preventive or a repressive power of judicial review. Preventive power of judicial review refers to the power of a court to pronounce over a statutory instrument before that instrument becomes law. The French *Conseil Constitutionnel* has jurisdiction to pronounce over Bills before they become law and its decisions are final and binding on all organs, with no appeal lying against them. Repressive judicial review, on the other hand, is exercised by a court which has jurisdiction to declare invalid an existing law which is in conflict with the Constitution. The United States Supreme Court and the German Constitutional Court have a repressive power of judicial review: in the United

States the existence of a "case or controversy" is a jurisdiction if the court is asked to adjudicate over an issue in which there is no adversarial relationship between the parties.[45]

The Constitutional Court of South Africa combines almost all of the above attributes. In the first place, South Africa has a centralised system of judicial review, since the Constitutional Court alone has jurisdiction to pronounce on the validity of Acts of Parliament. No other courts, except the provincial and local divisions of the Supreme Court, have jurisdiction to deal with constitutional issues and even their jurisdiction is limited by the fact that they may not pronounce on the validity of Acts of Parliament. The Appellate Division has no jurisdiction whatsoever over constitutional matters.[46] It would appear that the main reason for choosing a centralised system of judicial review was that many felt that the Appellate Division was tainted by a legacy of gross violations of human rights; it had sent many prominent figures in the liberation struggle to the gallows and to prisons. As a result, the Court had lost its credibility and legitimacy in the eyes of the majority and it seemed incongruous to vest such a court with the power to decide controversial political and human rights and constitutional law questions while retaining the Appellate Division's jurisdiction over civil, criminal and other cases. This is clearly expressed by Professor J van der Westhuizen who writes:

> "The legal system is widely alleged to be experiencing crisis. The majority of South Africans have come to perceive the laws of the country, the courts and the police, in fact the legal order as such ... as part and parcel of the apartheid system and an instrument of oppression and exploitation, rather than the embodiment of justice or a system of protection ... The mere possibility of entrusting a new bill of rights to the existing judiciary often invokes serious scepticism as to the bill of rights idea as such and causes the concept of judicial review to be suspected as but another device to perpetuate apartheid and to secure dominant class interests.[47]

> "In the third place, the recommendations (of the S A Law Commission, p24 of Project 58 summary of the Interim Report, August 1991) brushes over the fact that the Appellate Division, because of its role under Apartheid, has lost all legitimacy as a Court. In particular, it will not be easily acceptable as a Court for solving controversial political and constitutional issues by those whom it has been sending to prison because of their role as fighters for freedom and democracy." [48]

A further possible reason for the split jurisdiction was to enable the new democratic order to participate in the appointment of the judges who were to play such a vital role in the shaping of the new democracy. In the second place, the Court has both repressive and preventive powers of judicial review, since, apart from the power to determine the validity of Acts of Parliament, it also has jurisdiction to pronounce on the validity of Bills which have not yet become law. Thus, in addition to section 98(2)(*c*) of the 1993 Constitution, which empowers the court to inquire into the constitutionality of an Act of Parliament, section 98(2)(*d*) of the 1993 Constitution also authorises it to inquire into the constitutionality of a Bill before Parliament or a provincial legislature. This power must be distinguished from the power of the Canadian Supreme Court in terms of section 53 of the Supreme Court Act, which empowers it to hear and consider questions of law and fact referred to it by the Governor General in Council. This power of reference is not preventive, but repressive,[49] since only "law(s)" or Bills which have become law can be referred. The power derives from an Act of Parliament and not from the Constitution. Further, while the decision of the Constitutional Court is binding on everyone, including non-parties,[50] the view in Canada is that the answers to a reference "are only advisory and will have no more effect than the opinions of law officers".[51] Consequently, the opinion is neither binding on the parties to the reference nor does it have the same precedential weight as an opinion in an actual case.[52] The new Constitution has retained the centralised nature of judicial review but has given the Supreme Court of Appeal some constitutional jurisdiction. Furthermore, the Constitutional Court retains both repressive and preventive [53] powers of judicial review.

3.3.3 Procedures to be followed in order to gain access to the Court

Before the Constitution came into force, the power of the courts to inquire into the validity of Acts of Parliament was governed by section 34(3) of the Constitution, Act 110 of 1983, which provided:

> "Save as provided in sub-section (2), no court of law shall be competent to inquire into or pronounce upon the validity of an Act of Parliament." [54]

This section was a codification[55] of a rule established by the courts that, "[i]f a Legislature has plenary power to legislate on a particular matter no question can arise as to the validity of any legislation on that matter and such legislation is valid whatever the real purpose of that legislation is." [56]

The new Constitution has signalled an end to the era of parliamentary sovereignty. Section 4(1) of the 1993 Constitution proclaims that:

> "This Constitution shall be the supreme law of the Republic and any
> law or act inconsistent with its provisions shall, unless otherwise
> provided expressly or by necessary implication in this Constitution,
> be of no force and effect to the extent of the inconsistency."[57]

Parliament is now subject to the Constitution and its laws must conform to the Constitution. The power of the Court to pronounce on the constitutionality of Acts of Parliament is not limited to the question of the manner and form of legislation; it may also pronounce on the constitutionality of Acts of Parliament if the content of the legislation is in any way in conflict with the spirit, purport or letter of the Constitution.

The only limitation placed on the power of the courts is that not all courts may pronounce on the validity of Acts of Parliament; only the Constitutional Court has this power. Thus, if the constitutionality of an Act of Parliament is in dispute before any court, the matter must be suspended and the issue of the constitutionality of the Act of Parliament referred to the Constitutional Court.[58] According to section 102(1) of the 1993 Constitution, the conditions for referring an issue to the Constitutional Court are that the issue must be decisive for the case, the issue must be in the exclusive jurisdiction of the Constitutional Court and the lower court must consider it to be in the interest of justice that the issue be referred to the Court. These requirements for referring to the Constitutional Court are described by Ackerman J in *Bernstein & others v Bester NO & others*[59] as follows:

> "Section 102(1) of the Constitution does not empower a provincial or local division of the Supreme Court to refer a matter by agreement to the Constitutional Court, but only when the requirements set forth in the subsection are met ... The impression should be avoided that referrals can take place simply because parties have agreed thereto. In certain referrals to this court, the conclusion is difficult to avoid that this is in fact what has happened. Problems which had arisen in connection with such referrals were commented on in *S v Vermaas; S v Du Plessis*[60] and in *Ferreira v Levin*[61] this court pointed out that the power and duty to refer only arises when three conditions are fulfilled:
>
> (*a*)   there is an issue in the matter before the court in question which may be decisive for the case;
>
> (*b*)   such issue falls within the exclusive jurisdiction of the Constitutional Court; and
>
> (*c*)   the court in question considers it to be in the interests of justice to refer such issue to the Constitutional Court.
>
> The court has further held that it is implicit in section 102(1) that there should be a reasonable prospect that the relevant law or provision will be held to be invalid and while this is a sine qua non of a referral it is not in itself a sufficient ground, because it is not always in the interest of justice to make a referral as soon as the relevant issue has been raised."[62]

Section 100 of the 1993 Constitution makes provision for direct access to the Court, the prerequisites for which are concretised in Rule 17 of the Constitutional Court rules. These requirements are that the matter be of such urgency, or otherwise of such public importance, that any delay necessitated by the use of the ordinary procedures would prejudice the public interest or the ends of justice and good government.[63]

Once the Court has made a finding that a law referred to it or a provision thereof is inconsistent with the Constitution, it has full powers to declare such law or provision to be invalid to the extent of its inconsistency.

However, the Court also has the power, in terms of section 98(5) of the 1993 Constitution, to suspend the coming into operation of the order of invalidity and instead require Parliament to correct the defect in the law or provision.[64] The law then remains in force pending the correction or the expiry of the period specified and within which Parliament was required to correct the defect.[65]

The normal course for accessing the Court therefore is either by way of referral from the provincial or local division of the Supreme Court or on appeal from such a court. Because the magistrates' courts have no jurisdiction to handle constitutional issues, whenever such courts are confronted with constitutional issues, they either have to dispose of the matter as if the law whose constitutionality is being questioned was valid[66] or refer the matter to the local or provincial division of the Supreme Court.[67] The latter Court either decides the matter or, if there are issues which are in the exclusive jurisdiction of the Constitutional Court, refers those issues while suspending the proceedings pending the decision of the Court.[68]

The Appellate Division of the Supreme Court is precluded from deciding constitutional issues.[69] It has the power to refer to the Constitutional Court any issue which is within the jurisdiction of that Court. An interesting section of the 1993 Constitution, which touches on the relationship between the two courts, is section 35(3). This section provides that:

> "In the interpretation of any law and the application and development of the common law and customary law, a court shall have due regard to the spirit, purport and objects of this Chapter [on fundamental rights]."

In the now famous case of *Du Plessis & others v De Klerk & another*,[70] the Constitutional Court answered the question whether the rights contained in the Bill have horizontal application. In the view of the Court the rights do not, *in principle* (our emphasis), have horizontal application. The effect of the decision is that constitutional rights may not be invoked by private litigants against each other; whenever the state is involved, private litigants can always invoke chapter 3 of the 1993 Constitution and may do so to attack the common law if the state's action is based on the common law. Section 8 of the 1996 Constitution also addresses the horizontal application question.

3.4 CONCLUSION

With the adoption of the 1993 and 1996 Constitutions, South African constitutional law has seen the disappearance of the concept of parliamentary sovereignty and the ushering in of an era of constitutionalism in which the Constitution is supreme. The Constitutional Court is the institution created by the Constitution to guard and protect constitutional supremacy. Whereas under the 1993 Constitution the Appellate Division had no constitutional jurisdiction, under the 1996 Constitution it will have this jurisdiction. This will have the effect of making it possible for the Constitutional Court to decide issues after they have been exhaustively discussed by all the divisions of the Supreme Court and by the Supreme Court of Appeal. The effect of this will be to bring the Constitution to bear in all decisions of the courts and to make South Africa a real constitutional democracy.

3.5   SUGGESTED READING AND SOURCES

Asmal, K. 1991. *Constitutional Courts: A Comparative Survey.* Unpublished paper delivered at the Magaliesburg conference 1–3 February 1991.

Chaskalson, A. 1991. *A Constitutional Court: Jurisdiction, Possible Models and Questions of Access.* Unpublished paper delivered at the Magaliesburg conference 1–3 February 1991.

Dugard, J. 1991. *Judicial Power and a Constitutional Court.* Unpublished paper delivered at the Magaliesburg conference 1–3 February 1991.

Hogg, PW. 1992. *Constitutional Law of Canada,* 3 ed. Toronto: Carswell.

Mtshaulane, PM. 1992. *Judicial Review in a Future Democratic South Africa. (Perspectives and Prospects).* Doctoral thesis, unpublished, VU 1992.

Mtshaulana, Patric & Thomas, Melanie. 1996. The Constitutional Court of South Africa: An introduction. *Review of Constitutional Studies,* III (1) (Law journal published under the auspices of the law faculty, University of Alberta, Canada).

Prakke, L. 1971. *Toetsing in het Publiekrecht.* Academisch Proefschrift, UVA 1971, Van Gorcum, Assen.

Van der Westhuizen, J. 1991. The protection of human rights and a Constitutional Court for South Africa: Some questions and ideas. 1991 *De Jure* 24.

• •

ENDNOTES

1   See also sections 167 and 172 of the 1996 Constitution.

2   Dullah Omar: Opening Speech at the Constitutional Court on 14 February 1995.

3   Mtshaulana, P & Thomas, M. 1996. The Constitutional Court of South Africa: An introduction. *Review of Constitutional Studies* III (1) at 1.

4   Constitution of the Republic of South Africa, 1996.

5   The appointment of a Deputy President was provided for by section 1 of the Constitution of the Republic of South Africa Second Amendment Act 44 of 1995.

6   According to section 233(3) of the 1993 Constitution, "in consultation with" means "with concurrence of".

7   Section 233(4) provides that the phrase "after consultation with" means "such decision shall be taken in good faith after consulting and giving serious consideration to the views of such other functionary".

8   The court structure of South Africa consists of a Constitutional Court headed by the President of the Court; the Supreme Court, consisting of the Appellate Division and provincial and local divisions, headed by the Chief Justice; and the magistrates' courts.

9   Under the 1996 Constitution the President of the Court and his Deputy will be appointed by the President after consultation with the Judicial Service Commission and the leaders of the parties represented in the National Assembly.

10   Section 97(2)(*a*), read with section 99(6) of the 1993 Constitution, specifically dispenses with consultation with the Judicial Service Commission in relation to the first President appointed to the Court.

11   Similarly, for the appointment of the Chief Justice under the 1993 Constitution, the President in terms of section 98 of the Constitution appoints the Chief Justice in consultation with the Cabinet after consultation with the Judicial Service Commission. In this regard the discussion about whether Mandela had made a mistake by making known his candidate was based on a misconception of the nature of the procedure under the 1993 Constitution.

12   Under the 1996 Constitution adopted by the Constitutional Assembly in May 1996, the President shall appoint the four judges from a list compiled by the Judicial Service Commission and after consulting the President of the Constitutional Court and leaders of the parties represented in the National Assembly (section 174(4)).

13   Every provincial division of the Supreme Court is headed by a Judge President.

14   Whereas under the 1993 Constitution the profession appointed its own representatives, under the 1996 Constitution the President will have a wider discretion to appoint the representatives of the profession. In this way the number of people appointed by the executive has increased (section 178(1)(*e*) & (*f*).

15   Under the 1996 Constitution this position would be filled by a teacher of law designated by teachers of law at South African universities.

16   Under the 1996 Constitution the National Assembly has six representatives, three of whom must be members of the opposition parties. In addition, the National Council of Provinces has four delegates and these have to be supported by at least six provinces.

17   The procedure for the appointment of Constitutional Court judges has been simplified under the 1996 Constitution. All must be appointed from a list drawn up by the Judicial Service Commission interviewed by this body. From section 174(3) it is not clear whether the procedure to be followed by the Judicial Service Commission for the appointment of other judges also has to be followed for the appointment of the President of the Court and his Deputy and the Chief Justice and his Deputy.

18   Under the 1996 Constitution the Judicial Service Commission compiles a list which contains three names more than the number of judges to be appointed.

19   The tenure of office of the Constitutional Court judges and the method of appointment of the President and his or her Deputy will change under the 1996 Constitution. See note 17 above: the term of office in this case is twelve years (section 176).

20   "Judges of the Constitutional Court and the Supreme Court shall receive such remuneration as may be prescribed by or under law, and their remuneration shall not be reduced during their continuation in office."

21   Section 104(4).

22   Hogg. 1992. *Constitutional Law of Canada,* 3 ed. Toronto: Carswell, section 8.4. According to Hogg, judges of the Supreme Court are appointed by the Governor in Council.

23   In South Africa the legal profession consists of the Side Bar for attorneys and the Bar for advocates. Only members of the latter were eligible to be appointed as judges in the past. Members of the Side Bar are in direct contact with the general public, whereas members of the Bar have to be briefed by an attorney first and never take instructions directly form their clients.

24   *The Weekly Mail and Guardian*, 30 September 1994, 37.

25   The Minister of Justice and the four senators.

26   Although he was already a judge, he was subjected to the interviews, but his other four colleagues, who had been appointed by the President, were not interviewed.

27   *The Citizen*, 6 October 1994, 4.

28   *The Star*, 4 October 1994, 3.

29   Except the President and his Deputy (section 174(3)).

30   The President appointed several acting judges in his place. One of these was Kentridge AJ who became famous for his role as the defence lawyer in the Steve Biko inquest in the 1970s. He is presently a barrister in England and has served on the Bench in Botswana. The other two acting judges were Trengrove J, one of the few judges who resigned from his post in the Appellate Division, and Ngoepe J, one of the few black lawyers who seem to have made it.

31   *S v Khanyile & another* 1988 (3) SA 795 (N), *S v Davids; S v Dladla* 1989 (4) SA 172 (N) and *S v Rudman & another; S v Mthwana* 1992 (1) SA 343 (A).

32   Under the 1996 Constitution, the Appellate Division will be called the Supreme Court of Appeal. In addition to the jurisdiction it now has, it will also have the jurisdiction "to decide appeals in any matter", including Constitutional matters. In the latter case there will still be an avenue of appeal to the Constitutional Court.

33   Section 101(2) reads: "Subject to this Constitution, the Supreme Court shall have the jurisdiction, including the inherent jurisdiction, vested in the Supreme Court immediately before the commencement of this Constitution, and any furhter jurisdiction conferred upon it by this Constitution or by any law."

34   Section 98(2).

35   To this list section 167(4)(*d*) and (*e*) of the 1996 Constitution have been added. In terms of these subsections, only the Constitutional Court has power to decide whether or not Parliament or the President has failed to comply with their constitutional duty and the power to certify provincial Consititutions.

36   Section 101(5).

37   The matter falling within the exclusive jurisdiction of the Constitutional Court must be decisive for the case and the provincial division of the Supreme Court must consider it in the interest of justice to refer the matter to the Constitutional Court. In that case the division must suspend the case in so far as there may be issues which have not been referred. This suspension will be pending the decision of the Constitutional Court on the matters referred (section 102(2).

38   This section provides that the 1996 Constitution must comply with the Constitutional Principles contained in schedule 4 of the 1993 Constitution.

39   Certification of the Constitution of the Republic of South Africa, 1996, CCT 23/96, decided on 6 September 1996.

40   Para 482 of the judgment of the court.

41 This section gives workers the right to form trade unions and to participate in strikes. It also gives employers the right to form employers' organisations, but does not give them the right to engage in collective bargaining (eg lock-out).

42 Which entrenched the Labour Relations Act of 1995.

43 See Prakke *Toetsing in het Publiekrecht*; see also Mtshaulana *Judicial Review in a Future Democratic SA (Perspectives and Prospects)* at 27.

44 However, it must be stressed that there are differences between the two courts' jurisdictions in respect of non-constitutional issues. In the United States, the Supreme Court has held that, except in matters governed by the Constitution, the law to be applied in any case is the law of the state. The federal courts have no constitutional jurisdiction to develop a federal common law in the absence of constitutional issues (*Erie Railroad Co v Tompkins* (1938) 304 US 64). The position in Canada is different. The Supreme Court of Canada is the highest court of appeal for all provincial law matters and has jurisdiction to develop uniform common-law rules for all the provinces of Canada.

45 "Embodied in the words 'case' and 'controversies' are two complementary but somewhat different limitations. In part those words limit the business of the federal courts to questions presented in an adversarial context and in a form historically viewed as capable of resolution through the judicial process." (*Flast v Cohen* 392 US 83 (1968) at 95).

46 Section 101(5): "The Appellate Division shall have no jurisdiction to adjudicate any matter within the jurisdiction of the Constitutional Court."

47 Van der Westhuizen J at 1; see also the following unpublished papers presented at Conference: A Constitutional Court for South Africa, Magaliesburg, 1–3 February 1991: Dugard J *Judicial Power and a Constitutional Court*; Chaskalson *A Constitutional Court: Jurisdiction, Possible Models and Questions of Access*; and Asmal *Constitutional Courts: A Comparative Survey*.

48 Mtshaulana *Judicial Review in a future Democratic South Africa (Perspectives and Prospects)*.

49 The opinion relates to an existing law. Preventive judicial review, on the other hand, prevents unconstitutional laws from coming into being at all.

50 Section 98(4) of the 1993 Constitution.

51 *Attorney General of Ontario v Attorney General of Canada* 1912 AC 571.

52 Hogg op cit at 8.6(*d*).

53 NT 167 (4).

54 Subsection (2) contained the form and manner provision in terms of which a division of the Supreme Court was empowered "… to inquire into and pronounce upon the question as to whether the provisions of the Constitution were complied with in connection with any law which expressed to be enacted by the State President and Parliament …".

55 "The procedure express or implied in the South Africa Act so far as Courts of Law are concerned is at the mercy of Parliament like everything else … Parliament's will … expressed in an Act of Parliament cannot now in this country, as it cannot in England, be questioned by a Court of Law, whose function it is to enforce that will not to question it." *Ndlwana v Hofmeyr NO* 1937 AD 229, 237, 238.

56 *Collins v Minister of the Interior* 1957 (1) SA 552 (A) at 565D.

57 Section 2 of the 1996 Constitution is the supremacy clause. Unfortunately the words "unless otherwise provided expressly or by necessary implication …" have been left out. This omission will cause problems of interpretation where two clauses conflict.

58 Section 172(2) r/w 168(3) of the 1996 Constitution allows the Supreme Court and the Appellate Division to make an order concerning the constitutional validity of an Act of Parliament. Such order has no force and effect unless confirmed by the Constitutional Court.

59 1995 (9) SACLR 74 (CC) para 2.

60 1995 (4) SACLR 257 (CC); 1995 (3) SA 292 (CC); 1995 (7) BCLR 851 (CC) para 7–12.

61 *Ferreira v Levin NO & others; Vriyenhoek & others v Powell NO and others* 1995 (7) SACLR 63 (CC); 1996 (1) BCLR (CC) para 6–8.

62 *Mhlungu & 4 others v S* 1995 (5) SACLR 1 (CC); 1995 (3) SA 867 (CC); 1995 (7) BCLR 793 (CC) para 59 and *Ferreira v Levin* para 7 (see also *Zantsi v Council of State & 2 others* 1995 (6) SACLR 88 (CC) para 3–4).

63 *Zuma & others v S* 1995 (3) SACLR 1 (CC) para 11 at 35; also *Luitingh v Minister of Defence* 1995 (9) SACLR 44 (CC) para 15 at 69.

64 Section 172 of the 1996 Constitution.

65 This power was used by the Court in the case of *The Executive of the Western Cape Legislature & others v The President of the Republic of South Africa & others* Case no CCT 27/95, decided on 22 September 1995, where the Court declared invalid section 16A of the Local Government Transition Act and all proclamations which were made by the President under it. However, the Court gave Parliament thirty days in which to rectify the invalidity. Parliament was on recess at the time, but had to be reconvened and the proclamations legalised by passing them in the form of an Act of Parliament.

66 Section 103(2) of the 1993 Constitution.

67 Section 103(3). The magistrate must be of the opinion that it is in the interests of justice to refer the issue raised.

68 Section 103(4).

69 Section 168(3) of the 1996 Constitution brings a change in that the Supreme Court of Appeal has jurisdiction to hear constitutional appeals.

70 1995 (5) BCLR 658 (CC).

Chapter 4
Democracy and Policing

Medard Rwelamira

4.1   INTRODUCTION

*A*NY discussion of democracy and policing in South Africa today must take place within the context of the recent political changes.

The first democratic elections held in 1994 have not only had a tremendous impact on the broader political landscape but have also in many ways shaped attitudes towards political institutions, governance, social and political account-ability. Indeed, the 1994 elections represent a watershed between the new order based on democratic principles and constitutionalism, and the old apartheid era which was characterised by massive violations of human rights, of which police brutality was a significant feature. This chapter examines the challenges that face the police in the new democratic dispensation and the attempts to refashion and shape the Police Service to align it with democratic ideals. This, of course, cannot be regarded as a one-way process. The police, as a major institution of state power, should be influenced by the broader changes in the political process. Policing, in turn, can influence the direction and realisation of democratic targets, and the legitimacy of the political transi-tion itself. Thus, this chapter also examines the exercise of executive power in the South African Police Services and the attendant consequences for human rights. In this context, both judicial and legislative controls of that power are also examined. It is also argued that the protection of human rights does not rest merely on the entrenchment of formal guarantees in the Bill of Rights; rather, the citizenry should also have the institutional capacity to monitor and facilitate the achievement of fundamental rights.[1] More importantly, the public have a duty to expose human rights abuses when they do occur. Similarly, the governance and accountability of the Police Service as an institution for the administration of justice should be treated on a more realistic and rational plane, taking into account the legacy of apartheid of which it must still divest itself.

Policing in South Africa must therefore be viewed in the broader context of a democratic society. The process of building a democratic society should encompass an earnest endeavour to abandon the institutions of tyranny and to replace them with institutions capable of engendering unity, nation building and reconciliation. The liberation of South Africa requires more than the dis-mantling of apartheid:

> "It requires the establishment of new forms of governance that will promote the liberty assets of those susceptible to discrimination, manipulation and exploitation of others. The institutions of policing are central to the conception of liberty as a civic asset."[2]

4.2   KEY OBJECTIVES

The key objectives of this chapter are to enable students to:

- understand and discuss the influence of the Constitution on policing in general;

- understand and discuss the legal framework for police control;
- understand and discuss the relationship between police powers and accountability;
- understand and discuss the controls within the Police Service in relation to democracy;
- discuss the role of the community in policing.

4.3   APPLICABLE LAW

The 1993 Constitution, sections 8, 11, 23, 25(3), 221 and 222
The 1996 Constitution, sections 12 and 32
The Criminal Procedure Act of 1977, section 39(3) and 217
The South African Police Service Act of 1995, chapter 2 and section 3

4.4   INTERPRETATION AND DISCUSSION

4.4.1   Policing and the Constitution

The adoption of both the 1993 and 1996 Constitutions — especially the Bill of Rights — has set the firm basis for the protection of human rights. The individual can now not only challenge laws that unreasonably infringe individual rights but can also approach the courts for a remedy. In relation to the police, the protection being sought by an individual will invariably be protection against state interference with individual human rights. Under the Constitution, any person whose fundamental rights are infringed is entitled to apply to a competent court of law for appropriate relief. The Constitution also recognises the equality of persons, freedom and security of the person, freedom of expression, association and movement, the right of assembly, demonstration and petition. It protects the right to life, privacy and the right to freedom of conscience, religion, thought, belief and opinion. The Bill of Rights also contains elaborate provisions protecting the rights, dignity and integrity of detained, arrested and accused persons. It binds all legislative and executive organs at all levels of government. The latter is certainly one of the most important aspects of the Bill of Rights. It imposes on the courts not only an obligation to provide relief when such rights have been infringed but also empowers the courts to interpret and give content to the guarantees contained in the Bill of Rights. The courts are thus able to keep surveillance over legislative and executive competencies as well as to temper executive discretion. These powers have an important bearing on the exercise of police powers. The way the police exercise their powers and how the organisation as a whole is accountable for its actions are bound to have far-reaching constitutional and human rights implications.

4.4.2   The legal framework for police control

To most South Africans, particularly the formerly disenfranchised, the police are still regarded with suspicion and sometimes with outright hostility. During the apartheid era the police were used to suppress basic human rights. In the past the police force, as it was then called, was used more as an instrument to perpetrate violence than as an agent to promote peace. The police testimonies in the De Kock trial and before the Truth and Reconciliation Commission have shown beyond doubt that the police were a power unto themselves. There were no clear mechanisms to exact accountability, and even where such mechanisms existed, they were flouted with impunity. Not only were the police not punished for abusing their powers, they were often congratulated and promoted for work "well done". Over the years police accountability has been lacking. The apartheid era was characterised by a failure to make police institutions as responsible as other structures of the state. It is partly because of these considerations that the control of the police has been specifically provided for in the 1993 and 1996 Constitutions. The Constitution provides for the establishment and regulation by Act of Parliament of a South African Police Service to be structured at both national and provincial levels. Such a Service should function under the direction of the national government as well as the various provincial governments. Thus, at the level of government structure, the Police Service is under the civilian control of the Department of Safety and Security. Under the South Africa Police Service Act of 1995 which provides for the establishment, organisation, regulation and control of the Service, the Minister is empowered to establish a Secretariat for Safety and Security. The Secretariat is charged, *inter alia*, with the following functions:

(1) to advise the Minister in the exercise of his or her powers and the performance of his or her duties and functions;

(2) to promote democratic accountability and transparency in the Service;

(3) to promote and facilitate participation by the Service in the Reconstruction and Development Programme;

(4) to perform such functions as the Minister may consider necessary to ensure civilian oversight.

By bringing the Police Service directly under civilian responsibility, it has been subjected to the normal processes of political and constitutional accountability. Under individual and collective responsibility both the Minister and the government as a whole are responsible to Parliament for the conduct of the Police Service. This makes it possible to monitor on a continuous basis the behaviour as well as the performance of the police.

4.4.3 Police powers and accountability

The police have many powers under the law. These include the powers of arrest, search, seizure and the power to investigate the commission of crime. Under the Criminal Procedure Act of 1977 the police are vested with myriad powers, including the power to proceed to any place where they have reasonable suspicion that a crime has been committed, and then to conduct investigations. If they come across evidence that indicates that a crime has been committed, they have the power to arrest suspects.

The power of arrest is probably one of the most critical competencies that the police have. Arrest represents one of the major invasions and restrictions on individual freedom. Not only does it affect one's freedom of movement, it can also affect the dignity and privacy of the person. This was no more apparent than during the time of apartheid when political opponents, often innocent, were mercilessly arrested or placed under house arrest. Almost invariably arrest was used as an effective device to muzzle, if not completely silence, political opponents. Thus, because of its potential to affect negatively other rights such as the right to privacy, freedom of movement and association and the right to security of the person, the power of arrest has critical implications for the establishment of a democratic and constitutional legal order.

The new constitutional dispensation in South Africa is predicated on the need to create a society in which all South Africans are equal and are able to enjoy and exercise their fundamental rights and freedoms. Arrest represents a drastic interference with the personal liberty of an individual and is therefore valid only if it complies with the procedural requirements set out in the Criminal Procedure Act of 1977 and the Constitution of 1996. No general power of arrest has been accorded to any person. Arrest is justified only if the person effecting the arrest has a search warrant or if the arrest is justifiable under any of the rules of law which condone arrest without a warrant. The person effecting an arrest must in addition show good reasons to support its execution. Our courts have increasingly taken the view that arrest as a method of securing attendance should be sparingly used. In the recent case of *S v More*[3] Justice Marais took the view that summons should be preferred to arrest, particularly in cases where the gravity of the offence or the particular circumstance of the accused show that there is no good basis to suppose that the arrested person will abscond. This position is further reinforced by the constitutional provisions which require that a person be presumed innocent until found guilty. Justice Marais could not have put it more succinctly, when he said:

> "where the accused is known and his interests are such as to dispel any suspicion that he might decamp, there is usually no necessity for resorting to a method which however tactfully exercised, must result in some loss of liberty and in the imposition of some measure of indignity".

The consequence of arrest is usually that the person is in lawful custody or lawfully detained. Section 39(3) of the Criminal Procedure Act of 1977 provides that:

> "the effect of an arrest shall be that the person arrested shall be in lawful custody and that he shall be detained in custody until he is lawfully discharged or released from custody".

On the face of it, this seems to be an ominous position and indeed the consequences of arrest have been curtailed in a number of decisions. In *Nhlabati v Adjunk Prokureur-Generaal, Transvaal*[4] the Court pointed out that detention does not remain lawful merely on the strength of arrest. Similarly, the 1993 and

1996 Constitutions now provide additional safeguards. Not only is the detained person entitled to challenge the lawfulness of his/her detention in person before a court of law, but in addition, as an arrested person he/she has the right to be released from detention unless the interests of justice require otherwise. While the courts have taken the position that bail can be denied under appropriate circumstances (*S v Mabaza en 'n ander*),[5] they recognise the principle that bail is an entitlement which should not be lightly denied. In addition, a detained person has the right as soon as possible, but not later than 48 hours after his/her detention, to be brought before a court of law and be charged or informed of the reasons for his or her further detention, failing which he or she is entitled to be discharged or released. This has a number of implications. In the first place, the police can only keep someone in custody if there are compelling reasons for doing so, and even then these reasons must justify the denial of bail to such a detainee. In addition, the principle of presumption of innocence imposes a duty on the state to adduce sufficient and cogent reasons to justify the encroachment of individual liberties.

Another important aspect of the development of the democratic order has been the curtailment — if not total removal — of police secrecy, especially in relation to evidence in criminal proceedings. Before 1994 and the adoption of the Bill of Rights, evidence contained in police dockets was privileged and was not available to the accused for discovery purposes. The common law made no provision for discovery in criminal cases, and the docket privilege was entrenched in the law of evidence by the decision in *R v Steyn*.[6] In that case the Court held that, when statements are procured from a witness for the purposes of evidence in a contemplated lawsuit, these statements are protected against disclosure until at least the conclusion of the proceedings. This remained the position until the adoption and commencement of the Constitution in 1994.

One of the cardinal principles underlying the 1993 Constitution is transparency on the part of government organs and institutions. It is recognised that, in order to make government and government institutions accountable, it is imperative that the veil of secrecy over government operations be confined to the barest minimum, and even then carefully circumscribed. Thus, section 23 of the 1993 Constitution provides that: "Every person shall have the right of access to all information held by the state or any of its organs at any level of government insofar as such information is required for the exercise or protection of any of his or her rights."

Section 32 of the 1996 Constitution provides as follows:

"(1)   Everyone has the right of access to —

(a) any information held by the State; and

(b) any information that is held by another person and that is required for the exercise or protection of any rights.

"(2)   National legislation must be enacted to give effect to this right, and may provide for reasonable measures to alleviate the administrative and financial burden on the State."

Initially the courts were hesitant to interpret section 23 of the 1993 Constitution liberally. For example, in the cases of *S v Fani & others*,[7] *S v Lombard*[8] and *S v Dontas*,[9] the courts consistently defended the docket privilege and took the position that such a privilege was not necessarily inconsistent with fundamental rights. In the *Dontas* case, Justice Swart was of the opinion that such a privilege did not infringe the presumption of innocence as set out in section 25 of the 1993 Constitution, and that in any case the presumption applied only as far as the court was required to regard the accused innocent until his/her guilt had been proved.

However, in subsequent decisions, starting with the case of *S v Majavu*,[10] the courts shifted the pendulum in favour of the accused person. In that case Justice Heath held that the rights provided for in section 23 of the 1993 Constitution had to be considered together. After reviewing a number of international authorities, and in particular the Canadian decision in *R v Stinchcombe*,[11] he came to the conclusion that section 23 was not a criminal discovery measure. He argued that the rights provided for in section 23 of the 1993 Constitution had to be considered in conjunction with the rights envisaged by the provisions of section 25(3) of the 1993 Constitution which entitled the accused to a fair trial. In terms of the latter, the Court reasoned that what was envisaged by the right to a fair trial, apart from compliance with rules of procedure and the principles of law, was that the accused must be enabled or be given an opportunity to present his or her case properly and fully. Furthermore, in terms of the provisions of section 8 of the 1993 Constitution, every person has a right to equality before the law and equal protection by the law. This means that the accused has a right to enjoy equal protection under the law as that enjoyed by the state. After taking due cognisance of the spirit and objectives of the Constitution, and the "values which underlie an open and democratic society", he concluded that these would best be served by "transparency also of information in possession of the prosecution and the state". He was unequivocal in his assertion that the openness and accessibility of police dockets would also promote a situation where the police would realise that they must conduct their investigations properly and professionally. In the later decision of *S v Botha en andere*,[12] Justice Le Roux, while endorsing the reasoning of Justice Heath, put the matter very succinctly when he argued that the values of our "open and democratic society based on freedom and equality" demanded that the previously authoritarian style of prosecution espoused by the prosecuting authority was no longer appropriate and that, accordingly, the state could no longer remain the sole organ with the exclusive responsibility of deciding which statements could be furnished to the accused.

This trend in judicial reasoning is bound to have far-reaching implications especially in relation to the methods employed by the police when conducting criminal investigations. The practices of the past, whereby the state had exclusive control over all information available to the prosecution, can no longer be reconciled with new democratic ideals (*Phato v Attorney-General, Eastern Cape*

& another,[13] *Commissioner of South African Police Services v Attorney-General, Eastern Cape & others*[14] and *Shabalala v Attorney-General, Transvaal*[15]).

In addition to evidentiary controls imposed by the court there are other controls to be found in the Constitution. Section 11 of the 1993 Constitution and section 12 of the 1996 Constitution guarantee freedom and security of the person. No person can be subjected to torture of any kind, whether physical, mental or emotional, nor may anyone be subjected to cruel, inhuman and degrading treatment. These constitutional provisions certainly impose limitations not only on the methods that the police can use to obtain information from suspects during interrogation, but also have the effect of rendering evidence thus obtained inadmissible. Section 217 of the Criminal Procedure Act of 1977 provides that a confession will be inadmissible unless it is made freely and voluntarily and without undue influence. While a confession obtained in violation of section 11 of the 1993 Constitution is clearly inadmissible, the constitutional provision appears to be broad enough to cover other evidence obtained in contravention of the Bill of Rights. In the case of *S v Melani & others*[16] the Court seems to have accepted in principle that evidence obtained by means which infringe the rights of the accused may under certain circumstances be inadmissible. Similar restraints are imposed in cases of state emergencies. While the state of emergency introduced in 1985 and extended annually after 1986 was provided for in such a way as to avoid legal supervision and accountability, the present constitutional provisions regarding the declaration of a state of emergency are emphatic and categorical in their requirements for detailed control of discretionary power. While the Constitution provides for the suspension of certain rights during a state of emergency, other rights are non-derogatable. Such rights include the Bill of Rights section of the Constitution dealing with the equality clause, the right to life, human dignity and the right to freedom and security of the person. By subjecting all the measures taken in the state of emergency to legislative or judicial scrutiny, the executive organs of the state, including the police, would be required to justify their actions on objective grounds.

One must, however, quickly add that the presence of legal controls does not per se guarantee police accountability for their actions. Much will depend on the willingness of victims to report such abuses and on the courts' disposition to interpret the law in the context of democratic ideals. Secondly, even where the victims are prepared to report and bring charges in respect of these abuses, the costs of litigation will normally be prohibitive. Apart from the considerations of access to finance, lawyers and resources, the gravest difficulty that litigants are bound to face is that of proving the facts. This will apply equally to both civil and criminal proceedings.[17]

4.4.4 Controls within the Police Service

One of the major weaknesses in exacting police accountability during the apartheid era was the absence of independent organs to investigate allegations of police misconduct.[18] Whenever complaints were made against the police, it would be the police themselves who carried out the investigations, with the predictable result that culprits were seldom identified or punished. The situation was even worse when the complainants were black people since, in some cases, they were unlikely to attract the sympathy of white police officers. The latter were generally reluctant to investigate their fellow white officers. This mutual support and what has sometimes been described as institutional cohesion made it difficult, if not impossible, to subject police conduct to accountability to local communities or community structures. It is against this background that, during the negotiations for the 1993 Constitution, emphasis was placed on providing for some mechanism to scrutinise police conduct. Thus, section 222 of the 1993 Constitution provides for the establishment of an independent complaints mechanism under civilian control. Its functions are, *inter alia*, to ensure that complaints in respect of offences and misconduct allegedly committed by members of the Police Service are investigated in an effective and efficient manner.

The South African Police Service Act of 1995 has made provision for the establishment of the Independent Complaints Directorate. The Directorate is supposed to function independently and without interference from the Police Service. In addition to implementing the objectives contemplated in the Constitution, the Directorate is also charged with the responsibility of receiving complaints, investigating any misconduct or offence allegedly committed by any member of the Police Service and, where appropriate, referring such an investigation to the Commissioner concerned. Other responsibilities include investigating any death in police custody or as a result of police action. The Director may seek assistance from any officer in the Service, including the Attorney-General, in respect of any matter under investigation. At the end of each financial year the Director is required to present to the Minister a written report on the activities of the Directorate, which report will be tabled before Parliament.

It is hoped that the above supervisory mechanisms will complement the internal controls which deal with discipline, training and codes of conduct generally. Although such measures primarily focus on internal behaviour and discipline, they can also be extended to instances of abuse of discretion by police officials.

4.4.5   The role of the community in policing

One of the major challenges in the transformation of the South African Police Service is how to change it from an instrument of oppression into a community resource. The crisis of legitimacy that currently faces the Police Service is the consequence of a deep-rooted institutional complicity or organisational deviance which over the years has inhibited the SAP's capacity as a police organisation to become a protector of communities, especially of black communities. Throughout the apartheid era members of the South African Police Service were trained and motivated to control rather than protect communities.

In order to change this attitude, much more than legislative intervention will be required. More innovative approaches which emphasise "culture change" and dedication to community protection will have to be evolved if other programmes aimed at transforming the police are to succeed. For the police to gain legitimacy in the eyes of the communities, partnerships will have to be developed.

Section 221 of the 1993 Constitution provides for the establishment of community police forums. This requirement has now found detailed expression in the provisions of the South African Police Service Act of 1995. The objectives of such forums are, *inter alia*, to promote communication between the police and the community, to promote co-operation between the police and the community in order to meet the community's policing needs and to improve transparency and accountability of the Police Service. The idea behind the community police forums is certainly a noble one. However, their effectiveness as institutions, as well as their ability to exact accountability from the police, will depend on a number of factors. Firstly, it will depend on the availability of resources and the synergy that exists between the community and the police. Unless communities are prepared to accept the police as partners in the fight against crime and vice versa, the whole initiative is unlikely to succeed. Secondly, and probably of more crucial importance will be the extent to which the police are able to allow communities to influence their policies, choices and decisions. It will indeed be unfortunate if the perception develops that community police forums are little more than instruments of the police to control communities. Lastly, the communities, as well as the police, will need to have a clear understanding of their respective roles and how they relate to each other. However, the ultimate responsibility of maintaining law and order rests squarely with the police.

4.4.6   Conclusion

As the democratic transition takes root the challenges facing the Police Service are bound to increase both in nature and complexity. The need constantly to re-examine institutions and realign them with emerging democratic aspirations will become more critical. Already the police are under considerable pressure to adjust to the human rights culture introduced by the Constitution. The Bill of Rights has exerted pressure on old and familiar ways of dealing with crime and communities. The police are now required to maintain that delicate balance between law enforcement and respect for human rights and human dignity. At the same time one is only too aware of the fact that poverty and other injustices created by the system of apartheid are bound to exert considerable pressure on democratic institutions and, in the process, to generate popular impatience with the criminal justice system. How the police respond to calls for harsh and severe measures against suspects and criminals will be crucial for their image. At the same time, the police must review and initiate training programmes which emphasise human rights and community values. Programmes should also be arranged which expose them to policing practices in established democracies. This commitment must, however, be supported by the community. Indeed, both the community and the police need to be made aware of the values and wealth of the human rights and democratic traditions.

4.5 SUGGESTED READING AND SOURCES

Brogden, M. 1989. The origins of the South African Police: Institutional versus structural approaches. 1989 *Acta Juridica* 1.

Brogden, M & Shearing. 1993. *Policing for a New South Africa*.

Cachalia, A. 1994. *Fundamental Rights in the Constitution*. Cape Town: Juta.

Dugard, J. 1978. *Human Rights and the South African Legal Order*. Princeton University Press.

Haysom, N. 1989. Policing the police: A comparative survey of police control mechanisms in the United States, South Africa and United Kingdom. 1989 *Acta Juridica* 139.

Kapinga, W. 1990. The police force and human rights in Tanzania. *Third World Legal Studies*, 37.

Paul, JCN. 1990. Putting internal security forces under the rule of human rights law: The need for a code of universal principles regulating their governance. *Third World Legal Studies*, 233.

Schärf, W. 1989. Community policing in South Africa. 1989 *Acta Juridica* 206.

• •

ENDNOTES

1   Kapinga 37.
2   Brogden & Shearing 2.
3   1993 (2) SACR 606 (W).
4   1978 (3) SA 630 (W).
5   1994 (5) BCLR 42 (N).
6   1954 (1) SA 324 (A).
7   1994 (1) SACR 635 (E).
8   1994 (3) BCLR 126 (T).
9   1995 (1) SACR 473 (T).
10   1994 (2) SACR 265 (Ck).
11   992 LRC (Cnm) 68.
12   1994 (3) BCLR 94 (W).
13   1994 (5) BCLR 99 (EC).

14 1994 (2) SACR 734 (EC).

15 1995 (12) BCLR 1593 (CC).

16 1996 (2) BCLR 174 (EC).

17 Haysom 147.

18 Ibid.

Chapter 5
Interpretation

Cecile van Riet

SUMMARY

SECTION 35 of the 1993 Constitution and section 39 of the 1996 Constitution deal with the interpretation of the two Constitutions respectively. This chapter covers judicial review and discusses and analyses both interpretation clauses, as well as the role of international law in interpreting the Bill of Rights.

5.1   INTRODUCTION

The Constitution 1993 ushered in a new constitutional dispensation for South Africa. It represented a break with the Westminster parliamentary tradition, in terms of which the legislature was sovereign and the courts were obliged to apply the law, without having the power to pronounce on the validity of its content. The 1993 and 1996 Constitutions are supreme and this system of constitutionalism accords a vital role to the judiciary. In terms of "judicial review" the judiciary has the power to review legislation, as well as the actions of the government and administrative decisions. The Constitution, and especially the fundamental rights with their underlying values, provides the framework for this review.

When the preamble to the 1993 Constitution speaks of a "new order", it refers to a new political reality for all South Africans, founded on a new legal construct which, of necessity, will have to be interpreted in an original fashion. This new order is *sui generis*. Its future meaning will come to depend on the discovery and application of the values immanent in the Constitution: *the founding contract of a new society*.

> "The Constitution of a nation is not simply a statute which mechanically defines the structures of government and the relations between government and the governed. It is a 'mirror reflecting the national soul', the identification of the ideals and aspirations of a nation; the articulation of the values bonding its people and disciplining its government. The spirit and the tenor of the Constitution must therefore preside and permeate the processes of judicial interpretation and judicial discretion.[1]"

5.2   KEY OBJECTIVES

The key objectives of this chapter are to enable students to:
- understand and discuss judicial review;
- understand and discuss the interpretation clause;
- understand and discuss the role of international law in interpreting the Bill of Rights.

5.3   APPLICABLE LAW

The 1993 Constitution, section 35
The 1996 Constitution, section 39

5.4   INTERPRETATION AND DISCUSSION

5.4.1   Judicial review

Judicial scrutiny/review is a two-stage process: determining the scope of fundamental rights constitutes the first step in the process and the application of a general standard of limitation (in terms of the scope of the right) the second. The first stage deals with the question of whether the law that is being challenged violates any of the rights in the Bill of Rights. If this is so, we proceed to ask if this violation can be justified in terms of the limitation clause. The 1993 Constitution contained a general limitation clause in Section 33 and the 1997 Constitution in Section 36.

5.4.2   The interpretation clause

Certain principles of interpretation are contained in section 35 of the 1993 Constitution and section 39 of the 1996 Constitution.

Section 35 of the 1993 Constitution reads as follows:

"(1) In interpreting the provisions of this Chapter a court of law shall promote the values which underlie an open and democratic society based on freedom and equality and shall, where applicable, have regard to public international law applicable to the protection of the rights entrenched in this Chapter, and may have regard to comparable foreign case law.

"(2) No law which limits any of the rights entrenched in this Chapter, shall be constitutionally invalid solely by reason of the fact that the wording used prima facie exceeds the limits imposed in this Chapter, provided such a law is reasonably capable of a more restricted interpretation which does not exceed such limits, in which event such law shall be construed as having a meaning in accordance with the said more restricted interpretation.

"(3) In the interpretation of any law and the application and development of the common law and customary law, a court shall have due regard to the spirit, purport and objects of this chapter."

Section 39 of the 1996 Constitution reads as follows:

"(1) When interpreting the Bill of Rights, a court, tribunal or forum —

(*a*) must promote the values that underlie an open and democratic society based on human dignity, equality and freedom.

(*b*) must consider international law.

(*c*) may consider foreign law.

"(2) When interpreting any legislation, and when developing the common law or customary law, every court, tribunal or forum must promote the spirit, purport and objects of the Bill of Rights.

"(3) The Bill of Rights does not deny the existence of any other rights or freedoms that are recognised or conferred by common law, customary law or legislation, to the extent that they are consistent with the Bill."

The point of departure for any exercise in interpretation is *the text*:

"Nor am I equally sure, did the learned Judge intend to suggest that we should neglect the language of the Constitution. While we must always be conscious of the values underlying the Constitution, it is nonetheless our task to interpret a written instrument. I am well aware of the fallacy of supposing that general language must have a single 'objective' meaning. Nor is it easy to avoid the influence of one's personal intellectual and moral preconceptions. But it cannot be too strongly stressed that the Constitution does not mean whatever we might wish it to mean.

"We must heed Lord Wilberforce's reminder that even a constitution is a legal instrument, the language of which must be respected. If the language used by the lawgiver is ignored in favour of a general resort to 'values' the result is not interpretation but divination ... I would say that a constitution embodying fundamental rights should as far as its language permits be given a broad construction.[2]"

Any exercise in constitutional interpretation should commence with the text and, although a *literal approach* to constitutional interpretation may be feasible where provisions are plain and clear, this should be adopted with the cautionary note that a holistic and contextual approach should be used. It would be a violation of the Constitution if one of its provisions were to be construed in a manner which destroyed the whole basis of the Constitution, "... when by a different construction the beauty, cohesion, integrity and healthy development of the State through the Constitution will be maintained".[3]

In *S v Makwanyane*[4] the Court stated that the provisions of the Bill of Rights must not be interpreted in isolation but *in context*: the fact that the death sentence is imposed in a small number of murder cases (243 in the five years preceding the decision), when a very large number of murders are committed (according to police statistics, more than 100 000 for the same period), makes the imposition of the sentence (on the few unfortunate individuals amongst the many eligible ones) cruel. The fact that the death sentence permits killing and is an infringement of section 9 (the right to life) also indicates that section 11(2) (the right against cruel, inhuman or degrading punishment) is infringed. In employing this form of contextual interpretation, Justice Chaskalson allowed himself to focus on the infringements of sections 8, 9 and 10 and not simply on the meaning of section 11(2).

The Canadian case *R v Oakes*[5] serves to illustrate the importance of the limitation clause in terms of interpretation. Hogg[6] declares that it is not possible to insist that the rights enshrined in the Canadian Charter should be given a *generous interpretation* (wider scope), whilst insisting that the standard of justification for the limitation should be stringent. The fact that a high standard of justification for any limitation is placed upon the government entails a corresponding caution in defining the scope of the guaranteed rights. "Each right should be so interpreted as not to reach behaviour that is outside the purpose of the right — behaviour that is not worthy of constitutional protection."

Davis[7] therefore quite correctly rejects the bland assertion that constitutional interpretation requires a generous approach because "... it accords too little weight to the fundamental problem of constitutionalism, namely the balancing of the expression of the majority will as evidenced by the enactments of a legislature with the entrenched rights conferred in a bill of rights. It is necessary to examine carefully the manner in which a bill of rights itself seeks to promote the democratic enterprise. It is here that a *'purposive approach'* prompts superior guidance to the generous interpretation."

To interpret a provision generously would mean to give the widest possible meaning to the language. On the other hand, to interpret a provision in a purposive manner would mean that you interpreted it so that it could realise/promote/fulfil its purpose (the reason why it is enshrined). This enterprise is guided by the values which underpin the Constitution and ensures that the process is consonant with the thematic framework thereof — a far less mechanical undertaking.

The difference is clearly illustrated in *Andrews v Law Society*[8] and articulated well in *R v Big M Drug Mart*[9]:

> "The meaning of a right or freedom guaranteed by the Charter was to be ascertained by an analysis of the purpose of such a guarantee, it was to be understood, in other words, in the light of the interest it was meant to protect.
>
> "In my view this analysis is to be undertaken, and the purpose of the right or freedom in question is to be sought by reference to the character and the larger objects of the Charter itself, to the language chosen to articulate the specific right or freedom, to the historical origins of the concepts enshrined and where applicable to the meaning and purpose of the other rights and freedoms."

In *S v Makwanyane*[10] and *S v Zuma*[11] the Constitutional Court committed itself to the *purposive approach* to interpretation. The interpretation clauses of the 1993 and 1996 Constitutions require that the values which underpin fundamental rights in an open and democratic society based on human dignity, freedom and equality be identified and promoted in the interpretation. This involves value judgements[12] which may not be derived from or equated with public opinion. In *S v Makwanyane*[13] the Constitutional Court held that, while public opinion may be relevant, it is in itself no substitute for the duty vested in the Court to interpret the Constitution.

In *S v Zuma*[14] and *S v Mhlungu*[15] the Constitutional Court has also expressed itself to be in favour of a "generous, broad or liberal" approach to interpretation. It has, however, not indicated how it would resolve the tension between a generous and a purposive interpretation.

In section 39 of the 1996 Constitution, courts are instructed not only to promote the values that underlie an open and democratic society based on freedom and equality but also to value *human dignity*. The Constitutional Court stated in *Brink v Kitshoff* [16]:

> "As in other national constitutions, Section 8 is the product of our own particular history. Perhaps more than any of the other provisions in Chapter 3 its interpretation must be based on the specific language of Section 8, as well as our own constitutional text. Our history is of particular relevance to the concept of equality. The policy of apartheid, in law and in fact, systematically discriminated against black people in all aspects of social life. Black people were prevented from becoming owners of property or even residing in areas classified as 'white', which constituted nearly 90% of the land mass of South Africa; senior jobs and access to established schools and universities were denied to them; civic amenities, including transport systems, public parks, libraries, and many shops were also closed to black people. Instead, separate and inferior facilities were provided. The deep scars of this appalling programme are still visible in our society. It is in the light of that history and the enduring legacy that it bequeathed that the equality clause needs to be interpreted."

It seems as if the process of the drafting of the 1996 Constitution was in line with the development of a South African constitutional jurisprudence. The Constitution is the product of South Africa's peculiar history of discrimination and inequality and in that context *equality* and *human dignity* will be at the core of our constitutional values.

Both the 1993 and 1996 Constitutions are products of South Africa's peculiar problems and solutions. In *S v Makwanyane* [17] the Constitutional Court stated:

> "Our Constitution was the product of negotiations conducted at the multi-party negotiation process. The final draft adopted by the forum of the multi-party negotiating process was, with few changes, adopted by Parliament. The multi-party negotiation process was advised by technical committees, and the reports of these committees on the drafts are the equivalent of the *travaux preparatoires*, relied upon by international tribunals. Such *background material* can provide a context for the interpretation of the Constitution and, where it serves that purpose, I can see no reason why such evidence should be excluded. The precise nature of the evidence, and the purpose for which it may be tendered, will determine the weight to be given to it."

In the above-mentioned case a report of the Technical Committee on fundamental rights was used to show that the drafters of the Constitution left the right to life unqualified so that the Constitutional Court could decide on the constitutionality of the death penalty; it seems that documents which are clear, not in dispute, relevant and official can be used for the purposes of interpretation. The *Makwanyane* judgment and criteria certainly do not exclude the *Constitutional Principles* (Schedule IV of the 1993 Constitution) from being used as background materials in the interpretation process.

5.4.3   The role of international law in interpreting the Bill of Rights

Section 35(1) of the 1993 Constitution obliges the courts to have regard to public international law.

According to Dugard,[18] section 35(1) does not limit a court's enquiry to treaties to which South Africa is a party or to customary rules that have been accepted by the South African courts, but also to:

(*a*)   international conventions, whether general or particular, establishing rules expressly recognised by the contesting states;

(*b*)   international custom, as evidence of a general practice accepted as law;

(*c*)   the general principles of law recognised by civilised nations; and

(*d*)   judicial decisions and the teachings of the most highly qualified publicists of the various nations, as subsidiary means for the determination of rules of law.

He feels that such a conclusion follows logically from the use of the term "public international law" without qualification in section 35(1) and the language of section 116(*a*) of the 1993 Constitution. It seems that section 35(1) was meant to be this broad in order to give maximum effect to the otherwise incomplete catalogue of rights entrenched in chapter 3. In *S v Makwanyane*[19] the court seemed to agree with this and in In *Re: The School Education Bill of 1995 (Gauteng)*[20] Justice Sachs quoted from international sources, international instruments and the work of international organisations on developments with regard to the protection of minorities.

The wording of section 39(1) in the 1997 Constitution has changed to "... a court, tribunal or forum —

(*a*)   must promote the values that underlie ... .

(*b*)   must consider international law

(*c*)   may consider foreign law".

It would be interesting to see what — if any — effect this change will have on our recently established constitutional jurisprudence.

5.4.4   The rest of the interpretation clause

Section 35(2) of the 1993 Constitution dealt with what is known as a presumption of constitutionality, which allows a court to "read down" statutes or provisions which are "reasonably capable" of a more restricted/constitutional interpretation.[21] Justice Mokgoro warned that "reading down" may not be employed to subvert the intention of the legislator otherwise it amounts to judicial law-making[22] and Justice Sachs felt that it was an important mechanism "which permits constitutionality to be upheld at minimum legislative and social cost".[23] In section 39 of the 1996 Constitution this provision is omitted.

In terms of section 35(3) of the 1993 Constitution, legislation, the common law and customary law fall within the ambit of the Constitution and this raises the issue whether the Constitution has vertical application only, or also horizontal application. The debate has been settled by the decision of the Constitutional Court in *Du Plessis v De Klerk*[24] in which it was concluded that private persons and organisations were excluded.

Section 39(2) of the 1996 Constitution has more or less the same wording as section 35(3) of the 1993 Constitution, except that the word "application" has been omitted. Section 8(2) states that the Bill of Rights binds a natural or a juristic person and it seems that the Constitutional Court in the Certification Judgment[25] was rather vague on this point but did not foreclose their position. In terms of paragraphs 53 and 54 of that judgment, the possibility exists for direct horizontal application.

Both sections 35(3) of the 1993 Constitution and 39(2) of the 1996 Constitution state that in the interpretation of any law and the (application) and development of the common law and customary law, a court (tribunal or forum) shall have due regard to/must promote the spirit, purport and objects of the Bill of Rights.

Section 39(3) of the 1996 Constitution acknowledges the protection that exists in legislation and customary law, and especially common law, for the protection of rights and incorportates that protection to the extent that those rights are consistent with the Bill of Rights.

5.5   SUGGESTED READING AND SOURCES

Cachalia, *et al.* 1994. *Fundamental Rights in the New Constitution.* Cape Town: Juta.

Davis, D. 1994. Democracy — Its influence upon the process of constitutional interpretation. (1994) 10 *SAJHR* 103.

De Waal, J & Erasmus, G. The constitutional jurisprudence of South African courts on the application, interpretation and limitation of fundamental rights during the transition. Unpublished article.

Dugard, J. 1994. The role of international law in interpreting the Bill of Rights. (1994) 10 *SAJHR* 208.

Hogg, P. 1992. *Constitutional Law of Canada.* Scarborough: Carswell.

Marcus, G. 1994. Interpreting the chapter on fundamental rights. (1994) 10 *SAJHR* 92.

....

ENDNOTES

1   Mahomed, R in *S v Acheson* 1991 (2) SA 805 (NMHC).

2   Ackermann, R in *Ferreira v Levin* 1996 (1) SA 984 (CC).

3   *Attorney-General, Botswana v Unity Dow* cited in *Ntenteni v Chairman, Ciskei Council of State* 1993 (4) SA 546 (CKGD).

4   1995 (6) BCLR 665 (CC).

5   1986 26 DLR (4th) 200.

6   Hogg, P.

7   Davis, D.

8   BC 1989 1 SCR 143.

9   1985 (1) SCR 295 at 344.

10 See *S v Makwanyane* supra, para 9.

11 1995 (4) BCLR 401 (CC).

12 As recognised by Mahomed J in *Ex parte Attorney-General, Namibia: In Re Corporal Punishment by Organs of State* 1991 (3) SA 76 (Nm SC): "It is, however, a value judgement which requires objectively to be articulated and identified, regard being had to the contemporary norms, aspirations, expectations and sensitivities of the Namibian people as expressed in its national institutions and its Constitution, and further having regard to the emerging consensus of values in a civilized international community (of which Namibia is a part) which Namibians share. This is not a static exercise. It is a continually evolving dynamic. What may have been acceptable as a just form of punishment some decades ago, may appear manifestly inhuman or degrading today. Yesterday's orthodoxy might appear to be today's heresy."

13 Supra, para 88. See also *S v Williams* 1995 (7) BCLR 861 (CC) para 36–37.

14 Supra, para 14.

15 1995 (7) BCLR 793 (CC) para 8.

16 CCT 15/95 (unreported judgment of the Constitutional Court delivered in May 1996 para 40).

17 Supra, para 17.

18 Dugard J. 1994.

19 Supra, para 35.

20 1996 (4) BCLR 537 (CC).

21 *S v Bhulwana* 1995 (12) BCLR 1579 (CC) para 25–29.

22 *Case & another v Minister of Safety and Security & another* 1996 (3) SA 617 (CC) para. 76–80. (Obscene Photographic Matter).

23 *Executive Council of the Western Cape Legislature v The President of the Republic of South Africa* 1995 (1) BCLR 1289 (CC).

24 1995 (3) SA 850 (CC).

25 Certification of the Constitution of the Republic of South Africa, 1996. CCT 23/96.

Chapter 6
Mechanisms for Realising Rights under the Bill of Rights

Frans Viljoen

6.1 SUMMARY AND INTRODUCTION

*I*N terms of the 1993 and 1996 Constitutions South Africa is a constitutional democracy. The Constitution represents the highest law of the land. Included in the Constitution is a Bill of Rights, which enshrines various rights which are accorded to "everyone" in South Africa.[1] The mere fact that these rights were agreed upon during negotiations and have been codified is no guarantee that people's lives will be improved or will be affected by their inclusion.

Many factors will influence whether these rights become reality in our society. In the first place there must be legitimate, accessible institutions which people can approach. A further prerequisite is that people should know about their rights and about the possible institutions in which they can enforce their rights.

Courts, by their very nature, can easily intimidate or alienate people. It is therefore important to distinguish between judicial and non-judicial mechanisms or institutions. Non-judicial institutions are directed towards problem-solving outside the formal setting of a courtroom. To emphasise this dimension, the term "realisation" of rights, rather than "enforcement", is used. "Enforcement" evokes the image of two opposing sides in combat, the one intent on subduing the other with force. "Realisation" emphasises the impact of human rights in the reality of people's lives.

6.2 KEY OBJECTIVES

The key objectives of this chapter are to enable students to:
- discuss the non-judicial institutions responsible for realising human rights under the Bill of Rights;
- discuss the judicial mechanisms responsible for protecting human rights.

6.3 APPLICABLE LAW

The Constitution, 1996, sections 26, 27, 39, 166, 167, 170, 174, 183, 184, 185, 187, 193 and 194

The Constitution, 1993, sections 35 and 115

The Public Protector Act 23 of 1994, sections 6, 7 and 8

The Human Rights Commission Act 54 of 1994

The Promotion of National Unity and Reconciliation Act 34 of 1995

The Restitution of Land Rights Act 22 of 1994

6.4 INTERPRETATION AND DISCUSSION

6.4.1 Non-judicial institutions

6.4.1.1 Public Protector

Citizens in a modern bureaucratic state have many dealings with governmental departments, institutions and agents. The ordinary citizen should not have to approach a court to resolve an issue when suffering improper or prejudicial conduct at the hands of officials. Many democracies, following the lead of Scandinavian countries, have set up an institution to investigate allegations of improper and prejudicial conduct in state affairs and in public administration. In its original form, the person performing this function was called an ombudsman. The office of the Public Protector is the equivalent provided for in our Constitution.[2]

The Public Protector will investigate allegations of, for example, corruption, maladministration and undue delay by persons performing public functions. The Public Protector must then report and take appropriate action to remedy the situation.[3]

The Public Protector is appointed by the President. In terms of the 1996 Constitution, at least 60 per cent of the members of the National Assembly must support the candidate.[4] The appointment is for a non-renewable term of seven years.[5] A resolution supported by at least two thirds of the National Assembly is required to remove him or her from office before expiry of the seven-year term.[6] The first Public Protector to have been appointed is Mr Selby Baqwa.

The 1993 Constitution provided for the appointment of provincial public protectors. None of the provinces has, at the time of writing, appointed their own public protector.

6.4.1.2   Human Rights Commission

A Human Rights Commission (HRC) was established by legislation in 1995.[7] Its main aim is the promotion and protection of human rights in South Africa.

As far as its *protective* function is concerned, the HRC has the power to investigate and secure redress of violations of human rights.

This process can be initiated by someone reporting a complaint to the Commission, or at the initiative of the Commission itself.[8] The complaint has to be in writing. Staff of the Commission will assist persons not able to submit a written complaint. A complaint should contain:

- the name and address of the complainant;
- the identity number of that person;
- the name and address of any respondent;
- all the facts within the personal knowledge of the complainant.

The Commission will receive and *evaluate* the complaint. If no prima facie case is made out, the Commission may *refuse* the complaint. They may also decide to *refer* the matter to a different institution, if the Commission is not deemed the appropriate organ to dispose of the matter.

Complaints admitted by the Commission lead to an *investigation*. During an investigation *hearings* may be held to obtain information. A *report* is then drawn up, in which a *finding* will be given. The ideal is to solve the dispute through mediation or conciliation. Parties involved are invited to accept a "friendly settlement". This settlement is still scrutinised for compliance with the rights in and spirit of the Constitution.

If no friendly settlement can be reached, the judicial institutions come into play. The Commission may assist an aggrieved party in the process of *litigation*. Litigation is seen as a last resort.

As far as its *promotional* function is concerned, each commissioner is assigned a specific province that he or she has to visit regularly. The Commission is involved in research, lobbying and in the dissemination of information. Decentralised offices will be established in each of the nine provinces to further both the protective and promotional function of the Commission.

Socioeconomic (or "second generation") rights have been included in the 1996 Constitution. As these rights are not directly enforceable, but should be realised "progressively",[9] their implementation is problematic. The duty to oversee their realisation is that of the HRC. On a yearly basis state departments must report to the HRC on the measures that they have taken towards the realisation of these rights.[10] The HRC consolidates the information and reports to the National Assembly.

The present Chairperson of the HRC is Barney Pityana. Of the other ten commissioners initially appointed, three were part-time. The main office is in Johannesburg.

6.4.1.3   Other commissions

In terms of the 1993 Constitution,[11] a *Truth and Reconciliation Commission* (TRC) has been established.[12] The TRC is also concerned with the violation of human rights, but of a very specific nature. Only victims of human rights violations emanating from the conflicts of South Africa's political past may approach the TRC with complaints. It operates retrospectively, covering violations which took place between 1 March 1960 and 6 December 1993. The HRC should be approached for any current violation of human rights. While the HRC is a permanent institution, the TRC was from the outset intended as a temporary mechanism with a fixed and limited life span. The ultimate purpose of the TRC is also different, in that it aims at providing a picture of the gross human rights violations which occurred in our past, and aims at preventing their repetition in the future.

The 1996 Constitution provides for the institution of another two commissions whose task it will be to promote the rights of specific groups. They are the *Commission for Gender Equality* and the *Commission for the Promotion and Protection of the Rights of Cultural, Religious and Linguistic Communities.*

The function of the *Commission for Gender Equality* will be to promote respect for gender equality and to work towards its realisation.[13] The 1993 Constitution made provision for a similar institution.

The *Commission for the Promotion and Protection of the Rights of Cultural, Religious and Linguistic Communities* will serve the rights of these communities.[14] The primary objectives of this Commission will be to promote respect and tolerance, and to work towards the establishment of cultural councils for different communities. This Commission will be established in terms of national legislation.

In addition to these two commissions, the *Commission on the Restitution of Land Rights* must also be mentioned briefly. It was provided for in the 1993 Constitution, and was established by legislation.[15] People dispossessed of their land after 1913 due to racially based discriminatory laws may approach the Commission to claim back their land. The Commission should try to settle disputes through mediation and negotiation.[16] Litigation, in the Land Claims Court, is provided for as a last resort.

6.4.1.4   Civil society: The role of NGOs

The office of the Public Protector and the Human Rights Commission are institutions created and funded by the state. These institutions are examples of institutional checks and balances of state power. However, the realisation of rights should not depend on the state. If, for example, state funding is limited, the effective functioning of these institutions will be undermined. For that reason, civil society should be actively involved in the realisation of rights.

Individuals, groups and organisations without formal links with the state have created many ways of securing the rights of individuals. Examples are trade unions, newspapers, other publications, churches and NGOs.

NGOs are non-governmental organisations. They are funded by agencies not responsible to the South African government. Examples of NGOs involved in the protection of human rights are Lawyers for Human Rights, the Legal Resources Centre and the National Committee for the Rights of the Child (NCRC). Through these NGOs an individual's problems may be redressed, either through mediation or litigation.

6.4.2   JUDICIAL MECHANISMS

Courts give binding judgments. Anyone who does not comply with a court order is in contempt of court, which is a punishable offence. It is therefore more appropriate to use the term "enforcement" in this context, as the force of sanction gives backing to judicial pronouncements. Binding judgments may be the only appropriate way of redressing some serious violations of human rights or of forcing an offending party to co-operate in the process of mediation or conciliation.

The 1996 Constitution provides for a hierarchy of courts. Although the court structure is similar to that in the 1993 Constitution, some of the names have been changed. The four main levels of courts, in order of importance, are:[17]

- the Constitutional Court (in existence since its inauguration in February 1995);
- the Supreme Court of Appeal (previously the Appellate Division of the Supreme Court);

- high courts and, if established by legislation, high courts of appeal (previously local and provincial divisions of the Supreme Court);
- magistrates' courts.

The presiding officers in the first three courts are judges. Judges are appointed by the President on the advice of the Judicial Services Commission (JSC).[18] In the case of the Constitutional Court, the President must consult the President of that Court and the leaders of all political parties in the National Assembly before making appointments.[19] The Judicial Service Commission is a body representing the legal profession and political parties and consists of twenty-three members. When a vacancy for a judicial appointment arises, it is advertised. Applicants are publicly interviewed by the JSC. The JSC then makes a recommendation to the President. Previously, judges were appointed exclusively from the ranks of senior advocates. Today advocates without the title of "senior", attorneys and academics may also be appointed as judges.

Magistrates preside in the regional or district magistrates' courts. They are appointed by the Magistrates' Commission.

In making appointments those responsible have to consider the need for the judiciary to "reflect broadly the racial and gender composition in South Africa".[20]

6.4.2.1   The Constitutional Court

(a)   Constitutional jurisdiction

A new and separate court, the Constitutional Court, was created in terms of the 1993 Constitution. It is the highest court in all constitutional matters. That means that the last appeal in a matter involving the Constitution lies to this court. It also means that certain disputes can be resolved only by the Constitutional Court.[21]

- A dispute between "organs of state" (for example, between Parliament and the Human Rights Commission) concerning the constitutional status or powers of any of these "organs of state", is within the exclusive jurisdiction of the Constitutional Court.
- Only the Constitutional Court can give a final decision about the constitutionality of national or provincial legislation or bills.
- The constitutionality of amendments to the Constitution has to be scrutinised by this Court.
- Provincial constitutions have to be certified by the Constitutional Court.

(b)   Composition

The Constitutional Court consists of a President (Judge Chaskalson), a Deputy President and nine judges. At least eight judges must hear a particular case. At least four of the eleven members of the Constitutional Court must have been judges at the time of their appointment to the Court.

Judges of this Court are appointed for a non-renewable term of twelve years. If they reach the age of 70 before expiry of the twelve years, they have to retire.

6.4.2.2   The Supreme Court of Appeal

(a) *Constitutional jurisdiction*

Under the 1993 Constitution the Appellate Division (AD) of the Supreme Court (the Supreme Court of Appeal's predecessor) had no jurisdiction to hear any constitutional matter. This rigid distinction and sidelining of what before 1994 was the highest court, was criticised by commentators.

The decision in *Government of RSA v Basedeo*[22] illustrates how the AD itself contributed to this sidelining. In terms of the 1993 Constitution all courts, in interpreting legislation or developing the common law, had to have "due regard to the spirit, purport and objects"[23] of the chapter on fundamental rights. The AD was called to interpret section 49(2) of the Criminal Procedure Act in *Basedeo*'s case. Without referring to the Constitution, it observed that public policy called for a strict interpretation of the awesome powers granted in terms of that section.

In terms of the 1996 Constitution, the Supreme Court of Appeal may decide appeals in any matter (including constitutional matters). However, its finding on a constitutional matter will still be subject to appeal to the Constitutional Court. A decision invalidating legislation does not become final until the Constitutional Court has confirmed the ruling.

(b) *Composition*

The Supreme Court of Appeal consists of the Chief Justice, a Deputy Chief Justice and judges of appeal. When the 1993 Constitution came into force, the Chief Justice was Justice Corbett. With his retirement at the end of 1996, Justice Mahomed became Chief Justice.

6.4.2.3   The High courts

High courts may decide all constitutional matters except those that only the Constitutional Court may adjudicate. In other words, an application to have legislation declared unconstitutional may be made in this court. However, an order invalidating legislation does not have any force until the Constitutional Court gives a final pronouncement on the issue.

6.4.2.4   Magistrates' courts

Magistrates' courts are created by statute and do not have inherent jurisdiction to hear disputes: their jurisdiction depends on legislative provisions. Under the 1993 Constitution there was uncertainty about the competence of magistrates' courts to decide constitutional matters. In *Qozeleni v Minister of Law and*

Order[24] a full bench of the Eastern Cape Division of the Supreme Court concluded that they had. The court held that magistrates' courts should apply the law of the land, including the provisions on fundamental rights in the Constitution. Two judges of the Witwatersrand local division reached a different conclusion in *Bate v Regional Magistrate, Randburg.*[25] They held that magistrates' courts had no jurisdiction to adjudicate upon any violation of any fundamental right in the Interim Constitution.

The 1996 Constitution has resolved this uncertainty. Magistrates' courts now have jurisdiction to hear some constitutional matters.[26] Examples would be allegations that evidence had been obtained in violation of the right to a fair trial, that the trial had been delayed unreasonably, or that an accused is entitled to legal representation at state expense.

However, the jurisdiction of these courts is limited and can never extend to:
- a decision about the constitutionality of legislation; or
- an enquiry about the constitutionality of any conduct of the President.

6.5   SUGGESTED READING

The Constitution of the Republic of South Africa, 1996, chapters 2 and 9.

....

ENDNOTES

1   Chapter 2 of the 1996 Constitution.

2   Chapter 9 of the 1996 Constitution.

3   The Public Protector Act 23 of 1997, preamble, sections 6, 7 and 8.

4   Section 193(5)(*b*)(i) of the 1996 Constitution.

5   Section 183 of the 1996 Constitution.

6   Section 194(2)(*a*) of the 1996 Constitution.

7   Human Rights Commission Act 54 of 1994.

8   This procedure is set out in the *Government Gazette* of 4 October 1996.

9   Sections 26(2) and 27(2) of the 1996 Constitution.

10   Section 184(3) of the 1996 Constitution.

11   Section 115 of the 1993 Constitution.

12   Promotion of National Unity and Reconciliation Act 34 of 1995.

13   Section 187 of the 1996 Constitution.

14   Sections 185 and 186 of the 1996 Constitution.

15   Restitution of Land Rights Act 22 of 1994.

16   Section 13 of the Restitution of Land Rights Act of 1994.

17   Section 166 of the 1996 Constitution.

18   Section 174(6) of the 1996 Constitution.

19   Section 174(4) of the 1996 Constitution.

20   Section 174(2) of the 1996 Constitution.

21   Section 167(4) of the 1996 Constitution.

22   1996 (1) SA 355 (A).

23   Section 35(3) of the 1993 Constitution. See also section 39(2) of the 1996 Constitution.

24   1994 (3) SA 625 (E).

25   1996 (7) BCLR 974 (W).

26   Section 170 of the 1996 Constitution.

Chapter 7

The Generations of Fundamental Human Rights

Danfred Titus

SUMMARY

*T*HIS chapter explains the development of the various generations of rights. When studying this chapter you will notice that generations of human rights are but one of a variety of classifications of human rights. The other classifications include: classical and social rights, divic rights, political rights, economic and social rights, cultural rights, and fundamental and basic rights. There are also further classifications like freedoms, civil freedoms, and joint and separate rights.

The background and development of the various generations is outlined. The doctrines of John Locke, universally regarded as the father of the modern approach to human rights, are briefly explained, as are the shortcomings of this approach which resulted in the development of the second generation of human rights.

The Universal Declaration of Human Rights, the International Covenant on Civil and Political Rights, the International Covenant on Economic, Social and Cultural Rights and First Optional Protocol to the firstmentioned treaty are also examined.

The results of ratifying the treaties and the interaction between civil and political rights and economic, social and cultural rights are also explained.

7.1   INTRODUCTION

When speaking about generations of rights, general reference is made to:

* the civil and political rights of the International Covenant on Civil and Political Rights (ICCPR) as first-generation rights;
* the economic, social and cultural rights of the International Covenant on Economic, Social and Cultural Rights (ICESCR) as second-generation rights; and
* third-generation rights, as including the right to peace, the right to development, the right to a healthy environment and the right to share in the common heritage of mankind.

This terminology can be misleading in that it may denote a particular hierarchy. Generations succeed each other, and referring to human rights of the first, second and third generation may create the impression that the earlier generations have had their day.[1] Reference is also made to first-, second- and third-generation rights as blue, red and green rights.[2] In this chapter we shall firstly present the generations of fundamental human rights as part of the general classification of rights; secondly, we shall view the generations in terms of the development towards the International Bill of Rights, its ideological background and the component parts of the International Bill of Rights; thirdly, we shall discuss international case law; and lastly, we shall briefly discuss the liberal approach as presented in the South African context.

7.2   KEY OBJECTIVES

The key objectives of this chapter are to enable students to:

* indicate which rights are represented by the three generations of human rights;

- indicate which classifications, besides the classification into generations of rights, can be used to classify human rights;
- list the requirements which a right must meet in order to be formulated as a new human right;
- give a short explanation of the origin of third-generation human rights;
- discuss the component parts of the International Bill of Rights.

7.3 HUMAN RIGHTS INSTRUMENTS

The Universal Declaration of Human Rights
The International Covenant on Economic, Social and Cultural Rights
The International Covenant on Civil and Political Rights

7.4 INTERPRETATION AND DISCUSSION

7.4.1 Generations of human rights as part of the classification of rights

What should be borne in mind is that this reference to generations of rights is one of the many classifications of human rights. The following are other classifications.

7.4.1.1 Classic and social rights

Classic rights include civil and political rights and are directed at restricting the powers of the state over the individual. Social rights include economic, social and cultural rights. They require the active intervention of government in order to create the conditions necessary for human development, such as employment, education and health care. In other words, classic rights oblige the government to refrain from certain actions while social rights oblige it to provide certain guarantees. We may refer to classic rights as a duty to achieve a given result, and social rights in terms of a duty to provide the means.

7.4.1.2 Civil rights

This term is often used to refer to the rights set out in the first eighteen articles of the Universal Declaration of Human Rights. A further set of "physical integrity rights" is identified from this group relating to the right to life, liberty and security of the person, and offering protection against physical violence against the person, torture and inhumane treatment (by the government), arbitrary arrest, detention or exile, slavery and servitude, interference with one's privacy and right of ownership, restriction of one's freedom of movement, and the freedom of thought, conscience and religion.

The difference between these "physical integrity rights" and what is referred to as basic fundamental rights, lies in the fact that basic rights include economic and social rights and do not include rights such as protection of privacy and ownership.[3]

7.4.1.3 Political rights

In general, political rights are held to be those set out in articles 19 to 21 of the Universal Declaration of Human Rights. They include freedom of expression, freedom of association and assembly, the right to take part in the government of one's country and the right to vote and stand for election at genuine periodic elections held by secret ballot (articles 18, 19, 21, 22 and 25 of the International Covenant on Civil and Political Rights).

7.4.1.4 Economic and social rights

Socioeconomic rights are listed in articles 22 to 26 of the Universal Declaration of Human Rights and are rights which provide the conditions necessary for prosperity and wellbeing. They include the right to do work which one freely chooses or accepts, the right to a fair wage and a reasonable limitation of working hours, trade union rights, right to medical care, the right to an adequate standard of living (including social services) and to education (see articles 6 to 14 of the International Covenant on Economic, Social and Cultural Rights).

7.4.1.5 Cultural rights

The Universal Declaration of Human Rights lists cultural rights in articles 27 and 28 as the right freely to participate in the cultural life of the community, to share in scientific advancement, and the right to the protection of the moral and material interests resulting from any scientific, literary or artistic production of which one is the author (see also article 15 of the International Covenant on Economic, Social and Cultural Rights and article 27 of the International Covenant on Civil and Political Rights).

7.4.1.6 Fundamental and basic rights

Fundamental rights refer to such rights as the right to life and to the inviolability of the person. Within the United Nations, an extensive system of standards has developed, which, particularly since the 1960s, has been laid down in numerous conventions, declarations and resolutions, which bring already recognised rights and, increasingly, matters of policy which affect human development, into the sphere of human rights. This broad application of the term "human rights" carries with it the inherent danger of detracting from its practical significance. The definition of human rights can thus become too broad.

A separate group has therefore been established within the broad category of human rights, that is those referred to as "elementary", "essential", and "fundamental" human rights.

Another approach is to distinguish a number of "basic rights" which should be given absolute precedence in national and international policy. These include all the rights which concern people's primary material and non-material needs. If these are not provided, no human being can lead a dignified existence. Basic rights include the right to life, the right to a minimum level of security, the inviolability of the person, freedom from slavery and servitude, torture, unlawful deprivation of liberty, discrimination and other acts which impinge on human dignity. They also include freedom of thought, conscience and religion, as well as the right to suitable nutrition, clothing, shelter and medical care and other essentials crucial to physical and mental health.

There are also further classifications such as "freedoms", "civil liberties" and "collective and individual rights". The point to be made is that reference to generations of rights is part of a classification system of human rights. Bear in mind that human rights do not have a restrictive character, neither are they unchangeable; they are dynamic. New rights can certainly be the subject of discussion, and become accepted. At the same time, a word of caution is called for. Whenever new human rights are formulated, a number of preconditions should be taken into account.

- The proposed regulations should be of a fundamental nature, aiming at the protection of the inherent dignity of the human person.
- The issues at stake should be sufficiently specified and demarcated. For that purpose, it seems desirable that an identifiable person or group of persons be able to invoke the right in a practical manner, that there be an institution with which complaints may be filed and, finally, that the right may be translated into a reasonably objective claim.
- As clearly laid down in the United Nations' General Assembly Resolution 41/120 (4 December 1986), the human right in question should be consistent with the existing corpus of international human rights law and implementable through a realistic and effective implementation mechanism.

7.4.2   The development towards an international Bill of Rights

The development towards the International Bill of Rights provides a better understanding of the "generations of rights". The four major United Nations legal instruments[4] which exist to define and to guarantee the protection of human rights are:

- the Universal Declaration of Human Rights of 1948;
- the International Covenant on Economic, Social and Cultural Rights of 1966;
- the International Covenant on Civil and Political Rights of 1966; and
- the First Optional Protocol to the latter covenant.

Before discussing the component parts of the International Bill of Rights in more detail, let us first view the ideological background to the various generations.

7.4.2.1   First-generation human rights

It is generally accepted that the modern theory of human rights stems from John Locke. According to Locke, states are formed in terms of the so-called social contract, whereby men created states to provide themselves with the necessary protection from the uncertainty and danger inherent in the (hypo-thetical) state of nature in which they lived. Locke took the view that man was not absorbed totally into the new state as a result of the social contract, but in concluding it (the social contract) reserved certain rights, which the state was not permitted to infringe. If the state nevertheless infringed these rights, it was acting in conflict with the powers granted to it.

Human rights are therefore conceived as "prestate" rights. This means that human rights are by definition rights to freedom, and by definition they impose upon the state a duty of abstention. Therefore, human rights are con-ceivable only in the state–individual relationship.

This Lockean concept is considered to be a potent force of how Western society thinks about human rights. Locke at the same time developed the doc-trine of the separation of powers which Montesquieu later elaborated. This means that these rights could not simply be enforced against the government, they could also be enforced by the citizens. If the government entered the free domain of the citizen in breach of its authority, the citizen could approach the independent judiciary for assistance.

7.4.2.2 Second-generation human rights

The emphasis in this concept is the socialist theory which rejects the natural origin of citizens' rights and is unwilling to deduce them from either the nature of man or from the human mind. It equally rejects the idea that citizens' rights reflect the relationship between man and society or between an abstract "man" and the state. The basis is rather society organised in a state; these rights should reflect the relationship between the state and its citizens.

It would be appropriate at this stage to indicate some of the shortcomings in Locke's approach.[5]

- By taking as his point of departure a prestate state of nature, he gave a dis-torted picture of what society was really like. His view of society was atom-istic and individualistic: each separate individual made the social contract. In this, however, he totally failed to appreciate that man can never live in isolation without diminishing his humanness; being with other men is fun-damental to being a man.

- By placing such a heavy emphasis on the government's obligation to abstain from action so as not to impede the individual in his development, Locke missed the point that in order to give everyone the chance to develop, the government also has positive duties. (The state is, after all, there for *all* men.)

- Locke started out from a hypothetical liberty, equality and independence in the state of nature, but the reality is different. This is where Locke's model is criticised as purely egotistic, and his concepts of liberty and equality purely formal, with the greatest possible lack of liberty and inequality hid-den behind them. In other words, Locke's model of human rights was unable to bring about what it was intended to bring about, that is, the full development of every man, and respect for every man's human dignity. John McLachlan put it as follows: "Locke's democratic society found its final condemnation in the slums and squalor of Western cities and in the exploitation of human and physical resources purely in the interests of individual wealth and private property."[6]

7.4.2.3 Third-generation human rights

In November 1977, Karel Vasek called for the recognition of a third generation of human rights, namely solidarity rights.[7] Vasek worked with three different types of revolution.

The first revolution was the French Revolution of 1789, with the motto "liberty, equality and fraternity". The focus here was the so-called freedom rights, that is, the basic civil and political rights.

The Mexican Revolution and, particularly, the Russian Revolution focused upon the so-called equality rights, that is, the economic, social and cultural rights. These constituted the second-generation rights.

The third revolution is the emancipation of colonised and dominated peoples, which is linked to total interdependence. One world or no world. This brought into being the third generation of human rights which presented itself as the brotherhood of man demanding solidarity rights. These rights are the right to peace, the right to development, the right to a healthy environment and the right to share in the common heritage of mankind. This third generation of human rights is still met with resistance and scepticism. One argument was that the very idea of generations creates the impression that as generations succeed each other, earlier generations may have outlived their usefulness. Fears have been expressed that an overemphasis on these rights could provide an excuse for repressive regimes not to respect the classic civil and political rights, or economic, social and cultural rights. Furthermore, it was objected that by their very nature, solidarity rights cannot be invoked by individuals, and apply only to collectivities. An individual's right to peace would be difficult to contemplate.

On the other hand it is argued by proponents of third-generation rights that in many countries, Africa in particular, governments struggle to combat famine, illness and ignorance. They tend to overlook the classic liberties of the Western world but they find themselves in a fight against underdevelopment. In this fight they are in a state of emergency which permits derogations to be made. They recognise the importance of the realisation of social and economic developments and the securing of the classic rights and liberties. The "right to development" is then considered as a necessary corollary of the other fundamental human rights.

7.4.2.4 The component parts of the International Bill of Rights

The Universal Declaration of Human Rights is the basic international statement of the inalienable and inviolable rights of all members of the human family. It is intended to serve as "a common standard of achievement for all peoples and nations" in the effort to secure universal and effective recognition and observance of the rights and freedoms it lists.

Being a declaration, it was not intended to be a legally enforceable document, though parts of it are now generally accepted as being part of international customary law.[8] The Universal Declaration was adopted with forty-eight states in favour, no dissensions, but with nine states abstaining, one of which was the Union of South Africa.[9]

The development of the Universal Declaration of Human Rights from a "common standard of achievement" and a "Magna Carta of mankind", to an international standard of customary international law is also indicative of the progress made since 1946. Furthermore, the Universal Declaration established itself as the primary exponent of the international human rights concept and has become the authoritative catalogue of universally recognised human rights. While not all the provisions constitute customary international law, "most states (and scholars) would agree that failure to respect *some* of the provisions ... would constitute a violation of international law".[10] This, apparently, is the legal assumption the United Nations acted on when it took various measures in respect of violations of human rights by governments that had adhered to no international human rights agreement, *inter alia*, the numerous resolutions against apartheid in South Africa.[11]

The two Covenants provide the protection for specified rights and freedoms. They both recognise the rights of peoples to self-determination. Both Covenants have provisions barring all forms of discrimination in the exercise of human rights. And, above all, both have the force of law for the countries which ratify them. South Africa is not a party to either of these Covenants.[12]

We have also had opportunity to witness the development from the Universal Declaration towards the two International Covenants of 1966. According to Kooijmans,[13] one of the reasons that eighteen years elapsed before the nations of the world accepted the Covenants, was the different visions people have of human rights.

In 1948 the world community was relatively homogenous with the Western countries in the majority. The East European countries at that time abstained from voting on the Universal Declaration. Their argument was, *inter alia*, that insufficient attention was given to economic and social human rights. To the countries of the West human rights entail the classical freedoms, which require a duty of non-interference from government and which can be justiciable. The rights presented as economic and social, such as the right to labour and the right to social security, were not regarded as subjective rights but as social objectives.

With the increased entry of developing countries to the UN — countries which experienced the right to a dignified, humane existence as priority — the urgency for economic and social rights in a treaty also increased. And, according to Kooijmans,[14] the West was becoming increasingly convinced that economic and social rights were just as imperative for human development as the classical rights, although not exactly enforceable before a court of law. This, says Kooijmans,[15] is an example of the fact that political confrontation need not always lead to an impasse, but also to better understanding and even enrichment of one's own value system. It is submitted that, while these developments relate to the international legal order their relevance to municipal legal orders cannot be overemphasised, certainly not in South Africa with its different approaches to human rights.

Henkin[16] portrays the eighteen years' delay as, *inter alia*, a "tribute to respect for law". While states had been prepared readily to accept the hortatory Declaration of Human Rights, they were more cautious when it came to accepting the same terms in a legally binding instrument. The Covenants may therefore be regarded as constituting the serious consideration given by the nations of the world to the international law of human rights at the time. By July 1992 the International Covenant on Civil and Political Rights of 1966 had been ratified or acceded to by 112 states, the International Covenant on Economic, Social and Cultural Rights of 1966 by 113 states, and the First Optional Protocol by 66 states.[17]

The First Optional Protocol, although it came into force simultaneously with the International Covenant on Civil and Political Rights, is also an indication of the development of international human rights. It provides that a state party "recognizes the competence of the Committee to receive and consider communications from individuals subject to its jurisdiction, who claim to be victims of a violation by that State Party of any of the rights set forth in the Covenant" (article 1).

The Optional Protocol therefore represents the "dialectic link" between international law and municipal law of Partsch,[18] Meuwissen's[19] fundamental rights as the basis of municipal and international law, and also the "peculiarly sensitive point" of Falk.[20]

The International Covenant on Economic, Social and Cultural Rights involves economic, social and cultural rights, such as the right of every person to work and to free choice of employment; to fair wages; to form and join labour unions; to social security; to an adequate standard of living; to freedom from hunger; to health and education.

States which ratify this Covenant acknowledge their responsibility to promote better living conditions for their people. States report on their progress in the promotion of these rights. These reports are then reviewed by a committee of experts elected by the Economic and Social Council.[21] The fulfilment of these rights presupposes an active, "interfering" government policy. It is the responsibility of governments to see to employment opportunities, a social security system, housing, education, health, and so forth. The first-generation rights are formulated throughout as "everyone has the right to ...", "all persons ...", "anyone ...", and so forth. Second-generation rights, however, have a different formulation: "The State Parties to the present Covenant recognize the right of everyone ... and undertake to ensure ...".

Unlike the first-generation rights, these second-generation rights[22] cannot be considered to be self-executing, which means that they cannot be directly applicable to the individual. This statement, however, requires qualification.

Article 2(3) of the International Covenant on Economic, Social and Cultural Rights stipulates that the rights in the Covenant will be exercised without discrimination of any kind. It is therefore possible to submit discriminatory practices in terms of the rights under this Covenant in national courts. This amounts to a detour of some sort to have the implementation of these rights enforced by a court of law.[23] Two Dutch cases ("communications") before the Human Rights Committee (HRC) that vividly display this interplay between the rights under the two Covenants of 1966 are *Broeks v The Netherlands*[24] and *Zwaan de Vries v The Netherlands*.[25] In *Broeks* the state party challenged the fact that an individual complaint in respect of the rights to social security could be dealt with by the Human Rights Committee. It would be incompatible with the aims of both the Covenants and the Optional Protocol. The complainant ("author") on the other hand, argued that she was not complaining about the level of social security or other issues relating to article 9 of the International Covenant on Economic, Social and Cultural Rights (in terms of which state parties recognise the right of everyone to social security, including social insurance). Her claim was based upon the fact that she was a victim of unequal treatment prohibited by article 26 of the International Covenant on Civil and Political Rights.

The Committee observed that the question whether or not social security should be progressively established in the Netherlands was not at issue. What was at issue was whether the legislation providing for social security violated the prohibition against discrimination contained in article 26 of the International Covenant on Civil and Political Rights and the guarantee given therein that all persons should receive equal and effective protection against discrimination. The Committee expressed the view that the state party should offer Mrs Broeks an appropriate remedy.

In similar fashion in the *Zwaan de Vries* case the Human Rights Commitee was of the view that article 26 established an autonomous right regardless of the subject matter. It observed that the Covenant does not require states to establish social security schemes, but, once they do, only distinctions based on reasonable and objective criteria are allowed.

From the USA Henkin[26] also states that, although the second-generation rights are not constitutional rights in the USA, if the government decides to make available economic and social benefits, invidious discrimination in providing them would be a denial of the equal protection of the laws.

The Limburg Principles on the Implementation of the International Covenant on Economic, Social and Cultural Rights, 1986, also state that the equal protection clause in the Covenant requires immediate application.

To round off this discussion, Alston[27] presents the General Comment 3 (1990) of the Committee which monitors compliance with state parties' obligations under the International Covenant on Economic, Social and Cultural Rights and which is particularly instructive:

> "5. Among the measures which might be considered appropriate, in addition to legislation, is the provision of judicial remedies with respect to rights which may, in accordance with the national legal system, be considered justiciable. The Committee notes, for example, that the enjoyment of the rights recognized, without discrimination, will often be appropriately promoted, in part, through the provision of judicial or other effective remedies. Indeed, those State Parties which are also parties to the International Covenant on Civil and Political Rights are already obligated (by virtue of articles 2(1), 2(3), 3 and 26 of that Covenant) to ensure that any person whose rights or freedoms (including the right to equality and non-discrimination) recognized in that Covenant are violated, shall have effective remedy (article 2(3)(*a*)). In addition, there are a number of other provisions, including articles 3, 7(*a*)(i), 8, 10(3), 13(2)(*a*), 13(3), 13(4) and 15(3), which would seem to be capable of immediate application by judicial and other organs in many national legal systems. Any suggestion that the provisions indicated are inherently non-self-executing would seem to be difficult to sustain."

Therefore, even if you cannot approach a court of law on the lack of housing, you can approach the court on being discriminated against when housing facilities are allocated.

The International Covenant on Civil and Political Rights concerns civil and political human rights, the so-called classical rights or the first-generation rights whereby the government is requested not to interfere with the private life of the individual.

The rights concerned here are, for instance, the right of every human person to life, liberty and security of person; to privacy; to freedom from cruel, inhumane or degrading treatment and from torture; to freedom from slavery; to immunity from arbitrary arrest; to a fair trial; to recognition as a person before the law; to immunity from retroactive sentences; to freedom of thought, conscience and religion; to freedom of opinion and expression; to liberty of movement, including the right to emigrate; to peaceful assembly and to freedom of association.

This Covenant also has a First Optional Protocol which provides for individuals under certain circumstances to file complaints of human rights violations by ratifying states. That is, individuals are entitled to file complaints against their governments in cases of alleged violations. These complaints are then considered by the Human Rights Committee. We will return more extensively to the operation of this Committee below. The Second Optional Protocol to this Covenant concerns the abolition of the death penalty.

This, in brief, is the International Bill of Rights expressing the existence and operation of the international law of human rights.

The following illustration[28] indicates the various classifications of rights as reflected in international human rights law.

FIGURE 7.1   HUMAN RIGHTS STANDARDS

This schedule is not limitative and serves illustration and quick reference purposes only. The right-hand columns refer to the relevant articles/paragraphs in international instruments.

The left margin of the table reads vertically "CLASSIC RIGHTS" (outermost column) and "CIVIL RIGHTS" (second column).

Category	Right	1	2	3	4	5	6	7
	– right to self-determination		1	1			V4	
	– equality	1	2	3	14		C5,9	
	– women's rights					P1,1	M40	CEDAW
	– non-discrimination	2	26		14		C40	CERD
	– protection of children		24			7	C13	CRC
	– protection of minorities		27		14		C30	
INTEGRITY RIGHTS	– right to life	3	6		2			
	– no death penalty		P2		P6,1		C17	
	– no slavery	4	8		4			
	– no torture	5	7		3		C16	CAT
	– freedom of residence							
	– freedom of movement	13	12		P4,2		C20	
	– right to leave any country, return	13	12		P4.3			
	– protection of privacy, honour and reputation	12	17		8			
	– protection of property	17			P1,1			
	– freedom of thought, conscience and religion	18	18		9		C16	
	– right to seek asylum from persecution	14						Geneva 1951
	– right to nationality	15						
	– right to family life	16			12			
DUE PROCESS RIGHTS	– no arbitrary arrest, detention or exile	9	9		5			
	– right to effective remedy	8			13		V13,9	
	– right to fair trial	10						
	– equality before the courts	10	14				C5,9	
	– rights of the accused	11	14		6		M23	
	– *nulla poena sine lege*	11	15		7		C5,18	
POLITICAL RIGHTS	– opinion and expression	19	19		10		C9,1	
	– assembly and association	20	21		11		C9,2	
	– take part in government	21	25				C7	
	– equal access to public service	21					C7,5	
	– elect and be elected	25		P1,3		C5		➤

				1	2	3	4	5	6	7
S O C I A L	SOCIO-ECONOMIC RIGHTS	LABOUR RIGHTS	– right to work	23		6		1		
			– equal pay for equal work	23						
			– no forced labour		8		4	1		ILO111 ILO 29,105
			– trade union	23		8	11	5	C9	ILO87
			– organised and collective bargaining					6		ILO98
			– rest and leisure	24		7		2		
			– adequate standard of living	25		11				
			– right to food	25		11				
			– right to health	25		12		11		
			– right to housing	25		11				
R I G H T S			– right to education	26		13	P1,2			
	CULTURAL RIGHTS		– take part in cultural life	27	27	15				
			– to benefit from scientific progress			15				
			– protection of authorship and copyright	27		15				
			– freedom in scientific research and creative activity			15				

| | | 1 | 2 | 3 | 4 | 5 | 6 | 7 |

1. Universal Declaration of Human Rights
2. International Covenant on Civil and Political Rights
3. International Covenant on Economic, Social and Cultural Rights
4. European Convention for the Protection of Human Rights (+ Protocols)
5. European Social Charter
6. CSCE Documents
7. Other standards

V = Vienna
C = Copenhagen
M = Moscow
P = Protocol

7.4.3   The liberal approach

We have established the question of economic and social rights as one of the most significant areas of disagreement amongst the major political parties. We have also established through, *inter alia*, the cases of *Broeks v The Netherlands* and *Zwaan de Vries v The Netherlands* that, although second-generation rights are generally held not to be self-executing, this cannot be maintained without qualification.

It is submitted that, in the same way as the Western liberal democracies opposed the acceptance of second-generation rights in the debate leading up to the two covenants of 1966, the liberal approach in South Africa also finds itself at loggerheads with these rights.[29] We refer to Brooks,[30] in particular, to illustrate the possibilities that the international norms of human rights have in the South African human rights debate.

Second-generation rights, says Brooks, claim that you do not only have the right to unhindered exercise of your autonomy but also the right to demand that which will enable you to fully exercise that autonomy. These rights impose on others the positive duty to provide the right holder with adequate food, education and health care. If ownership of a motor car gave such positive rights in addition to negative property rights "then I could expect my car to be kept in petrol, maintained and repaired". Brooks[31] therefore does not accept the existence of such positive human rights as it would imply that "we should not only be left undisturbed and at peace but that the world owes each and every one of us a living".

Brooks[32] presents us with another example. If you have more than enough food, surely some of it should go to help the starving man at your gate rather than be used to entertain your well-fed friends? But does this confer a right upon the man at the gate? Suppose I have a duty to give 10 per cent of what I own to the poor, does this confer a right on anyone? It cannot, because 10 per cent of what I own divided by the number of the severely malnourished would not amount to more than the merest fraction of the world's smallest currency unit apiece.

The article by Brooks is placed in opposition to the argument of Sachs[33] for, *inter alia*, the acceptance of second-generation rights. Brooks considers the arguments of Sachs as giving "rise to liberal concerns".[34] It is submitted that these liberal concerns are focused upon the right to property and the reluctance to accept the validity of second-generation rights as fundamental human rights. It falls outside the scope of this study to pay proper attention to this crucial discussion. Suffice it to say that, whereas Locke regarded human rights as by definition fundamental freedoms against interference by the state and as operating only within the relation of individual to the state, Karl Marx concentrated his attack on the *laissez-faire* individualism with its enormous respect for private property which stood central in Locke's state.[35] We have already referred to Locke's hypothetical liberty as being out of step with reality (see paragraph 7.4.2.2).

It should therefore be clear that the acceptance of second-generation rights is not the irrational concern of the ANC or a refusal to "reject old-style Marxist socialism".[36] As we have pointed out, the deadlock between first- and second-generation rights was broken as early as 1966 and, as we saw in the cases of *Broeks* and *Zwaan de Vries* (supra), the international law of human rights has developed considerably since then.

It is submitted that the South African human rights movement can ill afford to remain aloof from the slums and squalor of South Africa's cities and other areas. The freedoms of the first-generation rights in South Africa cannot be allowed to mean the "right to be exploited and colonised" as it did for the "majority of the working classes and peoples of conquered lands".[37]

7.4.4   Conclusion

We have established that the underlying principle when considering the so-called generations of human rights is the indivisibility of human rights; that, in the case of economic, social and cultural rights, it is not a question of whether they constitute rights but that they are different only in implementation; and that, furthermore, justiciability should not necessarily be a hindrance in their recognition as fundamental human rights.

According to Robertson and Merrills,[38] it is now generally recognised that there is a crucial correlation between the enjoyment of human rights and economic development. Neither is possible without the other. There is little point in trying to decide whether one category of rights is more important than the other. What we should do instead is to recognise that the different categories of rights, be they civil, political, economic, social or cultural, are interrelated and that "all are desirable, and actually necessary, to the full realisation of the human personality".[39]

7.5   SUGGESTED READING AND SOURCES

Alkema, EA. 1981. *Schakelbepalingen — Enige Beschouwingen over Samenhang en Werking van de Rechten van de Mens.* Inaugural lecture, Professor Extraordinaire in Human Rights, University of Amsterdam.

Alston, Philip. 1991. The International Covenant on Economic, Social and Cultural Rights. In *Manual on Human Rights Reporting*, 39–77. New York: UN Centre for Human Rights & UN Institute for Training and Research; Geneva: United Nations.

Bernhardt, Rudolf & Jolowicz, John A (eds). 1985. International Enforcement of Human Rights. Reports submitted to the Colloquium of the International Association of Legal Science, Heidelberg, 28–30 August 1985, 1–19. Berlin: Springer Verlag.

Brooks, DHM. 1990. Albie Sachs on human rights in South Africa. *SAJHR,* 6 (1), 25–35.

Communication No 172/1984. 1990. In *Selected Decisions of the Human Rights Committee under the Optional Protocol (October 1982 — April 1988),* 196–201. New York: United Nations.

Communication No 182/84. 1990. In *Selected Decisions of the Human Rights Committee under the Optional Protocol (October 1982 — April 1988),* 201–214. New York: United Nations.

Falk, Richard A. 1964. *The Role of Domestic Courts in the International Legal Order.* Syracuse University Press.

Henkin, L. 1979. Rights: American and human. 79 *Columbia Law Review* 405, 418–419.

Henkin, L. 1987. The International Bill of Rights: The Universal Declaration and Covenants. In Rudolf Bernhardt & John A Jolowicz (eds), *International Enforcement of Human Rights.* Reports submitted to the Colloquium of the International Association of Legal Science, Heidelberg, 28–30 August 1985, 1–19. Heidelberg: Springer Verlag.

The International Bill of Rights. 1988. Geneva: United Nations' Centre for Human Rights.

Heringa, AW. 1983–84. Het discriminatieverbod als sociaal grondrecht. *Staatkundig Jaarboek* (The Netherlands), 193–209.

Humphrey, John. 1989. *No Distant Millennium; The International Law of Human Rights.* Paris: Unesco.

Klein, GP. & Kroes, M. 1986. *Mensenrechten in de Nederlandse Rechtspraktijk.* Zwelle: WEJ Tjeenk-Willink.

Kooijmans, PH. 1983–84. De VN-Commissie voor de rechten van de mens: Een kromme stok voor rechte slagen? *Staatkundig Jaarboek* (The Netherlands), 177–192.

Kooijmans, PH. 1990. Human rights — A universal panacea? Some reflections on the so-called human rights of the third generation. *NILR*, XXXVII, 313–329.

Marks, Stephen P. 1981. Emerging human rights: A new generation for the 1980s? *Rutgers Law Review* 33, 438.

Meuwissen, DHM. 1977. The relationship between international law and municipal law and human rights. *Netherlands International Law Review*, 189–204.

Partsch, Karl J. International law and municipal law. In *Encyclopaedia of Public International Law*, 10, 238–257.

Robertson, AH & Merrills, JG. 1989. *Human Rights in the World*, 3 ed. Manchester: Manchester University Press.

Sachs, Albie. 1990a. *Protection of Human Rights in a New South Africa.* Cape Town: Oxford University Press.

Sachs, Albie. 1990b. Towards a bill of rights in a democratic South Africa. (1990) 6 *SAJHR* 1.

Vasek, K. 1977. *Unesco Courier*, November 1977.

Van Banning, TRG (ed). 1992. *Human Rights Reference Handbook*. 2 ed. Netherlands Ministry of Foreign Affairs.

••••••••••••••••••••••

ENDNOTES

1   Kooijmans 1990 at 316–317.

2   Sachs 1990a at 9. For an in-depth discussion of the interrelation of these rights, see Kooijmans 1990 at 313–329.

3   Human Rights Reference Handbook 5.

4   1988. The International Bill of Rights. Geneva: United Nations Centre for Human Rights. A further element is the Second Optional Protocol to the International Covenant on Civil and Political Rights aiming at the abolition of the death penalty 1.

5   Kooijmans 1990 at 318–319.

6   Ibid.

7   UNESCO *Courier* November 1977.

8   Robertson & Merrills 96; Humphrey 204.

9   Law Commission Working Paper 25 at 58.

10   Henkin 1987 at 6.

11   Bernhardt & Jolowicz 6. This, however, was not the only assumption on which the United Nations acted *vis-à-vis* apartheid. Apartheid was also seen as a possible threat to international peace and security.

12   Law Commission Working Paper 25 at 59–60.

13   Kooijmans 1983–84 at 181–182; Henkin 1987 at 7.

14   Kooijmans 1990 at 181.

15   Kooijmans 1990 at 182. See also Alkema.

16   Henkin 1987 at 7.

17   1992. *The Netherlands Quarterly of Human Rights* (*NQHR*) 3 at 392–403, Annex I.

18   Partsch 257.

19   Meuwissen 189.

20   Falk 4 n 5.

21   1988. The International Bill of Rights. Geneva: United Nations Centre for Human Rights 2, read with part iv of the Covenant, articles 16–22.

22   General reference is made to the civil and political rights of the ICCPR as first-generation rights, the economic, social and cultural rights of the ICESCR as second-generation rights, and as third-generation rights *inter alia*, the right to peace, the right to development, the right to healthy environment and the right to share in the common heritage of mankind. This terminology can be misleading in that it may denote a particular hierarchy. Reference is also made to blue, red and green rights. Cf Sachs, 1990 at 9. For an in-depth discussion of the interrelation of these rights, cf Kooijmans 1990 at 313–29.

23   Klein & Kroes 9; Cf Alkema; also Heringa 193–209.

24   Communication No 172/1984. 1990. In *Selected Decisions of the Human Rights Commit-*

tee under the Attional Protocol (October 1982–April 1988) New York: United Nations 196–201.

25   Communication No 182/84. 1990. In *Selected Decisions of the Human Rights Committee under the Attional Protocol* (October 1982–April 1988) New York: United Nations 209–214.

26   Henkin 1979 at 418–419.

27   Alston 44.

28   Van Banning 19.

29   Cf Working Paper 25 regarding Western norms of civilisation at 199–203, and regarding the right to property at 452–64. Also Brooks 25–35.

30   Brooks 27.

31   Ibid.

32   Brooks 28.

33   Sachs 1990b at 1–24.

34   Brooks 25.

35   Kooijmans 1990 at 317–319.

36   Brooks 29.

37   Marks 438. Cf Kooijmans 1990 319 n 16.

38   Robertson en Merrills 13–14.

39   Ibid.

Chapter 8
The Limitation Clause

Gordon Hollamby

SUMMARY

*H*UMAN rights are not absolute: they can be limited or circumscribed. The limitation clause, contained in section 36(1) of the 1996 Constitution, determines the manner in which all the rights in the Bill of Rights can be limited. The rights in the Bill of Rights can be limited in terms of a law of general application, provided that the limitation is reasonable and justifiable in an open and democratic society based on human dignity, equality and freedom. In this balancing process the court takes into account all relevant factors, such as the nature of the right, the importance and purpose of the limitation, the nature and extent of the limitation, the relation between the limitation and its purpose, and less restrictive means to achieve the purpose. In taking account of these factors, competing values are weighed up in a process that has come to be known as the "test of proportionality".

Constitutional analysis under the Bill of Rights takes place in two stages. Firstly, the applicant is required to demonstrate that his or her human right(s) has (have) been infringed. If the court finds that the right(s) of the applicant has (have) been infringed, then the party seeking to uphold the restriction will be required to demonstrate that the infringement is reasonable and justifiable in terms of the limitation clause.

8.1 INTRODUCTION

It is trite that virtually no right, whether entrenched or not, can be absolute:[1] its boundaries must be set by the rights and freedoms and the interests of others. The state is involved in balancing these rights. That is what section 36 of the 1996 Constitution explicitly recognises by providing a mechanism for the limitation of the rights in the Bill of Rights.[2]

18.2 KEY OBJECTIVES

The key objectives of this chapter are to enable students to:
- define the purpose of a limitation clause;
- discuss the criteria in terms of which human rights may be limited;
- apply the two-stage approach to a set of facts;
- be conversant with the components of the general application test;
- be conversant with the factors to be taken into account in applying the proportional test.

18.3 APPLICABLE LAW

The 1996 Constitution, sections 7(3), 11, 12, 16, 19(3)(*b*), 37, 38 and 56(*a*)
The 1993 Constitution, section 33(1)
The South African Police Service Act 68 of 1995, section 35
The Criminal Procedure Act 51 of 1977, section 49(2)

8.4 INTERPRETATION AND DISCUSSION

8.4.1 The limitation clause

Section 36 of the 1996 Constitution reads as follows:

"(1)   The rights in the Bill of Rights may be limited only in terms of law of general application to the extent that the limitation is reasonable and justifiable in an open and democratic society based on human dignity, equality and freedom, taking into account all relevant factors including —

(a)   the nature of the right;

(b)   the importance of the purpose of the limitation;

(c)   the nature and extent of the limitation;

(d)   the relation between the limitation and its purpose; and

(e)   less restrictive means to achieve the purpose.

(2)   Except as provided in subsection (1) or in any other provision of the Constitution, no law may limit any rights entrenched in the Bill of Rights."

8.4.2 What is a limitation clause and why is it necessary?

A limitation clause provides the constitutional basis for the limitation of the rights in the Bill of Rights. It has a fourfold purpose.[3] Firstly, it functions as a reminder that the rights enshrined in the Bill of Rights are not absolute: the rights may be limited where the restrictions can satisfy the test laid out in section 36 of the 1996 Constitution. Secondly, the limitation clause tells us that rights may *only* be limited where and when the state objective behind the restriction is designed to reinforce the values which animate this constitutional devise. Those values include openness, democracy, freedom, and equality, as well as the more specific values reflected in the individual rights themselves. Thirdly, the test set out in the limitation clause — with a bit of judicial amplification — will allow for open and candid consideration of competing government, public, private, and constitutional interests. In other words, the limitation clause provides us with a mechanism for weighing or balancing competing fundamental values against one another. Fourthly, the limitation clause represents an attempt to solve the problem of judicial review by establishing a test which determines the extent to which the democratically elected branches of government may limit our constitutionally guaranteed rights and freedoms and the extent to which an unelected judiciary may override the general will and "write" the law of the land. By making the guidelines for judicial nullification of majoritarian decisions reasonably precise, the drafters hoped to provide at least a partial solution to the problem of judicial review.[4]

The reason for having a limitation clause might become more apparent if the following two examples are considered. Assume, for instance, that a member of the Police Service stands for and is elected as town councillor. This is in direct contravention of section 35 of the South African Police Service Act of

1995. If that member of the Police Service wants to attack the constitutionality of this provision, he or she must show that this section of the South African Police Service Act infringes his or her political rights as guaranteed in the 1996 Constitution.[5] Should he or she succeed, then the state (through the Minister of Safety and Security) has to show that section 35 of the South African Police Service Act is a reasonable and justifiable limitation on the political rights of the member.[6]

Another example will suffice to illustrate this further. In an attempt to arrest a murder suspect, a member of the Police Service shoots and kills the suspect. In the subsequent criminal trial, the member of the Police Service relies on the provisions of section 49(2) of the Criminal Procedure Act 51 of 1977[7] and he or she is acquitted. The family of the deceased, however, institutes a civil action against the member and the Minister of Safety and Security for damages based on the unlawful killing of the suspect.[8] In this civil action, it is argued that section 49(2) of the Criminal Procedure Act of 1977 is unconstitutional as it infringes sections 11[9] and 12[10] of the 1996 Constitution. What can the member do? The logical response would be to argue that section 49(2) of the Criminal Procedure Act of 1977 is a reasonable and justifiable limitation of the right to life and the freedom and security of the person.

In essence, then, the importance of the limitation clause flows from the simple fact that it provides the test that the courts must use to determine whether government infringements of the rights and freedoms enshrined in the 1996 Constitution are reasonable and justifiable and therefore constitutional.[11]

8.4.3 Interpreting and applying the limitation clause

The power of the courts to limit and balance human rights and freedoms does not give an unfettered discretion. It has to result in a finely balanced exercise that permits the unfolding of these rights and freedoms in a manner that will result in their optimal application in society. A limitation clause is necessary in order to ensure the meaningful enjoyment of human rights, not to create a new source of power to be used by the state to curtail them.[12]

As such the limitation clause must be distinguished from the derogation or suspension clause, contained in section 37 of the 1996 Constitution. The latter only applies in times of public emergency. A limitation clause, on the other hand, is of a permanent nature and its application forms part of the normal enforcement of fundamental rights and freedoms.

The basic structure of our Bill of Rights follows the Canadian example and is one of generally stated rights on the one hand and a separate limitation clause on the other. Accordingly, most useful comparative sources for understanding the operation of a general limitation clause are to be found in Canadian jurisprudence. However, as our courts have repeatedly warned,[13] foreign case law should not be followed blindly. Due to some important differences, judicial interpretations of the limitation clause in the 1993 Constitution may also no longer hold true.[14]

In any event, it is logical to interpret limitations and limitation clauses restrictively.[15] The general rule is the protection of the right or freedom: the limitation is the exception.

8.4.4   The two-stage approach

Constitutional analysis under the Bill of Rights takes place in two stages.[16] First, the applicant is required to demonstrate that his or her ability to exercise a fundamental right has been infringed.[17] This demonstration itself has several parts. To begin with, the applicant must show that the activity for which he or she seeks constitutional protection falls within the sphere of activity protected by a particular constitutional right. If he or she is able to show that the activity for which protection is sought falls within the value-determined ambit of the right, then the applicant must show, in addition, that the law or government action in question actually impedes the exercise of the protected activity.[18]

If the court finds that the law in question infringes the exercise of the fundamental right, the analysis may move to its second stage. In this second stage the party[19] looking to uphold the restriction will be required to demonstrate that the infringement is reasonable and justifiable. This last determination is made, not within the context of the right or freedom, but within the limitation clause.[20]

If, however, the government — or other respondent — does attempt to demonstrate that the restriction on the right or freedom is constitutionally justifiable, the limitation clause requires that the government or other respondent answer satisfactorily the following question. Is the restriction placed on the right "reasonable and justifiable in an open and democratic society based on human dignity, equality and freedom"? To pass constitutional muster, the government or other respondent must be able to convince the Court that this question is answered affirmatively, taking into account all relevant factors such as the nature of the right, the importance of the purpose of the limitation, the nature and extent of the limitation, and so forth.

To show how and why the limitation clause is likely to appear, if not star, in every piece of constitutional litigation, an example might be useful.[21] If, for example, the latest edition of *Hustler* has been banned,[22] it must first be shown that the official banning of that magazine amounts to an infringement of the freedom of expression.[23] The facts supporting these arguments will have to be adduced by the petitioner.

If these requirements have been met, the state will then have to demonstrate that the banning (limitation) is justifiable and therefore constitutional because it meets the requirements of section 36. In other words, the state will have to show that the limitation is reasonable and justifiable in an open and democratic society based on human dignity, equality and freedom. This latter part of the court's function will require that it evaluates the arguments and evidence produced by the state and determines the importance of the interest invoked as justification for limiting the enjoyment of the right under discussion. This involves the balancing of the enjoyment of a fundamental right against the interests of the state on which it relies for justifying the limitation. This last function goes to the heart of constitutional review. It requires that the values and purpose of the Constitution should be given full recognition and application.[24]

In sum, therefore, the court places the purpose, effects and importance of the infringing legislation on the one side of the scales and the nature and effect of the infringement caused by the legislation on the other. The more substantial the inroad into human rights, the more persuasive the grounds of justification must be.[25]

8.4.5   The onus of proof

It has been held[26] in respect of the criteria which must be addressed by the proponent of a limitation on a right that "... the onus of proof is on the party seeking the limitation, and the standard of proof is the civil standard, proof by a preponderance of probabilities". Where evidence is required to satisfy the requirements of a limitation clause, which will generally be the case, "it should be cogent and persuasive and make clear to the court the consequences of imposing or not imposing the limit ... A court will also need to know what alternative measures ... were available ...".[27]

8.4.6   Comparing the limitation clause in the 1993 Constitution with that of the 1996 Constitution[28]

Unlike other provisions in the Bill of Rights, the limitation clause in the 1996 Constitution[29] appears to differ substantially from that in the 1993 Constitution.[30] Some of these differences need highlighting.

Firstly, section 33 of the 1993 Constitution created two categories of tests.[31] Limitations to certain rights had to be both reasonable and necessary.[32] Others only had to be reasonable.[33] The effect of this was that a stricter test[34] was required with respect to certain rights. Limitations on these, more "important",[35] rights met with stricter judicial scrutiny and enjoyed extra protection from the judiciary. This is no longer the case. The limitation clause in the 1996 Constitution provides only one test that applies to all fundamental rights. That test is that rights may be limited only to the extent that the limitation is reasonable and justifiable in an open and democratic society based on human dignity, equality and freedom, taking into account all relevant factors.

Secondly, the limitation clause no longer prohibits the limitation from negating the essential content of the right.[36] However, nothing much hinges on this omission. As we have already seen, the content of a right is really no more than the values and practices the right is designed to support.[37] For example, freedom of speech might be said to serve such socially desired goals as political participation, an unfettered press, political stability, truth-seeking through critique and competition, cultural autonomy, self-realisation, and anti-orthodoxy. The practices which serve these values run the gamut from art exhibitions to commercials, public political protest to poetry readings, heavy text to two-word t-shirts — a very broad spectrum indeed.

8.4.7 The approach of the Constitutional Court

The Constitutional Court has moved very slowly and cautiously in its development of a limitations doctrine. In *S v Zuma*[38] Kentridge J writes that "I see no reason in this case ... to fit our analysis into the Canadian pattern" and then goes on to supply no pattern of "our" own. In *S v Makwanyane*[39] Chaskalson P appears to be even more emphatic in his refusal to define the terms found in section 33(1) of the 1993 Constitution. He quotes Kentridge's rejection of *R v Oakes*[40] and then goes on to say that there is "no reason ... to fit our analysis ... into the pattern followed by any of the other courts to which reference has been made." To be fair, the President of the Constitutional Court does discuss the concept of proportionality "which calls for the balancing of different interests"[41] and places it at the heart of limitation clause jurisprudence. The President of the Constitutional Court justifies his refusal to supply details about the limitations tests that the Court will employ on the grounds that "different rights have different implications for ... an open and democratic society based upon freedom and equality" and that "means that there is no absolute standard which can be laid down for determining reasonableness and necessity".[42] In *Case v Minister of Safety and Security*[43] the majority of the Constitutional Court[44] again refrained from attempting to delineate the precise circumstances under which a limitation might be reasonable and justifiable. In a dissenting judgment, however, Mokgoro J found the impugned provisions unconstitutional for bringing about a limitation of the right to freedom of expression, which limitation could not be saved by the limitation clause.[45]

On the other hand, our lower courts have been far less reticent about what they believe to be the appropriate limitation clause test(s) and have enthusiastically endorsed the *Oakes* decision.[46]

8.4.8 The requirements for constitutionally valid limitations

The following discussion will deal with the various requirements for constitutionally valid limitations, as laid down in section 36 of the 1996 Constitution.

8.4.8.1 Law of general application

According to section 36(1), only laws of general application may legitimately limit the rights entrenched in the Bill of Rights.[47] If a piece of legislation, a rule of common law, or an executive action does not qualify as a "law of general application", then a government violation of a right or freedom in the Bill of Rights cannot be saved under the limitation clause, no matter how reasonable or justifiable it may be.[48]

This threshold test for determining government justification of its actions is designed to do two things. Firstly, it is intended to promote and give effect to the rule of law. Secondly, it should filter out bills of attainder. Bills of attainder are laws which are designed to pick out specific, named individuals or easily ascertainable members of a group for punishment without judicial trial.[49] By requiring that laws which seek the benefits of section 36 of the 1996 Constitution be general in application, this threshold test ensures that law-making bodies themselves do not craft laws which infringe the human rights of named or easily ascertainable individuals. Thus, the requirement of generality not only appears to bar arbitrary and discriminatory behaviour by officials who wield discretionary power but also appears to put a brake on the arbitrary and discriminatory powers of law-making bodies themselves.

The important question, then, is how we go about differentiating a "law of general application" from a law which is not of general application. In theory a law of general application will satisfy the requirements of generality, non-arbitrariness, publicity, and precision.[50] In practice, this four-pronged test will be satisfied by most statutes, regulations and the common law, as well as by most actions which flow from the operation and necessary implication of statute, regulation and the common law.[51]

There are, however, instances in which legislation, the common law and executive action will fail to qualify as law of general application. Legislation may fail this threshold test where, for instance, the grants of power to government officials are not constrained by identifiable legal standards. For example, legislation might simply grant a censorship board the power to ban films, without specifying the criteria for banning.[52] Such an unfettered grant of power potentially fails the general application test on two grounds. Firstly, it logically entails arbitrary action. Secondly, the grant of power lacks precision.[53] Similarly, legislation or the common law may fail this threshold test where the law is vague. For example, a statute may give the police the power to stop individuals of "questionable moral character" from moving about South Africa, but fail to identify criteria by which a person might determine who qualifies as an individual of questionable moral character. Such a law, while general and public, is far too imprecise, far too vague to place the public on sufficient notice of what the law expects of them.[54]

> "Executive action will generally fail this test where police and other enforcement officers take actions which infringe fundamental rights without possessing clear legal authority to do so. Such actions might include the failure of the police to inform an arrested person that she has a right to counsel where no statutory or common law specifies the conditions under which such a failure could legally occur. Likewise, if an enforcement official were to take a confession without informing the accused of his right to remain silent in the absence of legal authority permitting such a departure from form, then the action would not be justifiable under s 33 (the limitation

clause). In both sorts of cases the executive actions appear to fail all four prongs of the law of general application test. They lack generality, publicity, precision and seem to be paradigmatic examples of official arbitrariness."[55]

8.4.8.2   Reasonableness

The reasonable restriction test should be driven by two primary — and somewhat opposed — concerns.[56] On the one hand, for the rights enshrined in the Bill of Rights to have real meaning the court must be willing to defend them vigorously and subject limitations to searching review. To make good this promise, the reasonable restriction test cannot be applied with the same generosity or deference as the American minimal scrutiny or rational relation tests.[57] On the other hand, the government should be allowed a "margin of appreciation"[58] to craft legislation and undertake action which serve pressing public interests.

The first requirement of a reasonable restriction test is that the government restriction in question be a means for effecting a substantial and pressing government objective. This requirement involves a determination by the court as to whether the objective being pursued by the government is sufficiently "substantial and pressing" to justify a restriction of a human right in an open and democratic society based on human dignity, equality and freedom. In effect, the limitation clause is telling us that the rights enshrined in the Bill of Rights may *only* be limited where and when the government objective behind the restriction is designed to reinforce the values which animate the 1996 Constitution and our Bill of Rights in the first place.

The second requirement is that the government restriction must be designed to impair the right in question as little as is reasonably possible. Nevertheless, the test should allow the government sufficient freedom to achieve its substantial and pressing goals, while at the same time forcing the government to take cognisance of the manner in which human rights may be deleteriously affected by its programmes or actions before it initiates them.

The final requirement is that the government restriction must not impose costs on burdened individuals or groups which are not reasonably proportionate to the expressed objective. Where a restriction realises little benefit and generates much hardship, a court should strike it down as disproportionate.[59]

8.4.8.3   Justifiable in an open and democratic society based on human dignity, equality and freedom

What is reasonably justifiable in an open and democratic society is an elusive concept. It is one that defies precise definition by the courts. There is no legal yardstick, save that the quality of reasonableness of the provision under attack is to be adjudged on whether it arbitrarily or excessively invades the enjoyment of the guaranteed right according to the standards of a society that has a proper respect for the rights and freedoms of the individual.[60]

Justification will require a value-based analysis although, in practice, the courts will rely on comparative legislation and jurisprudence in other democratic societies, international covenants and instruments.[61] The hallmarks of an open and democratic society are pluralism, tolerance, and broad-mindedness.[62] Although individual interests may on occasion be subordinated to those of a group, democracy does not simply mean that the views of the majority must always prevail: a balance must be achieved which ensures fair and proper treatment. Democratic societies approach this problem from the standpoint of the importance of the individual, and the undesirability of restricting his or her rights or freedoms.

Democracy is in certain circumstances compatible with restrictions on political freedoms and freedom of expression.[63] European societies (more than in the United States) have at times invoked such restrictions in order to protect community interests and to prevent sedition, libel, blasphemy, or obscenity. In Germany the doctrine of a capable or defensive democracy[64] has been developed, *inter alia*, in response to terrorism. In terms hereof democracy has to prevent the exploitation of democratic freedoms for the purpose of destroying democracy.[65]

8.4.8.4 Proportionality

The limitation of constitutional rights for a purpose that is reasonable and justifiable in an open and democratic society involves the weighing up of competing values, and ultimately an assessment based on proportionality. This is implicit in the provisions of section 36(1) of the 1996 Constitution. The fact that different rights have different implications for an open and democratic society means that there is no absolute standard which can be laid down for determining reasonableness and justification. Principles can be established, but the application of those principles can only be done on a case-by-case basis. This is inherent in the requirement of proportionality, which calls for the balancing of different interests.[66]

Section 36(1) lists the following as some of the relevant factors to be taken into account in determining whether a limitation of a right is reasonable and justifiable in an open and democratic society based on human dignity, equality and freedom:

- the nature of the right;
- the importance of the purpose of the limitation;
- the nature and extent of the limitation;
- the relation between the limitation and its purpose; and
- less restrictive means to achieve the purpose.

These factors should not be seen as an exhaustive list. This is clearly indicated by the word "including" in the subsection.

These factors are but embodiments of a proportionality test.[67] A proportionality test is applied to the limitation of fundamental rights by the Canadian courts,[68] the German Federal Constitutional Court[69] and the European Court of

Human Rights.[70] Although the approach of these courts to proportionality is not identical, all recognise that proportionality is an essential requirement of any legitimate limitation of a fundamental right. Proportionality is also inherent in the different levels of scrutiny applied by United States courts to governmental action.[71]

The requirement of proportionality, which calls for the balancing of different interests, received the blessing of the Constitutional Court in *S v Makwanyane*.[72] In discussing the limitation clause, the Court held that as part of the balancing process, the relevant considerations include:[73]

> "... the nature of the right that is limited, and its importance to an open and democratic society based on freedom and equality; the purpose for which the right is limited and the importance of that purpose to such a society; the extent of the limitation, its efficacy, and particularly where the limitation has to be necessary, whether the desired ends could reasonably be achieved through other means less damaging to the right in question." [74]

Indeed, section 36(1) is substantially a repetition[75] of what was said in the judgment of *S v Makwanyane*.[76]

8.4.9   The purpose of section 36(2) of the 1996 Constitution

On a quick reading this provision's ambit seems relatively straightforward. It purports to tell us that, in order for a law to limit legitimately a right entrenched in the Bill of Rights, it must satisfy the test set out in section 36(1) of the 1996 Constitution. Upon closer inspection, it is clear that the wording of the provision is in fact open to misinterpretation.

The phrase "any other provision of this Constitution" is the real source of trouble. The phrase seems to suggest that limitations on human rights and freedoms may be justified not by satisfying the rigorous test set out in section 36(1), but instead by reference to other provisions in the 1996 Constitution. For example, the relevant part of section 56(*a*) of the 1996 Constitution states that the National Assembly or any of its committees may "summon any person to appear before it to give evidence on oath or affirmation or to produce documents". This creates the possibility that such persons might be required to give incriminating evidence and, depending upon how the provisions of section 35[77] are construed, this power to coerce evidence could well have the effect of infringing a person's rights to remain silent and not to be a compellable witness. Similarly, the power to coerce the production of documents might be deemed to infringe the right to privacy[78] generally or its specific protection against the violation of private communications. In either case, however, this reading of the phrase "any other provision of this Constitution" would appear to permit the overriding of human rights by other provisions of the Constitution, without the requirement that they be justified by reference to the test laid out in section 36(1).[79]

8.5   CONCLUSION

In their day-to-day functions, members of the Police Service operate on those margins of society where liberties are at risk and where freedoms and rights often have to be curtailed and infringed if the police are to be effective. And yet, the police are not a law unto themselves: they are the servants and agents of both the state and the people. This rule protects both the police and the public. It protects the public from arbitrary and improper interference with their liberties and freedoms and it protects the police in the proper discharge of their duties. In this regard the limitation clause will play an increasingly important role.

8.6   SUGGESTED READING AND SOURCES

Blaauw-Wolf, L & Wolf, J. 1996. A comparison between German and South African limitation provisions. *SA Law Journal*, 1996 (113), 267–296.

Cachalia, A, *et al.* 1994. *Fundamental Rights in the New Constitution*. Cape Town: Juta.

Carpenter, G. 1995. Internal modifiers and other qualifications in bills of rights — some problems of interpretation. *SA Public Law*, 1995 (10), 260–282.

Chaskalson, M, *et al.* 1996. *Constitutional Law of South Africa*. Cape Town: Juta.

Devenish, G. 1995. An examination and critique of the limitation provision of the bill of rights as contained in the Interim Constitution. *SA Public Law*, 1995 (10), 260–282.

De Ville, J. 1994. Interpretation of the general limitation clause in the Chapter on Fundamental Rights. *SA Public Law*, 1994 (9), 287–312.

De Ville, J. 1995. The right to administrative justice: An examination of section 24 of the Interim Constitution. *SAJHR*, 1995 (11), 264–280.

De Waal, J. 1995. A comparative analysis of the provisions of German origin in the interim bill of rights. *SAJHR*, 1995 (11), 1–29.

Du Plessis, LM. 1996. The bill of rights in the working draft of the New Constitution: An evaluation of aspects of a constitutional text *sui generis*. *Stellenbosch Law Review*, 1996 (7), 3–24.

Du Plessis, LM & Corder, H. 1994. *Understanding South Africa's Transitional Bill of Rights*. Cape Town: Juta.

Hogg, PW. 1992. *Constitutional Law of Canada*, 3 ed. Scarborough: Carswell.

Kommers, DP. 1989. *The Constitutional Jurisprudence of the Federal Republic of Germany*. Duke: University Press.

MacDonald, R St J, Matscher, F & Petzold, H (eds). 1993. *The European System for the Protection of Human Rights.* Dordrecht: Martinus Nijhoff Publishers.

Nel, F & Bezuidenhout, J (compilers). 1995. *Human Rights for the Police.* Cape Town: Juta.

Sieghart, P. 1983. *The International Law of Human Rights.* Oxford: Clarendon Press.

South African Law Commission Final Report on Group and Human Rights. 1994. Pretoria: Government Printer.

Tribe, L. 1988. *American Constitutional Law,* 2 ed. Mineola: New York Foundation Press.

Van Wyk, D, *et al.* 1994. *Rights and Constitutionalism: The New South African Legal Order.* Cape Town: Juta.

Woolman, S. 1994. Riding the push-me pull-you: Constructing a test that reconciles the conflicting interests which animate the limitation clause. *SAJHR,* 1994 (10), 60–91.

....

ENDNOTES

1   Sieghart 87. See also Cachalia *et al* 106.

2   Section 7(3) of the 1996 Constitution states unequivocally that the rights in the Bill of Rights are subject to "the limitations contained or referred to in section 36, or elsewhere in the Bill".

3   Chaskalson *et al* 12–1.

4   Whether any solution to the counter-majoritarian problem is possible where judges possess the power to strike down legislation or enjoin executive action is a subject discussed at length in Chaskalson *et al* 11–6 and 11–9. See also Van Wyk *et al* 6 et seq.

5   Section 19(3)(*b*) of the 1996 Constitution.

6   See also *Molutsi v Minister of Law and Order* 1995 (12) BCLR 1658 (W) on the constitutionality of section 32(1) of the Police Act of 1958.

7   Section 49(2)of the Criminal Procedure Act 51 of 1977 reads as follows:

"Where the person concerned is to be arrested for an offence referred to in Schedule 1 or is to be arrested on the ground that he is reasonably suspected of having committed such an offence, and the person authorized under this Act to arrest or to assist in arresting him cannot arrest him or prevent him from fleeing by other means than by killing him, the killing shall be deemed to be justifiable homicide."

8   See also *Fose v Minister of Safety and Security* (CCT 14/96; heard on 10 September 1996; judgment reserved) where the Constitutional Court considered the possibility of awarding constitutional damages in similar circumstances.

9   The right to life.

10 The right to freedom and security of the person.

11   Van Wyk *et al* 640.

12   Ibid.

13   See *S v Melani* 1995 (5) BCLR 632 (E); *Nortje v Attorney-General, Cape* 1995 (1) SACR 446 (C); *Shabalala v Attorney-General, Transvaal* 1995 (1) SACR 88 (T).

14   The Constitutional Court has shown hesitation in interpreting the limitation clause. See, for instance, *S v Zuma* 1995 (2) SA 642 (CC), 1995 (4) BCLR 401 (CC); *S v Makwanyane* 1995 (6) BCLR 665 (CC); *Case v Minister of Safety and Security* 1996 (5) BCLR 609 (CC).

15   Sieghart 91. See also Van Wyk *et al* 642.

16   Our courts have been quick to adopt this two-step form of analysis. See *S v Zuma* 1995 (2) SA 642 (CC); 1995 (4) BCLR 401 (CC) para 21: Fundamental rights analysis under Chapter 3 (the Bill of Rights) "calls for a 'two-stage' approach. Firstly, has there been a contravention of a guaranteed right? If so, is it justified under the limitation clause?" See also *Matinkinca v Council of State, Ciskei* 1994 (4) SA 472 (Ck); 1994 (1) BCLR 17 (Ck) at 26, 34; *ANC (Border Branch) v Chairman, Council of State, Ciskei* 1994 (1) BCLR 145 (Ck) at 161D.

17   It must also be recalled that, in terms of section 38 of the 1996 Constitution not only an infringement but also a threat to any right entitles a person to appropriate relief.

18   Chaskalson *et al* 12–2.

19   Usually the government. It is important to note that the government need not litigate this second stage as it may concede the argument if it believes that the infringement cannot in fact be justified under the limitation clause.

20   Chaskalson *et al* 12–2.

21   For further examples, see Nel & Bezuidenhout para 8.4; Woolman 61 et seq.

22   On the possession of indecent or obscene pornographic material, see *Case v Minister of Safety and Security* 1996 (5) BCLR 609 (CC).

23   Section 16 of the 1996 Constitution guarantees the right to freedom of expression.

24   Van Wyk *et al* 643.

25   *S v Bhulwana; S v Gwadiso* 1995 (12) BCLR 1579 (CC).

26   *Edwards Books and Art Ltd v The Queen* [1986] 35 DLR (4th) 1 at 41.

27   *Regina v Oakes* [1986] 26 DLR (4th) 201 at 227.

28   See also Du Plessis 12–13.

29   Section 36(1) of the 1996 Constitution.

30   Section 33(1) of the 1993 Constitution.

31   Du Plessis & Corder 124.

32   The "stricter" test. See also the discussion of the meaning of the word "necessary" in *Coetzee v Government of the Republic of South Africa; Matiso v Commanding Officer, Port Elizabeth Prison* 1995 (4) SA 631 (CC), 1995 (10) BCLR 1382 (CC) at para 55 et seq.

33   The "standard" test.

34   See Du Plessis & Corder 126 et seq for background.

35   See also *Potgieter v Kilian* 1995 (11) BCLR 1498 (N) at 1526E–F.

36   The requirement is of German origin. See also De Waal 1; Blaauw-Wolf & Wolf 267.

37   Woolman 71.

38 1995 (2) SA 642 (CC), 1995 (4) BCLR 401 (SA) para 35. See also *S v Mbatha; S v Prinsloo* 1996 (3) BCLR 293 (CC) para 14 et seq.

39 1995 (3) SA 391 (CC), 1995 (6) BCLR 665 (CC) para 110.

40 (1986) 19 CRR 308.

41 *S v Makwanyane* 1995 (3) SA 391 (CC), 1995 (6) BCLR 665 (CC) par 104.

42 Ibid.

43 1996 (5) BCLR 609 (CC) para 93.

44 Per Didcott J; Chaskalson P, Mahomed DP, Ackermann, Kriegler and O'Regan JJ and Ngoepe AJ concurring.

45 At para 61.

46 See *Nortje v Attorney-General, Cape* 1995 (2) SA 460 (C), 1995 (2) BCLR 236 (C) at 248F–G; *Zantsi v Chairman, Council of State, Ciskei* 1995 (2) SA 534 (Ck) at 560; *Park-Ross v Director, Office for Serious Economic Offences* 1995 (2) SA 148 (C), 1995 (2) BCLR 198 (C).

47 The phrase "law of general application" appears to have been borrowed from Article 19(1) of the German Basic Law. See also Blaauw-Wolf & Wolf 275–278, 293–295; De Waal 18 et seq.

48 Chaskalson *et al* 12–17.

49 Chaskalson *et al* 12–18. See also *United States v Lovett* 328 US 303, 66 S.Ct 1073 (1946); *United States v Brown* 381 US 437, 85 S.Ct 1707 (1965); Tribe 64–665.

50 Chaskalson *et al* 12–18.

51 See *ANC (Border Branch) v Chairman, Council of State, Ciskei* 1994 (1) BCLR 145 (Ck) at 159; *Khala v Minister of Safety and Security* 1994 (4) SA 218 (W), 1994 (2) BCLR 89 (W) at 97. But see J De Ville at 275 who argues that, as written, "law of general application" covers only laws and not actions pursuant to laws; therefore actions pursuant to laws may not be justified under the limitation clause.

52 See *Re Ontario Film and Video Appreciation Society* (1984) 45 OR (2d) 80 (CA).

53 See *Irwin Toy Ltd v Quebec* [1989] 1 SCR 927, 58 DLR (4th) 577 at 606, 617: "Absolute precision in the law exists rarely, if at all. The question is whether the legislature has provided an intelligible standard according to which the judiciary must do its work."

54 Chaskalson *et al* 12–19.

55 Chaskalson *et al* 12–19 — 12–20.

56 Chaskalson *et al* 12–23.

57 See also Tribe 1443 et seq.

58 MacDonald, Matscher & Petzold 83–124.

59 Chaskalson *et al* 12–24.

60 *Woods v Minister of Justice, Legal and Parliamentary Affairs* 1995 (1) SA 703 (ZSC), 1995 (1) BCLR 56 (ZSC). See also *Nyambirai v National Social Security Authority* 1995 (9) BCLR 1221 (ZSC) at 1231E et seq.

61 SA Law Commission para 5.94.

62 *Handyside v United Kingdom* (5493/72) Judgment: 1 EHRR 737 (1976).

63 Van Wyk *et al* 646.

64 *"Streitbare Demokratie"*.

65 This extraordinary measure will presumably be taken only when there is a threat to the life of the (democratic) nation.

66 *S v Makwanyane* 1995 (3) SA 391 (CC), 1995 (6) BCLR 665 (CC) para 104.

67 For a discussion of the requirement of proportionality in the 1993 Constitution, see Cachalia *et al* 112–116.

68 Hogg 851–857.

69 Kommers 59, 425.

70 Sieghart 94.

71 Tribe 1454–1465, 1590–1593, 1610–1613.

72 1995 (6) BCLR 665 (CC) par 104. See also *S v Williams* 1995 (7) BCLR 861 (CC) para 60 and 92.

73 Per Chaskalson P at 708E–G.

74 This approach is now well established. See also *Ferreira v Levin NO; Vryenhoek v Powell* 1996 (1) BCLR 1 (CC).

75 *Re Certification of the Constitution of the Republic of South Africa*, 1996 (CCT 23/96; judgment 6 September 1996, as yet unreported) para 90.

76 1995 (6) BCLR 665 (CC).

77 This section guarantees the rights of arrested, detained and accused persons.

78 Section 14 of the 1996 Constitution.

79 For a better reading, see Chaskalson *et al* 12–31.

Chapter 9
Cultural Diversity and Human Rights

Danfred Titus

SUMMARY

*T*HIS chapter explores the question whether or not human rights are universal and whether it can be said that the concept of human rights is a Western construct with only limited applicability to the rest of the world. Notions of cultural relativism and cultural imperialism are analysed and possible solutions provided. The challenge is to come to grips with cultural diversity in respect of human rights and their universalisation in spirit and to overcome sociocultural barriers to genuine universality and transnationalisation. Cultural pluralism must be accommodated and tolerated and regarded as a source of spiritual enrichment of the global society and its human heritage.

9.1 INTRODUCTION

In the chapter dealing with the historical background of human rights we identified the Universal Declaration of Human Rights (UDHR) as the "common standard of achievement for all peoples and nations".[1] Some sections of the Declaration are now generally accepted as being part of international customary law.[2]

The question which this chapter poses is how universal are human rights? The experiences at the United Nations (UN) showed that the norms of the UDHR could be widely interpreted. The Western democratic states could not see eye to eye with the communist states on these norms. The Western European and North American governments placed greater emphasis on individual rights, while the Eastern Europeans favoured collective rights. African participants placed greater emphasis on third-generation rights, particularly the right to development.

With Western countries highlighting civil and political rights, in particular when criticising human rights abuses in developing countries, small wonder that these countries claim that human rights is a form of Western cultural imperialism.

The bottom line of it all is succinctly summed up in the Pollis and Schwab[3] argument:

- human rights is a Western construct with only limited applicability for the rest of the world;
- the UDHR is viewed as mainly irrelevant for societies with other values and cultural backgrounds;
- the entire concept of human rights should either be radically reformulated or abolished in its entirety.

In this chapter we discuss this problem from different vantage points, examine possible solutions, present arguments in answer to the critics, and finally move towards a possible convergence of cultures.

9.2 KEY OBJECTIVES

The key objectives of this chapter are to enable students to discuss:

- just how universal human rights really are;

- whether human rights is a form of Western cultural imperialism;
- cultural relativism;
- cultural diversity.

9.3   APPLICABLE LAW

The Universal Declaration of Human Rights
The International Covenant on Civil and Political Rights
The International Covenant on Economic, Social and Cultural Rights

9.4   INTERPRETATION AND DISCUSSION

9.4.1   Universality and cultural relativism: The common standard conflicting with different cultures

According to Marek Thee,[4] the universality of human rights has been taken for granted. Too often this common standard of the UDHR and of other international human rights instruments conflicts with disparate conceptions of rights and duties in different cultures around the world.

There are many instances where diverse religious beliefs, traditions and habits do not conform to accepted Western patterns and understanding of human rights. We see this in the status of women, in the relationship between state and citizen, family and society and in divergent attitudes to capital and labour. Thee[5] then concludes:

> "The international reality is of cultural relativeness meaning that dominant cultures in different parts of the globe command dissimilar moral standards of behaviour."

While Thee's point on the reality of cultural relativeness is well taken, we must briefly examine some arguments on universality. It is true that international human rights instruments — the UDHR included — are based on the assumption that they reflect universally accepted behavioural norms. This is crucial for the UN in its supervisory role of ensuring that state parties to the various human rights instruments meet their international obligations. Universal validity is essential to enable the UN to carry out its supervisory activities.

We see this assumption in the preamble of the UDHR, as well as in the two ensuing international covenants on human rights, the International Covenant on Civil and Political Rights, and the International Covenant on Economic, Social and Cultural Rights:

> "... the recognition of the inherent dignity and of the equal and inalienable rights of all members of the human family is the foundation of freedom, justice and peace in the world."

Nevertheless, the acceptance of these texts does not imply acceptance of the universal nature of human rights. Let us look at some of the criticisms[6] of the UDHR:

- it was drafted when most of the Third World nations were still under colonial domination; those nations that subsequently incorporated the standards of the UDHR in their constitutions or accepted them as members of the Organisation of African Unity or the Organisation of American States did so under Western pressure;

- the rights in the UDHR are said to reflect mainly Western ideological views, rather than values dominant in non-Western societies;
- the UDHR uses an individualistic approach to human rights, which is supposedly not suitable for societies that emphasise collective values.

9.4.1.1 Religion

A further area of universality conflicting with cultural relativism is that of religion. The question is whether the UDHR can also qualify as a universal moral code. The contention is that the norms and values expressed by the Declaration can be regarded as valid for all human beings.

The problem is that cultural antecedents of human rights still remain firmly embedded in Western culture and philosophy, in particular in eighteenth-century Enlightenment philosophy. The question is, therefore, how can the human rights doctrine claim a universal validity when it is based on Enlightenment thinking? Two examples will serve to illustrate the point.[7]

According to article 1 of the UDHR, all human beings are born free and equal as far as dignity and rights are concerned. If we look at this claim in terms of the notion of *karma* in Hinduism, a different picture emerges: *karma* implies that the birth of the individual is determined by the *karma* that has been developed in previous lives.

It is clear that the phrase "born free and equal" will have to be significantly reinterpreted. Furthermore, this cannot mean that for Hindus the Declaration cannot be valid on the point of freedom and equality. It does mean that, in order to determine its validity and practical consequences, Hindus can only interpret its claims within their own religious framework. Should they do otherwise, they will have to give up a very important element of their religious tradition.

The UDHR therefore will have to be

"... interpreted from all possible points of view and integrated into all possible traditional frameworks, in order to acquire universal validity. If not, it remains the product of an alien culture, valid only for those who adhere to the views inherent to that particular culture." [8]

The second example is found in article 18 of the UDHR, which states that all human beings have freedom of thought, conscience and religion. In many Western societies this right is interpreted in the wider context of individual freedom and equality. What this implies, among other things, is the equal status of men and women within the particular religious community. What we must take into account here is that some religious communities do not acknowledge equal status for women. It therefore appears that should the state decide to enforce equality for women, the right of these communities to religious freedom would be infringed.

While the latter problem can be dealt with successfully in the context of the limitations clause, the underlying point is that interpretation cannot be done from a particular cultural approach. The converse also appears to be true: that is, cultural interpretation need not exclude the application of universal human rights. The fact that the term *human rights* does not appear in the Bible and that the human rights concept of autonomy of the individual is anathema to the triad God, man, fellowman, cannot negate the biblical and Christian influences on human rights.

9.4.1.2   Cultural relativism

When we place the discussion back on the cultural relativist track, we see how far its adherents are prepared to go. According to them, local or regional cultural traditions in the fields of religion, politics, economics and law determine the existence and scope of civil and political rights enjoyed by individuals in society. They argue further that ethical and moral standards differ in different places and times. These differences can only be understood against the background of the different cultural contexts of which these norms and values are a part. The cultural context is assumed to determine the amount of attention that is given to human rights. It is further contended that something like a universal morality cannot be supposed to exist, because "the world has been characterised by a plurality of cultures".[9]

According to Baehr,[10] the above view can have far-reaching consequences for the validity of international human rights standards. If all depends on the local cultural context, there is little room left for the universal validity of international standards.

9.4.2   Beyond cultural relativism

Although one need not be in full agreement with the notion of cultural relativism, one must admit that the implementation of human rights in different cultural situations implies a stronger emphasis on human rights in some cases than in others. It is difficult to condemn cultural relativism outright.

We saw in the cold war days the dialogue between the East and the West. It was often pointed out then, as it is today in the North–South dialogue, that it makes little sense to emphasise freedom of the press in societies where most people don't know how to read or write.

Donnelly[11] has developed the notion of "weak cultural relativism". According to him, culture is considered to be an important source of the validity of a moral right or rule. It serves as a check on potential excesses of universalism. This does not say that "core rights" may be infringed, that is, the rights relating to the integrity of the human person. These include the right to life, the right not to be tortured or to undergo cruel, inhuman or degrading treatment or punishment, and the right to freedom of opinion.

There are few adherents of cultural relativism who will oppose the idea that these core rights be respected everywhere.

9.4.3 The criticism of the Western origin of human rights

According to Baehr[12] there is little doubt that the idea of the protection of fundamental human rights was first mentioned in Western writings. The concept of human rights has its roots in Western philosophy and Western ways of thinking, including Marxism. The debate now is whether or not, in the course of time, these rights have developed into universal norms of behaviour, which are accepted by human beings with different cultural backgrounds all over the world.[13]

Donnelly[14] notes the following in this regard:

"The human rights approach to human dignity has been referred to … as 'Western' (or 'modern') because it was first developed in Europe in the early modern period — more precisely, seventeenth-century England. It is important to stress, however, that the label 'Western' does *not* imply that the West has necessarily made more progress in implementing internationally recognised rights, that the West is not or has not been the source of many human rights problems and violations throughout the world, that cultural "Westernization" is essential or even necessarily helpful to realising human rights, or that the West deserves special praise or should feel special pride for 'discovering' (or inventing or creating) human rights."

Eric Heinze[15] is much more forthcoming in his response to the charge of "cultural imperialism" or Western domination:

"The criticism of 'cultural imperialism' assails a straw man through its assumption that human rights law presupposes a monolithic vision of human beings and human society. It attributes to human rights a claim which human rights law itself does not make (although, concededly, some enthusiasts may make it), then challenges that claim's legitimacy."

Heinze[16] also makes the following observations:

- Human rights law derives from minimum standards of proper treatment of citizens within static sociopolitical regimes. It does not claim nor require assumptions about the absolute good for all human beings in all times and places.
- Furthermore, even though minimum norms are prescribed, countries enjoy considerable latitude in implementing them and, even more important, they can shape their own destinies beyond the baseline of fundamental rights.
- Human rights law, therefore, not only embraces cultural and individual diversity but also provides the only normative framework for assuring that these multiple diversities can endure side by side without destroying each other.

- The contemporary system of human rights is necessarily secular; not to the extent of condemning humanity to desolate atheism, but only to the extent that is necessary to ensure that every belief and tradition can be preserved and pursued with due respect for the others. Instead of rejecting certain religious convictions and practices, universal human rights commands respect for all beliefs and traditions.

Heinze[17] concludes that "cultural imperialism"

> "… fails to distinguish between literal universality, which would require profound homogeneity of societies and norms throughout time and space, and recognised universality, which remains compatible with a vital, inviolable degree of cultural heterogeneity and transformation".

We have to recognise the objective value of the internationalisation of human rights. The following points raised by Heinze[18] are relevant in this regard:

- The internationalisation of human rights represents no more the imposition of values cherished in the West than of values long assailed and still never wholly safe in Western societies.
- Human rights have emerged more through bitter antagonism with Western tradition than through uncritical perpetuation of that tradition. Human rights must continue to be "imposed" as much in the West as elsewhere.
- The centuries-long emergence of the concept of human rights within Western culture has been a chronicle of constant defeats, as the brutal experiences of fascism, colonialism, racism, and the oppression of women demonstrate.
- These defeats have not diminished the normative legitimacy of claims to universality within Western jurisdictions.

This discussion obviously has many facets and it is certainly beyond the scope of this chapter to present all of them. What is abundantly clear, however, is that in South Africa we should continue this discussion with much more fervour and should not hesitate to draw from international experiences. South Africa has a history of turning culture into political ideology. There is no guarantee that this will not be the case again.

9.4.4   Universalism and cultural diversity: Potential for convergence?

We began our discussion with the statement that the universality of human rights has been taken for granted and examined the conflict of the UDHR with different cultures in the world. A second look at the UDHR reveals in article 29(2) the possibility of limiting the rights and freedoms:

> "… for the purpose of securing due recognition and respect for the rights and freedoms of others and of meeting the just requirements of morality, public order and the general welfare in a democratic society."

This gives one the impression that the authors of the UDHR did in fact understand the problems of the universal observation of human rights, "even in the Western world, because of systemic, developmental and cultural variations".19

The International Covenant on Civil and Political Rights, which is considered to be the most exhaustive international document of "Western" liberal-democratic rights, also states the following:

> "[I]n accordance with the Universal Declaration of Human Rights, the ideal of free human beings enjoying civil and political freedom and freedom from fear and want can only be achieved if conditions are created whereby everyone may enjoy his civil and political rights, as well as his social, economic and cultural rights." (para 3 of the Preamble)

We can observe today how second-generation rights have found their way into "Western" societies that initially opposed them and how first-generation rights are becoming cornerstones in former communist societies, while African and other countries with similar colonial experiences are making important contributions to international human rights. The question now is, whether this distinction between "Western" and "non-Western" is not becoming increasingly irrelevant.

The world is not static and neither are possible interpretations of the world or the norms which govern it. Is it then necessary to ask where the norms originate? Should we not rather, along with Heinze,20 enquire: "Where and in what respects, regardless of their origin, are they applicable in today's world?"

Without doubt cultural diversity is here to stay as is the tension with universality. We should therefore follow Heinze's suggestion. Thee21 also encourages us to keep this issue on the human rights agenda for the twenty-first century:

- Coming to grips with cultural diversity in respect of human rights and their universalisation in spirit and deed remains a formidable task.
- Overcoming sociocultural barriers to genuine universality and transnationalisation is a long-term endeavour.
- Arriving at cross-cultural universals requires accommodation and tolerance of cultural pluralism as a source of spiritual enrichment of the global society and its human heritage.
- Learning the art of rapprochement between different cultural traditions, religions and perceptions of life, and shaping an open, kind and democratic world is a civilisational pursuance.

On the potential for convergence of cultures, Thee argues further that this convergence and these value considerations, as well as common standards of interhuman behaviour, may be part of the general advance of mankind in the course of modernisation, socioeconomic progress and globalisation of economy and human concerns.

9.4.5   Conclusion

We have discussed universality and cultural diversity in broad terms. The focus has largely been on international developments. It is now for the new South Africa and the new South African Police Service, in particular, to contextualise this discussion in terms of our local conditions.

A last word, perhaps, from the victims of human rights violations. "When my rights are being violated, how can I say: 'Torture me, it's part of my culture or discriminate against me, my culture prescribes it.' Victims never talk this language, governments do."

9.5   SUGGESTED READING AND SOURCES

An-Na'im Abdullahi A, Gort, Jerald D, Jansen, Henry & Vroom, Hendrik (eds). 1995. *Human Rights and Religious Values — An Uneasy Relationship?* Michigan: Wm B Eerdmans.

Baehr, Peter R. 1995. *The Role of Human Rights in Foreign Policy.* New York: Macmillan.

Donnelly, J. 1989. *Universal Human Rights in Theory and Practice.* Ithaca: Cornell University Press.

Heinze, E. 1994. Beyond parapraxes: Right and wrong approaches to the universality of human rights law. In *Netherlands Quarterly of Human Rights,* vol 12(4), 369–391.

Pollis, Adamantia & Schwab, Peter. 1980. Human rights: A Western construct with limited applicability. In Pollis & Schwab (eds) *Human Rights: Ideological and Cultural Perspectives.* New York.

Robertson, AH & Merrills, JG. 1989. *Human Rights in the World. An Introduction to the Study of the International Protection of Human Rights,* 3 ed. Manchester: Manchester University Press.

Thee, M. 1993. The philosophical–existential issues of the human rights project — Challenges for the 21st century. In Bard–Adders, Andreassen and Theresa Swinehart *Human Rights in Developing Countries, Yearbook 1993.* Nordic Human Rights Publications.

....

ENDNOTES

1   See the preamble to the UDHR.

2   Robertson & Merrills 204.

3   Pollis & Schwab 3–18.

4   Thee 14.

5   Ibid.

6   Baehr 13–14.

7   An-Na'im Abdullahi A *et al* ix–x.

8   An-Na'im Abdullahi A *et al* ix.

9   Baehr 14.

10 Ibid.

11 Donnelly 15.

12 Baehr 15.

13 Ibid.

14 Donnelly 63–64.

15 Heinze 378–380.

16 Ibid.

17 Ibid.

18 Ibid.

19 Thee 15.

20 Heinze 380.

21 Thee 15–16.

Chapter 10
Vulnerable Persons – Part 1

Elaine Venter

SUMMARY

*A*CCORDING to the National Crime Prevention Strategy (NCPS) (Interdepartmental Strategy Team 1966) rape, domestic violence and crime against children require a special focus because of their prevalence and their negative impact on society as a whole. This chapter will focus on these groups of people in particular, with the intention of showing that in certain situations these persons will be more vulnerable than ordinary members of society, and will therefore warrant a different kind of treatment by the SAPS than ordinary citizens. This chapter aims to explain to the police official what makes these persons more vulnerable and why it is necessary to treat such people with more care, especially as far as the protection of their fundamental rights is concerned.

It is, however, important that the reader understand that the groups identified in this chapter do not constitute an exhaustive list of vulnerable persons in a community, but that the principles which apply to them can also apply to any member of the community who finds himself/herself the victim of circumstances which qualify him/her as a vulnerable person.

10.1 INTRODUCTION

In all the communities of the world there will always be certain people who are less able to protect themselves than other members of society. Such people are not only more vulnerable in relation to the rest of the community but also with regard to their relationship with the government and, more specifically, the police. This should be seen in the context of the *Annual plan of the South African Police Service 1996/7* in which it is stated that the SAPS must serve the community in a representative and non-discriminatory manner which fully recognises the human rights of all people.[1]

The reason for this vulnerability may be the result of the following factors: race, gender, sex, ethnic or social origin, colour, sexual orientation, age, disability, religion, conscience, belief, culture or language, poverty, etc.

As it is impossible to cover the particular circumstances of each of these groups, this chapter aims to discuss the relationship of the police service with a few specific groups.

10.2 KEY OBJECTIVES

The key objective of this chapter is to enable students to:
- understand the concept of a vulnerable person.

10.3 APPLICABLE LAW

The Constitution 1996, sections 9, 10, 12 and 28
The Correctional Services Amendment Act of 1996, section 29

International instruments:
(*a*) The Universal Declaration of Human Rights, article 9
(*b*) The International Covenant on Civil and Political Rights, article 9.2.9.3
(*c*) The African Charter on Human Rights, article 6
(*d*) The Body of Principles for the Protection of All Persons under Forms of Detention or Imprisonment, principles 2, 10, 12 and 13
(*e*) The Body of Principles on the Protection of Detainees, principle 37
(*d*) The Convention on the Rights of the Child, article 37b

10.4 INTERPRETATION AND DISCUSSION

10.4.1 The 1996 Constitution

Section 9: Equality
"(1) Everyone is equal before the law and has the right to equal protection and benefit of the law:
(2) Equality includes the full and equal enjoyment of all rights and freedoms. To promote the achievement of equality, legislative and other measures designed to protect or advance persons, or categories of persons, who are disadvantaged by unfair discrimination may be taken.
(3) The state may not unfairly discriminate directly or indirectly against anyone on one or more grounds, including race, gender, sex, pregnancy, marital status, ethnic or social origin, colour, sexual orientation, age, disability, religion, conscience, belief, culture, language, and birth.
(4) No person may unfairly discriminate on one or more grounds in terms of subsection (3). The state must adopt directly or indirectly against any one national legislation to prevent or prohibit unfair discrimination.
(5) Discrimination on one or more of the grounds listed in subsection (3) is unfair unless it is established that the discrimination is fair."

Section 10: Human dignity
"Every one has inherent dignity and the right to have their dignity respected and protected."

Section 12: Freedom and security of the person
"(1) Everyone has the right of freedom and security of the person, which includes the right —
(*a*) not to be deprived of freedom arbitrarily or without just cause;
(*b*) not to be detained without trial;
(*c*) to be free from all forms of violence from both public and private sources;
(*d*) not to be tortured in any way; and

(e)   not to be treated or punished in a cruel, inhuman or degrading way.

(2)   Everyone has the right to bodily and psychological integrity, which includes the right —

(a)   to make decisions concerning reproduction;

(b)   to security in and control over their body; and

(c)   not to be subjected to medical or scientific experiments without their informed consent."

Section 28: Children

"(1)   Every child has the right —

(a)   to a name and a nationality from birth;

(b)   to family care, parental care, or appropriate alternative care when removed from the family environment;

(c)   to basic nutrition, shelter, basic health care services, and social services;

(d)   to be protected from maltreatment, neglect, abuse, or degradation;

(e)   to be protected from exploitative labour practices;

(f)   not to be required or permitted to perform work or provide services that are inappropriate for a person of that child's age, or that place at risk the child's well-being, education, physical or mental health, or spiritual, moral, or social development;

(g)   not to be detained except as a measure of last resort, in which case, in addition to the rights the child enjoys under sections 12 and 35, the child may be detained only for the shortest appropriate period of time, and has the right to be —

(i)   kept separately from other detained persons over the age of 18 years; and

(ii)   treated in a manner, and kept in conditions, that take account of the child's age; and

(h)   to have a legal practitioner assigned to the child by the state and at state expense in civil proceedings affecting the child, if substantial injustice would otherwise result; and

(i)   not to be used directly in armed conflict, and to be protected in times of armed conflict.

(2)   A child's best interest is of paramount importance in every matter concerning the child.

(3)   In this section, "child" means a person under the age of 18 years."

10.4.1.1   Equality (section 9)

The right to equality forms a very important part of the Constitution, given the history of our country. However, equality before the law, equal benefits and protection do not mean that all persons must be treated in exactly the same manner. For example, a child and an adult will, of necessity, have to be treated differently. Different groups of people must be treated differently, and equals must be treated equally. For example, when two persons apply for a job and one is a male and the other female, they should be evaluated on grounds of merit and not on grounds of gender. But in the case where a child is arrested, a police official must take more care with the way the child is treated and with the manner of communication than would be the case when arresting an adult. To treat a child and an adult as equals thus implies that a child actually deserves special treatment.

10.4.1.2   Human dignity (section 10)

When the legal duty of the police to treat people with respect is seen in the context of Chapter 2 of the 1996 Constitution, it can be said that the police must treat all persons with dignity under all circumstances. A police official's conduct will be judged objectively against the background of section 10 of the 1996 Constitution. Once again the highest standard of conduct will be expected of police officials, who must treat all persons equally regardless of any personal convictions. All people will have to be treated with the highest degree of decency and dignity, since the Constitution has granted every person this right.

10.4.1.3   Freedom and security of the person (section 12)

As explained in previous chapters, it is generally accepted that the right to freedom and security of the person enjoys wider application than the right to physical integrity, and that it also includes psychological freedom. The right to protection against physical violation means that no person may be subjected arbitrarily to arrest, detention and search. In the widest sense, freedom of the individual refers to a person's right to be protected against arbitrary acts of the state which could violate or inhibit his/her physical and spiritual integrity.

10.4.1.4   The rights of children (section 28)

Until the adoption of the Universal Declaration of Human Rights and later conventions such as the Declaration of the Rights of the Child and the African Charter on Human and People's Rights, children had not enjoyed special protection in international human rights instruments or in domestic constitutions.[2] Over the last three decades there have been increasing efforts to formulate and to establish special safeguards for children on account of their particular vulnerability to violations of human rights arising especially out of inadequate social conditions, armed conflict, exploitation, hunger and disability.[3]

This section focuses on that factor which is of paramount importance in the treatment of children — what are the best interests of the child.

Section 28(1)(*g*) complies with the international community's views regarding the detention of juveniles.

A child is identified as a person younger than the age of 18.

10.4.2   The United Nations Convention on the Rights of the Child

The United Nations Convention on the Rights of the Child was signed and ratified by the South African government on 16 June 1995; as signatory, the government is bound to uphold the rights embodied in this Convention. In terms of the Convention any country which has ratified the Convention must submit a report on the status/position of the children in that country to the United Nations two years after ratification; South Africa will thus have to submit its report in June 1997. The most important sections relating to the position of the child in the context of policing are discussed below.[4]

The Convention focuses on the basic rights required by children in order to live, be protected, develop, and participate. Signatories to the Convention commit themselves to showing respect for the dignity, equality and rights of all people, including children, in order to ensure freedom, justice and peace.

Children need special protection and care because they are both mentally and physically young and inexperienced. The laws of the state must protect children before and after they are born. Many children are suffering and live in difficult conditions; these children need special care and attention.

Children need to grow up in a family where there is happiness, love and understanding. Children need peace, dignity, acceptance, freedom, equality and support. All signatories to the Convention must work together to protect children's rights around the world.

The Convention regards every person under the age of 18 years as a child with fundamental rights.

All children have basic human rights and must not be discriminated against in any way. For example, children of all races deserve equal treatment and opportunities in life. All children deserve a good education, quality health care and protection from abuse and neglect. It does not matter where children live, what colour they are, whether they are girls or boys, or whether their parents are married. All children deserve equal treatment and basic human rights.

The Convention also states that the state, the courts, parents and other adults must think about the good of the child at all times. They must always consider what is best for the child instead of what is best for them.

The state must make sure that the basic human rights of all children are protected as much as possible. The state should spend as much money as possible on children to make sure that they are able to survive, be protected, develop, and participate.

The following sections in the Convention are particularly relevant in the context of policing.

10.4.2.1 The right to privacy (article 16)

"The state shall protect the child against unlawful interference with his or her privacy, family, home, correspondence, honour and reputation."

10.4.2.2 The right to choice (articles 12, 14 and 30)

"The child has the right to freedom of religion, ideas, thought, conscience and expression. The freedom to choose is, however, limited to what is in the best interests of the child. Parents have the right to guide the child and assist him or her in making choices with due regard to the child's maturity and best interests."

10.4.2.3 The right of association and peaceful assembly (article 15)

"The child has the right to associate with people of his or her choice. No one shall prevent the child from exercising this right, except in situations where such association is detrimental to national security, public safety or public health, good morals, or the rights and freedoms of others. For example, a child may not insist on his or her right of association if he or she exercises it by associating with drug addicts and criminals."

10.4.2.4 Protection against degrading punishment (article 37)

"The child has the right to be treated with respect and dignity as a human person. To this end, the child shall be protected against torture and all other forms of cruel, inhuman or degrading treatment or punishment."

10.4.2.5 Protection against sexual exploitation and sexual abuse (articles 25 and 34)

"The child has the right to protection against all forms of sexual exploitation and sexual abuse. The state shall introduce measures preventing a child from being encouraged or forced to take part in any unlawful sexual activity or practices, prostitution, pornographic performances or materials. The state shall also prevent children from being stolen or sold for any purpose whatsoever."

10.4.2.6 Protection against harmful substances and exploitation in general (articles 33 and 36)

"The child has the right to protection against any form of exploitation which is harmful to his or her welfare. The state shall protect the child from drug abuse and prevent children from being used to produce and traffic drugs."

10.4.2.7 General provision

"The state shall promote the physical and psychological recovery and reintegration of abused and neglected children in an environment which fosters the health, self-respect and dignity of the child."

10.4.3 Children as victims

"At the Southern tip of the continent of Africa, a rich reward is in the making, an invaluable gift is in preparation, for those who suffered in the name of humanity when they sacrificed everything for liberty, peace, human dignity and human fulfilment. This reward will not be measured in money ...

"It will and must be measured by the happiness and welfare of the children, at once the most vulnerable citizens in any society and the greatest of our treasures. The children must, at last, play in the open veld, no longer tortured by the pangs of hunger or ravaged by disease or threatened with the scourge of ignorance, molestation and abuse, and no longer required to engage in deeds whose gravity exceeds the demands of their tender years."

(President Nelson Mandela, Excerpt from Nobel Peace Prize Acceptance Speech, 10 December 1993)

One must distinguish between crimes committed by children and crimes committed against children: crimes committed by children are investigated by the relevant unit (that is, Crime Investigation Service), while crimes committed against children are dealt with by the Child Protection Unit.[5]

The Child Protection Unit is a specialised unit, the members of which, in addition to the normal training, undergo in-service training in the form of a task-oriented course covering a period of three weeks. As they are trained to deal specifically with the child as victim, this section of the chapter will address the issue only in very general terms. The issue of the child victim is, however, very important, as the ordinary official will most certainly at some stage or other come into contact with such a child.

Pienaar[6] points out that a child's level of communication differs from that of an adult and that insensitive handling of a child victim can cause permanent damage to the child. She states further that the manner in which such a child is treated will determine to what degree the child victim will be able to handle and accept the trauma.

The police official will come into contact with the child as victim, when the child has been the victim of rape (8499 children Jan–Aug 1996), common assault (2951 children Jan–Aug 1996), indecent assault (2777 children Jan–Aug 1996), serious assault (2382 children Jan–Aug 1996) and other crimes, such as sodomy, incest, sexual offences, attempted murder, abduction and kidnapping, etc.[7]

As stated in section 28(1)(*d*) and section 28(2) of the 1996 Constitution, the child has a right to be protected from maltreatment, neglect, abuse or degradation; furthermore, what is in the best interest of the child should always be the most important priority.

The dignity of the child should always be at the forefront of the police official's mind; the status of the child should not be the determining factor. For instance, a child from the streets who has been raped or sodomised should be treated in the same manner as a child who comes from a wealthy background and who has suffered a similar ordeal.

The following basic guidelines will help the police official to give effect to the rights accorded to the child in terms of the 1996 Constitution.[8]

- The dignity of the child is very important. A child is much more vulnerable than any other member of the community, and a police official should therefore take particular care when communicating with a child.
- In many cases the child will not even realise that he/she is being abused or exploited, especially when a younger child or an ignorant child (such as a street child) is involved. The police official should not assume that a child living on the streets is a willing participant in certain activities; even if the child is a willing and consenting participant in, for instance, prostitution, the police official has a duty in terms of the Constitution to protect that child against abuse and exploitation, even against the will of the child. The police official should always be focused on acting in the best interests of the child.
- The police official should establish a relationship of trust with the child victim. This will only happen if the official treats the child in a manner respecting the dignity of the child. A relationship of trust is very important because it will help to dispel any fears that the child may have of the police official, the police station, or of dealing with extremely intimate and frightening issues such as sexual crimes.
- A police official will be expected to be extremely patient when dealing with a child, as the child's ability to recall and verbalise facts may be slow and may take anything from a few hours to several days. Remember that the perpetrator may have threatened the child with suicide, the killing of a pet, the killing of the child, abandonment, or even with imprisonment of the child, and the child may also be intimidated by the presence of the perpetrator in court.

Pienaar[9] points out that, according to psychologists, it is impossible to establish the emotional impact of a crime against a child and it should therefore be emphasised that the official should take great care as the investigator's conduct may either help the child to cope with the problem or cause more harm than the crime itself.

The need to protect and take care of the child victim arises not only from the police official's duty in terms of the Constitution and of the Convention on the Rights of the Child but also from the fact that victims who go untreated often become perpetrators of either retributive or displaced violence in the social or domestic spheres.[10] Nel points out that support of the victim forms a vital part of true community policing and is essential for the victim's further development and quality of life.[11]

While it is true that the police official is hampered by factors such as available resources, role uncertainty, boundary restrictions, bureaucracy, etc, it is also true that by being sensitive and respecting the child's dignity, by showing the respect which is particularly necessary because the official is dealing with a child, in short by just acting humanely, not only will the basic fundamental rights of the child be respected, but trust in and respect for the SAPS will also be created.

10.4.4   Street children

Today there are more than 10 000 homeless children living on the streets of South African cities and towns. Most of them have left their families to live on the streets due to factors such as physical, sexual, or emotional abuse in their homes, and the dire poverty of their families.[12] (It is very difficult to give accurate estimates of the number of children living and working on the streets because of their nomadic nature and high mobility.)

The need to uphold children's rights is never more pressing than when one is dealing with street children. These children can be either the victims or the perpetrators of crime, and sometimes even both.

There is often an erroneous perception that the very fact that a child lives on the streets means that he/she will inevitably be an offender. This is certainly not true, and it should be stressed that street children become potential offenders only if their needs are not met.[13] Brancken (NICRO) has pointed out that organisations working with street children often complain of the gross abuse of these children and of the negative attitudes encountered in the community when attempting to deal with their problems.

The situation can be very trying for police officials. On the one hand, there are the problems experienced by business people and other members of the community who are constantly harassed by children either begging for money or expecting payment for directing townsfolk to available parking bays. Very often, if payment is not forthcoming, cars are broken into or even stolen. Street children are often also involved in crimes ranging from bag snatching to rape and murder. They also pose a health risk to the community as they urinate in the streets and create "squatter" conditions in business and restaurant areas. As a result, the community expects police officials to rid the streets of this menace.

On the other hand, street children can also be victims and the police are expected to protect these children from abuse by crime syndicates, drug dealers, pimps and even ordinary citizens and business executives who take the law into their own hands and assault these children. Street children often indulge in glue sniffing which causes them to lose control over their actions and responses. Police officials are expected to treat these children with respect even when they spit on and swear at the police and have scant regard for the dignity of the police service.

The police official is expected not only to protect the community against the street children but also to protect street children against the community.

It is very important that the police official should fully understand the phenomenon of the street child and, in particular, the rights which apply to these children, in order to deal with them in the best possible manner. Of particular importance is an understanding of the vulnerability of street children and of the ways in which this problem can best be addressed.

A street child has the right to have his or her dignity respected (section 10 of the 1996 Constitution). A police official may thus inadvertently treat the child in accordance with this misconception, especially when the child is guilty of some misconduct. Seeing a street child urinating on the street and living in such unhygienic conditions that the child becomes a health risk, or catching the child in the act of stealing or participating in even more serious crimes such as assault, rape, etc, strengthens the negative perception of such a child.

The police official should, however, always remember that he/she is a professional and is not supposed to make a value judgement of any person accused of having committed a crime. The police official is expected to treat all persons equally (section 9 of the 1996 Constitution), regardless of their age or social standing. This means that the street child deserves just as much respect as the most influential or important member of the community.

The importance of treating a street child with the necessary dignity and respect cannot be emphasised enough. A street child is much more vulnerable than a person of standing, and it is much easier to infringe the rights of such a child, because he/she is less able to protect himself/herself than an ordinary citizen. When dealing with a street child, the police official's attitude will be severely tested: he/she must remain committed to professionalism and must be motivated by an inner resolve — not by the possibility of disciplinary action being taken against him/her.

10.4.4.1 Contact persons/organisations

NIPILAR (012) 328 5901/2
Itumeleng Assessment Centre (012) 343 1373

Kids' Haven (011) 421 4222
The Homestead (021) 419 9763/4

10.4.5 Juveniles

A juvenile is a young person who has contravened the law. Research has shown that such a child has often been the victim of child abuse, has usually been exposed from an early age to violence, particularly in the family environment, was neglected as a child (including emotional or physical neglect, particularly in infancy), and more often than not has been abandoned and forced into other means of survival, such as prostitution, drugs, theft and acts of violence.[14]

It has been estimated that between 50 and 75 per cent of police work involves adolescents, either directly or indirectly.[15] Dealing with juveniles is therefore an important part of policing.

10.4.5.1 Section 28(1)(g) of the 1996 Constitution

Section 28(1)(g) of the 1996 Constitution stipulates clearly that a child (that is, a person below the age of 18) should only be detained as a last resort. If the detention of a child is unavoidable, such child will be accorded the rights embodied in sections 12 and 24 and should not be kept in detention longer than is absolutely necessary. Section 28 of the 1996 Constitution states further that a child who is being detained should be treated in a manner consistent with the age of the child and should not be kept in the same cells as persons older than 18 years. Police stations, however, do not always have enough facilities available to keep detainees separate and this creates a very real problem. There is no clear answer, but it must be emphasised that only in absolutely exceptional circumstances will it be acceptable to detain children and adults in the same cells. The following factors must be taken into account:

- whether it is absolutely necessary to detain the child;
- the age of the child;
- the crime committed by the child;
- which other facilities are available.

10.4.5.2 The Correctional Services Amendment Act 14 of 1996

The Correctional Services Amendment Bill was signed into law as the Correctional Services Amendment Act 14 of 1996 (the "Amendment Act"), and came into effect on 10 May 1996.

The possibility of extended periods in detention in police cells was not provided for in this Act, and only limited periods of detention in prisons are permitted.

Section 29(2) provides that persons between the ages of 14 and 18 can be held prior to their first appearance in court for 48 hours, rather than 24 hours.

Section 29 states further that a juvenile must as soon as possible after his or her arrest be afforded the opportunity to obtain legal representation as contemplated in section 35 of the 1996 Constitution and section 3 of the Legal Aid Amendment Act of 1989. If read in isolation, "afforded to" can be interpreted as simply requiring the police official to allow the juvenile access to a telephone. This should, however, be read in conjunction with section 36 of the 1996 Constitution, and can thus be interpreted as requiring the police official, as soon as possible after the juvenile's arrest or detention, to inform him/her in a language that he/she understands of his/her right to legal representation, and to help him/her to get in touch with a legal practitioner.

In *S v Kondile* [16] the court applied the principle laid down by the Appellate Division in *S v M*,[17] that the failure to afford a juvenile the assistance of a parent or guardian might in the circumstances of the case amount to undue influence. The confessions made by two juveniles were found to be inadmissible. Although the accused had been advised of their rights to legal representation and of their right to remain silent, they were not given the opportunity to be assisted by their parents or guardians. There was no suggestion of any other type of improper influence. However, the court found that it was highly probable that the absence of parental assistance had influenced the accused in their decision to make a confession and to point out evidence.[18]

The Amendment Act also includes some international rules, for example:
"The highest priority shall be given to the most expeditious processing of the trial of a person." (Rule 17 of the United Nations Rules for the Protection of Juveniles Deprived of their Liberty (1990)).

"Detention pending trial shall be used only as a measure of last resort and for the shortest possible period of time." (Rule 13.1 Standard Minimum Rules for the Administration of Juvenile Justice (1985), also article 37(*b*) of the United Nations Convention on the Rights of the Child (1989)).

This emphasises the need for the speedy finalisation of trials by magistrates, investigating officers and other persons involved.

The prominence given to relevant international standards and norms is evident from the provision that the Minister of Correctional Services shall as soon as possible after the commencement of the Act ensure that regulations regarding awaiting-trial prisoners are brought in line with international standards.

10.4.5.3 Important international standards

Article 10 of the UN Standard Minimum Rules for the Administration of Juvenile Justice ("The Beijing Rules") requires:
"the parents or guardian of juveniles arrested to be immediately notified of the fact of arrest;
a judge or other competent official or body to consider, without delay, the issue of release;

and contacts between law enforcement officials and juvenile offenders to be managed in such a way as to respect the legal status of the juvenile and avoid harm to her/him, with due regard to the circumstances of the case."

The Convention on the Rights of the Child (adopted by UN General Assembly resolution 44/25 on 25 November 1989) also refers to the arrest of juveniles. Article 37.b states:

"No child shall be deprived of his or her liberty unlawfully or arbitrarily. The arrest, detention or imprisonment of a child shall be in conformity with the law and shall be used only as a measure of last resort and for the shortest appropriate period of time."

Of the above only the Convention is binding international law, but the other rules and standards do enjoy widespread support because they form a coherent set of norms and principles concerning the treatment of juveniles who contravene the law.

From the above it is clear that the police will in future be careful not to arrest children simply for loitering (slentering), for being a public nuisance, squatting, etc. This does not mean to say that children who break the law should not be arrested, but it does mean that in the case where a child is a first offender, and/or a minor crime has been committed, the police should rather try to put the child in the care of a parent than to keep him/her in the cells. When an arrest has been made, the parents or the guardian of the child should, where possible, be notified immediately. Juveniles should not be treated as adult criminals but as young offenders; the need to treat a child with more care and sensitivity cannot be overemphasised. It is true that in our violent society children have often committed some of the most violent crimes; in such circumstances it is understandable that the police official may overlook the fact that the perpetrator is still a child. At this point it should, however, again be emphasised that the police official should at all times endeavour to fulfil his/her duties as a professional. In the case of a juvenile offender, the police official is expected, in terms of the Constitution, to maintain professional standards and to respect the dignity of the juvenile, bearing in mind that this person is still considered to be a child in terms of the law. As the official is communicating with a child — and more often than not with a child who is ignorant of the law and of what different legal terms mean — it is important to ensure that the child understands what the different rights imply and what the consequences of his/her decisions will be.

In conclusion, it is clear from the Constitution, the Correctional Services Amendment Act, recent case law and applicable international instruments, that a juvenile should be treated differently from other offenders.

10.5   SUGGESTED READING AND SOURCES

Cachalia, *et al.* 1994. *Fundamental Rights in the New Constitution*. Cape Town: Juta.

Gardner, A & Mogotsi, Z. 1996. What do you know about children living on the streets? In *NIPILAR*.

Nel, JA. Snr Supt, SAPS. 1996. *The Role of the South African Police Service in Victim Support and Prevention*.

Petzer, G. *The Role of the Police within Current Policy*.

Pienaar, A. Supt, SAPS. 1996. *Crimes Against Children*.

SAPS. Annual Plan of the South African Police Services 1996/7.

Schwikkard, PJ. *Evidence*. SACJ (1995) 8 SAS.

UN. *United Nations Convention on the Rights of the Child*. In *NIPILAR*, 3 ed. Burlington: Dataprint.

Wolmarans, S & Jacobsz, R. *The Prevention of Juvenile Offending: Problems and Solutions*.

....

ENDNOTES

1   At 3.

2   Cachalia *et al* 100.

3   Ibid.

4   NIPILAR.

5   Pienaar 1.

6   Ibid.

7   Ibid, the statistics indicate only the reported cases, and furthermore, only those handled by the Child Protection Unit and specialised individuals.

8   Ibid.

9   Ibid.

10   Nel 3.

11   Ibid.

12   Gardner & Mogotsi 1.

13   Wolmarans & Jacobsz 13.

14   Wolmarans & Jacobsz 12.

15   Petzer 63.

16   1995 (1) SACR 394 (SEC).

17   1993 (2) SACR 487 (A).

18   Schwikkard 247.

Chapter 11
Vulnerable Persons – Part 2

Elaine Venter

11.1   REFUGEES AND ALIENS

11.1.1   Introduction

*H*AVING to flee or being expelled from one's own country is as old as the history of mankind. God expelled Adam and Eve from Eden and, in the New Testament, Joseph had to flee to Egypt with Mary and the baby Jesus. Other well-known figures such as Descartes, Hugo Grotius, Voltaire and Rousseau also joined the ranks of the refugees.

Today the number of refugees has grown to an estimated 17,5 million people and the majority are from Africa and Asia. In recent times refugee movements have increasingly taken the form of mass exoduses and 80 per cent of refugees are women and children.

11.1.2   Applicable law

Aliens Control Act 96 of 1991, sections 9, 23 and 47
The Prevention of Family Violence Act 133 of 1993
Universal Declaration of Human Rights, articles 9 and 14

11.1.3   Aliens

An alien is defined as:

> "an individual over whom a state (sic) has no jurisdiction, and no link exists between the individual and the state except in so far as the individual may be within the territory of that state".[1]

The Aliens Control Act 96 of 1991 is the primary legislation dealing with aliens. The Act defines an alien as a person who is not a South African citizen. The Act states further that any person who does not comply with the provisions of the Act or any person defined in the Act as a prohibited person shall be declared an illegal alien and will not be permitted to enter South Africa.[2]

The Act prohibits any alien from entering South Africa unless he/she is in possession of a temporary or permanent residence permit.[3]

Chapter VI deals with the removal of illegal aliens from the Republic and bestows considerable powers on the Minister of Home Affairs, determining that the Minister, should he consider it in the public interest, may order the arrest and removal from the Republic of any person who is not a South African citizen. Furthermore, the Minister's decision is not subject to appeal or to review by any court of law, and no person shall be entitled to be furnished with any reasons for such decision.[4]

The Department of Home Affairs administers the Act and, with the help of the SAPS and the SADF, repatriates between 60 000 and 90 000 illegal immigrants per annum, in terms of the said Act. Academics and human rights lawyers have strongly questioned the treatment and procedures used in the repatriation of illegal aliens, and have stated that the measures employed are unconstitutional.

11.1.4   Refugees

In the South African context refugees were only awarded formal recognition in 1993 when South Africa signed two agreements pertaining to refugees. The two agreements, namely

- The Basic agreement between the Government of the Republic of South Africa and the United Nations High Commissioner for Refugees concerning the presence, role, legal status, immunities and privileges of the UNHCR and its personnel in the Republic of South Africa[5]

and the

- Tripartite agreement between the Government of the Republic of South Africa, the Government of the Republic of Mozambique and the UNHCR for voluntary repatriation of refugees from the RSA[6]

currently govern the position of refugees.

Persons applying for refugee status have been given temporary permits in terms of the Aliens Act of 1991, which enables them to reside temporarily in South Africa.[7] The definition of a refugee as found in the OAU Convention has been adopted in the Status agreement. In terms of this agreement, the following persons are entitled to apply for refugee status:

- any person who has a well-founded fear of being persecuted for reasons of race, religion, nationality, membership of a particular social group or political party, and who is outside his/her own country;
- any person who is compelled to leave his/her place of habitual residence and to seek refuge outside his/her country of origin or nationality as a result of external aggression, occupation, foreign domination or events seriously disturbing the public order in either part or all of his/her own country (this includes any person fleeing because of civil war or because his/her country of origin is at war with another state).

A person seeking refugee status, but whose status has not yet been determined, will be called an "asylum seeker".

Persons who have committed serious non-political crimes outside South Africa before entering the country, persons who carry or smuggle arms or ammunition to South Africa and economic migrants will not be given the status of refugees.

The Tripartite Agreement deals specifically with the voluntary repatriation of Mozambiquan refugees.

11.1.5   The 1996 Constitution

A distinction should be drawn between rights that are accorded exclusively to persons who have citizenship (that is, political rights), and other rights that give "a person" access to a right (for example, the right to life). Both aliens and citizens alike can rely on the protection accorded by the latter.

There is a clear relationship between the refugee problem and the issue of human rights. Violations of human rights are not only among the major causes of mass exoduses but also rule out the option of voluntary repatriation for as long as they persist. Violations of the rights of minorities and ethnic conflicts are increasingly the root causes of both mass exoduses and internal displacements.[8]

Disregard for the fundamental rights of refugees and internally displaced persons is another dimension of the relationship between the two issues. Refugees have rights which should be respected prior to, during, and after the process of seeking asylum.[9]

Asylum seekers are often not even accorded the minimum standards of treatment. Inadequate refugee determination procedures and refoulement at airports and borders cause enormous problems for asylum seekers. At times refoulement is carried out in a grossly inhumane manner, for example forcibly returning asylum seekers to their countries of origin where their lives, liberties and security may be threatened. Boats of asylum seekers have often been pushed back to sea, causing them to die of hunger or to become easy prey for pirates and sharks. Other examples of ill-treatment include physical assaults, the detention of asylum seekers for extended periods without legitimate reason, and harsh interrogation procedures. Many refugees have died in military or armed attacks on refugee camps and settlements.

The Convention on the Rights of the Child makes specific provision for giving "appropiate protection and humanitarian assistance" to the refugee child. Women make up a large portion of the world's refugee population. They are frequently subjected to physical and sexual abuse in countries of refuge.

Many universally recognised human rights are directly applicable to refugees, for example the right to life, protection from torture and ill-treatment, the right to leave any country and the principle of non-refoulement.

These rights can be found in the International Bill of Rights:

"No one shall be subject to arbitrary arrest, detention or exile" (Universal Declaration of Human Rights, article 9).

"Everyone has the right to seek and to enjoy in other countries asylum from persecution" (Universal Declaration of Human Rights, article 14).

11.2   WOMEN: DOMESTIC VIOLENCE AND RAPE

"While in the conventional wisdom abuse tends to bring to mind an uneducated, unemployed, working class man hitting his wife mercilessly and repeatedly, literature and intervention with abusive men has revealed that the perpetrators of violence against women include men who hold respectable jobs and positions in society. ... These include lawyers, doctors, psychologists, psychiatrists, priests and business executives. We call such men monsters, yet nearly every woman has had contact with an abusive man at some point in her life. He looks and behaves like any other."

> "When you leave your child alone in the home she is not safe.
> And in the street, she is not safe. And in the school she is not safe.
> There is nowhere that she can walk and be safe. Girls are afraid
> somebody in a car will stop them and say 'get in'. When they walk
> in the street they are raped by men with guns. Sexual abuse hap-
> pens so much that some students stop going to school."
>
> Violence against Women in South Africa —
> *Human Rights Watch*, 1995, 48, 55.

11.2.1   Domestic violence

Because they are the ones who witness it daily, the police, more than anyone
else, know how enormous the problem of violence in South African society
actually is. This is especially true with regard to visible violence, but violence
against women has reached epidemic proportions without many people
being aware of its dimensions. This is because it takes place largely behind
closed doors. This is what is known as domestic or family violence and refers
to those cases where a woman is abused by the man with whom she shares
her life or cases where violence is used against children and elderly people.[10]

Statistics regarding the abuse of women by their partners vary from area to
area. For example, research carried out in Soweto in 1994 showed that one
out of every three women had been battered by their partners, while in the
Cape Metropolitan area a survey conducted by the Human Sciences Research
Council in 1994 found that 43 per cent of the 159 married women surveyed
had been subjected to marital rape or assault. Organisations such as People
Opposing Women Abuse (POWA) and the Advice Desk for Abused Women
estimate that one in every six women is regularly assaulted by her partner.[11]

What is, however, more worrying with regard to the issue of domestic violence is the fact that only 6 per cent of abused women report the abuse to
the police. A survey of 10 697 women (with a mean of 8,2 years of abuse by
their partners), conducted by the Advice Desk for Abused Women and the
National Women's Coalition, found that their reluctance to report the abuse to
the police and to government legal and social services stemmed directly from
the following factors:
- their negative experiences with the police;
- the inadequacy of the legal system in dealing with domestic violence;
- distrust of the legal and law enforcement systems;
- economic dependence;
- fear of retaliation;
- shame and self-blame;
- children;
- and even love, that is, wanting the abuse and not the relationship to end.[12]

Members of the SAPS cannot take sole responsibility for the fact that
women do not report or seek help for abuse. The SAPS can, however, inform,

sensitise and train their officials to treat victims of abuse in such a way that these victims, also those who have not approached the police, will develop the necessary trust in the system and the officials to not be afraid to seek help.

11.2.2 Rape

South Africa has one of the highest, if not the highest, statistics of reported rape cases in the world. For the period January to June 1996, 23 806 cases of rape and attempted rape were reported; this shows an increase of 23,3 per cent since 1994.[13] Less than one third of reported rapes reach the courts; of the cases prosecuted, only half — that is, less than 15 per cent of the reported cases — result in convictions.[14]

The police have been accused of contributing to the fact that rape survivors do not report rapes. It is widely reported that raped women have to face the further ordeal of relating their experiences to busy, indifferent and often judgemental police officers.[15] These reports may certainly be true in some cases and false in others, but even if they have been grossly exaggerated, these perceptions regarding the SAPS create an environment in which the victim believes that she cannot trust the police to enforce the law. If the victims of crime cannot trust the police, the police fail in one of their most important functions, namely upholding the law and protecting innocent members of the community (and particularly the more vulnerable members of the community). There is, furthermore, grave cause for concern if the community does not trust the police, as it vitally important that the community and the police should work together in solving crime.

There are many false perceptions regarding rape victims which make it even more difficult to lay a charge of rape. The following are some examples:

- Women ask to be raped. (Females from the age of a few months to the age of 80 are raped, and include housewives, nuns, mentally disabled women, professional women, etc. Rapists often seek out women who are trusting and will not fight back.)
- Rape is a crime of passion. (Rape is predominantly an act of violence, aggression and power, and the fact that many rapists fail to achieve an erection or to ejaculate only strenghtens this point.)
- Women cry rape to be vindictive. (Two American studies have found that only 2 per cent of all reported rapes are false.)

11.2.3 The Prevention of Family Violence Act 133 of 1993

This Act provides for a new and simplified form of interdict (that is, a court order which prohibits one person from infringing the rights of another, for example from causing injury to another person or damaging his/her property). The purpose of this measure is to enable the abused partner to apply to a judge or magistrate for an interdict against the abusive partner, ordering him not to commit certain harmful acts (such as sexual abuse) against the victim. The interdict can furthermore be extended to protect the children if they are being abused or threatened.[16] Application forms are available from any magistrate court, Supreme Court, or police station and assistance may be requested from police officials to help the victim make an application, affidavit, or sworn statement. When the court grants the interdict, a warrant for arrest is issued at the same time, the warrant being suspended for as long as the abuser obeys the interdict.[17]

The Act also stipulates that a wife can lay a charge of rape against her husband.

11.2.4   Definitions

Rape can be defined as intentional, unlawful sexual intercourse with a woman without her consent.

When analysing the concept of dignity, academics generally agree that it can be interpreted as self-esteem or the inherent worth of a human being. A person's dignity will obviously be impaired when that person is subjected to treatment which is cruel, degrading and humiliating, or to conduct which treats him/her as subhuman through the infliction of unusual punishment.[18]

The concept of torture implies severe pain or suffering, either physical or mental, and forms of intimidation and humiliation designed to destroy an individual's will and conscience. "Cruel" is defined in the *Collins English Dictionary* as "causing or inflicting pain without pity", while inhuman treatment is the deliberate causing of severe suffering, mental or physical, brutality, cruelty, etc.[19]

The concept of degrading treatment can be defined as treatment which grossly humiliates an individual or drives him/her to act against his/her will or conscience.[20]

11.2.5   The approach to be adopted by police officials

A victim of domestic abuse, violence or rape will in most (if not all) cases qualify as a person whose dignity has been seriously impaired, as a person who has been humiliated, degraded and tortured. When such a person seeks the help of the police, it is of the utmost importance that the official concerned should keep this in mind. The police official should realise that such a victim is extremely vulnerable and should treat her with extra dignity and care. This could be done, for example, by showing the victim that you take her story seriously, by believing the person, and by supporting and encouraging her to deal with the abuse or rape. This is reinforced by taking action, such as applying for an interdict, laying a charge of assault or rape, and enlisting the help of a social worker or other counsellor.

It is, however, extremely important that the official should be sensitive and realise that, just as in the case of a child, it is very easy to impair the dignity of a victim of abuse or rape (see above).

The police official should remember that he/she is a professional and that, no matter what his/her personal opinion may be, it is expected of him/her to act professionally, to be impartial, honest, accountable and responsible. The official should always refrain from passing judgement on the victim, especially where he/she abuses alcohol, is poor, or is not very literate.[21]

In conclusion, it should be emphasised that:

- a police official should always respect the other person's dignity (whether an alleged accused or a victim).
- in the case of a victim of abuse, the official should remember that he/she is dealing with a person whose dignity has already been impaired, who has been ill-treated and humiliated, and that the victim will therefore be much more vulnerable than an ordinary member of the community.

11.2.6 Contact persons/institutions

Resources Aimed at the Prevention of Child Abuse and Neglect (RAPCAN) (011) 685 4103.
Illitha La Bantu (011) 633 2383.
NICRO — Women support centre (011) 221 690.
Lifeline (011) 461 1111.

11.3 SUGGESTED READING AND SOURCES

Cachalia, *et al*. 1994. *Fundamental Rights in the new Constitution*. Cape Town: Juta.

De Sousa, J. 1991. *Behind closed doors*, CWB.

Elles, 1974. Aliens and the activities of the United Nations in the field of human rights. In *Human Rights Journal*.

Fedler, J. 1996. Why do we need laws to prevent family violence? 1.

'Focus on the abuse of women.' (May 1996) 5 RAPCAN.

Keen, J & Van der Sandt, T. *When love hurts*. NICRO.

Schutte, S. 1996. General information regarding rape: the Police response to rape.

Straight talk about woman abuse. In *TALKABOUT* No. 5, Pick 'n Pay.

UN. *Human Rights and Refugees*. United Nations Centre for Human Rights. Fact sheet no 20, June 1993.

Violence Against Women in South Africa. In *Human Rights Watch*. 1995 45.

....

ENDNOTES

1 Elles 291, 296.

2 Section 9.

3 Section 23.

4 Section 47.

5 Hereinafter referred to as "the Status agreement".

6 Hereinafter referred to as "the Tripartite agreement".

7 Section 41.

8 UN Centre for Human Rights, Fact Sheet No 20.

9 Ibid.

10 Fedler 1.

11 Human Rights Watch 45.

12 Human Rights Watch 47.

13 Schutte 6.

14 Human Rights Watch 90.

15 Ibid.

16 TALKABOUT 8.

17 Ibid.

18 Cachalia et al 34.

19 Ibid.

20 Ibid.

21 Fedler 7.

Chapter 12
Victims' Rights

Rika Snyman

SUMMARY

*I*N approximately half of the crimes that are committed the offender is never caught and victims have to accept that justice cannot be done. The question can be asked whether, in those cases where the offender is in fact apprehended and the case brought to trial, the victim is left with a feeling that justice has actually been done. The criminal justice process appears to be predominantly oriented towards the offender and the victim is deemed relatively superfluous. From the moment that the police decide to prosecute until the time that a sentence is passed, the victim is an outsider to the process and has a limited role to play.

The rights of the victims of crime in South Africa will be highlighted by investigating the position of such victims in sub-Saharan countries and in developed countries; by analysing the *United Nations Declaration of Basic Principles of Justice for Victims of Crime and Abuse of Power*; and by looking at the present position in South Africa. Finally, a victims' rights and justice model for South Africa is proposed.

12.1 INTRODUCTION

For many victims, their first exposure to crime is also their first exposure to the criminal justice system and it is an experience, coming on top of the original trauma of the crime, that can be bewildering and sometimes even frightening. In recent years victims of crime have raised questions about the lack of support, the absence of compensation and their diminished role in the criminal justice system.

12.2 KEY OBJECTIVES

The key objectives of this chapter are to enable students to:
- form a balanced concept of who the victim of crime is, and what is meant by victims' rights;
- understand that the position has changed since the precolonial era and that victims of crime are now receiving varying degrees of recognition in different parts of the world;
- form a conception of the content, meaning and value of the *United Nations Declaration on Basic Principles of Justice for Victims of Crime and Abuse of Power*; and
- acknowledge the model by which rights can be accorded to crime victims in South Africa, and the mechanisms to be put in place to ensure justice for these victims.

12.3 INTERPRETATION AND DISCUSSION
12.3.1 Definition of concepts
12.3.1.1 Victim

Despite the frequency and ease with which the term *victim* is used, it is not that easy to define. In certain crimes, like murder and housebreaking, there is an easily identifiable victim, but in crimes like corruption and drug trafficking, identifying who the victims are is more complicated. In law, the victim is the injured party who suffers loss as a result of a criminal act. The criminal law uses a purely objective criterion to determine who is victim and who offender. In criminological terms these two distinct categories may merge as criminology takes into account not only the objective but also the subjective elements in the crime. The dynamics and interaction that lead to the crime being committed should be considered to avoid simplistic and superficial labels of "victim" and "offender" being attached to individuals.[1]

Victims can be defined as persons who, individually or collectively, have suffered harm, including physical or mental injury, emotional suffering, economic loss or substantial impairment of their fundamental rights, through acts or omissions that are in violation of criminal laws operative within a specific country, including laws proscribing criminal abuse of power.[2]

12.3.1.2 Victims' rights

Some advocates of victims' rights argue that accused and arrested persons have too many rights and cite this argument as a justification for their call for specific rights for the victims of crime. This highlights the contest between victims' and offenders' rights, as though the establishment of rights for crime victims should come at the expense of the rights of offenders. Victims will, however, be poorly served by the curbing of offenders' rights.[3]

Victims' rights refer to a variety of rights and services which are afforded to victims of crime, such as, for example, information regarding available financial and social services, notification of case status, protection from harassment and intimidation, separate court waiting rooms, the speedy return of property held as the prosecutor decides not to prosecute, and being treated with compassion by criminal justice officials.[4]

12.3.2 Overview of victims' rights

The Bill of Rights, which forms an important part of the 1996 Constitution, fails to make any specific provision for the rights of the victims of crime. In this Bill of Rights, however, special provision is made for the protection of the rights of accused and detained persons, of women, and of children. This, coupled with the high crime rate in South Africa, has made many South Africans sceptical about the benefits of the Bill of Rights for the victims of crime.

An offence involves a triangular relationship between three parties, namely the offender, the victim and the state. Over the centuries the role of the state has become predominant and generally the primary relationship is between the offender and the state. The victim is often ignored and subjected to secondary victimisation.[5]

The formulation of victims' rights developed from a growing concern for the victims of crime. During the 1960s feminist organisations in England and in the United States of America established support services for the victims of domestic violence. In the early 1970s this concern was extended to the victims of child abuse and rape, and eventually to all victims of crime. This pressure for legal reform and the development of specific services for victims became known as the victim movement.[6]

12.3.2.1 The victim in sub-Saharan countries

In precolonial Africa the focus was on the crime victim rather than on the offender. Retribution for the harm caused by the crime took the form of reconciliation and restitution, and imprisonment was not used as a form of punishment.[7] Even when a serious crime like murder was committed, peaceful settlements were arranged that compensated the family of the deceased and punished the perpetrator at the same time. Research conducted by Mushanga on homicide in Uganda found that payment of cattle, goats, hoes, spears, and so forth, was made by the perpetrator and his clan to the family and clan of the victim.[8] Victims under indigenous criminal justice systems were cared for by their communities. When a person was attacked by criminals, all adult members were expected to respond and go to the rescue. When a person's property had been stolen, damaged or destroyed by a criminal, contributions towards replacing the most essential items were made by the community.[9]

Most of the available research on the rights of the crime victim has been carried out in developed countries in Western Europe, North America and Australia. Not much information has been made available by sub-Saharan African countries. Some sources suggest that the traditional and alternative systems of justice and of support continue to function, the rights of the crime victim thus being acknowledged in an informal manner. The victimisation surveys carried out in Dar es Salaam, Kampala and Johannesburg in 1992 noted that many offences were reported to community-based bodies rather than to the police.[10] Other sources, however, have noted that the rapid rural–urban migration and the internal conflicts in some countries like Rwanda and Zaire have severely disrupted these community ties, leaving the victim with no recourse other than the police.[11]

Only a few victims turn to the police if victimised. As can be inferred from the second international victimisation survey, the reporting rate in developing countries is very low. In sub-Saharan Africa in general, less than half of the robberies, only one third of the assaults, and less than one fifth of personal thefts are reported to the police. Moreover — and in contrast with the situation in developed countries — one of the primary reasons for the failure to report the commission of crime to the police is the negative attitude of the public towards the police.[12] The few victims who do turn to the criminal justice system run up against an almost total lack of services for victims. From the international victim survey it is evident that the failure to recognise the rights of victims and to supply support services is most prevalent in Africa.[13]

This failure to recognise the needs and rights of victims results in insensitive treatment by the different agencies in the criminal justice process, from the police, to the courts and the correctional services. In general, the victim only rarely has the necessary legal standing to appear in court, except in the role of witness. Even if the criminal case is successfully prosecuted, the victim rarely benefits. Imprisonment and corporal punishment are the predominant sanctions in sub-Saharan countries.[14] In many of these countries the only alternative would be a fine, which is also often converted into a prison sentence due to the poverty of the offender. Compensation orders and other sanctions that benefit the victim are possible in only a few African countries and are rarely, if ever, used. Few African countries have compensation schemes and victims are therefore left to find their own means of recovering from violent crime.[15]

12.3.2.2 The victim in developed countries

In 1985 the General Assembly of the United Nations adopted a *Declaration of the Basic Principles of Justice for Victims of Crime and Abuse of Power*. The Declaration lays down basic standards for the treatment of victims, including the right to information and fair treatment, consideration of their views, restitution and compensation, and the provision of victim services.[16]

The Council of Europe, to which thirty-two European countries are affiliated, has been active in establishing rights for crime victims. In 1983 the Council endorsed a "Convention on State Compensation" for victims of violent crime. The Council also made a series of recommendations on the role of the victim in criminal law and the criminal process, on assistance to victims and on crime prevention.[17]

Examples of provisions for crime victims within the criminal justice system are: considerate reception by the police, referral to support agencies, the provision of advice on preventive measures, the right to be notified of the outcome of the investigation or of ensuing criminal proceedings, the right to inform the court about the impact of the victimisation, and the right to receive restitution from the offender. In many parts of the United States of America victims also have a right to express an opinion on the most appropriate punishment for the offender. In most West European countries victims are not allowed to express opinions about the punishment. Instead, new procedures have been put in place to help the victim to secure restitution from the offender. Recent developments in the Netherlands are illustrative of the sophistication of the rights that crime victims are afforded. In 1995 a new law was enacted which will improve the chances of victims to receive restitution. Victims have the right to present claims for civil damages to the court, as is the case in most continental European countries. Under this new law the criminal tribunal can subsequently sentence the offender to the payment of restitution as part of the criminal verdict. If such an order is given, it is the duty of the prosecutors to collect the money. Jointly with this new law, the Dutch Minister of Justice issued new detailed guidelines for the police and the prosecutors about the required treatment of victims. Both the police and prosecutors are instructed to make the maximum effort to arrange restitution by the suspect/offender as early in the proceedings as possible. If compensation is paid, the prosecutor is supposed to consider a waiver of the prosecution. These new guidelines will be a stimulus for offender–victim settlements.[18]

12.3.3 The United Nations Declaration of Basic Principles of Justice for Victims of Crime and Abuse of Power

The *Declaration of Basic Principles of Justice for Victims of Crime and Abuse of Power* is an important statement of principles agreed to by the international community and should be incorporated into the laws of every country. The relevant sections pertaining to the rights of crime victims read as follows:

"A. Victims of crime

1   'Victims' means persons who, individually or collectively, have suffered harm, including physical or mental injury, emotional suffering, economic loss or substantial impairment of their fundamental rights, through acts or omissions that are in violation of criminal laws operative within Member States, including those laws proscribing criminal abuse of power.

2   A person may be considered a victim, under this Declaration, regardless of whether the perpetrator is identified, apprehended, prosecuted or convicted and regardless of the familial relationship between the perpetrator and the victim. The term 'victim' also includes, where appropriate, the immediate family or dependants of the direct victim and persons who have suffered harm in intervening to assist victims in distress or to prevent victimization.

3   The provisions contained herein shall be applicable to all, without distinction of any kind, such as race, colour, sex, age, language, religion, nationality, political or other opinion, cultural beliefs or practices, property, birth or family status, ethnic or social origin, and disability.

Access to justice and fair treatment

4   Victims should be treated with compassion and respect for their dignity. They are entitled to access to mechanisms of justice and to prompt redress, as provided for by national legislation, for the harm that they have suffered.

5   Judicial and administrative mechanisms should be established and strengthened where necessary to enable victims to obtain redress through formal or informal procedures that are expeditious, fair, inexpensive and accessible. Victims should be informed of their rights in seeking redress through such mechanisms.

6   The responsiveness of judicial and administrative processes to the needs of victims should be facilitated by:

   (*a*)   Informing victims of their role and the scope, timing and progress of the proceedings and the disposition of their cases, especially where serious crimes are involved and where they have required such information;

   (*b*)   Allowing the views and concerns of victims to be presented and considered at appropriate stages of the proceedings where their personal interests are affected, without prejudice to the accused and consistent with the relevant national criminal justice system;

   (*c*)   Providing proper assistance to victims throughout the legal process;

   (*d*)   Taking measures to minimize inconvenience to victims, protect their privacy, when necessary, and ensure their safety, as well as that of their families and witnesses on their behalf, from intimidation and retaliation;

   (*e*)   Avoid unnecessary delay in the disposition of cases and the execution of orders or decrees granting awards to victims.

7   Informal mechanisms for the resolution of disputes, including mediation, arbitration and customary justice or indigenous practices, should be utilized where appropriate to facilitate conciliation and redress for victims.

Restitution

8   Offenders or third parties responsible for their behaviour should, where appropriate, make fair restitution to victims, their families or dependants. Such restitution should include the return of property or payment for the harm or loss suffered, reimbursement of expenses incurred as a result of the victimization, the provision of services and the restoration of rights.

9   Governments should review their practices, regulations and laws to consider restitution as an available sentencing option in criminal cases, in addition to other criminal sanctions.

Compensation

12   When compensation is not fully available from the offender or other sources, States should endeavour to provide financial compensation to:

(a) Victims who have sustained significant bodily injury or impairment of physical or mental health as a result of serious crimes;

(b) The family, in particular dependants or persons who have died or became physically or mentally incapacitated as a result of such victimization.

13 The establishing, strengthening and expansion of national funds for compensation to victims should be encouraged. Where appropriate, other funds may be established for this purpose, including those cases where the State of which the victim is a national is not in a position to compensate the victim for the harm.

Assistance

14 Victims should receive the necessary material, medical, psychological and social assistance through government, voluntary, community-based and indigenous means.

15 Victims should be informed of the availablity of health and social services and other relevant assistance and be readily afforded access to them.

16 Police, justice, health, social service and other personnel concerned should receive training to sensitize them to the needs of victims and guidelines to ensure proper and prompt aid.

17 In providing services and assistance to victims, attention should be given to those who have special needs because of factors such as mentioned in paragraph 3 above."

A declaration does not confer or bestow rights, as it has as its main aim the identification, recognition and affirmation of rights which already exist, or should exist. Whatever basic rights victims of crime or of the abuse of power may have do not stem from the United Nations Declaration, as they existed prior to the Declaration and would have existed had the Declaration not been adopted. It is important to stress that the protection of, and assistance to, victims will have to become part of the core values of society and be deeply rooted in the general belief system.[19]

Implementing the provisions in the Declaration takes place in two stages. The first stage involves the realisation that one's own criminal justice system does not meet the standard set in the Victim Declaration. The attitudes of policy makers and practitioners need to be changed before any real changes are adopted. The media play a very important role by making known research results and by exposing the experiences of victims. The second stage of implementation involves the dissemination of information regarding the standards to be set; the development of policies and programmes; the adoption of legislation and guidelines; training and research; and the provision of the necessary facilities and resources.[20]

It must be borne in mind that the Declaration is not a blueprint for the ideal criminal justice system as it has inherent flaws and pitfalls. Joutsen (1996) identifies the following reasons why the Victim Declaration cannot provide such an ideal, or why a universally ideal system cannot be found.

- *The Victim Declaration remains an ambiguous road-map*
  In drafting the Declaration, the compilers recognised the fact that there are a great number of different criminal justice systems in the world, all of which use different mechanisms to achieve the same results. An example of this is the extent to which a complainant is allowed to express his/her views and concerns during the criminal justice process. In some countries the victim is allowed to initiate and pursue criminal proceedings; in other states the victim is allowed to play an active role in critical stages of judicial proceedings, and in others the victim can make an oral and/or written presentation to the court on the impact of the crime.

- *Victims have differing needs*
  Different victims have different expectations, hopes and concerns. This is not only true within a country but also internationally. In jurisdictions with a Germanic legal tradition, for example Austria, Germany and Sweden, victims play a relatively active role in prosecution, whereas in common-law systems the victim is simply treated as another witness. The differing needs of crime victims are particularly apparent in heterogenous countries where cultural traditions and values play an important role.

- *Reformers have different agendas*
  The victim movement consists of various interest groups who each have different goals that they would like to achieve. One group may focus on caring for victims and believe that reforms are needed to enable the community to assist the victim in recovery. A second emphasises the rehabilitation of the offender and is geared towards restitution and mediation. A third group may call for harsher punishment of the offender to bring it in line with the harm originally caused to the victim. A fourth group calls for strengthening the procedural position of the victim and changing the criminal justice system completely. The last category of interest groups emphasises crime prevention and aims to find out why a crime has been committed and to eliminate contributing factors.

- *Well-intended efforts fail to be realised in practice*
  Reforms are often proposed on the basis of theory or small-scale experiments without sufficient evaluation. A model that works in one country is often copied and directly implemented in another country, without adapting it to the specific requirements of the host society.

- *Lack of knowledge*
  As with many innovations in the criminal justice system, there is a lack of research on the effectiveness of victim assistance programmes. The methods of service delivery, its impact on the criminal justice system as a whole, and its effectiveness in addressing the needs of the crime victims are not sufficiently scientifically evaluated.

- *No system can be good enough for the victim*

  For many persons, becoming a victim of crime is such a frustrating and traumatising experience that no amount of assistance, no matter how well organised and sympathetic, can alleviate the victim's suffering. Research suggests that, even when the victim is afforded a strong position in the criminal justice system and his/her rights are fully recognised, victims tend to be dissatisfied with how the system operates.

  The development of victim policy is determined by the locus of the pressure for change. When this pressure comes from outside the government, specific interests and rights will be pursued — for example the feminist movement will call for women's rights. When the initiative lies with the government of a country, reforms are generally made in respect of payment of state compensation to victims and in areas directly subject to statutes, such as a change in court procedure (for example, allowing victim impact statements to be submitted in the sentencing phase).

12.3.4 The status of victims' rights in South Africa, and a victims' rights and justice model for South Africa

Although the victim support movement in South Africa has gained momentum over the past decades, not enough is yet being done to address the plight of victims and accord them any specific rights. Despite the sharp increase in crime and the escalation of violence, very little is being done for victims of murder, assault, kidnapping, robbery, burglary and domestic violence. The present support services for victims of crime and violence in South Africa are limited, fragmented, uncoordinated, reactive in nature and therefore also ineffective. The planning and establishment of these services are often not community-driven, and take place on an ad hoc basis which results in certain difficulties. Services do not cater sufficiently for differences in language, culture and world-view, and are mostly Eurocentric in nature. Certain services are overutilised, while others tend to be inaccessible with regard to their location and/or service fees, or are poorly marketed and therefore not often used. Certain categories of victims are highlighted while others are underplayed. Many service providers specialise in rape or child abuse, while few, if any, services are available for other victims. There is also a lack of long-term planning for new services. The community is often unaware of when an individual can be considered a victim, what their plight is and what services are available to them. Due to a lack of understanding and insensitivity on the part of many service providers, such as the South African Police Service, the Justice Department, and so forth, secondary victimisation occurs. Previous government policies, of which many are still operational, emphasised rules and regulations and were not person-centred. Until recently, violence, crime and the plight of victims were not afforded a high priority in government policy. This all contributes to the prevailing negative perceptions regarding government structures.[21]

The government's National Growth and Development Strategy (NGDS) has its origins in the Reconstruction and Development Programme (RDP) and seeks to consolidate, sequence and monitor long-term strategies in government departments. The NGDS defines six pillars of enabling policies which will help the government to prioritise those areas of activity which will raise the living standards of the majority of the population while at the same time promoting rapid growth. One of the six pillars is to ensure the safety and security of South Africans. The National Crime Prevention Strategy (NCPS) forms the core component within the NGDS pillar on Safety and Security and it is a medium- to long-term strategy to address the crime problem. Section 17 of the NCPS is devoted to a national programme for victim empowerment and support, and has as its main aim "the development of interventions and modifications in the criminal justice process which are aimed at the empowerment of victims". This empowerment will be achieved by addressing the negative effects of criminal activity on victims through programmes which mediate these effects and provide the necessary support and skills to address them. A meaningful role for the victim in the criminal justice process will have to be provided; the criminal justice system must be made more sensitive and service-oriented towards victims; and the criminal justice system's accessibility to crime victims must be enhanced.[22]

In South Africa very limited services are available to crime victims and they have been accorded very few rights. Naude (1995) has developed a model outlining those rights which will serve to achieve justice for all victims of crime in South Africa. The model consists of the following elements:

- Victims' rights should be entrenched in the Constitution or in a Victims' Charter to balance the rights accorded to the accused and detained person in the Constitution.
- A state compensation fund should be established to compensate victims of violent crimes for injuries suffered and for loss of income during the recovery period, or to compensate the victim's family if the victim was killed. State funds may be supplemented by means of a levy payable by all convicted criminals who can afford it.
- Compensation and restitution should be made an independent sanction option with priority over a fine, and should be strictly enforced if the offender cannot pay a fine which has been imposed; the court must give reasons for any refusal to grant such an option.
- Victims of serious violent crimes should be afforded an opportunity to make known their views with regard to the granting of bail or parole, and should be notified of an offender's impending release. If the victim is granted such an opportunity, the onus should be on the victim to inform the Department of Correctional Services of any change of address. All input should be made by means of a written statement.
- Legislation should be enacted and regulations and guidelines drafted to make provision for the following:

- that victims (or their families) be accorded the right to bring to the court's attention the harm that they suffered as a result of crimes of violence against the person (physical, emotional and psychological injury and financial losses suffered), and that such a submission be taken into account by the courts for sentencing purposes after the conviction of the offender. Details of the victim's career and employment status, age, gender, handicaps and personal character must also be included in the statement, as this may have made the victim particularly vulnerable;

- that victims be allowed to choose whether or not they wish to make such a submission to the court;

- that the court be granted the discretion to allow the submission of victim impact statements in cases of other serious crimes which do not involve violence;

- that such a submission be presented in the form of a written victim impact statement taken by a probation officer or a trained criminologist. Where necessary or relevant, such a statement should be accompanied by documentary evidence such as medical or psychological reports, statements of expenses incurred, and so forth;

- that all presentence reports include a separate victim impact statement, unless the victim has decided not to make a submission, in which case it must be so stated;

- that victim impact statements be disclosed to the defence;

- that disputed victim impact statements be handled in the same manner as other disputed evidence;

- that probation officers, prosecutors, magistrates and judges be informed and appropriately trained so that they are aware of the rights of the victim and of the use of victim impact statements, and that future legal training also include these aspects;

- that police officials be trained to include in all police statements full details of the harm suffered by the victims of crime, and that this information be included in the victim impact statement;

- that the public be educated and informed as to their rights in the criminal justice process;

- that continuous research be undertaken to monitor the effectiveness of the model once it has been implemented.

In order to ensure their effectiveness, these rights should be introduced as a whole, and not in a piecemeal fashion.

12.4   SUGGESTED READING AND SOURCES

Elias, R. 1992. Which victim movement? The politics of victim policy. In Fattah, EA (ed) *Towards a Critical Victimology*. New York: St Martin's Press.

Fattah, EA. 1991. *Understanding Criminal Victimisation*. Vancouver: Prentice-Hall.

Fattah, EA. 1992. The United Nations Declaration of Basic Principles of Justice for Victims of Crime and Abuse of Power: A constructive critique. In Fattah, EA (ed) *Towards a Critical Victimology*. New York: St Martin's Press.

Home Office. 1993. *Victim's Charter: A Statement of the Rights of Victims of Crime*. Home Office: London.

Interdepartmental Strategy Team. 1996. *National Crime Prevention Strategy*. Unpublished report: Pretoria.

Joutsen, M. 1996. *The United Nations Victim Declaration and the Search for an Ideal Criminal Justice System*. Paper presented at the Crimsa/Idasa Conference: Crime and Justice in the Nineties, 3–5 July 1996, Unisa, Pretoria.

Kirsta, A. 1988. *Victims. Surviving the Aftermath of Violent Crime*. Melbourne: Century.

Mushanga, TM. 1972. *Criminal Homicide in Uganda*. Kampala: East African Literature Bureau.

Mutambikwa, JG. 1996. *Some Significant Trends in the Sentencing Pattern of the Zimbabwe Judiciary during the Five Year Period of 1991–1995*. Paper presented to the National Sentencing Conference, Nyanga, Zimbabwe, 14–18 August 1996.

Naude, CMB. 1995. *An International Perspective on Victim Participation in the Criminal Justice Process with Specific Reference to Victim Impact Statements*. Research report, Department of Criminology. Pretoria: Unisa.

Nel, JA. 1996. *The South African Police Service Victim Support Programme Initiative: the way forward*. Paper presented to the Crimsa/Idasa Conference: Crime and Justice in the Nineties, July 3–5 1996, Unisa, Pretoria.

Nsereko, N. 1992. Victims of crime and their rights. In Mushanga, TM (ed) *Criminology in Africa*. Rome: Unicri.

Odenkunle, E. 1993. *Alternatives to Imprisonment in Africa*, edited by U Zvekic. Rome: Unicri.

Snyman, HF. 1996. *A Proposed Model of a National Body for Victim Assistance*. Paper presented to the National Workshop: Victim Empowerment and Support, 29–30 August 1996, Kempton Park.

UN. 1996. *Use and Application of the Declaration of Basic Principles of Justice for Victims of Crime and Abuse of Power*. Draft resolution adopted by the United Nations Commission on Crime Prevention and Criminal Justice, May 1996, E/CN.15/1996/L.16.Rev.1.

Van Dijk, J. 1996. *Victim Empowerment and Support in an Inernational Perspective*. Paper presented to the National Workshop: Victim Empowerment and Support, 29–30 August 1996, Kempton Park.

Zedner, L. 1994. Victims. In Maguire, M, Morgan, R & R Reiner (eds) *The Oxford Handbook of Criminology*. Oxford: Clarendon Press.

Zvekic, U & Del Frate, AA. 1995. *Understanding Crime: Experiences of Crime and Crime Control*. Rome: Unicri.

••••••••••••••••••••••

ENDNOTES

1   Fattah *Understanding Criminal Victimisation* 88–92.

2   UN (1992) 211 in Naude 15.

3   Elias 90.

4   Naude 16.

5   Joutsen paper presented 1996.

6   Zedner 1207.

7   Nsereko 21; Odenkunle 46.

8   Mushanga 138.

9   Nsereko 26.

10   Zvekic & Del Frate 20–22.

11   Joutsen paper presented 1996.

12   Joutsen paper presented 1996.

13   Van Dijk paper presented 1996.

14   Mutambikwa paper presented 1996.

15   Joutsen paper presented 1996.

16   Fattah *The United Nations Declaration* 401–403.

17   Naude 56.

18   Van Dijk paper presented 1996.

19   Fattah *The United Nations Declaration* 403.

20   Joutsen paper presented 1996.

21   Nel paper presented 1996.

22   Interdepartmental Strategy Team 65–67.

Chapter 13
Arrest and Detention – Part 1

Elaine Venter

SUMMARY

A PERSON can be detained without having been arrested and the Constitution provides adequate protection to such a person. Such a person will generally have the right to have his/her dignity protected and the right not to be subjected to ill treatment, inhumane treatment or even torture. Section 35(2) of the Constitution also affords specific protection to such a person. A detained person should, however, be distinguished from a person arrested in terms of the Criminal Procedure Act 51 of 1977. The reason for this is that, although a person arrested in terms of the Criminal Procedure Act of 1977 also has the right to the protection of his/her dignity and the right not to be ill treated, not to be treated inhumanely and not to be tortured, a specific distinction is made between arrested and detained persons in section 35 of the 1996 Constitution.

In terms of the Constitution the highest value of the community is not placed on the successful conviction of criminals, but on upholding the rights of individuals. It is therefore true that the Constitution ensures accountability, to the extent that the arbitrary exercise of power will be illegal and evidence resulting from such actions can be excluded.

When evaluating the rights specifically designed to protect detained, arrested and accused persons, it will be found that these rights primarily consist of those rights which such persons previously enjoyed in terms of the common law, the Criminal Procedure Act of 1977 and the so-called "Judges' Rules", as well as precedents set by the courts with regard to these laws before the Constitution was promulgated. However, the status of these rights has now changed because, since they have been codified in the Constitution, they have acquired the status of the highest law of the land.

Police officials will therefore be familiar with most of these rights, and will not find applying the laws strange and incomprehensible. They will be exercising the same functions as before, but with a much higher premium being placed on the responsibility to respect and adhere to these laws. Ideally, this will ensure that the conduct of police officials is worthy of the highest professional accolade.

13.1   INTRODUCTION

Essentially arrest involves depriving a person of his/her liberty by taking him/her into custody. From a human rights perspective the primary concern is that an arrest should be both legal and necessary. As far as detainees are concerned, detainees in police custody have ususally not yet been convicted and the presumption of innocence will therefore apply. For this reason, and out of respect for every individual's basic human dignity, the treatment of detainees by police officials must be both humane and legal.

13.2 KEY OBJECTIVES

The key objectives of this chapter are to enable students to define and understand:

- the difference between the "arrest" and "detention" of an accused person;
- the individual's right to liberty;
- the interrelationship between sections 10, 12 and 35 of the 1996 Constitution;
- the presumption of innocence and the fact that pretrial detention and arrest constitute a purely administrative action, thus highlighting the vulnerability and unconvicted status of detainees.

13.3 APPLICABLE LAW AND INTERNATIONAL INSTRUMENTS

Drug and Drug Trafficking Act 140 of 1992

Public Safety Act 74 of 1982

The 1996 Constitution, sections 10, 12 and 35

The Criminal Procedure Act 51 of 1977, sections 39–53

The Universal Declaration of Human Rights, article 9

The International Covenant on Civil and Political Rights, articles 9.2–9.3

The African Charter on Human Rights, article 9

The Body of Principles for the Protection of All Persons under Form of Detention or Imprisonment, principles 2, 10, 12 and 13

The Body of Principles on the Protection of Detainees, principle 37

The Convention on the Rights of the Child, article 37b

Principles on the Effective Prevention and Investigation of Extra-legal, Arbitrary and Summary Executions, principle 2

United Nations Standard Minimum Rules for the Administration of Juvenile Justice (Beijing Rules), article 10

13.4 INTERPRETATION AND DISCUSSION

13.4.1 Section 10 of the 1996 Constitution: Human dignity

> "10. Every one has inherent dignity and the right to have their dignity respected and protected."

Seen in the context of the 1996 Constitution, the legal duty of police officials to treat people with respect applies to *all* persons in *all* circumstances. The conduct of each and every police official will be judged objectively against the background of this section. The highest standard of conduct is expected of all police officials, who must treat all persons equally, regardless of their personal convictions. The Constitution affords every person the right to be treated with the highest degree of decency and dignity.

EXAMPLES

1   When arresting a person with a warrant (section 43 of the Criminal Procedure Act 51 of 1977), without a warrant (section 40 of the Criminal Procedure Act of 1977), and when arresting a person who has committed an

offence in court (section 178 of the Criminal Procedure Act of 1977), a police official should, as far as possible, address that person respectfully, and use the minimum force necessary to effect the arrest.

2 The provision made in the Standing Orders that women may only be searched by female officers (search of arrested persons, section 23 as well as section 29 of the Criminal Procedure Act of 1977), and other orders such as that body searches should take place in private if at all possible, are specifically designed to protect the dignity of the person concerned. It is to be expected that the provisions of the Constitution will necessitate many more such departmental orders which will serve to protect a person's dignity.

3 When using force (sections 39, 48 and 49 of the Criminal Procedure Act of 1977) during arrest, search (section 27 of the Criminal Procedure Act), crowd control and in self-defence, a police official should have an inherent respect for the dignity of the person concerned.

When the police official does not respect the dignity of the other person, abuse of power and authority is likely to occur.

13.4.2 Section 12 of the 1996 Constitution: Freedom and security of the person

"12.(1) Everyone has the right of freedom and security of the person, which includes the right —

(a) not to be deprived of freedom arbitrarily or without just cause;

(b) not to be detained without trial;

(c) to be free from all forms of violence from both public and private sources;

(d) not to be tortured in any way; and

(e) not to be treated or punished in a cruel, inhuman or degrading way.

(2) Everyone has the right to bodily and psychological integrity, which includes the right —

(a) to make decisions concerning reproduction;

(b) to security in and control over their body; and

(c) not to be subjected to medical or scientific experiments without their informed consent."

The focus will be on section 12(1), as it is this part of section 12 which specifically deals with the conduct of members of the South African Police Service. It is generally accepted that the right to freedom and security of the person enjoys wider application than the right to physical integrity, and that it also includes psychological freedom. The right of protection against physical violation means that no person may be subjected arbitrarily to arrest, detention and search. In the widest sense, freedom of the individual refers to the person's right to be protected against arbitrary acts of the state which could violate or inhibit the physical and spiritual integrity of an individual.

In *Ferreira v Levin NO & others and Vryenhoek & others v Powell NO & others* 1996 (1) BCLR 1 (CC) 4H–7H the interpretation of freedom so as to include psychological freedom was explained in the following manner:

"The word freedom should be interpreted as widely as possible. This does however not deny the essential role of the State to resolve the paradox of unlimited freedom by intervening. The primary purpose of the section would however still be to ensure that the physical integrity of the person was protected, and corresponds with the use of the term 'freedom and security of the person' in Public International Law. When the occasion however demanded it, and in context of the whole of the Bill of Rights, the Court will not hesitate to include psychological in the interpretation of the word."

Section 12(1)(*a*) of the 1996 Constitution gives a person the right not to be deprived of his/her freedom *arbitrarily* or without *just cause*.

EXAMPLES

1   When a police official effects an arrest (without a warrant, section 40 of the Criminal Procedure Act of 1977), the official must have good cause/just cause to believe that the person to be arrested has committed, is committing, or will be committing a crime.

2   Section 38 has been interpreted to provide for arrest as the last option in securing a person's attendance in court. There should thus be just cause before the alternative of arrest is used to secure the person's attendance in court; for example, the person may not have a fixed address, may be dangerous, or may skip the country.

The right not to be detained without trial (section 12(1)(*b*)) is closely related to the rights contained in section 35(2)(*d*) (the right to have the lawfulness of detention challenged in a court of law and to be released), and section 35(3)(*c*) (the right to a public trial before a court of law within a reasonable time after being charged). Other forms of detention are included which must also adhere strictly to legal rules which will survive the tests of Chapter 2 of the 1996 Constitution. Examples of these are the detention of mentally disturbed persons and illegal immigrants. An example of a legal rule which probably will not pass the test of constitutionality is section 12 of the Drugs and Drug Trafficking Act 140 of 1992, which authorises the detention of persons where there are reasonable grounds to believe that they may be withholding information in connection with a drug offence. Some of the provisions of the Internal Security Act 74 of 1982 which have been repealed, would also not have passed the test.

Section 12(1)(*d*), (*e*) absolutely forbids any state organ, and, by implication, more specifically the police, to subject any person to torture or cruel treatment. This section has very wide application resulting in the prohibition of all forms of torture or cruel treatment under threat of punishment. In South Africa, where the police have in the past been accused of the torture of suspects, tragically often with good reason, this section is of the utmost importance. It can be expected that the courts will place great emphasis on this right and will regard any violation thereof in a serious light.

On closer inspection of this section it appears that physical, psychological and emotional torture is forbidden. This includes all methods used on suspects for the procurement of information, an admission or a confession regarding a crime. The wording of this section makes it clear that not only are direct instances of torture and cruel treatment included but also indirect forms such as constant subjection to loud noise, deprivation of food and sleep, or any similar treatment. It is suggested that, in the light of these and other provisions, the police should re-evaluate their interrogation techniques and treatment of suspects. A certain degree of discomfort which could be considered normal during the interrogation process will not be prohibited, but any improper conduct before and during the interrogation will be illegal.

Policy for the treatment of detainees

The government signed the United Nations Convention against Torture and Other Cruel, Inhuman or Degrading Treatment or Punishment on 29 January 1993, thereby indicating an undertaking to adhere to the Convention.

State parties to the Convention also pledge to take effective legislative, administrative, judicial or other measures to prevent acts of torture in any territory under their jurisdiction. In addition, signatories agree to afford one another the greatest measure of assistance in connection with criminal proceedings arising from acts of torture, and to ensure that education and information regarding the prohibition of torture are fully included in the training of all persons involved in the custody, interrogation or treatment of any individual subjected to any form of arrest, detention or imprisonment.

This has necessitated a re-evaluation of the treatment of persons in the custody of the South African Police Service, as well as the approach of the police towards interrogation methods, detention, etc. The National Commissioner has requested that guidelines dealing specifically with the treatment of persons in the custody of the South African Police Service be drawn up. These guidelines will eventually be incorporated into National Orders.

EXAMPLE: GUIDELINE 3

A police official shall not obey an order to torture a person by a superior and, furthermore, where the official believes that a person is being tortured or that an attempt is made to do so, he should take all reasonable steps to put an end to it. This must immediately be reported to the station commissioner, and where the station commissioner is involved, another superior.

The South African Police Service has also signed an agreement with the International Committee of the Red Cross, giving the Red Cross unlimited, unannounced access to persons in detention. It is clear that the South African Police Service not only supports the right to protection against torture and other cruel, inhumane or degrading treatment, but that the Service is also committed to ensuring that this will be communicated and adhered to by all the members of the Service.

13.4.3 Section 35 of the 1996 Constitution: Arrested, detained and accused persons

"35.(1) Everyone who is arrested for allegedly committing an offence has the right —

(*a*) to remain silent;

(*b*) to be informed promptly —

(i) of the right to remain silent; and

(ii) of the consequences of not remaining silent;

(*c*) not to be compelled to make any confession or admission that could be used in evidence against that person;

(*d*) to be brought before a court as soon as possible, but not later than 48 hours after the arrest, but if that period expires outside ordinary court hours, to be brought before a court on the first court day after the end of that period;

(*e*) at the first court appearance after being arrested, to be charged or to be informed of the reason for the detention to continue, or to be released; and

(*f*) to be released from detention if the interests of justice permit, subject to reasonable conditions.

(2) Everyone who is detained, including every sentenced prisoner, has the right —

(*a*) to be informed promptly of the reason for being detained;

(*b*) to choose, and to consult with, a legal practitioner, and to be informed of this right promptly;

(*c*) to have a legal practitioner assigned to the detained person by the state, and at state expense, if substantial injustice would otherwise result, and to be informed of this right promptly;

(*d*) to challenge the lawfulness of the detention in person before a court and, if the detention is unlawful, to be released;

(*e*) to conditions of detention that are consistent with human dignity, including at least exercise and the provision, at state expense, of adequate accommodation, nutrition, reading material, and medical treatment; and

(f) to communicate with, and be visited by, that person's —

(i) spouse or partner;

(ii) next of kin;

(iii) chosen religious counsellor; and

(iv) chosen medical practitioner.

(3) Every accused has the right to a fair trial, which includes the right —

(a) to be informed of the charge with sufficient details to answer it;

(b) to have adequate time and facilities to prepare a defence;

(c) to a public trial in an ordinary court;

(d) to have their trial begin and conclude without unreasonable delay;

(e) to be present when being tried;

(f) to choose, and be represented by, a legal practitioner, and to be informed of this right;

(g) to have a legal practitioner assigned to the accused by the state, and at state expense, if substantial injustice would otherwise result, and be informed of this right;

(h) to be presumed innocent, to remain silent, and not to testify during the proceedings;

(i) to adduce and challenge evidence;

(j) not to be compelled to give self-incriminating evidence;

(k) to be tried in a language which the accused person understands or, if that is not practicable, to have the proceeding interpreted in that language;

(l) not to be convicted for an act or omission that was not an offence under either national or international law at the time it was committed or omitted;

(m) not to be tried for an offence in respect of an act or omission for which that person has previously been either acquitted or convicted;

(n) to the benefit of the least severe of the prescribed punishments if the prescribed punishment for the offence has been changed between the time that the offence was committed and the time of sentencing; and

(o) of appeal to, or review by, a higher court.

(4)   Whenever this section requires information to be given to a person, that information must be given in a language that the person understands.

(5)   Evidence obtained in a manner that violates any right in the Bill of Rights must be excluded if the admission of that evidence would render the trial unfair or otherwise be detrimental to the administration of justice."

In our earlier discussion of some of the other rights entrenched in Chapter 2 of the 1996 Constitution, we referred to the impact that these rights will have on the manner in which all persons — including detained, arrested and accused persons — are treated by police officials. In addition, section 35 extends certain specific rights to *detained, arrested* and *accused* persons. Section 35 should not be seen in isolation but against the background of all the rights protected by Chapter 2.

Before discussing the rights extended by section 35 to detainees, arrested and accused persons, we have to refer to the effect of the 1996 Constitution on the exclusion of evidence obtained in conflict with the provisions thereof and with other legal rules. The extent of the evidence which may be excluded is, however, extended by the provisions of Chapter 2 and specifically by section 35.

Before the commencement of the Constitution, it was expected of the police official to inform an accused, from the moment of arrest, that he/she did not have to answer any questions regarding the offence for which he/she was arrested and that he/she had a right to legal representation. Failure to inform the accused of these rights or of any other rights in terms of the Judges' Rules did not result in the exclusion by the court of any information given or pointing out by the accused as long as it was given voluntarily.

Section 35(3) of the 1996 Constitution, however, provides for the right of every accused to a fair trial. The constitutional protection of this right extends the authority of the courts to exclude illegally obtained evidence.

The exclusion of evidence means that the court will ignore such evidence for the purposes of deciding the guilt or innocence of the accused. The situation as far as such evidence is concerned is that it will be treated similarly to admissions or confessions obtained in conflict with the relevant provisions of the Criminal Procedure Act of 1977.

Where, in the process of gathering evidence, rights protected in terms of Chapter 2 of the 1996 Constitution are infringed, the courts, taking into account the extent and seriousness of the infringement, will not hesitate to exclude evidence thus obtained. This protection of the rights of individuals — and in particular the rights of detainees, arrested and accused persons — may result in the fact that persons who might otherwise have been convicted, may now be found to be innocent on a technical point.

The reason for this is that the basic premise underlying the protection of fundamental rights is that the highest value of the community is not placed on the successful conviction of criminals, but on upholding the rights of individuals. As far as the police official is concerned, this means that his/her activities and powers must be exercised with the primary object of protecting and upholding the rights of individuals; these rights may not be negated during the exercise of his/her duties or powers. The effect of the protection of individual rights is thus that it influences the manner in which the police official performs his/her duties. In the past police officials could get away with simply showing token respect for the protection of individuals' rights. The question whether or not a police official has exercised his/her duties with due observance of the protection of individual rights and interests will be evaluated objectively. The Constitution thus ensures accountability, to the extent that the arbitrary exercise of power will be *illegal* and evidence resulting from such actions will be excluded.

Although the 1996 Constitution, unlike the Criminal Procedure Act of 1977, does not state categorically that upholding the rights of an arrested person is a legal requirement for an arrest to be legal, it is nonetheless clear that this is the case. Furthermore, the requirements of the Criminal Procedure Act of 1977 were requirements for formal justice — that is, the requirements had to be observed for the arrest to be formally lawful. The requirements added by the Constitution are further requirements for material justice. Failure to comply with the legal requirements of the Criminal Procedure Act of 1997 would thus result in an unlawful arrest; the escape from custody of the arrested person would therefore be legal and he/she would be entitled to institute a civil claim for unlawful arrest. The effect of section 35(3) of the 1996 Constitution is that now, in addition, any evidence gathered in a manner contrary to the provisions of the Constitution could be inadmissable in a court of law. It is even possible that a court of law may, where the violation is of a serious nature, refuse to proceed with a criminal trial against the accused.

The difference between formal and material justice can be explained by the following example. A person is arrested on a murder charge. He is Chinese and speaks neither English nor Afrikaans. After his arrest he is not informed of the reason for his arrest nor of any of his other constitutional rights. He takes the police to his home and it is unlawfully searched without a warrant and a knife covered in blood is found. During the murder a struggle between the victim and the assailant had ensued and hair and tissue samples not belonging to the victim were found on the scene. Hair and tissue samples, as well as fingerprints, are taken from the arrested person. He is detained pending the outcome of tests by the forensic and fingerprint expert. A week later the results are made available and it appears that the fingerprints on the murder weapon and the hair and tissue samples match those of the person under arrest. A decision is made to charge the suspect.

Apart from the fact that some other rights of the accused were ignored, the arrest and the information gathered afterwards will be formally and materially illegal. The formal requirements for a legal arrest were not complied with as the accused was not informed of the reason for his arrest and he was not brought before a court within forty-eight hours of his arrest. Material requirements were also not met, because the arrested person was not promptly informed, in a language which he could understand, of the reason for his arrest, of his right to remain silent and of his right to legal representation. Before the inception of the Constitution the evidence regarding the findings of the investigation would probably have been admitted. The effect of the violation of the material requirements of the Constitution will be that the courts will be unwilling to hear a charge of murder against the accused and will refuse to authorise further detention. Furthermore, all the evidence which was gathered after the arrest will be excluded by the court.

Although the person may later legally be rearrested, the evidence regarding the fingerprints, hair and tissue samples, which ties the person to the crime scene, will possibly always be excluded by the court.

Chapter 14
Arrest and Detention – Part 2

Elaine Venter

14.1 SECTION 35 OF THE 1996 CONSTITUTION: ARRESTED, DETAINED AND ACCUSED PERSONS

14.1.1 Persons who have been arrested (section 35(1))

*I*N the past, legal arrest in terms of the Criminal Procedure Act 51 of 1977 comprised two basic elements, namely the physical deprivation of a person's freedom and informing the person of the reason for the arrest. Failure to satisfy these requirements would render the arrest unlawful and would mean that the arrested person could lawfully escape from custody and/or institute a civil claim for wrongful arrest.

14.1.2 Persons who are being detained, including sentenced prisoners (section 35(2))

By definition all arrested persons become detainees once they have been arrested. People may, however, also be detained in terms of a detention order issued by a competent authority; for instance, a mentally disturbed person may be detained by order of a magistrate and illegal immigrants by order of an immigration official. In such cases the requirements for legal arrest are satisfied by the detention order.

It is also held that a person who has not yet been arrested can be detained prior to being arrested (if he is arrested at all), because detention is interpreted as the most basic deprivation of a person's freedom. This would be the case where a roadblock is put up, and a person is taken to the police station for questioning or is even stopped and searched.[1] It is, however, imperative to inform a person that he/she is simply being detained and that this detention does not yet constitute arrest; it should further be explained that he/she is under no obligation to accompany the police, but is free to go should he/she prefer to do so.[2] It may, however, then be necessary for the police to arrest the person.

14.1.3 Accused persons (section 35(3))

When a decision is made to prosecute a person in detention, he/she becomes an accused person and the rights of section 35(3) are applicable.

14.1.4 Section 35(4)

In terms of section 35(4), whenever a police official is required by section 35 to inform a detainee, arrestee, sentenced or accused person of his/her rights, this information must be furnished in a language which the person concerned will understand. It would thus seem that, although the detained, arrested, accused or sentenced person has access to all the rights in section 35 of the 1996 Constitution, the police official is only bound to inform the person of a right where this is expressly stated. The rights concerned include the arrestee's right to be informed promptly of his/her right to remain silent (section 35(1)(i)), and of the consequences of not remaining silent (section 35(1)(ii)), the detained person's right to be informed promptly of the reason for his/her detention (section 35(2)(*a*)), the right to be informed of his/her right to consult with a legal practitioner of his/her choice (section 35(2)(*b*)), and the right to have a legal practitioner assigned to him/her at state expense if substantial injustice would otherwise result (section 35(2)(*c*)).

In terms of section 35(4), this information should be given in a language which the person understands. This means that a person should at least understand the rights that he/she has, but it does not mean that the person has a right to be addressed in his/her mother tongue. For example, a German person who understands English cannot expect the police official to address him/her in German, because section 35(4) simply stipulates that it must be in a language which he/she *understands*.3 If the German person, however, understands and speaks only German or even pretends to do so and the police official is not able to address him/her in German, that police official must enlist the services of an interpreter as soon as possible, as section 35 states that the information should be given to the person "promptly" (which can be interpreted as "as soon as possible").

14.1.5 Sections 35(1)(*a*), 2(*a*) and (4)

In terms of section 35(1)(*a*), (*b*)(i), (ii), the arrested person has the right to be informed promptly, in a language which he or she understands, of his/her right to remain silent and to be warned of the consequences of making any statement.

14.1.6 Section 35(1)(*a*), (*b*), (*c*) and section 35(2)(*b*), (*c*)

The right of the arrested person to remain silent and to be warned that any statement which he/she makes may be used in evidence against him/her, as well as the right not to be compelled to make a confession or an admission which could be used in evidence against him/her, are closely connected to the right to legal representation. The basic premise is that, when an accused decides to give information regarding the offence, despite having been informed of his/her right to remain silent, such a decision must constitute an informed choice. This means that he/she must know exactly the full extent of his/her right to remain silent and of his/her right not to be compelled to make a confession or an admission, and that he/she must understand fully the implications of providing information to the police.

The fact that a person cannot be forced to give evidence which will incriminate him/her is not unique to South Africa and other common-law jurisdictions, but is also found in the European codes.4 It traditionally formed part of the Judges' Rules.5

The right of an arrested person not to be compelled to bear witness against himself/herself goes further than the requirement that incriminating evidence should be provided voluntarily. In the first place it implies that the accused must be informed of his/her rights to the extent that the contents of these rights are fully understood. This aspect was mentioned above in the discussion of the right to legal representation and means, in effect, that when the accused decides to make a confession or an admission, despite his/her right to remain silent, it should be a well-informed decision.

Furthermore, the accused may not be unduly influenced in his/her decision to make a confession or an admission. The very fact that he/she has been arrested and detained will obviously have an effect on the emotional state of the person and, depending on the circumstances of his/her detention and the manner in which he/she was questioned (for example by use of psychological manipulation), it may cause a court of law to rule that the confession or admission was not given voluntarily and that it is therefore inadmissible.

Any method which involves bringing pressure to bear on an accused (except the usual request that he/she speaks the truth), may be seen by the court as undue influence, which means that such evidence can be excluded for the purposes of the trial.

From this it becomes clear that there is also a very definite relationship between this right (which forms part of the police investigation phase) and the right to a fair trial and the consequent admission of evidence at the trial. The manner in which the evidence was gathered will thus directly influence the admissibility of the evidence in court.

With regard to the relationship between these rights and the right to a legal representative, Cachalia[6] quotes the case of *Escobedo v Illinois* 378 US, in which the court held that a confession obtained at a police station was inadmissible because the police had deprived the defendant of his right to legal representation and had not effectively warned him of his right to remain silent. The defendant repeatedly requested a lawyer, but was denied this by the police. The police further denied the lawyer access to his client when he came to the station.

The police official should therefore inform the accused that he/she is entitled to legal representation and allow his/her lawyer access to him/her. This should be done promptly, which means immediately, or as soon as possible. For example, in a case where the accused only understands Mandarin, promptly means as soon as an interpreter is brought, which must be as soon as is humanly possible.

In cases where the person chooses not be represented, a particular duty rests on the official to explain the possible consequences of making a statement more fully than just by informing him/her that the evidence can be used against him/her. When the accused is an unsophisticated person, a juvenile, alien or mentally disturbed person, the court will be of the opinion that, before he/she could make an informed decision, concerted efforts would have had to have been made to make him/her understand that the evidence can be used in a court of law for the purpose of finding him/her guilty of the offence.

As far as the right of the accused to legal representation at the expense of the state is concerned, in the case of *S v Vermaas; S v Du Plessis*7 Didcott J rejected the claim that a right to legal representation at state expense implies a right to legal representation of one's own choice. He held that where the assistance of the state becomes imperative to prevent "substantial injustice", it will be up to the state to decide who to appoint as legal representative. The court failed to set out clear guidelines regarding when "substantial injustice" would actually result, and simply stated that the following should be taken into account: the possible ramifications of the case, the complexity or simplicity of the case, the accused person's aptitude to fend for him or herself, the gravity of the consequences, and any other contributing factor. The possibility of a jail sentence may, for example, be sufficient to constitute substantial injustice.

The rights which have been accorded to arrested persons do not imply that the police may not question an arrested person or that such a person may refuse to give his/her name and address to the police. It does, however, mean that unnecessary force, emotional manipulation and other unlawful methods may not be used to get a person to talk to the police.

14.1.7 Section 35(1)(*d*)

Section 39(3) of the Criminal Procedure Act of 1977 determines that the purpose of lawful arrest and detention by the police is not to punish the person but to ensure that he/she will appear in court; this should be read in conjunction with section 50 of the Criminal Procedure Act of 1977 which determines that such a person should be brought to a court of law within forty-eight hours.8 Section 35(1)(*d*) further provides that not only should a person be brought to court *within* forty-eight hours but that the person should appear in court *as soon as possible*. The period of forty-eight hours thus constitutes a maximum period and a duty rests on the police to bring the person to court at the earliest possible opportunity. If the police were in a position to bring a person to court but failed to do so, further detention may be found to have been unlawful.

Whenever a person is brought before a court, there is a duty on the court to explain to the person why he/she will be held for a longer period (if this is to be the case). This right relates to the right to bail, which will be discussed below.

14.1.8 Section 35(1)(e), (f)

The right to be released from detention with or without bail (unless the interests of justice require otherwise), is closely connected to an individual's right to freedom and security and also to the right to be presumed innocent until found guilty by a competent court. In the past it was accepted that an accused had no right to bail unless he/she could convince the court, on a balance of probabilities, that he/she should in fact be released on bail. In terms of legal precedent there were three main grounds on which bail could be refused, namely:

1 the risk of the accused's not attending the trial;
2 the possibility that, whilst out on bail, the accused could commit another crime; and
3 the fact that his/her freedom could defeat the ends of justice.

As a result of section 35(1)(e), (f) of the 1996 Constitution the situation has now changed. In the first place, the accused now has the right to bail; this right can only be limited if it is in the interests of justice. It is suggested that the reasons why it would not be in the interests of justice to allow bail in any given case remain the same (see above). In practice, in terms of this section, the onus is on the state to prove on a balance of probabilities that it would not be in the interests of justice to grant the accused bail.

When a person is arrested, it will have to be borne in mind that he/she may be granted bail — either police bail or bail allowed by the court — at his/her first court appearance. Even before the arrest, the arresting officer will have to consider whether or not an application for bail will be opposed. Furthermore, if the accused's bail application is to be opposed, the search for evidence to support the opposition to the bail application should take precedence after arrest has taken place.

As far as the police officer is concerned, the whole question of bail and whether or not it should be opposed should be regarded as an administrative decision. The provisions of section 33 of the 1996 Constitution that deals with just administrative action must thus be borne in mind.

14.1.9 Section 35(3)(a)

When the arrested person formally becomes an accused in a criminal matter, the right to be fully informed of the charges against him/her becomes part of his/her right to a fair trial. Before the person is formally charged, section 32 (access to information) — which provides that certain privileged information can be withheld from an accused — applies. However, once the accused has been formally charged, he/she must be able to prepare for trial and must be able to address the charges against him/her in order to be accorded a fair trial. This may mean that some information which was previously withheld will now have to be disclosed. When the investigation has been completed, the privileges and limitations placed on certain kinds of information in order to prevent interference with the case will no longer apply. However, some information which the accused will not require to be fully informed of the state's case again him/her, may still be used as evidence by the state and may thus be withheld until the last moment. If this information is not used in the trial, it does not have to be disclosed to the accused at all. Examples of this type of information are the following:

1   the identity of police informers;
2   information regarding the identities of persons who may reasonably fear intimidation or revenge;
3   information which, if it were to be disclosed, could jeopardise international relationships between the South African Police Service and police services or forces of other countries or other relevant international bodies or organisations;
4   new and sensitive investigative methods employed by the South African Police Service; all information regarding their methods remains privileged;
5   information which could violate the rights of co-accused and their rights to a fair trial;
6   where certain information is still required for investigative purposes, such information should not be provided, unless it is essential for the accused in the preparation of his/her defence.

Apart from the above-mentioned exceptions, all relevant information will have to be made available to the accused. It is important to note that information should only be disclosed after consultation with the investigative officer and the public prosecutor.

14.1.10   Section 35(3)(*h*), (*i*)

The rights accorded an accused in section 35(3)(*h*) and (*i*) (namely, to be presumed innocent, to remain silent during plea proceedings and not to testify during trial; to adduce and challenge evidence, and not to be a compellable witness against himself/herself) imply that a prejudicial inference can no longer be drawn whenever an accused refuses to testify in criminal proceedings brought against him/her. Of particular interest to the police officer is the fact that the effect of these sections may be that presumptions, which previously may have assisted in proving the case against an accused, will probably not survive a test of constitutionality.

14.2   INTERNATIONAL INSTRUMENTS

International human rights declarations, covenants and other agreements contain many provisions relating to, for example, international standards, etc. The relevant provisions are considered below.

14.2.1   Prohibition on arbitrary arrest

This is proclaimed in Article 9 of the *Universal Declaration of Human Rights*:
  "No one shall be subjected to arbitrary arrest, detention or exile"
and in Article 9 of the *International Covenant on Civil and Political Rights*:
  "Everyone has the right to liberty and security of the person. No one shall be subjected to arbitrary arrest or detention. No one shall be deprived of his liberty except on such grounds and in accordance with such procedures as are prescribed by law."

Each of these texts contains the following elements: the right to liberty and security of the person; a prohibition on arbitrary arrest; and a requirement that the grounds for arrest should be specified by law.

The Body of Principles for the Protection of All Persons under Any Form of Detention or Imprisonment defines arrest for its own purposes under "Use of Terms":

"'Arrest' means the act of apprehending a person for the alleged commission of an offence or by the action of an authority."

No other instrument defines the term, but the meaning given to it at the beginning of this chapter (that is, depriving a person of his/her liberty by taking him/her into custody) is implicit in those articles of each instrument which set out provisions on arrest.

14.2.2 Procedure

The procedure to be followed at the time of arrest and thereafter is set out in Article 9.2 and 9.3 of the *International Covenant on Civil and Political Rights* in the following terms:

"9.2 Anyone who is arrested shall be informed, at the time of arrest, of the reasons for his arrest and shall be promptly informed of any charges against him.

9.3 Anyone arrested or detained on a criminal charge shall be brought promptly before a judge or other officer authorised by law to exercise judicial power and shall be entitled to trial within a reasonable time or to release. It shall not be the general rule that persons awaiting trial shall be detained in custody, but release may be subject to guarantees to appear for trial, at any other stage of the judicial proceedings, and, should occasion arise, for execution of the judgement."

The Body of Principles for the Protection of All Persons under Any Form of Detention or Imprisonment refers to arrest as follows:

"Principle 2 — arrests are to be carried out in accordance with the law and by competent officials or persons authorised for that purpose;

Principle 10 — a person arrested is to be informed (at the time of arrest) of the reason for arrest, and (promptly) of charges against him;

Principle 12 — a record is to be made of:
- reason for arrest;
- time of arrest;
- arrival at place of custody and first appearance before judicial or other authority;
- identity of law enforcement official concerned; and
- precise information concerning place of custody.

>   Principle 13 — the person arrested is to be provided with infor-
>   mation on, and an explanation of, his/her rights and how to avail
>   him/herself of them."

14.2.3   Other safeguards

Article 9.4 of the *International Covenant on Civil and Political Rights* states:

>   "Anyone who is deprived of his liberty by arrest or detention shall
>   be entitled to take proceedings before a court, in order that the
>   court may decide without delay on the lawfulness of his detention
>   and order his release if the detention is not lawful."

This type of provision is repeated in the *American Convention* (Article 7.6), and the *European Convention* (Article 5.4), but not in the *African Charter*.

Principle 37 of the *Body of Principles on the Protection of Detainees* states:

>   "A person arrested on a criminal charge shall be brought before a
>   judicial or other authority provided by law promptly after his
>   arrest. Such authority shall decide without delay upon the lawful-
>   ness and necessity of detention."

Principle 2 of the *Principles on the Effective Prevention and Investigation of Extra-Legal, Arbitrary and Summary Executions* states:

>   "In order to prevent extra-legal, arbitrary and summary executions,
>   Governments shall ensure strict control, including a clear chain of
>   command and imprisonment as well as those officials authorised
>   by law to use force and firearms."

14.2.4   Juveniles

Article 10 of the *UN Standard Minimum Rules for the Administration of Juvenile Justice* ("The Beijing Rules") requires:

>   "the parents or guardian of juveniles arrested to be immediately
>   notified of the fact of arrest;
>   a judge or other competent official or body to consider, without
>   delay, the issue of release;
>   and contacts between law enforcement officials and juvenile
>   offenders to be managed in such a way as to respect the legal sta-
>   tus of the juvenile and avoid harm to her/him, with due regard to
>   the circumstances of the case."

The Convention on the Rights of the Child (adopted by UN General Assembly resolution 44/25 on 25 November 1989) also refers to the arrest of juveniles. Article 37(*b*) states:

>   "No child shall be deprived of his or her liberty unlawfully or arbi-
>   trarily. The arrest, detention or imprisonment of a child shall be in
>   conformity with the law and shall be used only as a measure of
>   last resort and for the shortest appropriate period of time."

14.2.5 Compensation

Article 9.5 of the *International Covenant on Civil and Political Rights* requires victims of unlawful arrest or detention to be given an enforceable right to compensation.

14.3 SUGGESTED READING AND SOURCES

Cachalia, A. *et al.* 1994. *Fundamental Rights in the New Constitution.* Cape Town: Juta.

Nel, F & Bezuidenhout, J. (compilers) 1995. *Human Rights for the Police.* Cape Town: Juta.

Universal Declaration of Human Rights: Centre for Human Rights, Geneva, United Nations, New York 1994.

International Covenant on Civil and Political Rights: Centre for Human Rights, Geneva, United Nations, New York 1994.

African Charter on Human and People's Rights: Centre for Human Rights, Geneva, United Nations, New York 1994.

The Convention against Torture and other Cruel and Inhuman and Degrading Treatment or Punishment: Centre for Human Rights, Geneva, United Nations, New York 1994.

Standard Minimum Rules for the Treatment of Prisoners: Centre for Human Rights, Geneva, United Nations, New York 1994.

Body of Principles for the Protection of all Persons under any Form of Detention or Imprisonment: Centre for Human Rights, Geneva, United Nations, New York 1994.

Convention on the Rights of the Child: Centre for Human Rights, Geneva, United Nations, New York 1994.

Principles on the Effective Prevention and Investigation of Extra-Legal, Arbitrary and Summary Executions: Centre for Human Rights, Geneva, United Nations, New York 1994.

....

ENDNOTES

1   Nel & Bezuidenhout 242.

2   Ibid.

3   *Delcourt v Belguim* (268/65) CD 22/48, decision of 11 October 1972 *Cort Suprema di Cassazione* Italy (no 6588). In the last-mentioned case the court held that, although the accused must be informed in a language he/she understands, this does not necessarily mean that it should be the language of the ethnic group to which he/she belongs.

4   Cachalia *et al* 80.

5   Ibid.

6   Cachalia *et al* 82.

7   1995 (2) SACR 125 (CC).

8   Nel & Bezuidenhout 234.

SUMMARY

*T*HIS chapter analyses the power of a member of the South African Police Service to use force in order to effect an arrest, to enter premises for the purpose of questioning a person with regard to an offence, or to conduct searches of persons or premises.

15.1 INTRODUCTION

In terms of section 205(3) of the 1996 Constitution, the objects of the South African Police Service are to prevent, combat and investigate crime, to maintain public order, to protect and secure the inhabitants of the Republic and their property, and to uphold and enforce the law. In the performance of these functions, members of the South African Police Service are from time to time confronted by resistance. The question that arises is whether such members may use force in order to overcome such resistance. In this chapter an attempt will be made to answer this question in the light of the Constitution and particularly in the light of the fundamental rights of every person as protected in chapter 2 of the Constitution.

15.2 KEY OBJECTIVES

The key objectives of this chapter are to enable students to:
- understand the general legal principles relating to the use of force by members of the South African Police Service;
- relate these general principles to the use of force for specific purposes, such as effecting an arrest, entering premises to question a person, and conducting a search;
- understand when a member of the Police Service may or may not use force in the performance of his or her duties;
- describe the requirements that must be met before the use of force will be deemed to be justified.

15.3 APPLICABLE LAW

The 1996 Constitution, sections 10, 11, 12, 14, 36 and 205(3)
The Police Act 1995, section 13(3)(*b*) and 67(1)(*a*)
The Criminal Procedure Act 51 of 1977, sections 20, 21, 22, 23, 26, 27, 39, 40, 48, 49 and 52

15.4 INTERPRETATION AND DISCUSSION

15.4.1 General

In terms of the Constitution of 1996, every person has the right –
- to life;[1]
- to respect for and protection of his or her dignity;[2]

- to freedom and security of the person, which includes the right to be free from all forms of violence from both public and private sources, not to be tortured or to be treated or punished in a cruel, inhuman or degrading way;[3] and
- to his or her personal privacy, which includes the right not to be subject to searches of his or her person, home or property or to the seizure of his or her possessions.[4]

The application of any force to a person or to his or her property, necessarily infringes upon at least one, and quite often more than one, of the above-mentioned rights. In terms of section 36 of the 1996 Constitution, the use of force against a person may therefore only take place in terms of law of general application which authorises the use of force and, in so doing, limits the said rights, provided that the law complies with the requirements laid down in section 36.

Section 13(3)(*b*) of the Police Act of 1995 provides that force may *only* be used by a member —

(*a*)   while such member performs an *official duty*;

(*b*)   provided that such member is *authorised by law to use force*; and

(*c*)   provided that such member uses only the *minimum force which is reasonable in the circumstances*.

At the outset, it must be pointed out that the use of force in defence of oneself or in defence of another person is not limited by the provisions of section 13(3)(*b*). Section 13(13) states quite emphatically that section 13 should not be construed as derogating from any power conferred upon a member by or under the Police Act of 1995, or any other law, including the common law. Members are therefore entitled to use force in defence of themselves or in defence of other persons, *provided that the circumstances comply with the requirements for private defence (self-defence) which are prescribed by law, and provided further that the force used was reasonably necessary in the circumstances to ward off the attack.* What is stated further in this chapter should therefore not be viewed at all as derogating from the power of members to defend themselves or to defend any other person.

Section 13(3)(*b*) should also not be interpreted to mean that a statutory provision which empowers a member to perform a certain action, must *expressly* authorise such member to use force to perform such action. The position in our law is that, where a statutory provision authorises a person to perform a certain function, all those powers that are reasonably necessary to perform that function will be deemed to be included in the power to perform the function, even though such powers may not expressly be mentioned in the empowering provision.[5] This principle may be explained by referring to the power to seize certain articles in terms of the Criminal Procedure Act of 1977. Sections 21, 22 and 23 of the said Act confer the power upon members to seize articles referred to in section 20 of the Act. Members are not expressly authorised in terms of the Act to use force in order to seize such articles. This does not mean that a member may not use such force as may be *reasonably necessary* to seize such articles. Accordingly, if a member is authorised to search a person and does so, and, during the course of the search, finds an article referred to in section 20 of the Criminal Procedure Act 1977 upon such person, but the person holds on to the article and refuses to let go of it, the member will be deemed to have the power to use such force as may be *reasonably necessary* in the circumstances in order to remove the article from the person and to seize it. It should be obvious that a very slight use of force ought to suffice (and should therefore be regarded as *reasonably necessary*) in the circumstances mentioned in the example. In these circumstances the use of force in order to overcome resistance against the seizure of the article will therefore be deemed to be included in the expressly conferred power to seize the article.

Section 13(3)(*b*) of the Police Act of 1995 prescribes that a member may make use of force only while performing an official duty. This means that a member may make use of force only where he or she does so for a lawful purpose. Although the use of force to lawfully arrest a person or to conduct a lawful search for a person or an article referred to in section 20 of the Criminal Procedure Act of 1977 may be lawful in certain prescribed (see below) circumstances, the use of force to intimidate or to punish a person, or to obtain a confession or information from a person, will *never* be a lawful purpose.

Although members are empowered by statute to use force in certain limited circumstances, the use of force should only be resorted to where there is no other reasonable alternative way of achieving the same objective without the use of force. In terms of section 13(3)(*b*) of the Police Act of 1995, a member may use only the *minimum force* which is reasonable in the circumstances. *Minimum force* will, in most instances, mean *no* force at all. If there is a reasonable alternative way of achieving the objective without the use of force, such alternative way *must* be used. This principle is known as the principle of subsidiarity.

The reference to *minimum force* in section 13(3)(b) further requires a member to only use the minimum degree of force which is reasonable in the circumstances to achieve the objective.

The use of a particular degree of force will be regarded as *reasonable in the circumstances* only if the member has reasonable grounds to believe that —
(*a*) the use of that degree of force is necessary in the circumstances to achieve the objective; and that
(*b*) the effects which the use of that degree of force could reasonably be expected to have are proportional to the objective to be achieved.

A member will only be regarded as having had reasonable grounds to form such a belief, if —
(*a*) such member based his or her belief on facts which existed at the time;
(*b*) the member honestly believed, in the light of those facts, that the use of that degree of force was necessary in the circumstances to achieve the

objective and that the effects, which the use of that degree of force was likely to have, were proportional to the objective to be achieved; and

(*c*)   any reasonable member, with the same level of training and experience, would, in the light of the facts, also have formed the same belief.

For the purposes of the above-mentioned test, a *fact* should be regarded as something which could be determined by using one's senses (that is, something that one personally sees, hears, smells, tastes, or touches). A fact need not be something which would form admissible evidence in a court of law. Even hearsay (that is, someone else informing the member that a certain state of affairs existed) could therefore constitute a fact. However, a member should not blindly believe everything that he or she is told. Where possible, a member should take steps to verify information given to him or her and only act after having done so.

15.4.2   The use of force to effect an arrest

In terms of section 40 of the Criminal Procedure Act of 1977, a member has the power to arrest a person without a warrant in the circumstances set out in that section. In terms of section 52 of the same Act, other legislation may also empower a member to arrest a person.

In terms of section 39 of the Criminal Procedure Act of 1977, unless the person to be arrested submits to custody, an arrest is effected by actually touching his or her body or, if the circumstances so require, by forcibly confining his or her body. Section 39 is qualified by section 49 of the same Act, which provides for the degree of force that may be used in effecting an arrest.

For the sake of clarity regarding the constraints applicable to the use of potentially lethal force, and in the light of the fundamental rights entrenched in chapter 3 of the 1993 Constitution and in chapter 2 of the 1996 Constitution, the South African Police Service proposed that section 49 of the Criminal Procedure Act 1997 be amended. This proposal was based on extensive international research which was undertaken by the South African Police Service. It is expected that Parliament will consider the proposal for the amendment of section 49 during the first half of 1997. Any amendment to section 49 which may be effected by Parliament will immediately be brought to the attention of all members.

Pending Parliament's pronouncement on an amendment to section 49, the South African Police Service issued instructions to all members concerning the use of force in effecting an arrest.[6] The relevant part of the instructions read as follows:

"2.   Force need not necessarily be applied during an arrest. If the person, who is to be arrested, submits himself or herself to custody, *no force* may be applied to effect the arrest (see section 39 of the Criminal Procedure Act). Force may only be applied against a person who is to be arrested, if such person resists the attempt to arrest him or her or flees to escape the arrest *and cannot be arrested without the use of force*. The purpose with the use of force in such circumstances may only be to confine the body of the person and may never be to punish him or her.

3. A member, who is by law authorised to arrest a person, may, in order to effect the arrest, where the person resists the arrest or flees in order to escape the arrest and cannot be arrested without the use of force, use such force *as may in the circumstances be reasonably necessary* to overcome the resistance or to prevent the person from fleeing: Provided that *the force so used, must be proportional to the seriousness of the offence* which the person to be arrested has committed or is reasonably suspected of having committed: Provided further that *the use of force which is likely to cause death is, in terms of this paragraph, only permissible where the person concerned is to be arrested for an offence referred to in paragraph 4 (below)*.

4. No member may use force which is likely to cause the death of the person to be arrested unless such person has committed or is reasonably suspected of having committed one of the following offences:

treason;

sedition;

public violence;

murder;

rape;

robbery, including robbery of a motor vehicle;

theft of livestock, excluding poultry;

theft of a motor vehicle;

kidnapping;

child stealing;

assault, when a dangerous wound is inflicted;

arson;

housebreaking;

any offence under any law relating to intimidation or terrorism or control over armaments, arms, ammunition, explosives, drugs or radio active material and in respect of which a punishment of imprisonment for a period of five years (or longer) may be imposed;

any offence involving serious violence or the use of a firearm or explosives or the threat thereof;

escaping from lawful custody, where the person concerned is in such custody in respect of any offence referred to in this paragraph or is in such custody in respect of the offence of escaping from lawful custody; and any conspiracy, incitement or attempt to commit any offence referred to in this paragraph, or complicity in the commission of such offence.

Note that the offences referred to in this paragraph differ from those contained in Schedule 1 of the Criminal Procedure Act.)

5. For the purposes of these instructions, discharging a firearm at a person shall be regarded as the use of force which is likely to cause death, irrespective of the part of the body aimed at.

6. If a member believes on reasonable grounds that the use of force will be necessary to effect an arrest, such member must, where it is reasonable in the circumstances to do so, issue a clear warning to the person who is to be arrested that force will be used against him or her unless he or she submits himself or herself to custody. This is particularly important in those circumstances where the member, who attempts to effect the arrest, reasonably believes that it will be necessary to use force (such as a firearm) which could result in the death of the person to be arrested. In such an event the said warning should inform the person to be arrested that lethal force will be used (eg that he or she will be shot at) unless he or she submits to the arrest. Furthermore, where a member reasonably believes that it will be necessary, in order to effect the arrest, to fire a shot at the person to be arrested, a warning shot must precede any shot fired at the person, unless the firing of a warning shot may endanger the lives of other people or could reasonably be expected to have the result that the person will escape the arrest.

7. The use of force will only be *reasonable in the circumstances* if the member believes on reasonable grounds that the use of force is necessary to effect the arrest. Such a belief must be based on facts which exist at the time when the force is used and of which the member concerned is aware at that time. Such facts may include the conduct of the person to be arrested, words used by him or her when he or she became aware of the intention to arrest him or her, information at the disposal of the member concerned, etc. These facts must also be such that any reasonable person would, when faced with the same facts, conclude that the use of force is necessary. A member may afterwards be required to explain what the facts were upon which he or she based the conclusion that the use of force was reasonably necessary.

8. Once a member has concluded that the use of force is reasonably necessary in the circumstances to effect the arrest, such

member must consider whether the use of the type and degree of force, which will be necessary to effect the arrest, is proportional to the seriousness of the offence committed by the person to be arrested. If the offence is of a trivial nature and it is clear that a high degree of force will be necessary to effect the arrest, the conclusion will be that the use of such a degree of force will be disproportionate to the seriousness of the offence and, accordingly, that *no force* should be used, *even though this may have the result that the suspect will escape the arrest.*

In this regard, special mention needs to be made of handbag snatching which may, in appropriate circumstances, qualify as robbery. It is still debatable exactly when handbag snatching will, in terms of South African law, constitute robbery and when it will constitute mere theft. Members must therefore never resort to force which may result in the death of the suspect (such as firing a shot at the suspect) in order to effect his or her arrest in such cases, unless there are serious aggravating factors present (such as the use of a firearm, knife or other dangerous weapon to remove the handbag from the victim or the infliction of serious injury during the robbery).

9.   As should be clear from the previous paragraph, the mere fact that an offence is mentioned in paragraph 4, does not in itself justify the use of force that may result in the death of the suspect where the arrest cannot otherwise be effected. Members will still have to consider whether the use of force that may result in the death of the suspect, will be justified in each and every case. Should the identity of the suspect, for instance, be known and it would be reasonably easy to find and arrest him or her at a later stage, the use of such force will never be justified, irrespective of the offence committed by him or her. If the offence is not one which is mentioned in paragraph 4, force which is likely to result in the death of the suspect may in any event never be used.

10. Existing Standing Orders which are inconsistent with the instructions contained in this circular, are hereby repealed to the extent that they are inconsistent therewith.

11. The instructions contained in this circular only deal with the use of force to effect an arrest and do not deal with situations where members use force in defence of themselves or others. All Standing Orders or instructions concerning the use of force by members in defence of themselves or others are therefore not affected at all by this circular and remain in force."

15.4.3   The use of force to enter premises

One of the most common methods of investigating an offence is by asking questions of persons who may possibly have information regarding the offence. Since every person is free to ask other persons questions, there is no need to provide for a special power for police officials to do so. Members may therefore ask questions of any person. However, it sometimes happens that a member suspects that a certain person has information regarding an offence, but cannot get to the person because he or she is on private premises. The question that arises is whether such member may enter the premises to question that person.

In terms of section 26 of the Criminal Procedure Act of 1977, a member may without warrant enter premises if he or she —

(*a*)   is investigating an offence or alleged offence;

(*b*)   *reasonably suspects* that a person who may furnish information with reference to any such offence is on such premises;

(*c*)   wishes to enter the premises for the purpose of interrogating such person and obtaining a statement from him or her; and

(*d*)   has obtained the necessary *consent* of the *occupier* of the premises in the case of a private dwelling.

The fact that a member must be investigating an offence does not mean that a docket must have been registered or that the member must have been designated as the investigating officer in respect of a docket that has been registered. If a person phones the police and alleges that he has heard shots being fired and persons screaming on the property of his neighbour, which property is inside the area of a municipality, a member may enter the land of the neighbour in order to investigate the alleged offence of discharging a firearm in a municipal area.

A member may only enter the premises of another if he or she *reasonably suspects* that a person as referred to in paragraph (*b*) (above) is on the premises. There is an important difference between "reasonsably suspects that" and "having reasonable grounds to believe that" a certain state of affairs exists. The difference lies in the words "suspects" and "believe". A person will easier "suspect" that a certain state of affairs exists than "believe" that it exists. A person will "suspect" something if he views it as a *possibility*, but will only "believe" it if he views it as *probable*. *Reasonably suspects* therefore means "viewing it as a reasonable possibility". A member will therefore *reasonably suspect* that such a person is on the premises, if he thinks that it is possible that such person is on the premises and any other reasonable member, having the same background and training as he or she, would, in the light of the information at the disposal of the member, also have regarded it as possible that the person is on the premises.

A member will only have the power to enter the premises if he or she does so for the purpose of interrogating the said person and taking a statement from that person. This purpose constitutes the *lawful purpose* referred to above in the discussion of section 13(3)(*b*) of the Police Act of 1995. Section 26 of the Criminal Procedure Act, 1977 does not authorise the entry of premises for any other purpose.

The proviso in paragraph (*d*) only refers to a private dwelling. This means that a member need not obtain prior consent from the occupier of open land or buildings which are not private dwellings. This, of course, does not mean that a member should not ask for permission to enter such premises. A member should always act in a manner which least infringes the fundamental rights of another. Therefore, if the occupier of the premises is available, the member should first attempt to obtain his or her permission to enter the premises before doing so. If the occupier grants his or her permission, the entry will not constitute an infringement of that person's rights. This is embodied in the principle of subsidiarity, which was explained above in the discussion of section 13(3)(*b*) of the Police Act of 1995.

Should permission be refused or if the occupier of the property cannot be reached, a member may nevertheless enter the premises in terms of section 26 where this can be done without the use of force. A member may therefore climb over a fence, open and enter through a gate, etc, to enter the premises without prior consent of the occupier of the premises, provided that the premises are not a private dwelling and it is done in the circumstances and for the purpose mentioned in section 26. The same applies to opening a door and entering through it in the case of an office building or the premises of a particular business.

In the case of an apartment building (flats), every apartment (flat) will qualify as a separate private dwelling which may not be entered without the consent of the occupier thereof. In the case of a hotel, motel or guest house, every single room which is occupied by a guest should be regarded as a separate dwelling.

Although the owner of premises will often also be the occupier thereof, this will not always be the case. If the premises are leased from the owner, the lessee and not the owner will be the occupier of the premises. In such a case not even the owner may give consent to the member to enter the premises. A member, however, need under normal circumstances not know who the owner or lessee of premises is before he or she asks for permission to enter the private dwelling. If a member knocks on the door, an adult person answering the door may normally be regarded as an occupier of the premises and his or her permission to enter the premises would normally suffice. Should it, however, be known to the member that the said person is not the occupier of the dwelling, the member must ask to see the occupier and ask for his or her permission to enter the dwelling.

A member will only be deemed to have consent to enter the dwelling if the occupier gave such consent voluntarily, while being at his or her full senses and while being aware of the purpose for which the consent is sought. If the member obtains consent while threatening the occupier, such consent will not be regarded as valid consent.

If the occupier of a private dwelling refuses permission to a member to enter the dwelling or if premises other than a private dwelling cannot be entered without the use of force, section 27(1) of the Criminal Procedure Act provides that a member may use such force as may be reasonably necessary to overcome any resistance to entry of the premises, provided that the member has audibly demanded admission to the dwelling and has revealed the purpose for which he or she seeks permission to enter the dwelling. This section specifically authorises the breaking open of a door or window to gain entry but does not limit the use of force to so doing. Should it therefore be reasonably necessary in order to gain entry to the premises to cut a chain which locks the gate to the premises that may also be done in terms of this section. This section covers both the case where the occupier refuses permission to the member to enter the dwelling or other premises and where the occupier is inside the dwelling or other premises, but simply ignores the request by the member to enter the dwelling. This situation is often encountered by members who receive a phone call from a wife who complains that her husband has assaulted her or one of her children and who, upon arrival at the house, are refused permission by the husband to enter the house. In such a case a member may use such force as may be reasonably necessary to enter the dwelling in order to question the complainant (the wife) and to take a statement from her. In this regard mention must be made of section 67(1)(*a*) of the Police Act of 1995, in terms of which a person who resists or wilfully hinders or obstructs a member in the exercise of his or her duty, is guilty of an offence which qualifies as a First Schedule offence as stated in the Criminal Procedure Act of 1977 and in respect of which a member may arrest a person without a warrant. Should the husband, in the above-mentioned example, therefore attempt physically to prevent the member from entering the dwelling or speaking to the wife, he may be arrested and be charged with the said offence.

Members should not confuse the situations provided for in sections 26 and 27 of the Criminal Procedure Act with situations where entry to premises and even to a private dwelling is gained in defence of another or in necessity. If the occupier of a private dwelling or any other person is held hostage on premises or inside a private dwelling, that degree of force which is reasonably necessary to gain entry to the premises or private dwelling in order to free the hostages may be used. In such a case, entry is gained, not in terms of sections 26 or 27, but as part of action in defence of another. Similarly, where a person is being attacked inside premises or a private dwelling, such force may be used as may be reasonably necessary to gain entry to the premises in order to protect the person who is being attacked. In such a case, sections 26 and 27 will not be applicable. Finally, where a house or other building is on fire, reasonable force may be used to enter the house or building in order to save persons inside the building. In such a case a member acts in necessity and sections 26 and 27 are not applicable. In all these instances, permission need normally not be asked before action is taken.

15.4.4 The use of force to search persons or premises

15.4.4.1 The use of force to search a person

As a general rule, a search should only be conducted in terms of a search warrant[7] unless a statute specifically authorises a search without a search warrant. Apart from sections 22, 23 and 24 of the Criminal Procedure Act of 1977, several other Acts of Parliament also authorise searches without a search warrant. This discussion will only focus on the use of force to conduct a search.

In terms of section 23(1)(*a*) of the Criminal Procedure Act of 1977, a member may search a person arrested by him or her and seize any article referred to in section 20 which is found in the possession of or in the custody or under the control of the arrested person.

It must be pointed out that, although section 23(1)(*a*) does not expressly authorise the use of force to conduct the search, it must be interpreted to imply the use of force *where the use of force is reasonably necessary to conduct the search*.[8]

If the arrested person submits himself or herself to such a search, it would normally not be necessary to use any force in order to conduct the search. The only exception would be where an object is found on the person and there are reasonable grounds to believe that the object contains an article referred to in section 20 and it is necessary to apply force to the object in order to determine whether it contains such an article. This would, for instance, be the case where a sealed or locked container is found on the arrested person or in his or her possession or under his or her custody or control, and there are reasonable grounds to believe that it contains drugs and its contents can only be determined after it has been broken open or some of its contents have been destroyed in a test to determine whether it contains a prohibited drug. In such an event, the arrested person must be given an opportunity to explain what the contents of the object are and force may only be applied to it if his or her explanation does not remove the reasonable grounds for the belief. If the object is locked, an attempt must, of course, first be made to obtain the key to the container and to open it with the key before force is applied to it. Any force applied to an object in these circumstances must be limited to the minimum force necessary to determine its contents and as little damage as possible should be caused.

If the arrested person resists the attempt to search him or her, such force as may reasonably be necessary to overcome the resistance may be used. For this purpose restraining measures, such as handcuffs, may be utilised.

An intimate search of the body orifices (mouth, rectum, vagina, etc) of an arrested person necessarily requires the use of a degree of force and may only be undertaken by a medical practitioner and, in any event, only if there are reasonable grounds to believe that an article referred to in section 20 is hidden in that part of the arrested person's body.

Searches of persons authorised in terms of sections 21 and 22 of the Criminal Procedure Act of 1977, should, as far as the use of force is concerned, be approached in exactly the same manner as a search in terms of section 23(1)(*a*).

15.4.4.2   The use of force to search premises in order to seize articles

Searches of premises are authorised in terms of sections 21 and 22 of the Criminal Procedure Act of 1977. In terms of section 27(1), force may only be used to gain entry to the premises in order to conduct the search or where the use of force is necessary to conduct the search itself. Section 27(1) therefore authorises the use of force for two purposes, namely —

(*a*)   to gain entry to the premises so that a search may be conducted on the premises; and

(*b*)   to conduct the search itself.

The use of force in terms of section 27(1) in order to gain entry to premises, has been dealt with in detail above and will not be discussed here. Attention is, however, drawn to the provisions of section 27(2) (the so-called no-knock clause). While it is a requirement in terms of section 27(1) that the member may use force to gain entry to the premises only after having audibly demanded entry and after having notified the occupier of the purpose for which he or she seeks to enter the premises, section 27(2) provides that force may be used to gain entry to the premises without doing so if the member is on reasonable grounds of the opinion that any article, which is the subject of the search, may be destroyed or be disposed of if entry is audibly demanded and the purpose for which entry is sought is stated. This would normally be the case where the article which is the subject of the search is very small or consists of a small quantity of drugs which could easily be destroyed or disposed of (for example by washing it down the drain or by swallowing it).

The use of force in order to overcome resistance to the search is also authorised by section 27(1). Should a person therefore resist the attempt to search the premises, such force as may reasonably be necessary in order to overcome the resistance and prevent the person from interfering with the search, may be used. Should a member be confronted by a locked container, cupboard or room, the occupier of the premises should first of all be approached to provide the key to open it. If the occupier of the premises refuses to provide the key, a member may use force to open the cupboard and search it only if —

(*a*)   there are no other reasonable alternative ways of opening it or of searching it without opening it; and

(*b*)   at least one of the articles for which the member is searching could reasonably be inside the container, cupboard or room.

There would, for instance, be no reasonable possibility that a hunting rifle could be inside a locked vanity case or a motor vehicle inside the locked drawer of a cupboard. Should force be used to open the vanity case or the drawer in these examples, the use of such force would be unlawful. Similarly, if a container is transparent and every object in it is clearly visible, it would not be reasonably necessary to break it open in order to search its contents.

15.4.4.3 The use of force to search premises in order to arrest a person

In terms of section 48 of the Criminal Procedure Act of 1977, a member may break open, enter and search premises for the purpose of effecting an arrest, if he or she —

(a) knows or *reasonably suspects* that the person to be arrested is on the premises;

(b) is authorised to arrest the person; and

(c) has audibly demanded entry into such premises and has made known the purpose for which he or she seeks but still fails to gain entry.

As far as the phrase *reasonably suspects* is concerned, you are referred to the discussion of that phrase as it appears in section 26 in paragraph 15.4.3 above.

A member will be authorised to arrest a person if a statute authorises a member to arrest such a person.

As far as the use of force to gain entry or to search the premises is concerned, the same principles discussed above in paragraph 15.4.4.2 will apply.

A short review of the provisions contained in international human rights instruments is essential, since South African courts of law are compelled to take cognisance of international law in interpreting the Constitution.[9]

15.4.5 International human rights instruments

15.4.5.1 The Universal Declaration of Human Rights, 1948

The importance of the provisions of this document lies in the fact that South Africa has been readmitted to the United Nations as a full member. Since the Universal Declaration was adopted in a resolution by the United Nations' General Assembly, it applies to all members of the United Nations. The general acceptance and authority of this instrument as a source of public international law should not be underestimated.

The Declaration calls upon "all peoples and all nations", as well as on "every individual and every organ of society" to respect human rights and to promote them by means of progressive measures at national and international level.

The provisions contained in the Universal Declaration of Human Rights concerning human rights that may be violated by the use of force are listed below.

- *The right to life, liberty, and security of person*
  "Everyone has the right to life, liberty and security of person."[10]
- *The right not to be ill-treated*
  "No one shall be subjected to torture or to cruel, inhumane or degrading treatment or punishment."[11]
- *Human dignity*
  "All human beings are born free and equal in dignity and rights. They are endowed with reason and conscience and should act towards one another in a spirit of brotherhood."[12]

15.4.5.2 The International Covenant on Civil and Political Rights

This Covenant is legally binding on all signatories. The South African President has indicated that he intends signing the two 1966 international covenants.

The provisions contained in this Covenant concerning human rights that may be violated by the use of force are the following.

- *The right to life*
  "Every human being has the inherent right to life. This right shall be protected by law. No one shall arbitrarily be deprived of his life."[13]
- *The right to freedom of person*
  "Everyone has the right to liberty and security of person. No one shall be subjected to arbitrary arrest or detention. No one shall be deprived of his or her liberty except on such grounds and in accordance with such procedures as are established by law."[14]
- *Human dignity*
  "All persons deprived of their liberty shall be treated with humanity and with respect for the inherent dignity of the human person."[15]

It should also be mentioned that the Covenant contains provisions which compel signatories to take certain steps. Signatories are bound to implement the rights contained in the Covenant by means of statutes and other enactments.[16]

Although the rights contained in the Covenant do in fact appear in the South African Bill of Rights, they should also find practical application in all new legislation promulgated after 27 April 1994.

15.4.5.3 The European Convention on Human Rights, 1950

Although South Africa is not legally bound to this Convention, the court cases are a valuable source of comparison. However, the application of findings by the European Human Rights Court does require a rudimentary knowledge of the relevant human rights provisions.

- *The right to life*
  "Everyone's right to life shall be protected by law. No one shall be deprived of his life intentionally save in execution of a sentence of a court following his conviction of a crime for which the penalty is provided by law."[17]

- *The right not to be ill-treated*
  "No one shall be subjected to torture or to inhumane or degrading treatment or punishment."[18]
- *The right to freedom and security of person*
  "Everyone has the right to liberty and security of person. No one shall be deprived of his liberty save in the following cases ..."[19]

Kelly v United Kingdom[20] will probably be one of the comparative court cases that a South African court of law could consider in the interpretation the South African Bill of Rights.[21]

In the *Kelly* case, the European Human Rights Court had to decide whether the force used by the British security forces during which the applicant's son was killed amounted to a violation of every person's right to life as guaranteed in section 2. In the first instance the court deliberated on whether or not the use of force in the prevention of crime as a police activity had been absolutely necessary in this case. Subsequently it had to decide whether the degree of force used was proportional or not. The court found that the actions of the British security forces in this case were justifiable.

15.4.5.4 The Banjul Charter on Human Rights, 1981

This Charter of human rights is the product of the Organisation of African Unity's attempts since 1979 to bind its members to the protection of human rights.

Although the functioning of the Charter is limited by inherent flaws, such as the fact that there is no court to hear violations of human rights, the provisions still have interpretive value.

The human rights that may be violated by the use of force are protected by the following provisions in the Banjul Charter on Human Rights.

- *Human dignity*
  "Every individual shall have the right to the respect of the dignity inherent in a human being ..."[22]
- *The right to life*
  "Human beings are inviolable. Every human being shall be entitled to respect for his life and the integrity of the person. No one may be arbitrarily deprived of this right."[23]
- *The right to freedom and security of the person*
  "Every individual shall have the right to liberty and to security of the person. No one may be deprived of his freedom except for reasons and conditions previously laid down in law ..."[24]

15.4.5.5 The Convention against Maltreatment and Other Forms of Inhumane and Degrading Treatment and Punishment, 1984

Although South Africa is not a party to this Convention at present, we will refer to it briefly since it is foreseen that this Convention will also be signed as part of the normalisation process of South Africa's position in the international community.

The Convention of the United Nations against Maltreatment and Other Forms of Inhumane and Degrading Treatment or Punishment is probably one of the most important human rights instruments regarding the use of force.

This Convention requires that any state which is a party to the Convention should take the necessary steps to prevent state officials from subjecting any person to cruel, inhumane or degrading treatment or punishment.[25]

Maltreatment is defined as any action deliberately inflicting pain or hardship, whether of a physical or a psychological nature, on a person for, *inter alia,* the purpose of obtaining information or a confession or an admission from him or her or from a third party.[26]

It should further be mentioned that the Convention provides that no exceptional circumstances, for example an instruction from a senior, may serve as justification for an act that amounts to maltreatment.[27]

The parties to this Convention undertake consistently and systematically to investigate the rules, instructions, methods and practices regarding cross-examination, arrests and detention.[28]

15.4.5.6 The United Nations' Code of Conduct for Law Enforcement Officials

The Code of Conduct for Law Enforcement Officials was adopted in a resolution by the General Assembly of the United Nations in 1979.[29]

The aim of this Code of Conduct was to strenghten national legislation and to assist in protecting human rights which may be violated by police officials in the pursuance of their duties.[30]

The Code of Conduct makes the following provision regarding the use of force:

"Law enforcement officials may use force only when strictly necessary and to the extent required for the performance of their duty."[31]

Commentary by authors concerning this article may be summarised under the following three points. In the first instance, it appears from article 3 that the use of force should be the exception rather than the rule. Secondly, the principle of proportionality should be used to determine whether or not the force was justifiable. Thirdly, firearms should be used only in exceptional cases, and never against children.[32]

15.4.6 International Standards for the Use of Minimum Force

These standards are contained in a publication aimed at the civil police component of the United Nations Protection Force in the former Yugoslavia (UNPROFOR).

The purpose was to provide them with a review of the existing international standards applicable in the execution of their duties.

The standards are based on the principles of international criminal procedure systems, human rights and humanitarian laws.

The provisions regarding the use of force and firearms are briefly as follows.

General provisions

- Each person has the right to freedom and security of the person;
- Each person has the right to participate in peaceful protest and has the right to freedom of association;
- A police official shall not use force or firearms if other methods would achieve the same results;
- A police official shall not use more force than absolutely necessary in order to achieve legitimate law enforcement objectives; and
- A police official shall not use a firearm with the intention of killing another person unless it is unavoidable in order save the life of the police official or another person.

A police official may use firearms only under the following circumstances

- To protect himself/herself or others against a threat against his/her or another person's life or against serious injury;
- To prevent the commission of a serious crime which may endanger the life of another person;
- To arrest a person who seriously threatens the life of another person and who resists attempts to arrest him or her; and
- To prevent the escape of a person who is a serious threat to the life of another person.

When police officials use firearms, they must comply with the following requirements

- The police official must identify himself or herself as a police official;
- The police official must give a clear indication that he or she intends using a firearm; and
- The police official must allow the suspect sufficient time to react to the warning.

A police official does not have to allow the suspect the necessary time mentioned above under the following circumstances

- Where such time allowed would seriously threaten the life of the police official;
- Where such time allowed would seriously threaten the life of or result in serious injury to another person; and
- Where it clearly would not be necessary under the circumstances.

Where it is clear that the use of force or firearms is an unavoidable factor, a police official shall follow the following procedures

- Exercise the necessary restraint and use the necessary force required only in order to achieve legitimate law enforcement;
- Show respect for human life and cause the minimum injury to the body of the other person;
- Cause minimum damage to property;
- Render aid to an injured person as soon as possible and obtain the necessary medical assistance as soon as possible; and
- Make sure that the family and friends of the injured persons are informed of the incident as soon as possible after the event.

The guidelines further state that, where a police official has used his/her firearm, he/she will draw up a report on the incident and provide his/her officer commanding with a copy as soon as possible.

The guidelines also provide that any person affected by the use of force is entitled to request the police to conduct a formal investigation or review of the incident.

Senior officers in command who knew, or should have known, that police officials under their command used force in an unlawful manner and did not take the necessary steps to prevent it, will be held responsible.

Where a police official was aware of the fact that the use of force and a firearm under specific circumstances would be unlawful, and he/she had sufficient opportunity to refuse to execute the order, the fact that he/she obeyed an order will not be sufficient justification in a court of law.

15.5 SUGGESTED READING AND SOURCES

Alderson, J, *Human Rights and the Police*. Strasbourg: Council of Europe Press.

Duffy. 1990. *Police and the European Convention on Human Rights*.

Du Toit, *et al*. 1987. *Commentary on the Criminal Procedure Act*. Cape Town: Juta.

Geldenhuys, T & Joubert, JJ. 1996. *Criminal Procedure Handbook*, 2 ed. Cape Town: Juta.

Kriegler, J. 1993. *Hiemstra. Suid-Afrikaanse Strafproses*, 5 ed. Durban: Butterworths.

Steyn. LC. 1981. *Die Uitleg van Wette*, 5 ed. Cape Town: Juta.

· ·

ENDNOTES

1   See section 11.

2   See section 10.

3   See section 12.

4   See section 14.

5   See Steyn LC 1981 *Die Uitleg van Wette,* 5th ed (Cape Town: Juta) at 209–211, as well as the cases referred to on those pages.

6   These instructions are contained in a Special Service Order which was sent out to members by means of a circular dated 14 August 1996 under reference 31/1/5/3.

7   See section 21 of the Criminal Procedure Act, 1977.

8   See footnote 5 and the accompanying text.

9   Section 39 of the 1996 Constitution.

10   Article 3 of the Universal Declaration of Human Rights.

11   Article 5 of the Universal Declaration of Human Rights.

12   Article 1 of the Universal Declaration of Human Rights.

13   Article 6 of the Covenant on Civil and Political Rights of 1966.

14   Article 9(1) of the International Covenant on Civil and Political Rights of 1966.

15   Article 10 of the International Covenant on Civil and Political Rights of 1966.

16   Article 2 of the International Covenant on Civil and Political Rights of 1966.

17   Article 2 of the European Convention for the Protection of Human Rights and Fundamental Freedoms of 1950.

18   Article 3 of the European Convention for the Protection of Human Rights and Fundamental Freedoms of 1950.

19   Article 5 of the European Convention for the Protection of Human Rights and Fundamental Freedoms of 1950.

20   App no 17579/90.

21   Section 39 of the 1996 Constitution.

22   Article 5 of the Banjul Charter of Human Rights of 1981.

23   Article 4 of the Banjul Charter of Human Rights of 1981.

24   Article 6 of the Banjul Charter of Human Rights of 1981.

25   Article 2(1) of the Convention against Maltreatment and all other Forms of Inhumane and Degrading Treatment and Punishment, 1984.

26   Article 1 of the Convention against Maltreatment and all other Forms of Inhumane and Degrading Treatment and Punishment, 1984.

27   Article 2(3) of the Convention against Maltreatment and all other Forms of Inhumane and Degrading Treatment and Punishment, 1984.

28   Article 11 of the Convention against Maltreatment and all other Forms of Inhumane and Degrading Treatment and Punishment, 1984.

29   General Assembly Resolution 34/169 17 December 1979.

30   Duffy. 1992. *Police and the European Convention on Human Rights,* Council of Europe, Strasbourg 21.

31   Article 3 of the United Nations Code of Conduct for Law Enforcement Officials.

32   Alderson, J. 1992. *Human Rights and the Police*. Strasbourg: Council of Europe Press, 182.

Chapter 16
Search and Seizure

Johan Koekemoer

SUMMARY

*I*T is an internationally accepted principle, and the standard which the 1996 Constitution sets, that, save in exceptional circumstances, prior authorisation should be obtained for search and seizure. The authority issuing the warrant should also be independent and impartial. The unreasonable and unjustifiable violation of a person's right to privacy, dignity, property, and freedom and security holds serious consequences, not only for police officials but also for the administration of justice. The challenge facing police officials is reconciling human rights with everyday policing.

16.1   INTRODUCTION

With the incorporation of a Bill of Rights in the 1996 Constitution, the South African Police Service has entered a new era of policing. The change from "force" to "service" is much more than a name change: it reflects a change of attitude towards policing and the community as a whole. In very basic terms, human rights will not necessarily cause the letter of statutes providing for search and seizure to change, but rather the circumstances under which search and seizure take place, and how they are carried out (that is, the why, when and how).

16.2   KEY OBJECTIVES

The key objectives of this chapter are to enable students to:
- discuss what the right to dignity, privacy, freedom and security of the person and property basically entails;
- to explain how human rights effect everyday policing;
- to discuss which statutes provide the police official with the authority to search and seize;
- to explain the importance of having respect for other people and for the law;
- discuss what the possible consequences of violating a person's constitutional rights are.

16.3   APPLICABLE LAW AND INTERNATIONAL INSTRUMENTS

The 1996 Constitution, sections 10, 12, 14 and 25
The Criminal Procedure Act 51 of 1977, sections 19 to 36
The South African Police Service Act 68 of 1995, section 13
    There are many other statutes, dealing with specific issues, which provide a police official with the authority to search and seize. The list of these statutes is so extensive that it cannot be printed here. However, the onus is on every police official to make sure that he or she is aware of the relevant statutes affecting his or her duties and to obtain copies of the statutes if necessary.

European Convention on Human Rights

Article 8 reads as follows:

"(1)   Everyone has the right to respect for his private and family life, his home and his correspondence.

"(2)   There shall be no interference by a public authority with the exercise of this right except such as is in accordance with the law and as is necessary in a democratic society in the interest of national security, public safety or the economic wellbeing of the country, for the prevention of disorder or crime, for the protection of health or morals, or for the protection of the rights and freedoms of others."

Article 5 reads as follows:

"Everyone has the right to liberty and security of person. No one shall be deprived of his liberty save ... in accordance with a procedure prescribed by law."

Universal Declaration of Human Rights

Article 12 reads as follows:

"No one shall be subjected to arbitrary interference with his privacy, family, home or correspondence, nor attacks upon his honour and reputation. Everyone has the right to the protection of the law against such interference or attacks."

International Covenant on Civil and Political Rights

Article 9 reads as follows:

"Everyone has the right to liberty and security of person. No one shall be subjected to arbitrary arrest or detention. No one shall be deprived of his liberty except on such grounds and in accordance with such procedure as are established by law."

Article 17 reads as follows:

"(1)   No one shall be subjected to arbitrary or unlawful interference with his privacy, family, home or correspondence, nor to unlawful attacks on his honour and reputation.

"(2)   Everyone has the right to the protection of the law against such interference or attacks."

16.4   INTERPRETATION AND DISCUSSION

16.4.1   Relevance of international and foreign law

The 1996 Constitution provides that, when interpreting the Bill of Rights, a court *must* consider international law and *may* consider foreign law. International law is found in international law instruments, such as those quoted above, and basically concerns internationally accepted general principles. Foreign law is the law applicable in a foreign country, for example the United

States of America. Thus, the laws providing police officials with the authority to search and seize will have to conform with internationally accepted standards. Although the cultural backgrounds and history of foreign countries differ from that of South Africa, their experience in bringing human rights and the exercise of state powers together can be invaluable.

16.4.2 Human rights that may be violated during search and seizure

In terms of section 36 of the 1996 Constitution, all the rights discussed below may be limited only in terms of law of general application to the extent that the limitation is reasonable and justifiable in an open and democratic society based on human dignity, equality and freedom.

16.4.2.1 Dignity

Section 10 of the 1996 Constitution reads as follows:

"Everyone has inherent dignity and the right to have their dignity respected and protected."

The rights protected by this section certainly include the right of persons to have their dignity respected by the state in its dealings with or treatment of them. Our common law interprets "dignity" as "self-esteem". Our courts have, however, linked it to status, honour, reputation or what amounts to esteem in others' eyes.[1]

Although the recognition of, or right to respect for, an individual's dignity is common in international human rights instruments, there is no exact definition of the word. What is clear, though, is that the international interpretation of the word is broader than our common law definition. Thus, apart from referring to self-esteem, it also entails the inherent worth of a human being and his or her humanity. Dignity is impaired when a person is subjected to treatment which is degrading or humiliating, or when he/she is subjected to conduct which treats the person as subhuman. Dignity, like privacy, is treated in international instruments as a personality right and a human attribute.

The right to respect for one's dignity interfaces with many — and indeed implies respect for all — of a person's rights. The conduct which impairs a person's dignity might simultaneously be the impairment of one's right to privacy. Accordingly, this right might be asserted as an additional ground in the challenge to some other law or practice which impairs a person's rights. This means that when a person challenges a search, with or without a warrant, on the grounds that it was an unreasonable infringement of his or her right to privacy, he or she might add the impairment of his or her dignity to strengthen the challenge.

This right is not absolute and may be limited in accordance with the provisions of section 36 of the 1996 Constitution. What does respect for a person's dignity mean for a police official conducting a search? It means treating the person being searched, or whose premises are being searched, like a human being and with respect. This includes handling any of the person's possessions or any other objects with the necessary care. The criterion a police official can use is to treat the person and his or her possessions as he or she would like himself or herself, or his or her possessions, to be treated.

16.4.2.2 Freedom and security of the person

Section 12 of the 1996 Constitution reads as follows:

"(1) Everyone has the right to freedom and security of the person, which includes the right —

(*a*) not to be deprived of freedom arbitrarily or without just cause;

(*b*) not to be detained without trial;

(*c*) to be free from all forms of violence from both public and private sources;

(*d*) not to be tortured in any way;

(*e*) not to be treated or punished in a cruel, inhuman or degrading way.

"(2) Everyone has the right to bodily and psychological integrity, which includes the right —

(*a*) to make decisions concerning reproduction;

(*b*) to security in and control over their body;

(*c*) not to be subjected to medical or scientific experiments without their informed consent."

The Supreme Courts of the USA[2] and India[3] have held that liberty denotes freedom from bodily restraint and encompasses those rights and privileges which have long been recognised as being essential for the orderly pursuit of happiness by free people. It is obvious that the search of a person will encroach upon a his/her right to liberty.[4] This section also warns a police official to use violence, if it is necessary, very sparingly. Subsection (*e*) emphasises the importance of having respect for a person's dignity.

16.4.2.3 Privacy

Section 14 of the 1996 Constitution reads as follows:

"Everyone has the right to privacy, which includes the right not to have —

(*a*) their person or home searched;

(*b*) their property searched;

(*c*) their possessions seized; or

(*d*) the privacy of their communications infringed."

The Parliamentary Assembly of the Council of Europe defined the right to privacy, contained in article 8 of the European Convention, as follows:[5]

"The right to privacy consists essentially in the right to live one's own life with a minimum of interference. It concerns private, family and home life, physical and moral integrity, honour and reputation, avoidance of being placed in a false light, non revelation of irrelevant and embarrassing facts, unauthorised publication of private photographs, protection from disclosure of information given or received by the individual confidentially."

It is clear that the scope of the right to privacy is very wide. The context in which we must view the right to privacy for present purposes is illustrated clearly by *Eisenstadt v Baird*[6] at 453:

"If the right of privacy means anything, it is the right of the individual, married or single, to be free from unwarranted government intrusion into matters so fundamentally affecting a person."

The specific intrusion we are dealing with here is the search and seizure of a person or his or her property. As the right to privacy is central to so many aspects of a person's being, the court will not take an infringement of this right lightly.

16.4.2.4 Property

The relevant part of section 25 of the Constitution 1996 reads as follows:

"(1) No one may be deprived of property except in terms of law of general application, and no law may permit arbitrary deprivation of property."

This section makes it imperative that police officials have the necessary grounds and authorisation for seizure of a person's property. This section, together with the violation of privacy and freedom and security of the person, will cause a police official endless problems if search and seizure do not take place on proper grounds and in a dignified manner.

16.4.3 Affording adequate protection for the human rights involved

As these rights are never absolute, and may be limited, the courts will do their utmost to protect people from unreasonable and unjustifiable search and/or seizure. The most effective protection against an infringement is prevention or authorisation before it happens. This is the basis for the warrant requirement. The courts consider it to be the most effective protection if an independent and detached judicial officer considers the merits of the infringement before it happens. That is why it is a requirement that a judicial officer or a justice of the peace grants a warrant before a search or seizure may take place. **It is an internationally accepted principle, and the standard which the 1996 Constitution sets, that a warrant (authorisation) should be obtained before search and seizure take place.**

The decision in *Park-Ross v Director: Office for Serious Economic Offences*[7] illustrates that the court has taken notice of this principle. Section 6 of the Investigation of Serious Economic Offences Act 117 of 1991, authorising search and seizure in pursuance of an enquiry, was judged to be unconstitutional, as it was not a reasonable and justifiable limitation of the right to privacy. It was recommended that the section be amended to provide that authorisation be obtained, before the search and seizure, from a magistrate or judge of the Supreme Court in chambers. The application for the warrant should set out, at least, under oath or affirmation, information such as the nature of the enquiry, and suspicions giving rise to such enquiry.

16.4.4   The South African situation

The constitutionality of search and seizure provisions in the Criminal Procedure Act of 1977 and in other legislation affording police officials these powers has not yet been challenged before the Constitutional Court. Section 21 of the Criminal Procedure Act of 1977 deals with the requirements for obtaining a search warrant and section 22 with the requirements to be complied with when searching without a warrant. The provisions in these sections are very similar to those in the majority of foreign countries which have a Bill of Rights. In *Ntantiso & another v Minister of Law and Order NO* [8] the issue was not the constitutionality of these sections, but Judge Froneman expressed the opinion that warrantless searches on the same basis as that provided for in section 22 of the Criminal Procedure Act of 1977 do not seem to have attracted the sanction of unconstitutionality in, for example, Canada. This illustrates what has been said before — that the provisions in the statutes will not necessarily change, but that the manner of execution definitely will.

As the Constitution requires prior authorisation for search and seizure, it is important that police officials put any resistance towards this principle behind them and closely abide by the provisions of the various statutes regulating their functions and duties. However, it often happens that a police official cannot find a magistrate in the early hours of the morning and then proceeds to search without a warrant. In the light of *S v Motloutsi* [9] the unavailability of a magistrate will no longer serve as a ground for search without a warrant. The judge mentioned that the police official could have obtained a warrant from a justice of the peace. A police officer is a justice of the peace.

It is submitted that police officials should start using the authority given to police officers in terms of section 21 of the Criminal Procedure Act of 1977. It is very important to bear in mind that the officer should not be part of the particular investigation. The object of issuing a warrant will be defeated if the authority issuing the warrant is not impartial. What applies to the magistrate applies to the police officer as well.

The court will not lightly set aside a warrant issued by a magistrate or a justice of the peace. The court will not even set the warrant aside if it deems the magistrate's or justice of the peace's decision to be incorrect. The court could, however, interfere with the decision if it appears that the magistrate or justice of the peace did not apply his or her mind to the matter. This means that the facts before the magistrate or the justice of the peace must provide reasonable grounds for believing that an article, as specified in section 20 of the Criminal Procedure Act of 1977,[10] is in the possession or under the control of or upon any person or upon or at any premises within his or her area of jurisdiction.[11] For a complete discussion and interpretation of some of the important issues involved in issuing a warrant, see *Mandela v Minister of Safety and Security* and *Van der Merwe v Minister van Justisie en 'n ander.*[12]

When it comes to the execution of a warrant, a police official should always have respect for a person's dignity. Although it may be difficult at times, a person should always be treated humanely and be regarded as innocent. Respect for a person's dignity also implies that a search should only take place during the day, if at all possible. When it is necessary to search at night, the police official should ensure that the warrant expressly states that the search may take place at night.

Section 22 of the Criminal Procedure Act of 1977, providing for search without a warrant, can basically be divided into two parts: a search conducted with the person concerned's consent, and a search undertaken on the reasonable belief that a warrant will be issued to the police official and that further delay will defeat the object of the search. Much of the uncertainty and the majority of problems which arise stem from searches conducted without a warrant. This has resulted in countless court cases. It is submitted that part of the problem lies in the fact that many police officials do not have a thorough understanding of the issues involved. Police officials will experience fewer problems if they have a proper understanding of the terms "consent" and "reasonable grounds to believe".[13]

A search conducted with the consent of the person concerned places a police official in a much better position than a search without such consent. It eliminates the procedural burden of proving the existence of reasonable grounds to search. Thus, a police official should, where practicable, make it clear that he or she is seeking the co-operation of the person concerned, and should ask for consent to search for the section 20 article. Although the consent causes the existence of reasonable grounds to be irrelevant, a duty still rests on the police official to conduct the search with proper regard for the individual's right to be treated in a dignified manner.

A good illustration of some of the issues involved in a search without a warrant is to be found the case of *S v Motloutsi.*[14] A suspect was arrested at 21:00 for allegedly committing the crime of armed robbery. At 03:00 police officials went to the house where the suspect rented a room. The owner of the house opened the door and consented to the search of the house. He showed the police officials that part of the house which was for the exclusive use of the suspect. In that particular part of the house, the police found bloodstained banknotes in the loudspeaker of a radio.

The court held that the police had conducted an illegal search, as a search warrant should have been obtained. The consequence of the illegal search was that the court refused to admit the banknotes as evidence. This is one of the most important effects of a violation of human rights. Apart from the fact that valuable resources have been wasted and the possibility of civil claims against the Police Service arises, crucial evidence may be excluded from court. This may lead to dangerous criminals going back to the streets, which contributes to the already soaring crime rate.

The police argued that a warrant was unnecessary as the owner did in fact give his permission for them to search the house. However, he only had direct control and possession of that part of the house which was not rented by the suspect. The only "person concerned" who could have given consent was the suspect himself. In the absence of his permission, a warrant was necessary to search that specific part of the house, unless it could have been justified under section 22(*b*) of the Criminal Procedure Act of 1977, which was not the case.

16.5 DEFINITIONS

16.5.1 Consent

Before a person can be said to have given consent, the following requirements have to be met.

- The person concerned must give consent *voluntarily* and without being *coerced* to do so. In addition, such a person must not be unduly influenced in order to persuade him or her to consent. If, at the time when a person is asked for permission to search, the necessary grounds for obtaining a search warrant are absent, a person should not be threatened by telling him or her that a search warrant will be obtained. If the person "consents" as a result of this threat, the court is likely to hold that no consent was given, as the person was coerced, by the use of false information, into giving consent. The court will most probably also refuse to admit the seized articles as evidence, due to the illegal entry, search and seizure by the police official. Other factors such as the number of police officials present, the manner of approach and the brandishing of firearms may also play a role in intimidating a person.

- The consent can either be *express* or *implied* by conduct. Permission is express when a police official requests permission to search and the person concerned states that the search may take place. When the person concerned invites the police official into or onto the premises by way of gestures this is a case of implied permission if the other requirements of consent are met. If a police official asks the person concerned for permission to *enter* his or her home and he or she gestures or invites the police official in, this does is not mean that consent to search and seize has been given. It is important for the police official to make it clear to the person concerned what his or her purpose is. However, when a police official is in a person's home with his/her permission, that official is there lawfully and any section 20 articles in plain view may be seized and used as evidence. No search takes place in such circumstances.

- The consent must be given *before* the search takes place. Consent may normally be *withdrawn* or *limited* before the search has been completed. Revocation of consent does not make the search prior to the revocation unreasonable/unlawful, and anything seized during that period has been lawfully seized. However, consent given after the search has taken place will not retroactively make the search lawful.

- The person consenting must have the *capacity* to consent. Capacity to consent means that the person must be capable of understanding the *nature*, as well as the *consequences*, of the act. The necessary capacity to consent may be lacking on account of youth, mental defect, intoxication or unconsciousness. For example, a police official cannot depend on the consent of a person who is so drunk that he/she can barely stand on his/her feet. It is quite possible that he/she does not comprehend the nature or the consequences of the act.

- The person consenting must be aware of the precise *nature of the act* to which he/she consents. A person can only be aware of the nature of the proposed conduct if the police official makes clear his/her intention to search and indicates what is being sought in the search. The consenting person must also be certain of the *identity of the person* conducting the search. If a person invites you into his/her home (by way of action or deed), well aware that you are a police official, and you see section 20 articles (for example, mandrax tablets) on the coffee table, these may be seized and used as evidence against the person. However, if you enter the person's home while he/she is under the impression that you are an insurance broker, no proper consent exists, which makes your entry into the home unlawful. Even if you do not conduct a search, the mandrax tablets will probably not be allowed in evidence against the person, as entry has been gained illegally.

- Mere *submission* does not constitute consent: there is a difference between submission and consent. Every consent involves submission, but it does not follow that mere submission involves consent. All the circumstances will be taken into account to determine whether the person's submission was the result of consent or whether it was the result of some other factors. This would be the case, for example, where you tell the person either that you have a warrant or that you will be able to obtain one, in circumstances where you do not actually have the necessary grounds to obtain a warrant.

16.5.2   Reasonable grounds to believe

- If a police official, on reasonable grounds, believes that a search warrant will be issued to him or her if he or she applies for such warrant *and* that the delay in obtaining such warrant would defeat the object of the search, such police official may search any person, container or premises for the purpose of seizing any section 20 article.

- A person can only be said to have reasonable grounds to believe if:
  i)   he or she really believes it;
  ii) his or her belief is based on verifiable facts; and
  iii) in the circumstances and in view of the existence of those grounds, any reasonable person would have held the same belief.
- The word "grounds" refers to "facts". This means that there will only be grounds for a certain belief if the belief can be reconciled with the available facts. As the existence of a "fact" is objectively determined, which means that one will have to look at the fact as it really is and not as someone thinks it is, a police official will have to make use of his/her five senses, namely sight, hearing, smell, touch and taste. Whether reasonable grounds to believe exist will depend on the circumstances of each case, but there must be some objective basis for it. *This clearly shows that a "hunch" or a "gut feeling" is not enough to serve as a "ground" on which one can search and seize.*
- It is important to note that there is a difference between reasonable grounds to *suspect* and reasonable grounds to *believe*. Suspicion is a state of conjecture (not knowing) or surmise where proof is lacking. It is not necessary to have substantial proof before one can be said to "believe", but the existence of a belief implies that there is more information available which turns conjecture or surmise into an acceptance that something is true.
- Normally there will be some verifiable information emanating from:
  i)   the suspect (description matches that of a recently reported thief);
  ii) his or her manner (furtive behaviour such as trying to hide something or loitering in an alley at the back of a shop);
  iii) surrounding circumstances (reports of a planned gang fight and the sight of known youths heading for the supposed venue);
  iv) third party (informant, complainant or witness);
  v)   the official's own observations or knowledge (for example, the smell of dagga).
- It will normally be a combination of the factors mentioned above. Neither knowledge of personal factors (for example knowledge of previous convictions, colour, age, manner of dress, etc) nor stereotyped images of certain persons as likely offenders (for example a certain gang) can support a reasonable belief *on its own*.
- Refusal to answer an official's questions might well increase suspicion, but on its own it cannot amount to reasonable suspicion, not to mention reasonable grounds to believe, since a person is under no general duty to answer police questions.
- A police official will have to consider the true facts before him or her and decide whether the true facts are, in his or her view, sufficient to warrant a belief that other facts exist, such as the presence of some prohibited drug on specific premises.

- The fact that the police official believes that certain facts exist is not sufficient to regard his or her belief as one based on "reasonable grounds". This will only be the case if it can be said that any reasonable person, who has more or less the same background knowledge, would have held the same belief in the circumstances.
- This only emphasises how far searching without a warrant, due to the inconvenience of having to obtain one first or due to the non-existence of true facts, falls below the standards required by the Criminal Procedure Act and the Constitution. Thus, before conducting a search without a warrant:
  - the police official must consider the facts before him/her and form the belief that certain other facts, such as the presence of narcotics on certain premises, do in fact exist;
  - the police official must believe on "reasonable grounds" that he/she will obtain a warrant if he/she applies for one; *and*
  - he/she must believe that, in the circumstances, the time lost in applying for a warrant will defeat the object of the search.

16.6   SUGGESTED READING AND SOURCES

Bevan, V & Lidstone, K. 1991. *The Investigation of Crime: A Guide to Police Powers*. London: Butterworths.

Cachalia, *et al.* 1994. *Fundamental Rights in the New Constitution*. Cape Town: Juta & Co.

LaFave, W R & Israel, JH. 1992. *Criminal Procedure*, 2 ed. St Paul Minnesota: West Publishing Co.

Nel, F & Bezuidenhout, J. 1995. *Human Rights for the Police*. Kenwyn: Juta & Co.

Van Dijk, P & Van Hoof, GJH. 1990. *Theory and Practice of the European Convention on Human Rights*, 2 ed. The Netherlands: Kluwer Law and Taxation Publishers.

Watt, D & Fuerst, M. 1996. *Tremeear's Criminal Code*. Canada: Carswell Thomson Professional Publishing.

....

ENDNOTES

1   *University of Pretoria v Tommy Meyer Films (Edms) Bpk* 1979 (1) SA 441 (A).

2   *Board of Regents v Roth* 408 US 564.

3   *Kharak Singh v State of Uttar Pradesh* (1964) 1 SCR 332, where the court held that the right to personal liberty includes freedom from restrictions or encroachments on his or her person, whether directly imposed or indirectly brought about by calculated measures.

4   See section 13 of the South African Police Service Act which provides police officials with the authority to cordon off an area, set up roadblocks, etc.

5   Van Dijk & Van Hoof 368.

6   405 US 438.

7   1995 (2) BCL 198 (C).

8   1995 (1) SACLR 119 (E).

9   1996 (2) BCL 220 (C).

10   "The State may, in accordance with the provisions of this Chapter, seize anything –

    (*a*)   which is concerned in or is on reasonable grounds believed to be concerned in the commission or suspected commission of an offence, whether within the Republic or elsewhere;

    (*b*)   which may afford evidence of the commission or suspected commission of an offence, whether within the Republic or elsewhere; or

    (*c*)   which is intended to be used or is on reasonable grounds believed to be intended to be used in the commission of an offence."

11   A police official has national jurisdiction and in this regard is not as restricted as a magistrate is.

12   1995 (2) SACR 397 (W); 1995 (2) SASV 471 (O).

13   See para 16.5 for a detailed explanation of both terms.

14   Supra.

Chapter 17
Admissions, Confessions and Pointing Out

Roux Krige

SUMMARY

*T*HIS chapter deals with the controversial and very relevant topic of admissions and confessions. We look at both extra-judicial and intra-judicial admissions, as well as mediate admissions. We consider the nature of the admission, the way in which the statement must be dealt with and requirements for admissibility. We also look at the constitutional requirements for the admissibility of confessions, emphasising the role of the 1993 and the 1996 Constitutions. The chapter concludes with a short discussion on pointing out.

17.1   INTRODUCTION

The success of court cases can often depend on the admissibility or inadmissibility of admissions or confessions. It is very important that every police official should know as much as possible about this topic. The commencement of the Constitution has also brought a new dimension to this topic, and in particular the effect of section 25 of the 1993 Constitution and section 35 of the 1996 Constitution.

17.2   KEY OBJECTIVES

The key objectives of this chapter are to enable students to:
- define admissions, confessions, and pointing out;
- discuss the requirements for admissibility of admissions and confessions;
- distinguish between extra-judicial, intra-judicial and mediate admissions;
- discuss the constitutional requirements for the admissibility of admissions and confessions.

17.3   APPLICABLE LAW

The 1993 Constitution, sections 7, 23 and 25
The 1996 Constitution, sections 32 and 35
The Criminal Procedure Act 51 of 1977, sections 112, 115, 209, 217, 218, 219A, 220 and 334

17.4   INTERPRETATION AND DISCUSSION
17.4.1   Admissions

Admissions are divided into extra-judicial admissions on the one hand and intra-judicial admissions on the other.

17.4.2   Extra-judicial admissions

Evidence from extra-judicial admissions by an accused may be adduced against him/her in a subsequent trial as evidence, *provided* that the requirements for admissibility have been met.

17.4.2.1 The nature of an admission

An extra-judicial admission is in essence an admission made outside the court. This may take place any time before the commencement of the trial, or may even have taken place before a decision was taken to charge or prosecute a person. An admission may be verbal or in writing.

17.4.2.1.1 Definition

An admission is a statement from which an unfavourable deduction can be made against the declarant (person making the statement).

17.4.2.1.2 Analysis of the definition

A statement that a declarant makes in a favourable light is not an admission in the legal sense of the word. However, a statement may partly favour and partly prejudice the declarant. For instance, the statement may contain both incriminating and exculpatory evidence. In such a case the declarant has the right to the whole statement being placed before the court. The court would therefore have to take both the exculpatory and the incriminating evidence into account. The statement as a whole must be taken into account — *Valachia*.[1] The weight that the court attaches to the exculpatory sections will depend on the circumstances in every case.

In order to determine whether a statement in a particular case is an admission in the legal sense of the word, we must look at the charge against the accused. If the statement is an admission of one or more elements (but not all) of the offence, it is an admission or admissions with reference to that offence. When *all* the elements of the offence are admitted, it is not an admission but a confession. We will deal with confessions later in more detail (section 17.4.5).

When considering whether a particular statement is an admission or a confession, the definition of the relevant offence should always be kept in mind. The definition of murder, for instance, is "unlawfully and deliberately to cause the death of another person". When a person therefore admits that he stabbed the deceased with a knife and that stabbing the deceased with a knife caused the death of the deceased, these are simply admissions to a charge of murder because they contain only two elements of the relevant offence, namely conduct and causality. They do not constitute a confession because not all elements of the offence have been admitted to.

An admission may also be deduced from the behaviour of the person. In criminal cases, however, the courts are wary of making an unfavourable deduction from the behaviour of the person. Such a deduction must be reasonable in the circumstances. The courts have a discretion to make such deduction from the behaviour of a person, in given circumstances. For instance, an unfavourable deduction may be made where the accused person remains silent in cases in which he/she could be expected to answer — *Barlin*.[2] However, one should keep in mind that the arrested person has the right to remain silent.[3]

A statement must be judged objectively to determine whether it indeed constitutes an admission. The intention of the declarant when making the statement is irrelevant. This means that even if the declarant is unaware of the fact that he/she is making an admission, it is an admission if, evaluated objectively, it constitutes a statement from which an unfavourable deduction can be made. Whether such an admission can be used later in a trial as evidence against the declarant is another question that must be considered in the light of admissibility requirements for an admission. The admissibility requirements for an admission or confession must not be confused with the question of whether the specific statement is indeed an admission or a confession. First one must determine whether the statement is a confession or an admission before one can look at the requirements for admissibility. The type of statement will determine what the admissibility requirements are, since these differ in the case of an admission and that of a confession.

17.4.2.2 Requirements for the admissibility of an admission

17.4.2.2.1 Constitutional requirements for the admissibility of admissions

To prevent unnecessary repetition, we will discuss these requirements under confessions, since the requirements are the same unless otherwise indicated. See constitutional requirements for admissibility of confessions below.

17.4.2.2.2 Admissibility requirements in terms of the Criminal Procedure Act of 1977

The admissibility requirements are contained in section 219A of the Criminal Procedure Act of 1977.

This section provides that evidence from an extra-judicial admission is admissible against the declarant (accused) if the admission was made voluntarily.

The common law definition of *voluntarily* in this section means that no promises were made or threats issued. Force must derive from a person in a position of authority in order to make the admission inadmissible — *Barlin*[4] and *Yolelo*.[5] A person in a position of authority is any person who may influence the course of the trial. This refers not only to state authority. However, it does not include members of a prison gang — *Peters*.[6] In this respect it differs from *freely and voluntarily* in a confession in terms of section 217 of the Criminal Procedure Act of 1977. See *confessions* below, in which we discuss the words *freely and voluntarily* (section 17.4.5.4.4.1).

17.4.2.3   The onus of proof

The onus of proof is on the state to prove that the admission was made voluntarily. The criterion for proof is *above reasonable doubt*. The section also stipulates that an admission made before a magistrate will, under certain circumstances, create a presumption that the admission was made voluntarily, and the onus of proof will therefore be on the accused to prove the contrary. This presumption with regard to a confession, however, was declared unconstitutional in the Constitutional Court in *Zuma*.[7] One must necessarily deduce that this will also apply with regard to admissions in terms of section 219A of the Criminal Procedure Act of 1977. The state must therefore prove that it was the accused who made the admission and that he/she made it voluntarily. We will discuss these aspects in more detail under confessions since they apply there too (section 17.4.5.5).

There are no further restrictions on admissions. In other words, an admission may be made by anyone, whether a member of the public or any member of the Police Service.

17.4.2.4   Trial within a trial

It is established practice that a trial is held within a trial to decide the admissibility of the admission. Further aspects with regard to the admissibility of admissions and the trial within a trial are discussed more fully under confessions since, with certain exceptions, they correspond with those of confessions (section 17.4.5.6).

17.4.3   Intra-judicial admissions

Intra-judicial admissions are admissions made during the pleading process or in the course of the trial.

17.4.3.1   Admissions after a plea of guilty in terms of section 112 of the Criminal Procedure Act of 1977

Once an accused has pleaded guilty, the court may, in the case of a minor offence, and *must*, in the case of a more serious offence, question the accused to determine whether the accused indeed intended to plead guilty and actually pleads guilty to all the elements of the offence. If the court is satisfied that the accused pleaded guilty to all the elements of the offence, the court may find him/her guilty. If the court is not satisfied that the accused pleaded guilty to all the elements of the offence, the court will enter a plea of not guilty in terms of the Criminal Procedure Act of 1977.[8]

Admissions made by the accused during his/her plea of not guilty in terms of section 112 of the Criminal Procedure Act of 1977 remain formal admissions. These admissions do not have to be proved by the state.

17.4.3.2   Admissions after a plea of not guilty in terms of section 115 of the Criminal Procedure Act of 1977

When an accused pleads not guilty in terms of section 115 of the Criminal Procedure Act of 1977, the procedure is as follows.

The accused may reveal the basis of his/her defence, if he/she wishes. He/she is not compelled to do so and no unfavourable deduction may be made from the fact that he/she exercises his/her right to remain silent. The accused always has a right to remain silent.[9]

If the court decides to reveal the basis of its defence it may do so. If the court feels that the accused has made admissions that are in direct conflict with the charge sheet, the court may ask the accused whether those admissions can be entered as admissions to the charges in the charge sheet.[10] However, such admissions must relate directly to the primary facts in issue, and may not simply constitute circumstantial evidence — *Sesetsi.*[11] The latter restriction applies only with regard to section 115 procedure. The accused need not agree to the entering of the admissions as admissions to those charges. Such admissions as are entered as admissions to those charges with the consent of the accused become formal admissions. These formal admissions corroborate the allegations in the charge sheet and do not have to be proved by the state. When the accused agrees that they be entered as formal admissions, this is sufficient evidence of the fact and if they remain standing at the end of the case (that is, if they are not withdrawn), they are *conclusive proof* — *Sesetsi.*[12] This is because they place the relevant fact or facts beyond dispute. Such admissions are admissions as intended in section 220 of the Criminal Procedure Act of 1977.[13]

However, if the accused refuses to have these admissions entered as formal admissions, the state must prove the allegations. The admissions are then referred to as informal admissions. They do not place the facts beyond dispute since the state must still prove them. Again, no unfavourable deduction may be made from the fact that the accused refuses to have such admissions entered as formal admissions. This does not mean that informal admissions are without value. However, they can be used for limited purposes only, such as corroboration in terms of section 209 of the Criminal Procedure Act of 1977 — *Mjoli*.[14] The accused may also be cross-examined on these, particularly where his/her evidence deviates substantially from his/her plea explanation in terms of section 115 of the Criminal Procedure Act of 1977, because the informal admissions are part of the evidence — *Sesetsi, supra.*

When the court considers the effect of an intra-judicial admission in terms of section 115 of the Criminal Procedure Act of 1977, it must take both the incriminating as well as the exculpatory sections into account — *Cloete*.[15] The latter court therefore overrules *Sesetsi*[16] on this point.

17.4.3.3 Admissions in terms of section 220 of the Criminal Procedure Act of 1977

It often happens that, during a trial, the accused decides to make certain admissions. The accused or his/her legal representative may make an admission during the course of the trial in terms of section 220 of the Criminal Procedure Act of 1977. Such an admission is then sufficient evidence of the fact. The admission is made formally and the intention is that it should be regarded as a formal admission.

However, such an admission can be withdrawn if a reasonable explanation is given of why it was done incorrectly, such as duress, error or undue influence. The point of dispute must then be proved by the state.

However, the accused may at no point be compelled to make an admission in terms of this section. He/she still has the protection of the 1993 Constitution[17] and the 1996 Constitution.[18]

17.4.4 Vicarious admissions

Vicarious means indirect. In the law of evidence the word means that someone can be held responsible for the actions or remarks of someone else. This may happen where a particular relationship exists between the person who made the admission and the other person against whom the admission is made, such as the relationship between employer and employee and that between legal adviser and client. There is some mutual identity of interests between these people. The content of an admission made in such a case by the declarant is imputed to the principal as if the principal made the admission. Express authorisation for such an admission is not a requirement. However, it must be within the apparent scope of the authorisation or relationship. The person against whom such an admission is made may also expressly accept or ratify (confirm) the admission.

In principle such an admission is admissible only against the person who made the admission. As a common-law exception to the hearsay rule, an admission made by one person may in certain circumstances apply against another.

17.4.5   Confessions

17.4.5.1   The nature of a confession

The term *confession* is used only for an extra-judicial statement that conforms with the requirements set out in the definition of a confession. The term is not used for an intra-judicial plea of guilty. It is also used in criminal cases only. The term is therefore not used in civil cases. The term has a technical legal meaning. A confession may be made verbally as well as in writing, but it may not be presumed from behaviour.

17.4.5.1.1   Definition

A confession is a straightforward admission of guilt that, if made in court, would amount to a plea of guilty — *Becker*[19] and *Mokoena*.[20]

17.4.5.1.2   Analysis of the definition

This means that a confession is an admission of all of the elements of the offence. The test is objective and not subjective — *Yende*.[21] The statement per se must comply only with the requirements for a confession. It deals with the facts asserted by an accused, rather than the intention behind the statement. The intention with which the statement is made is not relevant in determining whether the statement is indeed a confession or not. The nature and consequences of the statement are the deciding factor — *Yende, supra*. The statement must be read as a whole, without overemphasising any one part, and every word must be given its ordinary meaning — *Motloba*.[22]

A straightforward admission of guilt means that all possible grounds for defence are expressly or implicitly excluded — *George*.[23] In *Xulu*[24] the accused was charged with possession of dagga. The accused admitted extra-judicially that he was responsible for the dagga. The court found that this did not constitute a confession since he did not admit that he did not have a permit in accordance with the relevant Act to own the dagga. The Act makes provision for dagga to be legally owned with a permit. The court found that the accused had not excluded this possible basis for defence. See *George*.[25]

Where a particular act is an offence, unless authorised by a permit or licence, an admission of that act in itself is not usually a confession since it is not an admission that the accused had no permit or licence.

In order to determine whether a particular statement is an admission or a confession, reference is always made to the specific offence. A confession to one offence may be simply an admission with regard to another offence. The definition of the offence must therefore always be kept in mind in order to determine whether the statement is a confession or an admission with regard to that *particular offence*. The definition of murder, for instance, is to illegally and deliberately cause the death of another person. Where the accused on a charge of murder, for instance, has said that he stabbed the deceased with a knife because he always wanted to teach him a lesson, this is nevertheless not a confession to a charge of murder. It may indeed be a confession to a charge of assault. However, if the accused said that he stabbed the deceased with a knife, that this caused the death of the deceased, that he knew that it was an offence and that he intended to do it, he has *expressly* excluded the possibility of any grounds for defence, and his statement is therefore a confession to a charge of murder. Rape is the illegal and deliberate carnal intercourse by a man with a woman without her consent. For instance, an admission with regard to a charge of rape may be that the accused had intercourse with the woman, but this is not a confession, since it does not exclude the possible grounds for defence, namely consent, and therefore it is not an admission of all the elements of the offence. Consent as a basis for defence is not excluded by the statement. It is therefore not a confession. The offence would have been committed only if the accused did not have consent. It is indeed an admission to a charge of rape, since it admits to at least one of the elements of the offence. Have another look at the discussion of admissions above (section 17.4.2.1.2).

In *Grove-Mitchell* [26] the accused said that he emptied his revolver on his wife and shot her full of holes. The court found that this was not a confession since it did not exclude the possibility of self-defence or non-criminal responsibility. In other words, the element of illegality was not admitted.

In *S v F* [27] the court found that an admission of intercourse with the consent of a girl of 13 years was not a confession in contravention of section 14(1)(*a*) of the Sexual Offences Act 23 of 1957 (intercourse with a girl under the age of 16 years), because the Act allowed the accused certain grounds for defence in section 14(2), and that from the statement of *carnal intercourse with consent* no deduction could be drawn that the accused had waived these statutory grounds for defence, and it was therefore not a straightforward admission of guilt. Consequently it was not a confession, but an admission of that offence.

Accompanying circumstances may be taken into account to determine the actual intention of a statement. The requirement that all grounds for defence should expressly be excluded must be modified here. This can mean that words that are an admission *in vacuo* may in the light of all the circumstances be construed as a full confession. For instance, if the accused said that he murdered the deceased, he has *by implication* excluded the possibility of any grounds for defence, and this is therefore a confession of murder.

A written confession may also be contained in more than one document. In such a case the two documents must be read together —

Rossouw.[28] Where the one qualifies the other, they must be read together. As far as exculpatory sections are concerned, the court may reject these after consideration if there are grounds for not believing them. Where they do not qualify or explain the other part, but are simply contradictory, other considerations apply, particularly when some time elapsed between the two statements. The past and the future cannot artificially be linked as a unit — *Mkize.*[29]

17.4.5.2 A statement relating to more than one offence

As we have seen above, it is possible that one and the same statement can constitute an admission with regard to one offence and a confession with regard to another. Where the accused is charged with an offence for which a legal verdict is possible and the statement that he/she has made is a confession to a lesser offence but an admission of the more serious offence, the statement must always be handled as a confession — *S v F, supra*. For instance, where the accused is charged with murder, a legal verdict of assault is possible. If the accused said that he did not want to kill the deceased but simply wanted to assault him, this is a confession to assault and an admission with regard to the murder. If they were judged separately, the statement could be regarded as an admissible admission with regard to the main charge and an inadmissible confession with regard to the lesser offence, since the requirements for admissibility differ. A statement in such a case should therefore always be dealt with as a confession — *S v F, supra*.

17.4.5.3 The way in which a statement must be handled

The first step in handling a statement is to determine whether it was made by the accused. The second step is to determine whether the statement is an admission or a confession. The principles according to which this is determined should not be confused with the requirements for admissibility. The requirements for admissibility cannot contribute in any way to determining whether the statement is a confession or an admission. These requirements are relevant only once it has been decided whether the statement is an admission or a confession. It is vitally important to realise that if it is found that the statement is a confession and this confession is found to be inadmissible because, for instance, it was made to a peace officer, the statement may not be handled as an admission. Once a confession, always a confession, and it must comply with the requirements for admissibility of a confession; if not, it is inadmissible as a confession and may not be adduced (tendered) as evidence, save as provided by section 217(3) of the Criminal Procedure Act of 1977. Not even parts of the confession may be adduced as an admission.

17.4.5.4   Admissibility requirements for a confession

17.4.5.4.1   General

A confession made by one person is not admissible as evidence against another person.[30]

The statement of one person may, however, be held against another in the following cases —

(i) where the person in respect of whom the admission or confession is made accepts in word or deed the truth of the statement and makes it wholly or partially his/her own; and

(ii) where there was a conspiracy to commit an offence: a statement by one conspirator regarding the offence is admissible as evidence against another conspirator — *Sibanda*.[31] See *Mayet*.[32]

17.4.5.4.2   Judges' rules

The magistrate should find out from the accused whether he/she has had contact with a legal representative and, if not, should inform him/her fully of his/her rights to legal representation and enquire whether he/she wishes to make use of this right before he/she makes a statement — *Mbambeli*.[33] The form used by magistrates to take down statements should make provision for a note as to whether the accused was informed about his/her right to legal representation — *Januarie*.[34]

Although judges' rules do not constitute statutory requirements, they are practical tips that are actually prescriptions laid down by the courts. Judges' rules are administrative indicators and do not have the force of law — *Kuzwayo*.[35] However, this does not mean that they can be ignored. Disregard of the judges' rules cannot on its own invalidate the confession. Nonetheless, it is a factor that the court will consider when deciding whether the state has discharged its onus to prove that the requirements of admissibility have been met. The weight of the disregard of the rules will depend on the circumstances in each case — *Nkosi*;[36] *Colt*;[37] *Gcali*.[38]

Persons taking down statements must be impartial — *Mbele*.[39] It is always extremely unwise to take a detained or arrested person to a member of the SAPS who is part of the investigating team for the making of a confession. Even if the person who is to make the confession has a perception that he/she is making it before a member of the investigating team, it is desirable that he/she be taken to another officer for the entering of the confession — *Latha*.[40] Where possible, the police should use the services of a magistrate when a confession is taken — *Mchunu*.[41] Failure to do this may in certain circumstances throw light on the question as to whether the requirements for admissibility were followed or not. However, this in itself does not constitute an additional basis for admissibility in decreeing a confession admissible — *Mchunu, supra*. Where the statutory and constitutional requirements for admissibility have been met, the court is obliged to find the confession admissible. The court does not have a discretion to exclude it on other grounds — *Sidiki*.[42]

Depending on the circumstances, failure to grant a young person the support of a parent or guardian, where reasonably possible, when a confession is made, leads to the conclusion that the confession was not made voluntarily or without the minor having been unduly influenced — *M*.[43]

17.4.5.4.3 Constitutional requirements for the admissibility of confessions

This discussion applies to extra-judicial admissions too, except where otherwise indicated.

Members of the SAPS are specifically compelled to take the fundamental rights of every person thoroughly into account when carrying out their powers, duties and activities.[44]

Only the rights of detained and arrested persons that could possibly relate to the taking of admissions and confessions will be highlighted. Since there are important differences between the Constitution of 1993 and the Constitution of 1996, the rights will be indicated separately.

(a) The 1993 Constitution

Always bear in mind that the rights of an arrested person include the rights of a detained person.[45]

Every person who is detained shall have the right —

(i)   to be informed promptly in a language which he or she understands of the reason for his or her detention;[46]

(ii)   to be detained under conditions consonant with human dignity, which shall include at least the provision of adequate nutrition, reading material and medical treatment at state expense;[47]

(iii) to consult with a legal practitioner of his or her choice, to be informed of this right promptly and, where substantial injustice would otherwise result, to be provided with the services of a legal practitioner by the state;[48]

(iv)   to be given an opportunity to communicate with, and to be visited by, his or her spouse or partner, next of kin, religious counsellor and a medical practitioner of his or her choice;[49] and

(v)   to challenge the lawfulness of his or her detention in person before a court of law and to be released if such detention is unlawful.[50]

Every person arrested for the alleged commission of an offence shall, in addition to the rights which he or she has as a detained person, have the right —

(i)   promptly to be informed in a language which he or she understands, that he or she has the right to remain silent and to be warned of the consequences of making any statement;[51]

(ii)   as soon as is reasonably possible, but not later than forty-eight hours after the arrest or, if the said period of forty-eight hours expires outside ordinary court hours or on a day which is not a court day, the first court day after such expiry, to be brought before an ordinary court of law and be charged or informed of the reason for his or her detention, failing which he or she shall be entitled to be released;[52]

(iii) not to be compelled to make a confession or admission which could be used in evidence against him or her;[53] and

(iv) to be released from detention with or without bail unless the interests of justice require otherwise.[54]

(b)   The 1996 Constitution

Under this Constitution the rights of a detained person, in contrast with the Constitution of 1993, are not included under the rights of an arrested person.

Any person arrested in terms of the alleged commission of an offence has the right —

(i)   to remain silent;[55]

(ii)   to be informed promptly of — [56]

    (*a*) his or her right to remain silent; and

    (*b*) the consequences of any statements;

(iii) not to be compelled to make a confession or admission which could be used as evidence against him or her;[57]

(iv) to be brought before a court of law and charged as soon as is reasonably possible, but not later than forty-eight hours after the arrest or, if the said period of forty-eight hours expires outside ordinary court hours, on the first court day after such expiry;[58]

(v)   to be charged on the first court day after such arrest or informed of the reason for his or her further detention, or to be released; and [59]

(vi) to be released from detention if this serves the interests of justice, subject to reasonable conditions.[60]

Every detained person has the right to —

(i)   be informed immediately of the reason for his or her detention;[61]

(ii)   choose and consult with a legal practitioner, and to be informed of this right immediately;[62]

(iii) have a legal practitioner allocated to him or her by the state, at state expense, if substantial injustice would otherwise result, and to be informed of this right promptly;[63]

(iv) challenge the lawfulness of his or her detention before a court and, if the detention is unlawful, to be released;[64]

(v)   be held under conditions of detention that are consistent with human dignity, including at least exercise and the provision, at state expense, of adequate accommodation, nutrition, reading material and medical treatment;[65] and

(vi) communicate with, and be visited by, his or her — [66]

    (*a*)   spouse or partner;

    (*b*)   next of kin;

    (*c*)   religious counsellor of his or her choice; and

    (*d*)   a medical practitioner of his or her choice.

It should immediately be clear that various judges' rules are guaranteed in these sections of the various Constitutions. If these rights of a detained or accused person are not explained and the relevant person makes an admission or a confession, we can accept that the relevant statement will not be admissible in a court as evidence against such person. Where a person performing the arrest, for instance, fails to inform the arrested person or prisoner of his/her right to legal representation of his/her choice or of his/her right to remain silent and the arrested person makes an admission, such admission will be inadmissible in the later trial, unless the arrested person agrees to it. This situation holds for all the rights contained in both Constitutions.

Since the Constitution of 1993 has vertical application only,[67] one can deduce that the duty to ensure that these rights are enforced applies only with regard to officials of the state who perform arrests and not to the public in general.[68] Although the position with regard to the 1996 Constitution is uncertain on this aspect at the time of writing, it would appear that private persons will also be included since it is possible to find horizontal application too.

The protection offered by the Criminal Procedure Act of 1977[69] to a person making a confession is wider than that offered by the 1993 Constitution and the 1996 Constitution, since both Constitutions provide protection only to detained and arrested persons, while the Criminal Procedure Act of 1977 provides protection to any person. In addition, the 1993 Constitution and the 1996 Constitution make provision only for the confession to have been made voluntarily.[70] The Criminal Procedure Act of 1977 stipulates that such confession had to have been made freely and voluntarily, with the declarant being in his/her sound and sober senses, and without undue influence,[71] and finally that a confession made to a peace officer is inadmissible unless confirmed and put in writing in the presence of a magistrate or justice of the peace.[72]

An inadmissible confession of one accused, however, could well be made available to a co-accused to enable the co-accused to prepare his/her case and to cross-examine the accused if he/she decided to give evidence. Neither section 219 nor section 217 of the Criminal Procedure Act of 1977 prohibits such confession from being made available for this purpose, particularly if it could contribute to proving the innocence of the co-accused — *Smith*,[73] *Jeniker* (1)[74] and *Jeniker* (2).[75] However, it cannot be used against the accused as proof of the truth of the content of the statement.

We feel that it is at present in any event possible for the co-accused in terms of the 1993 Constitution and the 1996 Constitution to have access to such inadmissible confession. The 1993 Constitution[76] and the 1996 Constitution[77] stipulate that every person has the right to access to all information held by the state insofar as such information is required for the exercise or protection of any of his/her rights. It may also be justified by the fact that the accused has the right to a fair trial.[78]

17.4.5.4.4 Admissibility requirements for a confession in terms of the Criminal Procedure Act of 1977

The admissibility requirements are contained in section 217 of the Criminal Procedure Act of 1977.

This section provides that evidence from a confession made by a person with regard to the commission of an offence that relates to that offence is admissible in criminal proceedings if the requirements are met, including those of the proviso.[79]

The requirements are that the confession must have been made freely and voluntarily by a person in his/her sound and sober senses without that person having been unduly influenced.[80]

The proviso is that a confession made to a peace officer is not admissible unless confirmed and put in writing in the presence of a magistrate or justice of the peace.[81] This proviso does not apply with regard to admissions.[82]

A peace officer appointed in terms of section 334 of the Criminal Procedure Act of 1977 is expressly mentioned and included in this section.[83] A peace officer is usually a junior police official or non-commissioned officer (constable, sergeant, inspector). Peace officers are found, among others, in the South African National Defence Force, the Department of Correctional Services, nature conservation bodies and so on. A confession made to a peace officer is inadmissible unless confirmed and put in writing in the presence of a magistrate or justice of the peace.[84] This is the only case in which a confession must be reduced to writing to be admissible. Confessions to members of the public, magistrates and justices of the peace do not need to be in writing. They may be verbal. A confession addressed to a magistrate or justice of the peace by mail is regarded as addressed to him, although it may not reach the magistrate or justice of the peace directly — *Blyth*.[85] A confession may be contained in more than one document, namely where two documents actually constitute one statement — *Rossouw*.[86]

The Act [87] also makes provision for a presumption, namely that a confession made before a magistrate and put in writing under certain circumstances places the onus of proof on the accused to prove that the confession was not made voluntarily or that he/she was not in his/her sound and sober senses or that he/she was subject to undue influence to make the confession. However, this presumption was declared unconstitutional by the Constitutional Court in *Zuma*.[88] In its judgment the Court referred to various sections in the 1993 Constitution.[89] Section 217(1)(*b*)(ii) therefore does not need any further discussion in this regard.

17.4.5.4.4.1 *Freely and voluntarily*

Freely and voluntarily in section 217 gives the accused greater protection than *voluntarily* with regard to admissions in terms of section 219A of the Criminal Procedure Act of 1977. In section 217 the duress that makes the confession inadmissible does not necessarily have to come from someone in a position of authority. It can also, for instance, derive from members of a prison gang — *Peters*[90] — although our courts have already decided that a person in a position of authority is any person who has some measure of authority, for instance, that of a father towards a son, an uncle towards a nephew or an employer towards an employee — *Robbertson*.[91] Apart from this difference, it does not appear that there was intended to be any real difference between *voluntarily* in section 219A on the one hand and *freely and voluntarily* in section 217 on the other — *Mpetha (2)*.[92] *Voluntarily* refers to a voluntary act of will — *Mpetha* (2), *supra*. The ordinary dictionary meaning of the word is therefore sufficient.

17.4.5.4.4.2 *In his/her sound and sober senses*

In his/her sound and sober senses means that the accused must have the ability to know and realise what he/she has said. The fact that he/she was under the influence of alcohol or drugs will not necessarily invalidate the admissibility of the confession. If he/she was sober enough to know what he/she said, this requirement will have been satisfied. The fact that the accused had consumed alcohol could possibly affect the evidential value of the confession.

17.4.5.4.4.3 *Without having been unduly influenced*

This requirement is not the same as the concept of *freely and voluntarily*. The requirement of undue influence reaches further than the above requirement. *Person of authority* is not an ingredient in this requirement. Undue influence can be exercised by any person. Trivial undue influence must be ignored, as well as undue influence that clearly had no effect on the will of the accused. However, the fact that an accused does not complain in court about a particular influence exerted on him/her during the making of the statement does not necessarily mean that the court must ignore it as a possibility — *Mpetha* (2).93

Promises of some benefit or another if the accused makes the confession constitute undue influence. Undue influence also occurs when a person in a position of authority encourages the accused in an improper manner to make a confession. To encourage someone to tell the truth is not undue influence. Whether the influence was improper will depend on the circumstances in every case. Generally, however, anything that occurs in court that conflicts with the principles on which criminal law is based is improper. If there is any reasonable doubt about the suitable criterion, the accused is entitled to the benefit of the doubt — *Mpetha, supra.* Holding out the hope of bail to the accused does not necessarily constitute undue influence — *Nyembe.*94

The fact that the magistrate recording the confession did not inform the accused about the right to legal representation and did not ask him/her whether he/she had seen a legal adviser and, if not, ask whether he/she wished to make use of this right, does not indicate that the confession was made under undue influence. However, it is desirable that the magistrate act according to the rules — *Mbambeli.*95

However, a threat that a person will be detained unless he/she makes a confession does constitute undue influence — *Wanna.*96

Any influence that would tend to persuade the accused to say something that is perhaps not the truth can be seen as undue influence for the purposes of this section — *Niewoudt* (4).97

17.4.5.5   The onus of proof

The onus of proof that the confession was made freely and voluntarily with the accused in his/her sound and sober senses and without undue influence rests on the state — *Zuma.*98 The state must also prove that the confession was not made to a peace officer or that, where it was indeed made to a peace officer, that it was confirmed and put in writing in the presence of a magistrate or justice of the peace.99 The criterion according to which the state must acquit itself of this onus is above reasonable doubt. It is established practice that a trial is held within a trial to establish the admissibility of the confession.

17.4.5.6   Trial within a trial

A trial within a trial usually — but not necessarily — takes place at the end of the case of the state. The only question before the court in the trial within the trial is whether the confession was made freely and voluntarily, while the accused was in his/her sound and sober senses and without having been unduly influenced thereto. Because the onus of proof is on the state, the state will lead with the presentation of evidence. The state will therefore call its witnesses first. If the confession was recorded by a member of the Police Service, all those members involved with the accused before the confession was noted must give evidence on whether the requirements for admissibility were met.

The presiding officer may have no knowledge of the content of the confession before he/she rules the confession admissible, with one exception. This exception is in cases in which the accused in the trial within the trial alleges that the content of the confession was dictated to him/her. In such a case the state may put the content of the confession to the accused to prove that it is not the truth, in other words, simply to test the credibility of the accused — *Latha*,[100] *Talane*,[101] and *Lebone*.[102] In such a case the presiding officer will necessarily take note of the content of the statement. However, it may be used only to test the credibility of the accused; it may not be taken any further — *Mafuya* (2), *supra*. It may not be used to prove that the content of the statement is true — *Latha, supra* and *Lebone, supra*. It is used only to indicate that the accused is the author of the statement — *Tjiho*.[103]

When the state has concluded its trial within a trial, the accused can submit his/her case to the court through witnesses. He/she himself/herself may also give evidence. At the end of this trial, both parties have the opportunity to address the court in a submission. The court will then rule the confession either admissible or inadmissible. The court may withhold the reasons for its finding until the end of the main trial or give them immediately. If the court rules the confession or admission inadmissible, the statement is inadmissible and may not be used as evidence.

If the court rules the admission or confession admissible —

(i)   the person who recorded the confession will be called as a witness to read out the content of the confession before the court;

(ii)   in the case of a verbal confession, the person who recorded the confession will be called to testify on the content of the confession to the court;

(iii)   where the confession was made before a magistrate and this is apparent from the document, the prosecutor or advocate for the state will read the document into the record.[104]

   (*a*)   In order to prove that the confession was recorded by a magistrate, the state may either lead viva voce evidence or rely on section 231 of the Criminal Procedure Act of 1977 — *Jika*.[105]

           With an admission, the fact that the person who recorded the statement was a magistrate cannot be proved simply by submission of the document by the prosecution — *Dhlamini*.[106]

An accused may not be cross-examined in the trial within a trial on the merits of the main trial to test his/her credibility. However, where the accused repeats evidence that he/she gave in the trial in the trial within the main trial, he/she may be cross-examined on this to test his/her credibility — *Sabisa*.[107] A witness may also be cross-examined in the main trial on any contradictions between his/her evidence in the trial within a trial and his/her evidence in the main trial — *Gquma*.[108] However, such cross-examination may not exceed simply testing the witness's credibility.

It should be kept in mind that an accused has the right to have the question as to the admissibility of a confession decided in a separate trial. The evidence in the trial within a trial should therefore not be transferred to the main trial — *Sithebe*.[109] The main trial and the trial within a trial should be kept separate in substance as well as in form and the trial within a trial should be limited to evidence relating to the admissibility of the confession — *Shezi*.[110] What an accused says in the trial within a trial cannot be used against him/her on the merits — *Malinga*[111] and *De Vries*,[112] and the accused may also not rely on such evidence when it comes to the merits — *Mlomo*.[113]

The court may not provisionally allow a confession in the hope that further evidence will be led in the main trial to make the confession admissible. The court must rule the confession either admissible or inadmissible immediately after the trial within a trial. However, where a confession is ruled admissible, this is "provisional" in the sense that later evidence may arise that requires the confession to be excluded — *Ntuli*.[114]

17.4.5.7 Admissibility of an inadmissible confession

The Criminal Procedure Act of 1977[115] stipulates that an inadmissible confession is indeed admissible if —

(i) the accused submits evidence of a statement that constitutes part of or relates to the relevant confession; and

(ii) this is favourable for the accused.

The accused may make an inadmissible confession admissible by way of questions or statements to state witnesses, or he/she may do this while delivering his/her own evidence. It is the function of the court to decide whether this would indeed be favourable for the accused in the particular case.

17.4.5.8 The necessity to confirm a confession in terms of section 209 of the Criminal Procedure Act of 1977

When the court rules a confession admissible, the content of the confession becomes admissible evidence against the accused. However, an accused may not simply be found guilty of the offence on which he/she is charged and to which he/she has confessed on the strength of his/her confession alone. Section 209 of the Criminal Procedure Act of

1977 stipulates that an accused may be found guilty simply on the strength of his/her confession to an offence if such confession is confirmed in a material aspect *or*, where the confession cannot be so confirmed, by other evidence if such evidence proves that the offence was indeed committed. For instance, where an accused makes a confession that she murdered her husband by poisoning him with arsenic, confirmation for the offence can be found in the autopsy report if it is found that the deceased died as a result of poisoning by arsenic — *Blyth*.[116] In this example the post mortem report also confirmed the confession in a material aspect.

This section provides only for statutory corroboration in the event of a confession. The section applies only to confessions and not to a plea of guilty in court — *Talie*.[117] Corroboration may take any form. It can, for instance, be found in the evidence of an accomplice or even in an informal admission made in terms of section 115 of the Criminal Procedure Act of 1977 — *Mjoli*.[118] The purpose of section 209 is to attempt to eliminate the risk that a false confession will lead to a conviction — *Erasmus*.[119]

In principle it is possible for one confession to be used to corroborate another in terms of section 209. However, the circumstances in each case will determine whether this can be done in a certain case or not — *Erasmus, supra* and *Khumalo*.[120]

Compliance with the requirements of section 209 does not simply mean that a conviction will follow. There is still the question about whether one can safely rely on the allegations of fact in the confession and whether the guilt of the accused has been proved above reasonable doubt — *Blom*[121] and *Erasmus, supra*.

17.5   POINTING OUT

Section 218(1) of the Criminal Procedure Act of 1977 stipulates that evidence may be led of a fact or thing determined, irrespective of whether or not it was established as a result of an inadmissible admission or confession. However, evidence can be led only on the fact and *not* established as a result of a pointing out or pointer by the accused.

A pointing out is an admission through conduct. It must therefore meet the admissibility requirements of admissions irrespective of whether or not something was discovered by the pointing out. This means that pointing out should at present be made voluntarily to be admissible — *Januarie, supra; Prokureur-Generaal, Natal v Khumalo*.[122] This finding has resulted in section 218(2) of the Criminal Procedure Act of 1977 no longer serving any purpose. We therefore do not discuss this section. All the legal principles with regard to extra-judicial admissions therefore also apply now to pointing out.

17.6 SUGGESTED READING

Kriegler, J. 1993. *Hiemstra Suid-Afrikaanse Strafproses*, 5 ed. Durban: Butterworths.

· · · · · · · · · · · · · · · · · ·

ENDNOTES

1   1945 AD 826.

2   1926 AD 459.

3   Section 25(2)(*a*) of the 1993 Constitution; section 35(1)(*a*) of the 1996 Constitution

4   1926 AD 459 at 462.

5   1981 (1) SA 1002 (A).

6   1992 (1) SACR 292 (EC)

7   1995 (1) SACR 568 (CC).

8   Section 113.

9   Section 25(3)(*c*) of the 1993 Constitution; section 35(3)(*b*) of the 1996 Constitution.

10 Section 115(2)(*b*) of the Criminal Procedure Act of 1977

11 1981 (3) SA 353 (A).

12 Ibid.

13 Section 115(2)(*b*).

14 1981 (3) SA 1233 (A).

15 1994 (1) SACR 420 (A).

16 1981 (3) SA 353 (A).

17 Section 25(3)(*c*): right to silence during the trial.

18 Section 35(3)(*b*): right to silence during the trial.

19 1929 AD 167.

20 1994 (1) PH H13 (A).

21 1987 (3) SA 367 (A).

22 1992 (2) SACR 634 (B).

23 1993 (2) PH H62 (C).

24 1956 (2) SA 288 (A).

25 1993 (2) PH H62 (C), where the accused was also charged with possession of dagga and the court took the same stance. The accused admitted possession but did not exclude the possible grounds for defence provided by an Act. This may be far-fetched, but if there is a possible defence in terms of an Act, this must be expressly excluded before the statement can be regarded as a confession.

26 1975 (3) SA 417 (A).

27 1967 (4) SA 639 (W).

28 1994 (1) SACR 626 (EC).

29 1992 (2) SACR 347 (A).

30 Section 219 of the Criminal Procedure Act of 1977.

31 1993 (1) SACR 691 (ZS).

32 1957 (1) SA 492 (A), where the accused hired an agent to get someone to kill her husband. The first attempt at recruitment failed, after which the agent got two other people to carry out the assignment. The court found that what the agent had told the first person, together with identification of the accused as the principal, was admissible against the principal (accused) as evidence.

33 1993 (2) SACR 388 (EC).

34 1991 (2) SACR 682 (SEC).

35 1949 (3) SA 761 (A).

36 1994 (1) PH H22 (N).

37 1992 (2) SACR 120 (EC)

38 1992 (1) SACR 372 (Tk).

39 1981 (2) SA 738 (A).

40 1994 (1) SACR 447 (A).

41 1994 (1) PH H48 (N).

42 1994 (1) PH H15 (EC).

43 1993 (3) SACR 487 (A).

44 Sections 13(1) and 13(13) of the South African Police Service Act 68 of 1995; members of the SAPS should study this section (particularly section 13(8)(*d*) and (*g*) strictly against the background of section 25 of the 1993 Constitution and section 35 of the 1996 Constitution.

45 Section 25(2) of the 1993 Constitution.

46 Section 25(1)(*a*).

47 Section 25(1)(*b*).

48 Section 25(1)(*c*).

49 Section 25(1)(*d*).

50 Section 25(1)(*e*).

51 Section 25(2)(*a*).

52 Section 25(2)(*b*).

53 Section 25(2)(*c*).

54 Section 25(2)(*d*).

55 Section 35(1)(*a*) of the 1996 Constitution.

56 Section 35(1)(*b*).

57 Section 35(1)(*c*).

58 Section 35(1)(*d*).

59 Section 35(1)(*e*).

60 Section 35(1)(*f*).

61 Section 35(2)(*a*).

62 Section 35(2)(*b*).

63 Section 35(2)(*c*).

64   Section 35(2)(*d*).

65   Section 35(2)(*e*).

66   Section 35(2)(*f*).

67   *Du Plessis v De Klerk* 1996 (3) SA 850 (KH); 1996 (5) BCLR 658 (KH).

68   Section 7(1) en (7(2) of the 1993 Constitution.

69   Section 217.

70   Section 25(2)(*c*) of the 1993 Constitution and section 35(1)(*c*) of the 1996 Constitution.

71   Section 217(1).

72   Section 217(1)(*a*).

73   1927 OPD 16.

74   1993 (2) SACR 461 (C).

75   1993 (2) SACR 464 (C).

76   Section 23 1993 Constitution.

77   Section 32(1) of the 1996 Constitution.

78   Section 25(3) of the 1993 Constitution; section 35(3) of the 1996 Constitution.

79   Section 217(1).

80   Ibid.

81   Section 217(1)(*a*).

82   Section 219A.

83   Section 217(1)(*a*).

84   Ibid.

85   1940 AD 355.

86   1994 (1) SACR 626 (EC).

87   Section 217(1)(*b*)(ii) of the Criminal Procedure Act of 1977.

88   1995 (1) SACR 568 (KH).

89   Sections 25(2)(*a*): the right to silence and the right to be warned; 25(2)(*c*): not to be compelled to make a confession; 25(3)(*c*): the right to silence during the course of the trial; 25(3)(*d*): the right not to be a compellable witness against oneself.

90   1992 (1) SACR 292 (EC) (see the discussion under "voluntary in admissions, above).

91   1981 (1)SA 460 (C).

92   1983 (1) SA 576 (C).

93   Ibid.

94   1982 (1) SA 835 (A).

95   1993 (2) SACR 388 (EC).

96   1993 (1) SACR 582 (Tk).

97   1985 (4) SA 519 (C).

98   1995 (1) SACR 568 (KH).

99   Section 217(1)(*a*) of the Criminal Procedure Act of 1977.

100   1994 (1) SACR 447 (A).

101   1986 (3) SA 196 (A).

102   1965 (2) SA 837 (A) followed in *Mafuya*(2) 1992 (2) SACR 381 (W) and *Gxokwe* 1992 (2) SACR 355 (C).

103   1992 (1) SACR 639 (Nm).

104   Section 217(1)(*b*) of the Criminal Procedure Act of 1977.

105   1991 (2) SACR 489 (EC).

106   1981 (3) SA 1105 (W).

107   1993 (2) SACR (TkA).

108   1994 (2) SACR 182 (C).

109   1992 (1) SACR 347 (A).

110   1994 (1) SACR 575 (A).

111   1992 (1) SACR 138 (A).

112   1989 (1) SA 228 (A).

113   1993 (2) SACR 123 (A).

114   1993 (2) SACR 599 (W).

115   Section 217(3).

116   1940 AD 355.

117   1979 (2) SA 1003 (C).

118   1981 (3) SA 1233 (A).

119   1994 (1) PH H5 (EC).

120   1983 (2) SA 379 (A).

121   1992 (1) SACR 649 (EC).

122   1994 (2) SACR 801 (A).

Chapter 18
The Constitutionality of the Ascertainment of Bodily Features

Dalene Clark

SUMMARY

*I*N line with practices of international policing agencies, section 37 of the Criminal Procedure Act 51 of 1977 empowers a South African police official to ascertain bodily features in specified circumstances.

The constitutionality of these practices is disputed due to the fact that section 37 of the Criminal Procedure Act legally authorises acts which might otherwise give rise to criminal and delictual liability. It is argued that the ascertainment of bodily features impairs the right to privacy, human dignity, the right to freedom and security of the person, and the right not to give self-incriminating evidence, and therefore that this evidence is unconstitutional.

Admittedly section 37 of the Criminal Procedure Act makes serious inroads upon the bodily integrity and right to privacy of an accused. But these inroads should be seen in the light of the fact that the ascertainment of the bodily features and "prints" of an accused often forms an essential component of the investigation of crime and is in many respects a prerequisite for the effective administration of any criminal justice system, including the proper adjudication of a criminal trial.

After balancing the above-mentioned constitutional rights with the alledged limitation thereof it was concluded that the ascertainment of bodily features, as provided for in the Criminal Procedure Act of 1977, will generally be found to be constitutional. The proviso to this statement is that once it has been found that there is an infringement of a fundamental right, this infringement should be consonant with the limitation either embodied in the specific right or as found in the limitation clause.

18.1 INTRODUCTION

This chapter focuses on the constitutionality of the ascertainment of bodily features (section 37 of the Criminal Procedure Act of 1977). In so doing the ambit of the constitutionally protected rights to privacy, dignity, freedom and security of the person and the privilege against self-incrimination are examined to ascertain if, and to what extent, these rights are infringed upon by practices authorised by section 37.

18.2 KEY OBJECTIVES

The key objectives of this chapter are to enable students to:
- understand the necessity of ascertaining bodily features;
- identify the specified circumstances under which bodily features may be ascertained;
- understand the constitutional limitation of the right to privacy in the spheres of registration of bodily features and medical intervention;
- grasp the concept *dignity* and the reason why dignity in this context will not be subject to the limitation clause;
- understand why the ascertainment of bodily features does not amount to self-incrimination.

18.3 APPLICABLE LAW AND INTERNATIONAL INSTRUMENTS

The 1996 Constitution, sections 10, 12, 14, 35, and 36
The Criminal Procedure Act 51 of 1977, section 37
The South African Police Service Act 68 of 1995, section 13
The European Convention on Human Rights and Fundamental Freedoms
(ECHR), articles 3 and 8
Fifth Amendment to the American Constitution

18.4 INTERPRETATION AND DISCUSSION

There are occasions when it is the duty of police officials, when investigating crime and enforcing laws, to take fingerprints and photographs and/or to secure body samples. Body samples which may be relevant to an investigation are the contents of fingernails, toenails, hairs, blood or urine. The aim of the collection of this data — or rather the ascertainment of bodily features — is the identification of the offender or the obtaining of evidence which could link the suspect irrevocably to the crime scene or to the unlawful act which was committed.

The ascertainment of bodily features has been a long-established practice in policing agencies internationally. In line with this trend, section 37 of the Criminal Procedure Act of 1977 empowers a South African police official to ascertain bodily features in specified circumstances. Authoritative subsections in section 37 read as follows:

"(1) Any police official may —

(a) take the finger-prints, palm-prints or foot-prints or may cause any such prints to be taken —

(i) of any person *arrested upon any charge*;

(ii) of any such person *released on bail or on warning* under section 72;

(iii) of any person *arrested* in respect of *any matter* referred to in paragraph (*n*), (*o*) or (*p*) of section 40(1);

(iv) of any person upon whom a *summons* has been served in respect of any offence referred to in *Schedule 1* or any offence with reference to which the *suspension, cancellation or endorsement* of any *licence or permit* or the disqualification in respect of any licence or permit is permissible or prescribed; or

(v) of any person convicted by a court or deemed under section 57(6) to have been convicted in respect of any offence which the Minister has by notice in the *Gazette* declared to be an offence for the purposes of this subparagraph;

> (b) make a person referred to in paragraph (*a*)(i) or (ii) available or cause such person to be available for identification in such condition, position or apparel as the police official may determine;
>
> (c) take such steps as he may deem necessary, in order to ascertain whether the body of any person referred to in paragraph (*a*)(i) or (ii) has any mark, characteristic or distinguishing feature or shows any condition or appearance: Provided that no police official shall take any blood sample of the person concerned, nor shall a police official make an examination of the person concerned, where the person is a female and the police official concerned is not a female.
>
> (d) take a photograph, or may cause a photograph to be taken of a person referred to in paragraph (*a*)(i) or (ii).
>
> (2) (a) Any medical officer of any prison or any district surgeon or, if requested thereto by any police official, any registered medical practitioner or registered nurse may take such steps, including the taking of a blood sample, as may be deemed necessary in order to ascertain whether the body of any person referred to in paragraph (*a*)(i)[1] or (ii)[2] of subsection (1) has any mark, characteristic or distinguishing feature or shows any condition or appearance.
>
> (b) If any registered medical practitioner attached to any hospital is on reasonable grounds of the opinion that the contents of the blood of any person admitted to such hospital for medical attention or treatment may be relevant at any later criminal proceedings, such medical practitioner may take a blood sample of such person or cause such sample to be taken."

In terms of section 13(1) of the South African Police Service Act of 1995 members are enjoined as follows: "Subject to the Constitution and with due regard to the fundamental rights of every person, a member may exercise such powers and shall perform such duties and functions as are by law conferred on or assigned to a police official."

In view of the supremacy of the 1996 Constitution,[3] it is necessary to test the constitutionality of section 37 of the Criminal Procedure Act of 1977 and to determine whether it is inconsistent with any of the rights listed in the Bill of Rights contained in Chapter 2 of the 1996 Constitution. If this section is found to be unconstitutional, members of the South African Police Service will not be able to exercise the powers, duties and functions mentioned in this section.

Objections to the ascertainment of bodily features are based on the premise that it impairs the right to privacy,[4] human dignity,[5] the right to freedom and security of the person,[6] and the right not to give self-incriminating evidence,[7] and therefore that this evidence is unconstitutional.

18.4.1 The right to privacy (section 14 of the 1996 Constitution)

Section 14 of the 1996 Constitution provides for a general right of privacy, together with a direct guarantee of a right to privacy with regard to home life, private communications and the prohibition of unlawful entry and search.[8]

In comparison, article 8 of the European Convention on Human Rights and Fundamental Freedoms (ECHR) provides that "everyone has the right to respect for his private … life".

18.4.1.1 Registration of bodily features of persons

Section 37(1) of the Criminal Procedure Act of 1977[9] empowers a police official to ascertain bodily features only in specified circumstances.

In confirmation of this point, Spoelstra J states in *Nkosi v Barlow NO en andere* 1984 (3) 144 (TPA) at 148:

"Artikel 37(1) se duidelike bewoording magtig 'n polisiebeampte om vir 'n regmatige doel, die vingerafdrukke van 'n persoon wat in hegtenis is of wat op borgtog vrygelaat is, te neem. Solank as wat daardie vereistes teenwoordig is, duur die bevoegdheid voort. Ek vind niks in die bepaling wat aantoon dat die bevoegdheid beëindig word voor skuldigbevinding nie. Na skuldigbevinding moet 'n bevel van die hof verkry word (Art 37(4)).

"Dit dui daarop dat die polisiebeampte se bevoegdheid by skuldigbevinding of vryspraak beëindig word."

Retention of this evidence on a central register is restricted by section 37(5) of the Criminal Procedure Act of 1977 which makes provision for the obligatory destruction of prints — as well as the record of steps taken in terms of section 37 of the Criminal Procedure Act in the following circumstances:

(i)   the person concerned is found not guilty at his or her trial; or

(ii)   the conviction is set aside by a superior court; or

(iii)   the accused is discharged at a preparatory examination; or

(iv)   no criminal proceedings with reference to which such prints or photographs were taken or such record was made are instituted against the person concerned in any court; or

(v)   the prosecution declines to prosecute such person.

The existing law of general application pertaining to the ascertainment of bodily features, namely the Criminal Procedure Act of 1977, does not make provision for the registration of members of the public who do not have criminal records and, furthermore, where any of the circumstances in section 37(5) are applicable the Criminal Record Section is obliged to destroy prints. The opinion is held that the existing law makes every attempt to minimise any necessitated infringement of the right to privacy.

Looking abroad, Strasbourg case law allows registration by the police and the judiciary. The European Commission of Human Rights (ECHR) has found that this does not conflict with Article 8 of the ECHR, not even when the registration concerns persons who do not have any criminal record.[10], [11]

The ECHR has held that the keeping of records, including fingerprints and photographs relating to criminal cases of the past, is necessary in a modern democratic society for the prevention of crime and is therefore in the interests of public safety (Application No 1307/61, COll 9, at 53). In this case, the applicant had been tried on a criminal charge in connection with which the relevant records had been compiled, although his conviction was ultimately quashed.

In a case where suspected terrorists were lawfully detained and their fingerprints and photographs taken involuntarily, even though they had not been charged with or convicted of criminal offences, it was found by the ECHR that, in the circumstances of the case, such action was "in accordance with the law" and "necessary in a modern democratic society" for the "prevention of ... crime" (report of the Commission of 18 March 1981, Application Nos 8022/77, 8025/77, 8027/77, DR 25, at 15). As to the retention of such fingerprints and photographs after release (in the case of persons against whom no suspicion existed), it was found that, balancing the relatively slight interference with the applicants' right to privacy (due to the nature of the records) against the pressing need to combat terrorist activity, this could be considered necessary in the interest of public safety and for the prevention of crime.

Although the right to register persons under South African law is more restrictive than the position under comparative law, it still potentially infringes a person's right to privacy. In terms of paragraph 2 of Article 8 of the ECHR, limitations to the right to privacy are only authorised if they are prescribed by law and are necessary in a democratic society in the interests of public safety. The opinion is held that, taking into account the interests of public safety, section 14 of the 1996 Constitution may be reasonably and justifiably limited in terms of section 36 of the Constitution (the limitation clause).

18.4.1.2 Medical intervention

Another example of interference with private life is compulsory subjection to a medical examination. This intervention also impacts on the right in subsection 12(2)(*b*), which provides that "everyone has the right ... to security in and control over their body".

Section 37(2) of the Criminal Procedure Act of 1977[12] makes provision for medical intervention. Du Toit[13] submits that a police official may assist a registered medical practitioner or registered nurse to draw a blood sample from an "unwilling" person in circumstances where the police official requested the doctor or nurse to take the sample and the person concerned is someone referred to in section 37(1)(*a*)(i) or (ii). Reasonable force would presumably be permissible if such a person should refuse to have a blood sample taken or behave in such a manner as to make it clear that he/she does not want to co-operate. There are no statutory provisions compelling a person under sanction of penalty to submit to the taking of a sample of his/her blood. Section 37 of the Criminal Procedure Act merely grants rights to certain specific persons to take blood samples or to cause such blood samples to be taken. A refusal or unwillingness to co-operate might lead to an adverse inference.

In a situation where force in terms of section 37 becomes necessary the police official must act in accordance with section 13(3)(*b*) of the South African Police Service Act of 1995 which states that:

"Where a member who performs an official duty is authorised by law to use force, he or she may use only the minimum force which is reasonable in the circumstances."

In international law the European Commission of Human Rights states that:

"A compulsory medical intervention, even if it is of minor importance, must be considered as an interference with this right."

So far the only complaints which have been submitted to the Commission have been those of persons who had to undergo such an examination as suspects. Applicants were told that such examinations constitute a normal and frequently also desirable element of the investigation of a case.[14] Firstly, it should be ascertained whether such examinations are authorised by law and, secondly, whether subjection thereto could be justified on the basis of one of the grounds of limitation. In Application 8239/78[15] the Commission considered a blood test aimed at the determination of the alcohol content of a person's bloodstream in connection with traffic legislation as justified "for the protection of the rights of others".

Where a person refused to provide a sample of his blood in a case of driving a motor vehicle and being suspected of doing so under the influence of alcohol, he was convicted of an offence of refusing to give such blood sample contrary to domestic laws. The ECHR held, amongst other things, that the legislation of the state concerned was designed "for the protection of the rights of others" and "more particularly road safety and the health of other people". It concluded that, while compulsory blood testing may be seen as constituting a violation of private life within the meaning of Article 8, paragraph 1 of the ECHR, it may also be seen as necessary for the protection of the rights of others, within the meaning of Article 8, paragraph 2 (Application No 8339/78, DR 17 at 184). In other words, for the reasons given above, the limitation of this right was justifiable.

In *Breithaupt v Abram*[16] the United States Supreme Court made the following pronouncement with regard to blood tests:

"Modern community living requires modern scientific methods of crime detection lest the public go unprotected. The increasing slaughter on our highways, most of which should be avoidable, now reaches the astounding figures only heard of on the battle-field. As against the right of an individual that his person be held inviolable, even against so slight an intrusion as is involved in applying a blood test of the kind to which millions of Americans submit as a matter of course nearly every day, must be set the interests of society in the scientific determination of intoxication, one of the great causes of the mortal hazards of the road. And the more so since the test likewise may establish innocence, thus affording protection against the treachery of judgement based on one or more of the senses."

In the light of the foregoing international case law and section 36 of the 1996 Constitution, it is contended that medical intervention in terms of section 37 of the Criminal Procedure Act of 1977 will only be deemed constitutional if the importance of the purpose of the limitation, for example protection of the rights of others, is proved and that the least restrictive means to achieve the purpose were used. It is held that if the last-mentioned fact can be proved, the momentary loss of control over a person's body in the event of the person's refusing medical intervention will be deemed reasonable and justifiable.

18.4.2   The right to dignity and the right to freedom and security of the person (sections 10 and 12 of the 1996 Constitution)

For the purpose of this discussion, it is contended that the right to dignity is jointly entrenched in section 10 and subsection 12(1)(e) of the 1996 Constitution, and that such dignity may not be impaired by the state through any conduct which can be described as cruel, inhuman or degrading.

Section 10 and subsection 12(1)(e) of the 1996 Constitution read as follows:

"10.   Everyone has inherent dignity and the right to have their dignity respected and protected."

"12.(1)   Everyone has the right to freedom and security of the person, which includes the right —

(e)   not to be treated or punished in a cruel, inhuman or degrading way."

When deciding whether the ascertainment of bodily features, in this case the taking of fingerprints, conflicted with the entrenched protection of a person's dignity, Claasen J found in *S v Huma*[17] that "...I do not regard the taking of a person's fingerprints as a form of punishment. The taking of fingerprints cannot therefore be dealt with in the same way as inhuman, cruel or degrading punishment. Taking fingerprints cannot fall into the same category as, for instance, corporal punishment or incarceration or other kinds of punishment." As the aim of ascertaining bodily features, whether it be taking a blood sample or the taking of a photograph, is in no way to punish a person, the opinion is held that none of the actions in terms of section 37 of the Criminal Procedure Act of 1977 can be regarded as punishment.

The question remains as to whether actions in terms of this latter section could amount to cruel, inhuman or degrading treatment impairing a person's dignity in contravention of sections 10 and 12(1)(*e*) of the 1996 Constitution.

"Cruel treatment" has been defined by the *Collins English Dictionary* as "causing or inflicting pain without pity". The meaning of the word "inhuman", according to the *Oxford English Dictionary,* is "destitute of natural kindness or pity, brutal, unfeeling, cruel, savage, barbarous". In *Tyrer v United Kingdom* 2 EHRR 1, the European Court on Human Rights stated that suffering to which a person is subjected must attain a particular level before it can be classified as "inhuman". In *Denmark et al v Greece*[18] inhuman treatment has been defined as treatment which deliberately causes severe suffering, mental or physical, which in a particular situation is unjustifiable. In terms of the *Oxford English Dictionary,* "to degrade" means "to lower in estimation, to bring into dishonour or contempt; to lower in character or quality; to debase".

Internationally, the right embodied in section 12(1)(*e*) is absolute, non-derogable and unqualified. All that is therefore required to establish a violation of the relevant section is a finding that the state concerned has failed to comply with its obligation in respect of any one of these modes of conduct. No limitation is possible.

Article 3 of the European Convention on Human Rights provides that: "No one shall be subjected to ... inhuman or degrading treatment ...", and this fundamental provision should be kept in mind at all times when the taking of body samples is required by domestic law and procedure. Article 3 of the ECHR corresponds with section 12(1)(*e*) of the Constitution which reads as follows: "not to be treated ... in a cruel, inhuman or degrading way".

No physical pain accompanies most of the processes used to ascertain bodily features, for example taking a photograph or fingerprints. As stated by Claasen J in *S v Huma*,[19] "by comparison, the taking of a blood sample constitutes more of an intrusion into a person's physical integrity than the mere taking of one's fingerprints. When a blood sample is taken the skin is ruptured and it is accompanied by a small element of pain." If blood is acquired in accordance with section 37, it will be done by medical staff and therefore not in a cruel, inhuman or degrading manner.

When evaluating whether section 37 is in conflict with the aforementioned constitutional sections, the following should be kept in mind. This evidence is often an essential component of the investigation of crime and is in many respects a prerequisite for the effective administration of any criminal justice system including the proper adjudication of a criminal trial. The manner in which the features are ascertained must naturally fall within the parameters of acceptable and civilised standards of modern society. If bodily features are gathered in an inhumane or degrading manner, there is no question that this action will be found to be unconstitutional and that the evidence will be excluded in trial. In accordance with international jurisprudence, no limitation of subsection 12(1)(*e*) will be condoned. If the person's dignity, as stated in section 10, is impaired in accordance with the limitation clause, it is felt that it will be deemed to be reasonable and justifiable.

18.4.3   The privilege against self-incrimination

For the purpose of determining whether or not the ascertainment of bodily features constitutes a violation of the privilege against self-incrimination, the following sections in the Constitution should be borne in mind. Subsections 35(1)(*b*)(ii) and (*c*) of the 1996 Constitution provide for the following:

"Everyone who is arrested for allegedly committing an offence has the right —

(*b*)(ii)   to be informed promptly of the consequences of making any statement;

(*c*)   not to be compelled to make a confession or admission which could be used in evidence against that person."

Furthermore section 35(3)(*j*) provides that:

"Every accused has a right to a fair trial, which includes the right —

(*j*)   not to be compelled to give self-incriminating evidence."

As stated by Judge Combrink in *S v Maphumulo & another*[20] "the right which an accused person has not to be compelled to make a confession or an admission against his interest in criminal proceedings has now been enshrined in the Constitution. But it has been part of our common law for many generations, and finds expression in the maxim *nemo tenetur se ipsum prodere*. It means that no-one is bound to incriminate or betray himself." When looking at the question whether the taking of the accused's fingerprints would amount to a confession or admission by him, Judge Combrink found that "... it is necessary to draw a very clear distinction between the bodily appearance and physical characteristics of an accused person and his statements or communications ... where an accused is identified by a scar across his face, or a crooked nose, or an artificial leg, evidence of that might be placed before a court in support of a criminal charge against him. Such evidence is obviously a far cry from a statement whether by conduct or expressly made by an accused person, in which he makes an admission of involvement in a criminal offence or confesses it."[21]

According to Du Toit *et al*,[22] "[t]he common-law privilege against self-incrimination is confined to communications, whereas section 37 of the Criminal Procedure Act deals with the ascertainment of an accused's bodily or physical features or conditions which are not obtained as a result of a communication emanating from the accused".

In *In re R v Matemba* 1941 AD 75 it was said:

"Now where a palm print is being taken from an accused person he is entirely passive. He is not being compelled to give evidence or confess when his photograph is being taken or when he is put upon an identification parade or when he is made to show a scar in Court."

In *Nkosi v Barlow*[23] Judge Spoelstra referred to Wigmore[24] who explains that an inspection or ascertainment of bodily features does not violate the privilege against self incrimination.

"... because it does not call on the accused as a witness — ie. upon his testimonial responsibility. That he may in such cases be required sometimes to exercise muscular action — as when he is required to take off his shoes or roll up his sleeve — is immaterial ... What is obtained from the accused by such action is not testimony about his body, but his body itself ... Unless some attempt is made to secure a communication — written, oral or otherwise — ... the demand upon him is not a testimonial one."

In the Supreme Court of the United States the permissibility of identification by fingerprints or by palm-prints is beyond doubt.[25]

The use of a picture of the accused taken by a police officer, after his arrest and while in the custody of the officer, for the purpose of identification, was held not to violate his privilege against self-incrimination in *Schaffer v United States*,[26] the court saying:

"In taking and using the photographic picture there was no violation of any constitutional right. There is no pretence that there was any excessive force or illegal duress employed by the officer in taking the picture. We know that it is the daily practice of the police officers and detectives of crime to use photographic pictures for the discovery and identification of criminals, and that, without such means, many criminals would escape detection or identification. It could as well be contended that a prisoner could lawfully refuse to allow himself to be seen, while in prison, by a witness brought to identify him, or that he could rightfully refuse to uncover himself, or to remove a mark, in court, to enable witnesses to identify him as the party accused as that he could rightfully refuse to allow an officer, in whose custody he remained, to set an instrument and take his likeness for purposes of proof and identification. It is one of the usual means employed in the police service of the country, and it would be matter of regret to have its use unduly restricted upon any fanciful theory or constitutional privilege."

In *Novak v District of Columbia*[27] it was found that, irrespective of the accused's consent, the taking of a urine specimen from a person accused of driving an automobile while intoxicated was held not to violate the prohibition of the Fourth Amendment against unreasonable search and seizure, nor, where the specimen was given voluntarily, to violate the privilege against self-incrimination guaranteed by the Fifth Amendment, the court assuming, but not deciding, that the latter privilege would be violated if the specimen was given involuntarily.

In *Schmerber v California* [28] the US Supreme Court found that:

"We therefore must now decide whether the withdrawal of the blood and admission in evidence of the analysis involved in this case violated petitioner's privilege. We hold that the privilege protects an accused only from being compelled to testify against himself, or otherwise provide the State with evidence of a testimonial or communicative nature, and that the withdrawal of blood and the use of the analysis in question in this case did not involve compulsion to these ends."

According to Judge Claasen in *S v Huma*,[29] "[i]t must be remembered that the common-law principle against self-incrimination, as codified in the Fifth Amendment to the American Constitution ('... nor shall be compelled in a criminal case to be a witness against himself ...') is almost the same as that contained in section 25(3)(*d*) of our Interim Constitution". (Note that section 25(3)(*d*) of the Interim Constitution corresponds with section 35(3)(*j*) of the 1996 Constitution). After adducing all the arguments placed before him, Judge Combrink found in *S v Maphumulo* [30] that "I have concluded, accordingly, that the taking of the accused's fingerprints, whether it is voluntarily given by them or taken under compulsion in terms of the empowerment thereto provided by section 37(1), would not constitute evidence given by the accused in the form of testimony emanating from him, and such would not violate his rights as contained in section 25(2)(*c*) [note that this is the equivalent of section 35(1)(*c*) of the Constitution 1996], or section 25(3)(*d*) [section 35(3)(*j*) of the 1996 Constitution] of the Constitution". Judge Combrink then continues and finds that "[i]n the result, the police are in the circumstances entitled in terms of the power conferred upon them by the provisions of section 37(1), to take the accused's fingerprints forcibly if necessary. In doing so, however, the police are enjoined to exercise discretion and care, and to have due regard of the accused."

18.5   CONCLUSION

Section 37 of the Criminal Procedure Act of 1977 makes serious inroads on the bodily integrity and right to privacy of an accused. But these inroads should be seen in the light of the fact that the ascertainment of the bodily features and "prints" of an accused often forms an essential component of the investigation of crime and is in many respects a prerequisite for the effective administration of any criminal justice system, including the proper adjudication of a criminal trial. An important consequence or effect of section 37 of the Criminal Procedure Act is that acts which might otherwise give rise to criminal and delictual liability are legally authorised. Such acts should, however, be performed within the limits of the authority of section 37 of the Act. A police official, for example, may not take a blood sample (see section 37(1)(*c*) of the Criminal Procedure Act). The defence of "authority" will in such an instance not be available to a police official who is subsequently charged with assault.

In conclusion it is held that the ascertainment of bodily features as provided for in the Criminal Procedure Act of 1977 will generally be found to be constitutional. The proviso to this statement is that, once it has been found that there is an infringement of a fundamental right, this infringement should be consonant with the limitation either embodied in the specific right or as found in the limitation clause.

An interesting question to which there is not a simple or perhaps any answer, is the question of what should be done in the exceptional cases where persons on grounds of fear, concern for health, or religious scruple might prefer some other means of testing, such as the "breathalyser" test instead of a blood test. Until the Constitutional Court has passed judgment on this matter, it is felt that if there is an alternative method of testing, such method should be used.

Every legal system has to grapple with a tension between respect for individual freedom and the urgent need to combat crime effectively. A society in which dangerous criminals mostly go free because of procedural technicalities will be neither safe, nor just. It has become a cliché to call for the growth of a human rights culture. However, without an awareness of the value and importance of human rights and the strong will to preserve them amongst judges, the legal profession and the public, any Bill of Rights will be worth little more than the paper on which it is written. With a human rights culture and the desire continually to strive for democracy, South Africa may have a legal system respected by its citizens and by all civilized people.

Alderson[31] says, "free people expect much from their police". The police in such societies stand at the point of balance, "on the one hand securing human rights and, on the other, exercising their lawful powers given to them by governments in the name of the people, to protect the people and their institutions". On the one hand, the police are there to implement and fulfil the fundamental human rights of people but, on the other hand, they have the authority to encroach and infringe on those very same fundamental human rights. This makes the police very unique among human rights actors. The courts have a particular responsibility, lawyers have their role, NGOs theirs, but the police have a very special role.[32]

18.6   SUGGESTED READING AND SOURCES

Alderson, J. 1984. *Human Rights and the Police.* Council of Europe.

Beaudoin, Gerald A & Reutushny, Ed. 1989. *Canadian Charter of Rights and Freedoms,* 2 ed. Carborough, Ontario, Canada: Carswell.

Cachalia *et al.* 1994. *Fundamental Rights in the New Constitution.* Cape Town: Juta.

Du Toit, E, *et al.* 1991. *Commentary on the Criminal Procedure Act.* Cape Town: Juta.

Kriegler, J. 1993. *Hiemstra. Suid-Afrikaanse Strafproses,* 5 ed. Durban: Butterworths

Van Dijk, P, *et al.* 1990. *Theory and Practice of the European Convention on Human Rights,* 2 ed.

Wigmore, 1940 (revised). *A Treatise on the Anglo American System of Evidence in Trials at Common Law.*

Titus, DJ. 1994. *Human Rights and the South African Police.* Paper delivered on 27 June 1994 at the Human Rights Conference: SA Police College.

····················

ENDNOTES

1 "(i) of any person arrested upon any charge".

2 "(ii) of any such person released on bail or on warning under section 72".

3 Section 2 of the 1996 Constitution.

4 Section 14 of the 1996 Constitution.

5 Section 10 of the 1996 Constitution.

6 Section 12 of the 1996 Constitution.

7 Section 35(3)(j) of the 1996 Constitution.

8 Cachalia *et al* at 43.

9 See 18.4 above.

10 See Appl 5877/72, *X v United Kingdom,* Yearbook /XVI (1973), at 328 (388), where the complaint concerned the taking, and storing in a file, of photographs of the applicant by the police for possible future identification purposes. The Commission evidently considered it decisive here that the photographs had not been released for publication or used for purposes other than police ends.

11 Van Dijk, Godefrickus & Van Hoof.

12 See 18.4 above.

13 Du Toit 3–13.

14 Appl 986/61, *X v Federal Republic Germany,* Yearbook V (1962) at 192 (198).

15 *X v The Netherlands* D & R 6 (1979) at 184 (189).

16 352 US 432, 1 L ed 2d 448, 77 S Ct 408.

17 1995 (2) SACR 411 (W) at 414–415.

18 (3321–3/67; 3344/67 YB 12 *bis*), as cited in Cachalia *et al* at 38 and 39.

19 1995 (2) SACR 411 (W) at 416 d–e.

20 1996 (2) BCLR 167(N) at 170 E.

21 *S v Maphumulo* at 171 B–D.

22 Du Toit *et al* 3–1.

23 1984 (3) SA 148 (T) at 154F–H.

24 1984 (3) SA 148 (T) at 154F–H.

25 Annotations in 16 ALR 370 and 63 ALR 1324, as well as annotation in 3 ALR 1706.

26 (1904) 24 App DC 417, cert den 196 US 639, 49 L ed 631, 25 S Ct 795.

27 (1946, Mun Ct App Dist Col) 49 A2d 88, reviewed on other grounds 82 App DC 95, 160 F2d 588.

28 384 US 757, 16 L ed 2d 908, 86 S Ct 1826.

29 At 419B.

30 At 172J–173B.

31 Alderson 19.

32 Titus, paper delivered.

Chapter 19
The Right to Information

Helene Lötz

SUMMARY

*I*N the past the public right to information held by the government was ruled and regulated by common law. While other countries have passed various statutes with the purpose of protecting the citizen's right to know, in South Africa many statutes have been enacted precisely to prevent the citizen from obtaining information.

The Constitution of 1993 created a right of access for individuals to information in government possession. This right creates two distinct problems. In the first place, the citizen's right to be informed could encroach upon other people's right to privacy. Secondly, matters of state security must of necessity remain confidential in the public interest. The problem of balancing these rights was left to our courts to resolve.

Since the inception of the Constitution, several applications have been brought in the Supreme Court invoking section 23 in order to obtain access to information contained in police dockets. The question of the extent of the information which may be disclosed was referred to the Constitutional Court in the *Shabalala*[1] case.

In the 1996 Constitution access to government information will be regulated by section 32. This section will allow the individual seeking information far wider rights.

19.1 INTRODUCTION

In the past the public had little or no access to information in the possession of the state. With the inception of the 1993 Constitution and the initiatives towards transparent government, the position has changed drastically. The Constitution, and other legislation to be enacted in the near future, will protect the individual's rights and interests in this regard. There are, however, certain kinds of information which have to remain confidential in the public interest.

19.2 KEY OBJECTIVES

The key objectives of this chapter are to enable students to:
* discuss the position regarding access to information held by the government before the inception of the 1993 Constitution;
* discuss international law;
* interpret section 23 of the 1993 Constitution;
* discuss the post-constitutional decisions by the Supreme Court and the Constitutional Court;
* interpret section 32 of the 1996 Constitution.

19.3 APPLICABLE LAW

19.3.1 South Africa

The Constitution, Act 200 of 1993, sections 23,25(3), 35

The Constitution of 1996, section 32
The Criminal Procedure Act 51 of 1977, section 202
The Protection of Information Act 84 of 1982
The Open Democracy Bill of 1996

19.3.2 Canada

Access to Information Act of 1982
Canadian Charter of Rights and Freedoms Schedule B to the Constitution Act
of 1982, section 7

19.3.3 United States of America

Freedom of Information Act of 1966
Privacy Act 5 USC 552a of 1988
Open Meetings Act 5 USC 552b of 1988

19.4 INTERPRETATION AND DISCUSSION

19.4.1 The position in South Africa before the 1993 Constitution

According to Baxter, no general legislation exists which allows the individual access to information in government possession. On the contrary, various statutes actually prohibit such access.[2] An example of such legislation is the Protection of Information Act.[3]

There are, however, various statutes which permit access to documents and records in the possession of administrative bodies, for example licensing and transport authorities.

Baxter states that "secrecy is an undoubted cause of maladministration, yet it still permeates many facets of the administrative process" and further states that "this is particularly true in South Africa". Even after abuses of power have come to light, secrecy has been allowed to continue.[4]

Even though secrecy leads to the concealment of information which should be available to the public, the sensitive or strategic nature of certain kinds of information requires that such information remain confidential. Examples are matters relating to defence, fiscal policy, international relations, information held in confidence and information of a personal nature.[5] During the litigation process it is recognised that a common-law privilege is attached to certain documents which need therefore not be disclosed.

Generally speaking, the issue of privileged documents has come to the fore in criminal trials. In accordance with common-law principles, the access to police dockets, for example, has been limited — a fact which could seriously prejudice the accused in his/her preparation for trial.

The police, in particular, often need the protection of privilege so that they can actively pursue their duty of preventing and detecting crime. This privilege is not intended to protect the members of the police service themselves, but rather to protect their sources of information and their methods of investigation.

This privilege has been recognised by our courts since 1933 when in the *Abelson*[6] case it was found that it was in the public interest to maintain secrecy regarding certain methods used by the police. In 1954 the privileges recognised by our courts were: (i) state secrets; (ii) information regarding the identity of informers; and (iii) the confidential communication between client and legal representative.[7] In this case the recognised privileges were extended to the statements of state witnesses.

In the *Peake* case[8] it was found that public interest is a common-law privilege, a view which was later supported by section 202 of the Criminal Procedure Act 51 of 1977.

In *Campbell & others*[9] it was found that statements obtained from state witnesses were privileged and that documents in police dockets were prima facie not open to disclosure. In *S v Jija*,[10] however, the court stated that disclosure was the rule and privilege the exception.

The so-called public interest privilege which is recognised in common law and by statute has the effect of causing certain evidence to be exempted from disclosure.

The protection against disclosure applies in both civil and criminal trials. In civil trials the parties are compelled by the Rules of Court to full disclosure before trial, with the exception of documents to which the attorney/client privilege applies.

In criminal trials, however, disclosure has traditionally been more limited and the practice of preparatory examination, which gave the accused the opportunity to establish the extent of the evidence against him/her, has fallen into disuse. The position according to case law was thus that the accused could generally not gain access to police dockets in order to prepare his/her defence.

19.4.2 The international position

19.4.2.1 The position in Canada

The Access to Information Act of 1982 regulates access to information in Canada. In section 2, under the heading "Purpose of Act", it is stated:

> "The purpose of this Act is to extend the present laws of Canada to provide a right of access to information in records under control of a government institution in accordance with principles that government information should be available to the public, that necessary exceptions to the right of access should be limited and specific and that decisions on the disclosure of government information should be reviewed independantly of government."

As far as disclosure in criminal trials is concerned, it was stated in *R v Stinchcombe*[11] that justice would be better served where both parties were able to address the relevant issues, where complete information was available, and all parties could prepare for trial. In *NLRB v Robbins Tyre and Rubber Co*[12] it was said that a "trial by ambush could be a disservice to the truth."

In the *Stinchcombe* case it was stated that there are no valid reasons for the view that there is no broad duty to disclose. Supported by section 7 of the Canadian Charter of Rights and Freedoms, the opportunity to make full answer and defence is regarded as one of the pillars of criminal justice and serves to ensure that the innocent are not convicted. The obligation to disclose is not absolute, as there is a discretion to withhold certain information. The courts, on the other hand, have a discretion to reveal information.

19.4.2.2   The position in the United States of America

In her article "Vryheid van inligting in die VSA", Du Plessis[13] summarises the position in the USA as follows:

> "In this article the Freedom of Information Act of the USA is studied, to consider whether a right to information can be protected by statute. It is found that there is justification for the existence of this Act. The Act limits the right to information by means of certain exceptions in the public interest."

In her article the writer further states that the USA was one of the first countries to introduce legislation to protect the right of the individual to information. The Freedom of Information Act was promulgated in 1966. This Act regulates the access to records or documents in possession of a state department or agency.[14]

Two other statutes, the Privacy Act[15] and the Open Meetings or so-called Sunshine Act,[16] have similar functions. The Privacy Act allows an individual the right of access to his/her personal files to ensure the proper administration thereof, while the Sunshine Act ensures that public matters which are discussed at state department level are open to public scrutiny.

True democracy necessitates the political participation of the citizens. Since it is not possible for citizens to participate in the actual governing process, the only alternative is for the citizen to control the elected government by constantly receiving information of governmental activity.[17]

Some limits have to exist and some of the exceptions are national security, privacy of the individual, law enforcement and foreign policy.[18] A balance must be maintained between the public right to be informed, on the one hand, and secrecy in the public interest on the other.

19.4.3   The position in South Africa after the 1993 Constitution

In the 1993 Constitution access to information in possession of the government is provided for in section 23, which reads as follows:

> "Every person shall have the right of access to all information held by the state or any of its organs at any level of government in so

far as such information is required for the exercise or protection of any of his or her rights."

This section of the Constitution has two built-in qualifications which limit access to information, namely:

- the right has vertical application only, that is, between the state and the person requesting the information; and
- the information must be required for the purpose of the exercise or protection of the person's rights.

The rights referred to in this section are not limited to the rights accorded by Chapter 3, but include all fundamental rights.

Soon after the commencement of the 1993 Constitution, a number of applications were brought in the Supreme Court for access to police dockets in criminal cases.[19] In *Khala v The Minister of Safety and Security*[20] the applicant was arrested in 1992 and later released without being charged; as a result, the applicant instituted action for unlawful arrest and detention. The SAP refused the applicant's request for access to the police docket and application was brought for an order that the defendant be directed to make available for inspection and copy certain documents which were not disclosed.

The court interpreted the Constitution and specifically the provisions of section 23. With reference to the *Qozeleni* case (*supra*), the court found that, without the necessary information, the applicant would not be able to determine whether the contents of the docket would be useful in the trial and that disclosure of the information would be necessary to exercise and protect his rights. The court found that the plaintiff clearly required the information contained in the police docket and had a right, in terms of section 23, to obtain access to the required information.

Under the heading "docket privilege", the court stated that before 1954 the privileges recognised by our courts were: (i) evidence of state secrets, (ii) the identity of informers in criminal proceedings, and (iii) professional privilege, that is, communication between a legal adviser and his/her client.

The only privilege recognised as far as police dockets were concerned was "informer privilege". This privilege was extended in *Rex v Steyn* (*supra*) to include the statements of witnesses, and was further extended from time to time.

In an attempt to prevent access to the police docket, the defendant submitted an additional affidavit by the Commissioner of the South African Police in which reference was made to the high crime rate in South Africa; this meant that it was not in the public interest to make certain kinds of information available. In discussing this the judge concluded that it was indeed public policy that certain kinds of information should remain confidential, but distinguished between information which is privileged and that which is not privileged.

The court declared that allowing the applicant access to the police docket would cause risk to the state should the state decide to proceed with the criminal trial. Even though the court found that the rights of the applicant outweighed the interests of the state, an order for full disclosure was not made. The state was given the opportunity to claim privilege in particular documents.

In the *Shabalala* case (*supra*) the five accused were charged with murder. They applied for copies of the relevant police dockets, including witness statements and lists of exhibits in possession of the state. The state refused access and maintained that, in terms of *R v Steyn* (*supra*), there exists a "blanket docket privilege" which protects the contents of a police docket. The applicants maintained that section 23 of the 1993 Constitution, read together with section 25(3) (right to a fair trial) and section 35 (the interpretation clause), entitled them to access to the police docket.

The application was refused and the following question relating to docket privilege was referred to the Constitutional Court:

- whether section 23 of the 1993 Constitution could be used to exercise the right to a fair trial as provided for in section 25(3), and, if so, whether the accused could have access to the police docket.

The Constitutional Court ordered the following with regard to the police.

- The "blanket docket privilege", as expressed in *R v Steyn* (*supra*), is unconstitutional, as it protects all information from disclosure in all circumstances.
- Ordinarily an accused is entitled to information which could serve to prove his/her innocence or to assist in his/her defence. This would include access to witness statements. But, in certain circumstances, the prosecution may be able to justify their refusal to disclose information on the grounds that the information sought is not necessary for the purposes of a fair trial.
- If the state can show that the disclosure of information could create a reasonable risk that such access could lead to (a) the disclosure of state secrets; (b) the disclosure of the identity of informers; (c) the intimidation of witnesses; or (d) that it could prejudice the proper ends of justice, the court has a discretion to refuse or allow such an application.

It should be remembered that all courts are now bound by this decision of the Constitutional Court until such time as this Court should decide to amend the judgment.

19.4.4   The Constitution of 1996

In the 1996 Constitution access to information is regulated by section 32, which reads as follows:

> "(1)   Everyone has the right of access to —
>   (*a*)   any information held by the state; and
>   (*b*)   any information that is held by another person and that is required for the exercise or protection of any rights.

"(2)   National legislation must be enacted to give effect to this right, and may provide for reasonable measures to alleviate the administrative and financial burden on the state."

It is clear that the qualifications of section 23 of the 1993 Constitution have been removed as far as information in possession of the state is concerned. In the 1996 Constitution a person requesting information from the state will not have to prove that their request is for the purpose of protecting or exercising their rights. Furthermore, the rights will have both vertical and horizontal application, in that they will apply between state and subject as well as between the individual and private persons, which will include legal persons (that is, companies).

It should be remembered that the fact that the qualifications of section 23 will be omitted in the future does not mean that any information will be disclosed to any person requesting such information. Other rights in the Bill of Rights, such as human dignity (section 10), privacy (section 14) and the limitations clause (section 36), will continue to limit the right provided for in section 32. As determined in section 32(2), legislation will be enacted in the form of the Open Democracy Bill of 1996 to regulate the disclosure of information. In such an Act it is envisaged that, although all persons have the right of access to information held by the state, certain exceptions will be permitted such as, for example, the defence and security of the Republic, legal professional privilege, international relations, law enforcement, records given in confidence, to mention but a few.

It must also be borne in mind that the information contained in police dockets is not the only information held by the SAPS. Personnel records, files held in the archives, computer information in the Crime Administration System, fingerpints and records of previous convictions held by the Crime Record Centre are but a few examples of the type of information which is held by a government department such as the SAPS. All information held is subject to the following restrictions: the decision by the Constitutional Court in the *Shabalala* case, the other rights entrenched in the Bill of Rights,and other legislation of general application.

It remains to be seen whether the Constitutional Court will find a reason to alter the decision in the *Shabalala* case after the inception of the 1996 Constitution.

19.5   SUGGESTED READING AND SOURCES

Baxter, L. 1984. *Administrative Law*, 2 ed. Cape Town: Juta.

Cachalia, A, Cheadle, H, Davis, D, Haysom, N, Maduna, P, & Marcus, G. 1994. *Fundamental Rights in the New Constitution*. Cape Town: Juta.

Chaskalson, M, Kentridge, J, Klaaren, J, Marcus, G, Spitz, D & Woolman, S. 1996. *Constitutional Law of South Africa*. Cape Town: Juta.

Du Plessis, W. 1987. *TRW* vol 12 December 179.

Mathews, AS. 1978. *The Darker Reaches of Government*. Cape Town: Juta.

Shils, EA. 1956. *The Torment of Secrecy*. Glencoe: Free Press.

....

ENDNOTES

1   *Shabalala v The Attorney-General of the Transvaal & The Commissioner of the South African Police* CCT/23/94; 1995 (1) SA 608 (CT).

2   Baxter 235.

3   Act 84 of 1982.

4   Baxter 234.

5   Baxter 233.

6   1933 TPD 227.

7   *R v Steyn* 1954 (1) SA 324 AD.

8   1962 (4) SA 288 (K).

9   1991 (1) SACR 435 NM.

10 1991 (2) SA 52.

11 1992 68 CCC (3d) I.

12 437 US 214, 57 LED 2d 159.

13 Du Plessis 179.

14 5 USC 552 1988.

15 5 USC 552a 1988.

16 5 USC 552b 1988.

17 Mathews 1–6.

18 Shils 24–26.

19 *The State v Pumla Fani & others* 1994 (3) SA 619 (E); *Sipho Walter Qozeleni v The Minister of Law and Order* 1994 (3) SA 625 (E); *Mkhuseli Majavu v The State* 1994 (4) SA 268 (Ck).

20 1994 (4) SA 218 (W).

Chapter 20
Bail

Jeanette Neveling

Jan H. Bezuidenhout

SUMMARY

*B*AIL has become a sensitive, if not contentious, issue in constitutional debate. The public very often only learns of heinous crimes when the media report on the outcome of the accused's bail application. When bail is granted, it sometimes leaves a strong perception that human rights benefit the perpetrator to the disadvantage of law-abiding citizens.

There are two distinct approaches to the issue of bail. Those who subscribe to a crime control approach to the criminal justice system want to see severe restrictions upon any process that allows suspects to regain their freedom after they have been apprehended. In contrast to this approach, the due process model of criminal justice advocates strict observance of an accused's rights and freedoms at every stage of the proceedings. What is needed is a balance between these two approaches.

This chapter investigates the effects of constitutionalism on the issue of bail, in particular the effects thereof on the nature of the application, burden of proof and other evidentiary aspects, procedural aspects and the duties and discretionary powers of the court. Factors that will render further detention in the interests of justice as well as reasonable bail conditions are also explored and analysed.

Particular attention is given to the role of the SAPS. The Constitution and amendments to the Criminal Procedure Act of 1977 have conferred new duties and responsibilities upon the police to ensure that fundamental rights are upheld, including the right to be released from detention.

20.1 INTRODUCTION

Bail has become a sensitive, if not contentious, issue in constitutional debate. The controversy may arise as a response to the continuous spiralling of South Africa's crime rate which has left many with a paralysing feeling that crime has overwhelmed the capacity of law enforcement to contain it.[1] This, coupled with indications that the number of convictions is decreasing, has left a strong perception, especially among the public, that human rights benefit the perpetrator, to the disadvantage of law-abiding citizens, especially when they learn that hardened criminals are walking the streets shortly after they have been apprehended by the police.[2] Very often the public only learns about a heinous crime when the media report on the outcome of the bail application of the suspect.

Cowling[3] rightly underlines the pivotal role the police can and must play in this regard, ultimately contributing to changed perceptions. He points out that the police are required to conduct a thorough investigation into the question of bail and to adduce evidence that will convince the court that the interests of justice require that bail should not be granted. If such evidence is not produced, the accused will in all likelihood be released.

There are two distinct approaches to the issue of bail. Those who subscribe to a crime control approach to the criminal justice system want to see severe restrictions upon any process that allows suspects to regain their freedom after they have been apprehended. This approach is set against liberty pending the outcome of the criminal trial.

In contrast to the above approach, the due process model of criminal justice advocates strict observance of an accused's rights and freedoms at every stage of the proceedings.[4] Those emphasising due process and the protection of human rights want to ensure that the suspect spends as little time as possible in custody pending the outcome of the criminal trial. Unnecessary detention not only deprives individuals of their freedom; it also takes them away from their families and they lose income which is particularly severe where they are sole income-earners or breadwinners. They are furthermore hindered in their preparation for trial.

Finding a balance and some degree of proportionality between these two approaches would provide an ideal position.[5] This view was confirmed by Van Schalkwyk J in *Ellish en andere v Prokureur-Generaal, Witwatersrand*[6] when he stated that the 1993 Constitution required of the presiding officer to ensure that a balance is maintained between the interests of society, who expects justice, and an individual's freedom. This approach is also prescribed by the Criminal Procedure Act of 1977. Section 60(9) of the Act provides that a court shall decide whether the refusal to grant bail and the detention of an accused in custody are in the interests of justice by *weighing the interests of justice against the right of the accused to his or her personal freedom* and, in particular, the prejudice he or she is likely to suffer if he or she is to be detained in custody.

It is, however, a complex relationship in which trade-offs between individual freedoms and interests of justice have to take place in accordance with the principles of reasonableness and fairness. There are, however, no simple solutions to solving tensions between constitutional values. The focus will thus be on the changing rules of evidence and criminal justice in pursuit of this balance within the constructs of constitutionalism.

20.2 KEY OBJECTIVES

The key objectives of this chapter are to enable students to:

- define bail;
- discuss the purpose and effect of bail;
- identify constitutional provisions applicable to bail;
- discuss the right to be released from detention;
- give a broad overview of international and comparative law relating to bail;
- identify and discuss provisions of the Criminal Procedure Act of 1977 relevant to the right to be released from detention;
- discuss the rules of evidence in respect of bail applications;
- discuss the concepts of "interests of justice" and "reasonable conditions";

- discuss factors to be taken into consideration when deciding whether or not to grant bail.

20.3   APPLICABLE LAW AND INTERNATIONAL INSTRUMENTS

The 1993 Constitution, sections 11, 25 and 35
The 1996 Constitution, sections 12, 35 and 39
The Criminal Procedure Act 51 of 1977, sections 50 and 58–71
The South African Police Service Act 68 of 1995, section 13
Canadian Charter of Rights and Freedoms, 1982
Bail Reform Act 1972
Canadian Criminal code
Bail Act, 1976 (Britain)
Constitution of the Republic of Botswana
Constitution of the Kingdom of Lesotho
Constitution of the Kingdom of Swaziland
Constitution of the Republic of Zimbabwe
Constitution of the Republic of Namibia
The Universal Declaration of Human Rights, articles 3 and 11
The International Covenant on Civil and Political Rights, articles 9(3) and 14(2)
The American Declaration of the Rights and Duties of Man, articles I and XXV
The American Convention on Human Rights, articles 7(1) and 7(5)
The European Convention for the Protection of Human Rights and Fundamental Freedoms, article 5(3)
The African Charter on Human and Peoples' Rights, article 6
The Declaration of the Basic Rights of Asean Peoples and Governments, article I
The Universal Declaration of Islamic Human Rights, chapter 1 (I)

20.4   INTERPRETATION AND DISCUSSION
20.4.1   Purpose and effect of bail

The primary purpose of detention is to ensure that a person who is arrested for allegedly having committed a crime, will appear at his or her trial, so that he or she can be charged, tried and convicted or acquitted. The purpose of bail is to ensure that an accused will reappear in court for his or her trial.[7]

Release on bail is furthermore a means of giving effect to the presumption of innocence which is fundamental to our criminal justice system and which is entrenched in our Bill of Rights.[8] Mahomed AJ in *S v Acheson*[9] points out that an accused person cannot be kept in detention pending his/her trial as a form of anticipatory punishment, because it is presumed in law that an accused is innocent until he or she has been found guilty by a court.

The non-penal character of bail is highlighted by Du Toit *et al*,[10] emphasising that continued incarceration does not imply the imposition of a penalty or sentence.

The granting of bail advances personal liberty in keeping with the constitutional right to freedom and security of the person.[11] Du Toit *et al*[12] describe the purpose of bail as the striking of a balance between the interests of society and the liberty of an accused. From a practical point of view release on bail places the accused in a better position to prepare for his or her trial, to remain employed, to maintain family ties and generally to keep his or her life intact.[13] The purpose of bail is to minimise interference in the lawful activities of the accused.[14]

Bail has been described as follows:

"[A] contract in terms of which an accused who is being held in custody is set at liberty upon his payment of, or his furnishing of a guarantee, to pay a fixed sum of money and, further, upon his express or implied undertaking to comply with the general conditions and the specific conditions relating to his release. The State, on the other hand, undertakes to respect the liberty of the accused…"[15]

The effect of bail is thus that an accused who is in custody is released from custody upon payment of, or the furnishing of a guarantee to pay, the sum of money determined for his or her bail.[16] In turn, the accused is compelled to appear at the place and on the date and at the time appointed for his or her trial or to which the proceedings relating to the offence in respect of which he or she is released on bail are adjourned. Bail endures until a verdict is given and the accused sentenced. Should a sentence not be imposed immediately after the verdict and the court extends bail until sentence, it will remain operative until such time. Bail may, however, be cancelled prior to a verdict being given when, for example, an accused fails to observe bail conditions.[17]

20.4.2 Constitutional provisions regarding bail

20.4.2.1 The 1996 Constitution

Section 35(1)(*f*) of the 1996 Constitution provides that everyone who is arrested for allegedly committing an offence has a right

"to be released from detention if the interests of justice permit, subject to reasonable conditions".

Its predecesor, section 25(2)(*d*) of the 1993 Constitution, made specific reference to bail. It recognised the "right to be released from detention with or without bail, unless the interests of justice require otherwise". This express reference to the right to bail has been described as "something of a constitutional rarity", since such a right is derived in the case of most constitutions from general principles of due process and liberty.[18]

20.4.2.2 Limitation and derogation

Section 35(1)(*f*) is, as are all other rights, subject to section 36 of the 1996 Constitution, the so-called general limitation clause. The latter provides that the rights contained in the Bill of Rights may be limited only in terms of laws of general application and to the extent that the limitation is reasonable and justifiable in an open and democratic society based on human dignity, equality and freedom. All relevant factors are to be taken into account, including the nature of the right, the importance of the purpose of the limitation, the nature and extent of the limitation, the relation between the limitation and its purpose and less restrictive means to achieve the purpose.[19]

A factor that has been described as an overriding consideration which carries considerable weight is the interests of justice. Although not specifically listed in the general limitation clause, it appears as an internal modifier under section 35(1)(*f*).[20] It has been suggested that statutory provisions purporting to limit or oust the court's discretion in determining whether the granting or refusal of bail will be in the interests of justice will not pass as permissible limitations in terms of the Constitution.[21] Section 35(1)(*f*) furthermore provides that the right to be released from detention is subject to reasonable conditions.

A further permissible derogation of section 35(1)(*f*) is found in section 37 of the 1996 Constitution which deals with states of emergency. It provides, *inter alia*, that no Act of Parliament, authorising the declaration of a state of emergency, may permit or authorise any derogation from certain rights listed under the Table of Non-Derogable Rights. However, as section 35(1)(*f*) is not listed in this table, derogation thereof in consequence of a state of emergency is authorised, subject to the provisions of section 37(6). The latter provides for the release of a detained person after review of his or her detention by the court as soon as reasonably possible, but not later than ten days after the person was detained, unless it is necessary to continue the detention to restore peace and order.[22] This is similar to the position under section 34 of the 1993 Constitution which provided that the rights in chapter 3 could be suspended in consequence of the declaration of a state of emergency to the extent necessary to restore peace and order.

20.4.2.3   Right of an accused to access to information contained in the police docket and in possession of the state

Both the 1993 Constitution[23] and the 1996 Constitution[24] contain a right to access to information held by the state. The effect of this on bail was discussed in *Nieuwoudt v Prokureur-Generaal van die Oos-Kaap*.[25] In this case Nieuwoudt and others requested the Attorney-General for access to the contents of the police docket and copies of witness statements, which request was denied. The court affirmed the need for openness and accessibility.[26] The state made vague claims regarding the importance of not disclosing the contents of the police docket and the identities of witnesses; there was no indication what number of witnesses would be required to testify in other cases and also no indication of when it would be possible to reveal their identity or the contents of their statements. The state merely stated that it could not be done at that stage. The court ruled that the vague claims could not outweigh the need of Nieuwoudt and the other applicants for access to the information sought to enable them to apply for bail and ordered that the Attorney-General furnish the information sought.

20.4.3 International and comparative law relating to bail

20.4.3.1 International law *and* comparative law

As was mentioned earlier, bail can be seen as a means of giving effect to the presumption of innocence, as well as advancing personal liberty and freedom. The right to freedom and security of the person and the right to be presumed innocent are dealt with extensively in international law. Article 3 of the Universal Declaration of Human Rights[27] stipulates that everyone has a right to life, liberty and security of the person. Section 11 thereof contains the right to be presumed innocent until proven guilty. Article 9(3) of the International Covenant on Civil and Political Rights[28] stipulates in respect of arrested or detained persons that it shall not be the general rule that the person awaiting trial shall be detained in custody. His or her release may be subject to guarantees to appear for trial. Article 14(2) embodies the right to be presumed innocent until proven guilty according to law.

On a continental level both the American Declaration of the Rights and Duties of Man[29] and the American Convention on Human Rights[30] contain the right to life, liberty and security of the person,[31] the right not to be deprived of liberty except in the cases and according to the procedures established by pre-existing law[32] and the right to be presumed innocent.[33] Similar rights are also embodied in the European Convention for the Protection of Human Rights and Fundamental Freedoms,[34] the African Charter on Human Rights and Peoples' Rights.[35] The European Convention[36] provides that an arrested or detained person is entitled to be released pending trial if not tried within a reasonable time. Release may be conditioned by guarantees to appear for trial.[37]

The Declaration of the Basic Rights of Asean Peoples and Governments[38] declares in this regard that it is the duty of government to respect and guarantee the life, liberty and security of the person. The Universal Declaration of Islamic Human Rights[39] affirms that man(kind) is born free and that no inroads shall be made on anyone's liberty except under the authority and in the due process of the law.

Section 39 of the 1996 Constitution stipulates that when interpreting the Bill of Rights a court must consider international law and may consider foreign law. In *Berg v Prokureur-Generaal van Gauteng*[40] it was held that circumspection is required when resorting to comparable foreign law. The different context and social milieu within and different historical background against which other constitutions were drafted give rise to the danger of unnecessarily importing doctrines associated with foreign constitutions which are inappropriate in the South African setting. It was further held that the Constitution ought first and foremost to be interpreted according to the principles of South African law.

20.4.3.2 Canadian Charter of Rights and Freedoms

Human Rights in Canada are protected in the Charter of Rights and Freedoms of 1982. Section 1 provides that the rights and freedoms set out in the Charter are subject only to such reasonable limits prescribed by law as can be demonstrably justified in a free and democratic society. Section 11(*e*) furthermore provides that any person charged with an offence has the right not to be denied reasonable bail without a just cause. However, the issue of the onus in bail applications is governed by the Bail Reform Act of 1972.[41]

The above-mentioned Bail Reform Act brought about a shift of onus to the state to justify the detention of an accused person. The reason for the shift was the apparent disturbing relationship between pretrial detention and the outcome of trials. An overwhelming number of detained persons were found not guilty.[42] As a result of public dissatisfaction with this shift, the Bail Reform Act was amended in 1975, shifting the onus to the detained person in specific instances.[43] The Bail Reform Act is still in force in spite of the adoption of the Charter of Rights and Freedoms of 1982.

Evidentiary issues regarding bail applications, as well as the function of the presiding officer, are stipulated in section 518(1) of the Canadian Criminal Code. It provides, *inter alia*, the following:[44]

(i)   the accused may not be examined or cross-examined by the presiding officer or any other person regarding the offence with which he or she is charged;

(ii) subject to the aforementioned, the presiding officer may make any enquiries, on oath or otherwise, of and concerning the accused as he or she considers desirable;

(iii) the prosecutor may, in addition to any other relevant evidence, lead evidence to prove previous convictions and to show the circumstances of the current alleged offence;

(iv) the presiding officer may receive evidence obtained as a result of an interception of a private communication.

20.4.3.3 English law

In the United Kingdom the Bail Act of 1976 regulates bail and the right to bail, which is not an absolute right. It provides that a person shall be granted bail except as provided in Schedule 1. Schedule 1 lists certain offences and draws a distinction between offences for which imprisonment is an option and those to which imprisonment does not apply. In respect of those offences for which imprisonment can be imposed, paragraph 2 of the Schedule provides that the accused need not be granted bail if the court is satisfied that there are substantial grounds for believing that the accused, if released on bail, would:

(*a*)   fail to surrender to custody; or

(*b*)   commit an offence while on bail; or

(*c*)   interfere with witnesses or otherwise obstruct the course of justice.[45]

Where imprisonment is not an option, the accused need not be granted bail if he or she failed to comply with previous or current bail conditions.[46]

The presiding officer is compelled in terms of paragraph 9 of Schedule 1 to take the following factors into account when deciding whether or not to grant bail:

(*a*)   the nature and seriousness of the offence;

(*b*)   the character, antecedents, associations and community ties of the accused;

(*c*)   the accused's record regarding the fulfilment of his or her obligations under previous grants of bail in criminal proceedings;

(*d*)   the strength of the evidence of his or her having committed the offence.[47]

20.4.3.4   Some southern African constitutions

Provisions regarding the release of an arrested person are also found in the constitutions of other southern African states. Here are some examples.

COUNTRY	CONSTITUTIONAL PROVISION
Republic of Botswana	Any person who is arrested or detained … and who is not released, shall be brought as soon as is reasonably practicable before a court; and if any person arrested or detained as mentioned in paragraph (*b*) of this subsection is not tried within a reasonable time, then, without prejudice to any further proceedings that may be brought against him, he shall be released either conditionally or upon reasonable conditions, including in particular such conditions as are reasonably necessary to ensure that he appears at a later date for trial or for proceedings preliminary to trial. (Section 5(3))
Kingdom of Lesotho	If any person arrested or detained upon suspicion of his having committed, or being about to commit a criminal offence is not tried within a reasonable time, then, without prejudice to any further proceedings that may be brought against him, he shall be released either conditionally or upon reasonable conditions, including in particular such conditions as are reasonably necessary to ensure that he

appears at a later date for trial or for proceedings preliminary to trial. (Section 3(5))

Kingdom of
Swaziland

If any person arrested or detained as mentioned in subsection (3)(b) is not tried within a reasonable time, then, without prejudice to any further proceedings that may be
brought against him, he shall be released either unconditionally or upon reasonable conditions, including in particular such conditions as are reasonably necessary to ensure
that he appears at a later date for trial or for proceedings
preliminary to trial. (Section 5(5))

Republic of
Zimbabwe

Any person who is arrested or detained ... and who is not
released, shall be brought without undue delay before a
court; and if any person arrested or detained upon reasonable suspicion of his having committed or being about to
commit a criminal offence is not tried within a reasonable
time, then, without prejudice to any further proceedings
that may be brought against him, he shall be released
either conditionally or upon reasonable conditions, including in particular such conditions as are reasonably necessary to ensure that he appears at a later date for trial or for
proceedings preliminary to trial. (Section 13(4))

Republic of
Namibia

In Namibia bail is still regulated by the Criminal Procedure
Act of 1977 which remained in force after the independence
of Namibia. The Criminal Procedure Amendment Act of
1991 only brought about minor amendments. The Namibian
constitution does not have a specific provision dealing with
bail, save for article 7, which provides that no person shall
be deprived of personal liberty except according to procedures established by law, and article 11, which *inter alia*,
provides that no person shall be subject to arbitrary arrest or
detention and that all persons who are arrested and
detained in custody should be brought before a magistrate
within forty-eight hours or as soon as possible thereafter
and that no person shall be detained beyond such period
without the authority of a magistrate or judicial officer.

20.4.4 Statutory provisions relevant to the right to be released from detention

20.4.4.1 Section 59 of the Criminal Procedure Act

Section 59 of the Criminal Procedure Act of 1977, which pertains to bail
before an accused's first appearance in a lower court, provides, *inter alia*:

"(1)(*a*) An accused who is in custody in respect of an offence,
other than any offence referred to in Part II or Part III of

Schedule 2 may, before his or her first appearance in a lower court, be released on bail in respect of such offence by any police official of or above the rank of non-commissioned officer, in consultation with the police official charged with the investigation, if the accused deposits at the police station the sum of money determined by such police official.

(b) The police official referred to in paragraph (a) shall, at the time of releasing the accused on bail, complete and hand to the accused a recognizance on which receipt shall be given for the sum of money deposited as bail and on which the offence in respect of which the bail is granted and the place, date and time of the trial of the accused are entered.

(c) The said police official shall forthwith forward a duplicate original of such recognizance to the clerk of the court which has jurisdiction."

Section 59 deals with so-called police bail. This section empowers a police official to release an accused on bail. Section 35(1) of the 1996 Constitution, which deals with the issue of bail, merely refers to the rights of persons arrested for allegedly committing offences. It is submitted that section 59 nevertheless gives effect to the provisions of section 35(1) of the Constitution and that arrested and accused persons for the purposes of section 59 carry the same meaning.

Section 59(1)(a), which was amended by the Criminal Procedure Second Amendment Act of 1995, ascribes an active role to both the police official considering bail as well as the investigating officer charged with the investigation. Before any decision regarding bail can be reached they will have to consult by whatever means. This obviously impacts on the availability of investigating officers for consultation outside their hours of duty. Furthermore, it is suggested that a police official is obliged to consider whether to grant bail in every instance where the offence falls within the ambit of section 59.[48]

It is suggested that section 50(6) of the Criminal Procedure Act of 1977 places a further duty upon police officials involved in arresting alleged offenders to inform them *as soon as possible* of their right to institute bail proceedings, and if they are not granted bail under section 59, to request to be brought before a lower court as soon as is reasonably possible so that their bail application can be considered.

Section 59 has certain inherent limitations.

1 It only applies to situations before an accused appears in court for the first time.

2 The powers contained in this section are conferred only upon a police official of the rank of non-commissioned officer or above. The South African Police Service Act of 1995 defines a commissioned officer as "a

commissioned officer appointed under section 33(1)", that is, those appointed by the President, and includes temporary officers. Both the Criminal Procedure Act of 1977 and the South African Police Service Act of 1995 are silent on the ranks considered to be included under non-commissioned officers. Du Toit *et al* [49] are of the opinion that this section refers to a police official of the rank of sergeant and above. This view was confirmed in the unreported decision of *S v Magwaza*.[50]

3   A police official may only grant bail in respect of offences not listed in Part II and Part III of Schedule 2. Offences included in Part II and III are rape, robbery and murder, to name but a few. Also included is theft involving an amount or value in excess of R200,00. It can be seen that section 59 really only applies to truly minor or fairly trivial offences.

4   This section only refers to a "sum of money". The police official cannot permit the accused to furnish a guarantee, with or without sureties, instead.[51]

5   The police officer cannot impose conditions other than determining the sum of money to be deposited as bail. However, a court before which a charge is pending is authorised to add further conditions of bail on application by the prosecutor, irrespective of whether bail was granted by that court, any other court or under section 59.[52] The court need not extend the bail granted under section 59 beyond the first appearance.[53] If, however, it remains in force, it will be in the same manner as if granted by the court under section 60.

It has been suggested that a claim for damages will arise in circumstances where bail is wrongly refused and the refusal is wilful and malicious, for example where the police official refuses to exercise his or her discretion.[54]

It must be emphasised that the procedure envisaged by section 59 is informal and of an administrative nature, but with a quasi-judicial element.[55] Because the considering and granting of bail is a quasi-judicial act, the rules of natural justice will apply. Furthermore, as it is an administrative act which the police official performs when considering bail, section 33 of the 1996 Constitution will apply. Section 33 deals with just administrative action and provides among others that everyone has the right to lawful, reasonable and procedurally fair administrative action. This section further provides that, where rights have been adversely affected, for example when bail is refused, such affected person has the right to be given reasons in writing. It is suggested that a police official should keep proper record of proceedings.[56]

Lastly, police officials should at all times bear in mind the provisions of the South African Police Service Act of 1995. Section 13(1) provides that a member of the police service may exercise such powers and shall perform such duties and functions as are by law conferred or assigned to him or her, subject to the Constitution and with due regard to the fundamental rights of every person. Section 13(3)(*a*) provides that official duties shall, with due regard to powers, duties and functions, be performed in such a manner as is reasonable in the circumstances.

20.4.4.2 Section 60 of the Criminal Procedure Act

Section 60 of the Criminal Procedure Act deals with bail applications of accused persons in court. Section 60(1) provides as follows:

"(*a*) An accused who is in custody in respect of any offence shall, subject to the provisions of section 50(6) and (7), be entitled to be released on bail at any stage preceding his or her conviction in respect of such offence, unless the court finds that it is in the interests of justice that he or she be detained in custody.

(b) If a court refers an accused to another court for trial or sentencing, the court referring the accused retains jurisdiction relating to the powers, functions and duties in respect of bail in terms of this Act until the accused appears in such other court for the first time.

(c) If the question of the possible release of the accused on bail is not raised by the accused or the prosecutor, the court shall ascertain from the accused whether he or she wished that question to be considered by the court."

The Criminal Procedure Second Amendment Act of 1995 extensively amended the provisions of the Criminal Procedure Act of 1977 dealing with bail. The amendments emerged from the recommendations of the South African Law Commission on the reform of the South African law regarding bail.[57]

The constitutional right to be released from detention permeates section 60.[58] This section will be dealt with in detail in the ensuing paragraphs.

20.4.5 Rules of evidence in respect of bail applications

20.4.5.1 Nature of application

Bail applications are not criminal proceedings, but simply judicial proceedings in which evidence can be adduced in an informal way.[59] In *S v Pienaar*[60] Botha J described the proceedings as follows:

"Bail applications are something *sui generis*. By the nature of things they are mostly urgent. No rigid format or procedure has been prescribed and nor is it advisable to do so. It is the function of the judicial officer concerned, having regard to the circumstances of the case, to give such directions as will ensure that all parties concerned can put their views across."

This view was also followed and confirmed in *Ellish en andere v Prokureur-Generaal, Witwatersrand*.[61] Bail proceedings are thus of an inquisitorial nature.[62]

20.4.5.2 Burden of proof

Procedural provisions regarding bail are contained in sections 58 to 71 of the Criminal Procedure Act of 1977. These sections are still applicable.

Prior to the coming into operation of the 1993 Constitution there were no statutory enactments regarding the burden of proof in bail applications. The attitude of the courts was that bail will always be granted where possible, and will lean in favour of, and not against, the liberty of the accused — provided that it is clear that the interests of justice will not be prejudiced thereby. [63]

The approach was, however, that the accused bore the onus of proving on a balance of probabilities that, if bail was granted, the interests of justice would not be prejudiced.[64]

The coming into operation of section 25(2)(*d*) of the 1993 Constitution gave rise to a number of disputes and contradictory judgments. It was contended on the one hand that the wording of section 25(2)(*d*) implied that the right to be released could be denied only where facts were proved, establishing the qualifying exceptional circumstances described in the words " unless the interests of justice require otherwise".[65]

There was a view, on the other hand, that there was no onus in bail applications.

The courts dealt with this question in depth. In *Magano & another v The District Magistrate of Johannesburg, Johnson NO & others,*[66] Van Blerk AJ ruled that section 25(2)(*d*) conferred upon an accused the right to apply for bail, which is independent of his or her right under the Criminal Procedure Act of 1977 to apply for bail. He ruled that this constitutional right could only be denied an accused person where the state proved that the interests of justice required otherwise.

In *Prokureur Generaal Witwatersrand v Van Heerden en 32 ander*[67] Eloff JP held that the framers of the 1993 Constitution intended that the right contained in section 25(2)(*d*) would have to be balanced against the demands of society. Bail applications are not criminal proceedings but simply judicial proceedings. The nature of such proceedings precluded the placing of an onus on either party.

An appeal against the judgment of Eloff JP was lodged to a full bench.[68] On appeal it was held that the approach adopted by Eloff JP was correct. *No onus exists in a bail application.* It is expected of the presiding officer to exercise his or her discretion by weighing the interests of the applicant in his or her freedom against the interests of the community in the administration of criminal justice. Regarding procedure, section 25(2)(*d*) of the 1993 Constitution required the state to start by leading evidence. If, at the end of the proceedings, the scales were evenly balanced, the applicant had to be granted bail. This was the case, not because of a failure to discharge any onus, but because of the provisions of section 25(2)(*d*).[69]

In *S v Mbele*[70] the effects of the amendments[71] to section 60 of the Criminal Procedure Act of 1977 were examined. Stegmann J in his judgment confirmed that the ruling in the *Ellish* case remained in effect *except* where a bail application was governed by the provisions of section 60(11) of the Criminal Procedure Act of 1977. Section 60(11) stipulates that, where an accused is charged with an offence referred to:

"(*a*) in Schedule 5;

(*b*) in Schedule 1, which was allegedly committed whilst he or she was released on bail in respect of a Schedule 1 offence, the court shall order that the accused be detained in custody until he or she is dealt with in accordance with the law, unless the accused, having been given a reasonable opportunity to do so, satisfies the court that the interests of justice do not require his or her detention in custody."

Where this section applies, the burden of proof rests on the accused to satisfy the court on a preponderance of probabilities that it will be in the interests of justice that he or she is not detained. It was further ruled that, where this section applies, the court may not act in an inquisitorial or inquiring way and may not enter the arena. The question is simply whether or not the accused has discharged the onus resting on him or her.

Section 60(11) refers to cases where an accused is charged with an offence such as murder involving a dangerous weapon or firearm, rape, robbery with aggravating circumstances, as well as robbery of a vehicle, theft, fraud and forgery involving more than R500 000,00, as well as crimes relating to drugs and firearms.

Edeling J in *Prokureur-Generaal, Vrystaat v Ramakhosi*[72] held that section 60(11) is in direct conflict with section 60(1)(*a*), which in turn is a repetition of section 25(2)(*d*) of the 1993 Constitution, and therefore unconstitutional. Section 25(2)(*d*) confers on a detained person a prima facie right to be released. Only if it is not in the interests of justice can bail be refused. However, he feels that it is an issue which has to be decided by the Constitutional Court. Leveson J in *S v Mbele*[73] conceded that on the face of it a direction that an accused should be detained in custody pending the outcome of the proceedings unless the accused satisfies the court that the interests of justice do not require his or her detention, as is the case under section 60(11), appears to be in conflict with section 25(2)(*d*) of the 1993 Constitution. He states, however:

"But I think it more proper to read the whole section as being adjectival, i e as simply requiring that in order to be released from detention the accused must satisfy the court that it is in the interests of justice that this be done."

20.4. 5.3 Type/quality of evidence

(a) Evidence by means of affidavit

In *Moekazi & others v Additional Magistrate, Welkom, & another*[74] it was held that a bail application can be brought on affidavit. If the state wishes to oppose the application, it can file answering affidavits or adduce *viva voce* evidence. In this regard Eloff JP in *Prokureur-Generaal van die Witwatersrandse Afdeling v Van Heerden*[75] criticised the magistrate presiding at a bail application for not drawing a stronger negative inference against the accused who preferred not to adduce *viva voce* evidence but to submit only vague affidavits. In *S v Hudson*[76] the court held that, where an accused applies for bail and confirms on oath that he has no intention of absconding, due weight has to be given to the statement on oath. Implicit reliance cannot, however, be placed on the mere say-so of the accused but the court should examine the circumstances. It should nevertheless be borne in mind that evidence need not be attested.[77]

(b) Opinion evidence

In a bail application the court may in suitable cases place reliance upon the investigating officer's opinion, even though his opinion is unsupported by direct evidence.[78] It should be borne in mind that opinion evidence, other than that of experts, is as a rule inadmissible. There are three basic requirements for the admissibility of opinion evidence at bail applications:[79]

(i)   the witness must be competent;

(ii)   the grounds for his or her opinion must be stated, either by means of direct or indirect evidence;

(iii) the court must not be bound by the opinion of the witness.

An investigating officer testifying for the continued detention of an accused by, for example, expressing the opinion that the accused may evade his or her trial or will undermine or jeopardise the objectives or proper functioning of the criminal justice system, is bound by the above-listed requirements.[80]

(c) Hearsay evidence

In spite of the fact that hearsay evidence is generally inadmissible, there are arguments in favour of the admissibility of hearsay evidence at bail proceedings.[81] Hearsay evidence is admissible on the basis of urgency because the accused needs to be assisted as a matter of priority. Hearsay evidence should, however, not be admitted in an unlimited way as it could severely prejudice the accused.[82] In *S v Mbolombo*[83] the court confirmed that hearsay evidence may be adduced.

(d) Duty on the state to adduce evidence

There is no rule compelling the state to adduce evidence where the correctness of the information is questioned by the accused. It is the duty of the presiding officer to consider the probative value or weight of the evidence. If the evidence is sufficiently reliable and convincing to form the grounds for a decision, it will override the accused's denial.[84] Therefore, if the information furnished by the state sounds convincing, the accused cannot simply deny such information. The nature of the accused's response will, however, depend on factors such as the nature of the case, the seriousness of the offence and the custom to grant bail in respect of certain offences. No general rule exists in this regard.[85] Where the nature of the offence is such that it does not favour the granting of bail, the accused will have to be more forth-coming in his or her response. This is so, not because there is a burden of proof on the accused, but because in finding a balance between the interests of the accused and those of justice, it might mean that bail will be refused.[86]

In *Prokureur-Generaal van die Witwatersrandse Plaaslike Afdeling v Van Heerden en andere*[87] the magistrate presiding at the bail application was strongly criticised for expecting the state to adduce evidence and contradict all aspects covered by the accused during cross-examination of state witnesses.

20.4.5.4　Procedural aspects

In *Prokureur-Generaal van die Witwatersrandse Plaaslike Afdeling v Van Heerden en andere*[88] it was held that, if the state opposes a bail application, it seems logical and fair to expect the state to motivate and substantiate its viewpoint. If the state does not do so, it can be inferred that the interests of justice do not require the detention of the arrested person.

On the other hand, should the state adduce evidence and it is of such a nature that it can be expected of the arrested person to provide an answer or some explanation, he or she should be given an opportunity to place such evidence before the court. If the arrested person elects not to do so, the court will be entitled to draw a negative inference.

The presiding officer also has the inherent power *and discretion* to make a decision, in the interests of justice, to recall witnesses himself or to allow the parties to recall witnesses.[89]

The presiding officer can also allow either the state or the arrested person to answer to allegations made by the other party.[90]

20.4.5.5　Duties and discretionary powers of the court

As the nature of the bail proceedings is inquisitorial, it follows that the presiding officer plays an active role.[91] It is the function of the judicial officer concerned, having regard to the circumstances of the case, to give such direction as will ensure that all parties concerned can put their views across.[92] This will enable the presiding officer to reach a proper decision. He or she therefore cannot just sit back and receive whatever evidence the parties are able to tender or wish to place before him or her. At times he or she might even have to seek actively corroborating evidence on, for example, an accused's personal background or previous convictions.[93]

In the unreported bail application of *Esterhuizen v The State*[94] it was held that the magistrate should have indicated his specific uncertainties and problems to the parties concerned during the application to afford them an opportunity to provide answers or explanations.

The Criminal Procedure Second Amendment Act of 1955 incorporated certain provisions in this regard into section 60 of the Criminal Procedure Act of 1977. Section 60(2) provides that a court may:

> "(*a*) postpone any such proceedings as contemplated in section 50(6) or (7);
>
> (*b*) in respect of matters that are not in dispute between the accused and the prosecutor, acquire in an informal manner the information that is needed for its decision or order regarding bail;
>
> (*c*) in respect of matters that are in dispute between the accused and the prosecutor, require of the prosecutor or the accused, as the case may be, that evidence be adduced."

Section 60(3) provides that if the court is of the opinion that it does not have reliable or sufficient information or evidence at its disposal or that it lacks certain important information to reach a decision on the bail application, the presiding officer *shall* order that such information or evidence be placed before the court.

The court should always exercise its powers by bearing in mind the fact that the Constitution is not simply some kind of statutory codification of the past, but that it constitutes a decisive break from the past towards a constitutionally protected culture of openness, democracy and universal human rights for all South Africans.[95]

The court ultimately has a *duty* to weigh up the personal interests of the accused against the interests of justice, notwithstanding the fact that the prosecution does not oppose the granting of bail.[96]

The court also has a *duty* to inform an unrepresented accused of his or her right to apply for bail and the procedure to be followed. Section 60 of the Criminal Procedure Act is clear on this issue. It states:

> "60(1)(*c*)   If the question of the possible release of the accused on bail is not raised by the accused or the prosecutor, the court shall ascertain from the accused whether he or she wished that question to be considered by the court."

Section 60 is, after all, meaningless to those oblivious of their rights in terms thereof.[97] Du Toit *et al*[98] point out that a failure to do so could result in an unfair trial constituting a complete failure of justice, depending, of course, on the merits of each case.

Furthermore, the court is competent and obliged to hear bail applications over weekends, on public holidays and outside normal hours. This applies not only to the accused's first compulsory appearance in court but also to the first appearance at his or her request in terms of section 50 of the Criminal Procedure Act of 1977.[99]

20.4.5.6 The use of evidence adduced at a bail application during the subsequent trial

In *S v Botha & others*[100] the state sought to tender evidence in a criminal trial, namely the transcript of the evidence which an accused had given in a bail application. Prior to and during the bail application the accused was not made aware of his right against self-incrimination.

The trial court had to determine whether the accused would have a fair trial if the record of the bail application were admitted in evidence. It was held that the accused could not have a fair trial if he were to be cross-examined on incriminating evidence he had given at the bail application in ignorance of his right to refuse to answer the incriminating questions.[101] It was held that an accused who testifies at a bail application retains the privilege against self-incrimination.

The strength of the prosecution's case is an important factor to be considered during a bail application, which in turn depends partly upon the ability of the accused to refute it. In a bail application the applicant also has a right to remain silent, but if he or she declines to testify, a consequence might be that he or she would fail to demonstrate that the prosecution's case was not as strong as it was made out to be. Accordingly, if the evidence given by an applicant at a bail application were to be admissible later at the trial, the applicant would face a dilemma at the bail application: a failure to testify might result in a refusal of bail, while a decision to testify in order to get bail would mean foregoing the right to remain silent and the privilege against self-incrimination.[102] The court was of the opinion that, in the interests of a fair trial, this choice should not have to be made. The way to avoid burdening anyone with that choice is to insulate the bail application proceedings from the main trial in the same way as an inquiry into the voluntariness of a confession is kept distinct from the issue of guilt by insulating the inquiry into the voluntariness in a compartment separate from the main trial.

The court held that the accused would not have a fair trial if the record of the bail application were to be admitted in evidence.[103]

The above decision must be viewed in the light of the fact that a certified record of the evidence of a bail application is admissible against the accused in terms of section 335 of the Criminal Procedure Act of 1977 at a subsequent trial.[104]

20.4.6 Granting or refusal of bail to arrested persons

20.4.6.1 "Interests of justice"

Section 35 of the 1996 Constitution provides that an arrested person has the right to be released from detention if the *interests of justice* permit, subject to reasonable conditions. This was also the position under section 25(2)(*d*) of the 1993 Constitution. Edeling J in *Prokureur-Generaal, Vrystaat v Ramakhosi*[105] confirmed that, although an individual's right to liberty and therefore also his or her right to be released are points of departure when considering bail, the interests of justice are an overriding consideration. In *Ellish en andere v Prokureur-Generaal, Witwatersrand*[106] it was held that the notion "in the interests of justice" had a meaning which placed it outside the category of provable facts, calling for a value judgment which required the presiding officer to exercise a discretion.

In *Lek v Estate Agents Board* [107] the notion "in the interests of justice" was defined as follows:

> "The phrase 'in the interests of justice' indicates that it [the court] should exercise a discretion in which fair play as between man and man is a paramount consideration. The word 'justice' is defined in the *Shorter Oxford English Dictionary* as: 'The quality of being morally just or righteous; the principle of just dealing; just conduct; integrity; rectitude'."

20.4.6.2 Guiding factors

The approach to be taken by the court in deciding whether or not to release a detained person on bail and the necessity of considering certain guiding factors in taking this decision was summarised as follows by Van der Merwe J in *Maharaj v S* [108]:

> "I am of the opinion that the court, either as a court of first instance or as a court of appeal, should look at the evidence as a whole and then consider whether it will be in the interests of justice in general to grant bail to an applicant or not. In deciding that question a court will obviously look at the question whether the accused will stand his trial, whether he will interfere with state witnesses and whether he has a propensity to commit crime whilst out on bail, *et cetera*. No *numerus clausus* of facts can be enumerated because various different facts of the case must be kept in mind. At the end a court will have to exercise a discretion, judicially exercised, in deciding whether to grant bail or not."

This holistic approach is reflected in the Criminal Procedure Second Amendment Act of 1995 which sets out the factors which should be taken into account when exercising the discretion referred to above. These factors are a compilation of those factors and guidelines enunciated in numerous judgments over the last two decades.

It must to be emphasised that the factors listed in the amendments to section 60 of the Criminal Procedure Act of 1977, brought about by the Criminal Procedure Second Amendment Act of 1995, do not appear to establish a *numerus clausus* of factors, but still give the presiding officer flexibility to exercise his or her discretion by taking into account any other factors which in his or her opinion should be taken into account.[109]

The refusal to grant bail and the detention of an accused in custody shall be in the interests of justice where *one or more* of the following grounds are established:[110]

> (i)   *Where there is the likelihood that the accused, if he or she were*
> *released on bail, would endanger the safety of the public or*

> *any particular person or the public interest, or would commit*
> *a Schedule 1 offence*

In considering whether this has been established, the court may, where applicable, take into account the following:[111]

- the degree of violence towards others implicit in the charge against the accused;
- any threat of violence which the accused may have made to any person;
- any resentment the accused is alleged to harbour against any person;
- any disposition to violence on the part of the accused, as is evident from his or her past conduct;
- any disposition of the accused to commit offences referred to in Schedule 1, as is evident from his or her past conduct;
- any prevalence of a particular type of offence;[112]
- any evidence that the accused previously committed an offence referred to in Schedule 1 while released on bail; or
- any other factor which in the opinion of the court should be taken into account.

> (ii)   *Where there is the likelihood that the accused, if he or she were*
> *released on bail, would attempt to evade his or her trial*

In considering whether this ground has been established, the court may, where applicable, take into account the following factors:[113]

- the emotional, family, community or occupational ties of the accused to the place at which he or she is to be tried;
- the assets held by the accused and where such assets are situated;
- the means, and travel documents held by the accused, which may enable him or her to leave the country;[114]
- the extent, if any, to which the accused can afford to forfeit the amount of bail which may be set;
- the question whether the extradition of the accused could readily be effected should he or she flee across the borders of the Republic in an attempt to evade his or her trial;[115]
- the nature and the gravity of the charge on which the accused is to be tried;[116]
- the strength of the case against the accused and the incentive that he or she may in consequence have to attempt to evade his or her trial;[117]
- the nature and gravity of the punishment which is likely to be imposed should the accused be convicted of the charges against him or her;[118]
- the binding effect and enforceability of bail conditions which may be imposed and the ease with which such conditions could be breached; or
- any other factor which in the opinion of the court should be taken into account.

> (iii)   *Where there is the likelihood that the accused, if he or she*
> *were released on bail, would attempt to influence or intimi-*
> *date witnesses or to conceal or destroy evidence*

In considering whether this ground has been established, the court may, where applicable, take into account the following factors, namely:[119] —

- the fact that the accused is familiar with the identity of witnesses and with the evidence which they may bring against him or her;[120]
- whether the witnesses have already made statements and agreed to testify;
- whether the investigation against the accused has already been completed;
- the relationship of the accused with the various witnesses and the extent to which they could be influenced or intimidated;
- how effective and enforceable bail conditions prohibiting communication between the accused and witnesses are likely to be;
- whether the accused has access to evidentiary material which is to be presented at his or her trial;
- the ease with which evidentiary material could be concealed or destroyed; or
- any other factor which in the opinion of the court should be taken into account.

    (iv) Where there is the likelihood that the accused, if he or she were released on bail, would undermine or jeopardise the objectives or the proper functioning of the criminal justice system, including the bail system

In considering whether this ground has been established, the court may, where applicable, take into account the following factors, namely: [121]

- the fact that the accused, knowing it to be false, supplied false information at the time of his or her arrest or during the bail proceedings;
- whether the accused is in custody on another charge or whether the accused is on parole;
- any previous failure on the part of the accused to comply with bail conditions or any indication that he or she will not comply with any bail conditions; or
- any other factor which in the opinion of the court should be taken into account.

In considering the above four questions, the court shall decide the matter by weighing the interests of justice against the right of the accused to his or her personal freedom and, in particular, the prejudice he or she would be likely to suffer if he or she were to be detained in custody, taking into account, where applicable, the following factors:[122]

- the period for which the accused has already been in custody since his or her arrest;
- the probable period of detention until the disposal or conclusion of the trial if the accused is not released on bail;
- the reason for any delay in the disposal or conclusion of the trial and any fault on the part of the accused with regard to such delay;
- any financial loss which the accused may suffer owing to his or her detention;

- any impediment to the preparation of the accused's defence or any delay in obtaining legal representation which may be brought about by the detention of the accused;
- the state of health of the accused; or
- any other factor which in the opinion of the court should be taken into account.

Lastly, the following remark of Mahomed J in *S v Acheson*[123] must be borne in mind where a bail application has been unsuccessful:

> "I am unable to agree with the suggestion that I am precluded from considering bail for the accused, merely because the accused was previously unsuccessful in this court. Each application must be considered in the light of the circumstances which appear at the time when the application is made. A Judge hearing a new application is entitled, is indeed obliged, to have regard to all the circumstances which impact on the issue when the new application is heard."

An accused who feels aggrieved by the refusal of a court to grant bail can appeal against such a refusal. The appeal may, however, not lie in respect of new facts which arose or were discovered after the refusal.[124]

20.4.6.3 "Reasonable conditions"

As mentioned above, section 35 of the 1996 Constitution provides that an arrestee has the right to be released from detention if the interests of justice permit, *subject to reasonable conditions*. This is reflected in section 60(12) of the Criminal Procedure Act of 1977 which empowers a court to make the release of an accused on bail subject to certain conditions which, in the court's opinion, are in the interests of justice.

There are four basic principles that govern bail conditions:[125]

(i) The bail conditions may not be *contra bonos mores*.
(ii) Bail conditions should be neither vague nor ambiguous.[126]
(iii) Bail conditions should not be *ultra vires*, that is, outside those conditions permitted by law.
(iv) Bail conditions must be practically feasible.[127]

A court before which a charge is pending in respect of which bail has been granted, may, in terms of section 62 of the Criminal Procedure Act of 1977, at any stage add further bail conditions on application by the prosecutor. The court may furthermore upon application of the prosecutor or the accused increase or reduce the amount of bail determined under section 59 or 60 of the Criminal Procedure Act of 1977 or amend bail conditions imposed under section 62.[128]

An accused who feels aggrieved by the conditions imposed by a court can appeal against such conditions, including amended or supplemented conditions.[129]

20.4.7   Guidelines regarding the amount of bail

Section 60(13) of the Criminal Procedure Act of 1977 provides that a court releasing an accused on bail may order that the accused:

"(*a*)   deposit with the clerk of the court or the registrar of the court, as the case may be, or with a correctional official at the prison where the accused is in custody or with a police official at the place where the accused is in custody, the sum of money determined by the court in question; or

(*b*)   shall furnish a guarantee, with or without sureties, that he or she will pay and forfeit to the State the amount that has been set as bail, or that has been increased or reduced in terms of section 63(1), in circumstances in which the amount would, had it been deposited, have been forfeited to the State."

Our courts have ruled that the following factors should be taken into account when determining the amount of bail.

(i)   The seriousness of the crime allegedly committed.[131]

(ii)   The accused's means.[132]

(iii) Where a presiding officer decides to grant bail in the case of a serious offence, the officer will have to set an amount high enough to discourage the accused from absconding. At the same time, the amount should not be such that it can never be met by the accused. Such an amount will be an unreasonable condition and will fall outside the ambit of the constitutional limitation of "reasonable conditions". The bail amount must be expensive ("duur") but not unaffordable. A balance must be struck between the human rights of the accused and the safety of the community, as well as the combating of crime.[132]

(iv)   An administrator of justice must evidently bear in mind the possibility that the applicant might be guilty and should not lose sight of the fact that the applicant could possibly be in possession of the loot obtained through the commission of an offence. It would, for example, be irresponsible to set bail in the amount of R10 000,00 where a person is suspected of an armed robbery of R400 000,00. The fact that the temptation to abscond and forfeit the bail could be unacceptably great, must be considered in the interests of justice. This necessarily brings about a predicament for the applicant, namely that he or she cannot pay the bail without implicating himself or herself. The question arises whether paying the bail will in effect mean that the accused will forego his or her right not be compelled to make a confession or admission which could be used in evidence against him or her (section 25(2)(*c*) of the 1993 Constitution). In *S v Mbolombo*[133] the court ruled that the accused will just have to resign himself or herself to this diminution of his or her rights in these circumstances as a result of the weighing up of his or her own interests and those of the community.

An accused who feels aggrieved by the amount of bail set by a court can appeal against such amount.[134]

20.5   SUGGESTED READING AND SOURCES

Chaskalson, M, *et al.* 1996. *Constitutional Law of South Africa.* Cape Town: Juta.

Cowling, M. 1996. A constitutional right to bail? *The Human Rights and Constitutional Law Journal of Southern Africa,* vol 1 no 1 March 1996.

Du Plessis, LM & De Ville, JR. Personal rights: Life, freedom and security of the person, privacy and freedom of movement. In Van Wyk, D, *et al. Rights and Constitutionalism.* Cape Town: Juta.

Du Toit, E, *et al.* 1996. *Commentary on the Criminal Procedure Act.* Cape Town: Juta.

Kriegler, J. 1993. *Hiemstra. Suid-Afrikaanse Strafproses,* 5 ed. Durban: Butterworths.

Nel, TJ. 1987. *Borghandleiding.* Durban: Butterworths.

Nel, F & Bezuidenhout, J (compilers). 1995. *Human Rights for the Police.* Cape Town: Juta.

Patel, EM & Watters, C. 1994. *Human Rights: Fundamental Instruments & Documents.* Durban: Butterworths.

Schmidt. *Bewysreg,* 3 ed. Durban: Butterworths.

Trotter, GT. 1992. *The Law of Bail in Canada.*

Van Wyk, D, *et al.* 1994. *Rights and Constitutionalism.* Cape Town: Juta.

....

ENDNOTES

1   An example of such public outcry is "Sacob calls for a Ministry of Crime" *The Citizen* 25 September 1996, page 1, where appeals were made for a single Ministry of Crime to address this distressing situation.

2   Shortly after the commencement of the 1993 Constitution the following article appeared in *Rapport* of 2 October 1994 under the title "Laws actually protect criminals, say police".

It read: "What is supposed to protect law-abiding citizens is often actually greatly assisting criminals ... Serious problems are being experienced with accused who are released on bail only to become immediately involved in violent crimes again ..." (Own translation). See also Olivier 280 and Cowling 36.

3   At 39.

4   Nel & Bezuidenhout 153.

5   This view is shared by Cowling 36.

6   1994 (5) BCLR 1 (W) at 12A–C.

7   See also Du Toit *et al* 9–2.

8   Section 35(3)(*b*).

9   1991 (2) SA 805 (NmHC).

10   At 9–5.

11   Section 12 of the 1996 Constitution; Du Plessis & De Ville at 237 state that the protection of freedom of the person is most concretely embodied in safeguards woven into the criminal process, comprehensively so in section 25 of the 1993 Constitution.

12   At 9–2.

13   Cowling 36.

14   *S v Petersen & another* 1992 (2) SACR 52 (C) at 55E.

15   Du Toit *et al* 9–1.

16   In *S v Mabuza* [1996] 4 All SA 163 (T) the court emphasised the difference between the granting of bail and the release from detention upon payment of the bail amount. Only in the latter instance can it be said that the accused is released on bail.

17   Section 66 of the Criminal Procedure Act of 1977.

18   Cowling 37.

19   Section 36(1).

20   *Prokureur-Generaal, Vrystaat v Ramakhosi* [1996] 4 All SA 207 (O) at 218b–c.

21   Cachalia *et al* 83. Cachalia *et al* refer to the now repealed section 30 of the Internal Security Act of 1982 which permitted the Attorney-General to issue an order that a person may not be released on bail or warning if the Attorney-General considered it necessary in the interests of the security of the state or the maintenance of law and order. In this respect Du Toit *et al* 9–14A point out that the now repealed section 61 of the Criminal Procedure Act of 1977 was similarly controversial, as it obliged a court to refuse bail when the Attorney-General acted in terms of section 61. Section 61 empowered the Attorney-General to prevent the granting of bail in respect of certain offences. The objections raised are valid: the power to release an accused on bail is an essentially judicial one and section 61 deviates from the fundamental principle of separation of powers. Du Toit *et al* 9–15 predicted that section 61 would be declared unconstitutional. As mentioned, it was subsequently repealed by the Criminal Procedure Second Amendment Act of 1995.

22   Section 37(6)(*e*).

23   Section 23.

24   Section 32.

25   1996 (3) BCLR 340 (SE).

26   Which is even greater when an accused bore an onus, as was contended by the Attorney-General in respect of bail.

27   Adopted and proclaimed on 10 December 1948 by the General Assembly of the United Nations.

28   Entered into force on 23 March 1976.

29   Adopted at the Ninth International Conference of American States in 1948.

30   Which came into force on 18 July 1978.

31   Article I of the American Declaration and article 7(1) of the American Convention.

32 Article XXV of the American Declaration and article 7(5) of the American Convention provide that a detained person shall be released without prejudice if not tried within a reasonable time, subject to guarantees to assure his or her appearance for trial.

33 Article XXVI of the American Declaration and article 8(2) of the American Convention.

34 Which came into force on 3 September 1953.

35 Which came into force on 21 October 1986.

36 Article 5(3).

37 Article 6 of the African Charter.

38 Adopted on 9 December 1983. See article I.

39 Proclaimed on 15 September 1981. See chapter 1 (II).

40 1995 (11) BCLR 1441 (T). See also *Nortje & another v Attorney-General of the Cape & another* 1995 (2) BCLR 236 (C).

41 Trotter 6.

42 Trotter 13.

43 Trotter 133–134.

44 Trotter 13, 133–143.

45 Chatterton 41, 45.

46 Chatterton 42.

47 Chatterton 43.

48 Nel & Bezuidenhout 273.

49 At 9–6.

50 Delivered on 15 July 1996 in the Transvaal Provincial Division, case number 780/96.

51 Bail money may, both in terms of section 59 and 60, also be paid by any person other than the accused for the benefit of the accused.

52 Section 59(2) read with section 62.

53 Kriegler 143.

54 Du toit *et al* 9–6 who refer to *Shaw v Collins* 1883 SC 389.

55 Kriegler 143; Nel & Bezuidenhout 273.

56 Nel & Bezuidenhout 273.

57 Project 66.

58 Edeling R in *Prokureur-Generaal, Vrystaat v Ramakhosi* [1996] 4 All SA 207 (O) at 217h–i confirms that section 60(1) corresponds in all material aspects to section 25(2)(*d*) of the 1993 Constitution.

59 *Ellish en andere v Prokureur-Generaal, Witwatersrand* 1994 (5) BCLR (W) 6H–J.

60 1992 (1) SACR 178 (W) 180J–181A.

61 1994 (5) BCLR 1 (W).

62 *S v Mbolombo* 1995 (5) BCLR 614 (C) at 616B; *S v Prokureur-Generaal, Vrystaat v Ramakhosi* [1996] 4 All SA 207 (O).

63 *S v Smith* 1969 (4) SA 175 (N) at 177E–F. *S v Hlongwa* 1979 (4) SA 112 (D) at 113G–H.

64 *S v Hlongwa* 1979 (4) SA 112 (D) at 113H. *S v Mqubasi & others* 1993 (1) SACR 198 (SOC) at 199H.

65 *S v Magano & another v The District Magistrate of Johannesburg; Johnson NO and others* 1994 (2) BCLR 125 (W) at 128G.

66 1994 (2) BCLR 125 (W).

67 1994 (2) SACR 469 (W).

68 *Ellisb en andere v Prokureur-Generaal, Witwatersrand* 1994 (5) BCLR 1 (W) which was delivered on 19 August 1994.

69 This approach was also adopted in *S v Njadayi* 1994 (5) BCLR 90 (E) and *S v Mabaza en 'n ander* 1994 (5) BCLR 42 (W).

70 1996 (1) SACR 212 (W). See also *S v Vermaas* 1996 (1) SACR 528 (T).

71 Brought about by the enactment of the Criminal Procedure Second Amendment Act of 1995.

72 [1996] 4 All SA 207 (O) at 222e–g.

73 1996 (1) SACR 212 (W) at 218J.

74 1990 (2) SACR 212 (O).

75 1994 (2) SACR 469 (W) at 480J.

76 1980 (4) SA 145 (D & CLD) at 148D–E.

77 *S v Mbolombo* 1995 (5) BCLR 614 (C) at 616E.

78 *S v Hlongwa* 1979 (4) SA 112D at 113H.

79 See Nel 69 who confirms that these requirements set out by Schmidt are also applicable to bail proceedings.

80 See also Nel 68–69.

81 See the discussion in Nel 61–66.

82 Nel 65; Du Toit *et al* 9–12.

83 1995 (5) BCLR 614 (C) at 616E.

84 *S v Mbolombo* 1995 (5) BCLR 614 (C) at 616E–F.

85 *S v Mbolombo* 1995 (5) BCLR 614 (C) at 616H–I.

86 *S v Mbolombo* 1995 (5) BCLR 614 (C) at 617A.

87 1994 (2) SACR 469 (W) at 480I–J.

88 1994 (2) SACR 469 (W) at 480C–E.

89 At 481B.

90 *S v Mabaza en 'n ander* 1994 (5) BCLR 42 (W) at 54I–J.

91 *S v Mbolombo* 1995 (5) BCLR 614 (C) at 616F.

92 *S v Pienaar* 1992 (1) SACR 178 (W) at 180J–181A.

93 *Ellisb en andere v Prokureur-Generaal, Witwatersrand* 1994 (5) BCLR 1 (W) at 6D–E.

94 Delivered in the Witwatersrand Local Division on 26 August 1994, case number A787/94 at 2, lines 13–23.

95 *Shabalala v Attorney-General of Transvaal* 1995 (2) SACR 761 (CC) at 774E–F.

96 Section 60(10).

97 *S v Ngwenya* 1991 (2) SACR 520 (T). See also Kriegler 151.

98 At 9–7.

99 *Twayie v Minister van Justisie* 1986 (2) SA 101 (O) which was confirmed in *S v Du Preez* 1991 (2) SACR 372 (Ck) and *Novick v Minister of Law and Order & another* 1993 (1) SACR 194 (W).

100 1995 (11) BCLR 1489 (W).

101 At 1494D.

102 At 1495E–G.

103 At 1496D.

104 *S v Adams* 1993 (1) SACR 611 (C).

105 [1996] 4 All SA 207 (O) 218b–c.

106 1994 (5) BCLR 1 (W) 14G.

107 1978 (3) SA 160 (C) at 171C–E. This definition was also employed in *Ellish en andere v Prokureur-Generaal, Witwatersrand* 1994 (5) BCLR 1 (W) at 14C–D.

108 Unreported judgment in the TPD on 7 March 1994, case number A394/94 at 3.

109 See, for example, section 60(5)(*b*), 60(6)(*j*), 60(7)(*b*), 60(8)(*d*) and 60(9)(*g*).

110 Section 60(4)(*a*)–(*d*). Many of these factors were listed as considerations in *S v Acheson* 1991 (2) SA 805 (NmHC) at 822B–823C.

111 Section 60(5)(*a*)–(*b*).

112 See *S v Patel* 1970 (3) SA 565 (W); *S v Anderson* 1991 (1) SACR 525 (C) at 527C–D.

113 Section 60(6)(*a*)–(*j*).

114 *S v Nichas* 1977 (1) SA 257 (C); *S v Hudson* 1980 (4) SA 145 (D).

115 *S v Mataboge & others* 1991 (1) SACR 539 (B).

116 *S v Grigoriou* 1953 (1) SA 479 (T); *S v Nichas* 1977 (1) SA 257 (C).

117 *S v Mabaza en 'n ander* 1994 (5) BCLR 42 (W) at 56H; *S v Nieuwoudt en andere v Prokureur-Generaal van die Oos-Kaap* 1996 (3) BCLR 340 (SE) at 34I–J.

118 *S v Grigoriou* 1953 (1) SA 479 (T); *S v Nichas* 1977 (1) SA 257 (C); *S v Hudson* 1980 (4) SA 145 (D) at 146H.

119 Section 60(7)(*a*)–(*b*).

120 *De Jager v Attorney-General, Natal* 1967 (4) SA 143 (D).

121 Section 60(8)(*a*)–(*d*).

122 Section 60(9)(*a*)–(*g*).

123 1991 (2) SA 805 (NmHC) at 821G–H.

124 Section 65 of the Criminal Procedure Act of 1977.

125 Du Toit *et al* at 9–18.

126 *S v Russel* 1978 (1) SA 223 (C) at 226E.

127 *R v Fourie* 1947 (2) SA 574 (O) at 557.

128 Section 63 of the Criminal Procedure Act of 1977.

129 Section 65 of the Criminal Procedure Act of 1977.

130 *S v Budlender* 1973 (1) SA 264 (K); *S v Mbolombo* 1995 (5) BCLR 614 (C) at 616B.

131 *S v Mohamed* 1977 (2) SA 531 (A); *S v Mbolombo* 1995 (5) BCLR 614 (C) at 616B.

132 *R v Du Plessis* 1957 (4) SA 463 (W); *R v Vermeulen* 1958 (2) SA 326 (T); *S v Mbolombo* 1995 (5) BCLR 614 (C) at 617C–E.

133 1995 (5) BCLR 614 (C) 617J.

134 Section 65 of the Criminal Procedure Act of 1977.

Chapter 21
Administrative Justice

Ettienne Raubenheimer

SUMMARY

*T*HIS chapter deals with the administrative justice clause in the 1996 Constitution. The position of administrative law in the legal system is identified and it is also defined and its function described. The changes and resultant consequences brought about by the Constitution are discussed. The administrative justice clause is analysed in three parts, namely:

- lawful administrative action;
- procedurally fair administrative action;
- justifiable administrative action.

The influence of administrative justice on the police official is also examined.

21.1 INTRODUCTION

Public law is that division of the law that regulates the legal relationships between the state authority and the subject. This is a very wide field with various subdivisions. The subdivision under discussion is administrative law. The function of administrative law is to regulate the organisation, powers and actions of the state administration.[1] Baxter divides administrative law into general and particular administrative law.[2] General administrative law covers the general legal principles and serves the following functions:

- regulation of the organisation of the administrative institutions;
- determining the fairness and efficacy of the administrative process;
- governing the validity of and the liability for administrative action and inaction;
- governing the administrative and judicial remedies applicable to such action or inaction.

Each division of administrative law consists of legislation, legal principles and policies developed with regard to a specific area of administration. There is a constant interplay between general and specific administrative law. This interplay can best be explained by comparison with criminal law, where there is also a constant interplay between the general principles for criminal liability and the specific requirements of every crime. This chapter focuses mainly on general administrative law.

21.2 KEY OBJECTIVES

The key objectives of this chapter are to enable students to:

- identify the functions of administrative law;
- discuss the interplay between general and specific administrative law;
- discuss the doctrines that form the cornerstones of South African state administration;
- explain what is meant by a constitutional order of government;
- explain the material constitutional state;
- discuss the requirement that administrative action must be lawful;
- discuss the content of the requirement of procedural fairness;

- explain what is meant by justifiable administrative action;
- explain the influence of the administrative justice clause on the police official with reference to a specific set of facts.

21.3 INTERPRETATION AND DISCUSSION

21.3.1 The effect of the Constitution on administrative law

The strongest influence on South African administrative law has undoubtedly been the English law. The doctrine of parliamentary sovereignty and the doctrine of the separation of powers were both borrowed from English law. These two doctrines formed the cornerstones of South African state administration. The doctrine of parliamentary sovereignty provides that the legislature, as the law-making branch of government, is bound only by procedural rules when making laws. This means that there are no material limitations on the laws that parliament can make as long as the correct procedure is followed. This doctrine was replaced by a constitutional form of government in the 1993 Constitution.[3] South Africa is now a constitutional state where the Constitution, and not the legislature, is supreme. Section 4 states clearly that the Bill of Rights binds all legislative, executive and judicial organs of the state. The doctrine of the separation of powers provides that the different branches of government, namely the legislature, executive and judiciary, should be kept apart. This guards against the misuse of power in that one branch of government cannot usurp the functions of another. This doctrine is of fundamental importance in any democracy and has been kept intact.

The Constitution of 1993 creates a constitutional state[4] in the material sense. The main feature of the material constitutional state is that it binds the state authority to compliance with higher norms. The exercising of state authority must lead to the creation of a materially fair legal situation. The main aim of the material constitutional state is to ensure the protection of the freedom of the individual.[5] This approach to constitutional law means that each branch of the government must always act in accordance with the values embodied in the Constitution.[6]

It is exceptional to find a clause in a Bill of Rights that guarantees administrative justice. Such clause is indeed to be found in the South African Bill of Rights, as well as in the Namibian constitution, whereas no such guarantee is found in the constitutions of the USA and Canada.[7]

A constitution almost invariably provides an accurate indication of a country's past and of the future envisioned by that country. It indicates a movement away from certain doctrines, values and ways of doing things. In South Africa the movement is away from a culture of authority to a culture of justification. The latter implies that any exercise of power must be justified: the leadership of the country must be able to defend their actions and not base their power on fear instilled by their position of authority. The community must be founded on persuasion and not coercion.[8]

The inclusion in the South African Bill of Rights of this clause that guarantees administrative justice is not only a recognition of the need for a transparent and accountable state administration but also indicates an awareness of a recent global phenomenon, namely the growth of the executive state and the need to protect the individual against the executive state. This inclusion places South Africa in the forefront of human rights legislation.

21.3.2   The administrative justice clause

Administrative justice is guaranteed in section 33 of the proposed 1996 Constitution, which reads as follows:

"33 (1)   Everyone has the right to administrative action that is lawful, reasonable and procedurally fair.

(2)   Everyone whose rights have been adversely affected by administrative action has the right to be given written reasons.

(3)   National legislation must be enacted to give effect to these rights, and must

(*a*)   provide for the review of administrative action by a court or, where appropriate, an independent and impartial tribunal;

(*b*)   impose a duty on the state to give effect to the rights in subsections (1) and (2); and

(*c*)   promote an efficient administration."

Schedule 6 of the 1996 Constitution contains the transitional arrangements. Section 23(2) of this schedule stipulates as follows:

"(2)   Until the legislation envisaged in sections 32(2) and 33(3) of the new Constitution is enacted —

(*b*)   section 33(1) and (2) must be regarded to read as follows:

Every person has the right to —

(*a*)   lawful administrative action where any of their rights or interests is affected or threatened;

(*b*)   procedurally fair administrative action where any of their rights or interests or legitimate expectations is effected or threatened;

(*c*)   to be furnished with reasons in writing for administrative action which affects any of their rights or interests unless the reasons for that action have been made public; and

(*d*)   administrative action which is justifiable in relation to the reasons given for it where any of their rights is affected or threatened.

(3) Sections 32(2) and 33(3) of the 1996 Constitution lapse if the legislation envisaged in those sections, respectively, is not enacted within three years of the date the new Constitution took effect."

The effect of the transitional arrangements is that the administrative justice clause contained in section 24 of the 1993 Constitution is kept intact until such time as the legislation envisaged by section 33(3) is enacted. If this legislation is not enacted within three years after the date on which the new Constitution takes effect, section 33(3) will lapse and the administrative justice clause will then consist of sections 33(1) and (2).

The following rights are protected by the administrative justice clause:
- the right to lawful administrative action;
- the right to reasonable and procedurally fair administrative action;
- the right to be given reasons in writing where administrative action has adversely affected rights; and
- the right to the review of administrative action either by a court or by an independent and impartial tribunal.

21.3.3   Analysis of the administrative justice clause

21.3.3.1   Lawful administrative action

There are various possible interpretations of this section. The first is that this section prohibits the promulgation of ouster clauses by the administration. An ouster clause is a clause in terms of which judicial review of administrative action is excluded, with the effect that the administration bears the responsibility of ensuring administrative lawfulness.[9] According to Mureinik, the object of the lawful administrative action clause is to guard against the implementation of ouster clauses by creating a constitutional right to lawful administrative action, with the effect that review of administrative action cannot be excluded by legislation.[10]

Another interpretation, based on the positivistic approach, is that the administrative action must comply with the provisions of the enabling statute only.[11] This narrow approach does not conform to the principle of legality in terms of which lawful administrative action must comply with the provisions of the empowering statute, as well as with the rules and regulations of the common law.[12]

According to the wide approach, lawfulness is an all-encompassing concept embracing all the requirements for valid administrative action.[13]

The Constitution is the supreme law of the country.[14] This means that administrative action must first and foremost be reconciled with the spirit of the Constitution and must serve to promote the underlying values of an open and democratic society based on human dignity, equality and freedom.[15]

The 1993 Constitution contains an inherent limitation on the right to administrative justice in the sense that individuals are only entitled to this right if their rights or interests are affected or threatened. It is suggested that "rights" must be interpreted more widely than just the rights contained in the Bill of Rights. The scope of this limitation will depend on the interpretation that the courts attach to "interests". The 1996 Constitution adopts a wider approach in that it states that "everyone" has the right to administrative justice.

According to Mureinik, one of the results of the requirement that administrative action must be lawful is that administrative actions which were never before subjected to judicial control may now be subjected to such control.[16]

21.3.3.2 Procedurally fair administrative action

The right to be heard before the administrative decision is made is the essence of procedural fairness. This requirement entails the application of the rules of natural justice. These rules comprise the common-law rules of *audi alteram partem* and *nemo iudex in sua causa.* In essence, these rules require that:

- the person affected by the decision must be given the opportunity to be heard, which includes being given notice;
- full disclosure of all relevant facts, whether detrimental or otherwise must be made;
- the administrative authority making the decision must be free from bias and must be unprejudiced.

These rules are to be applied not only where existing rights and freedoms are affected but also where the party has a legitimate expectation — a status less than a right.[17] The effect of this inclusion is that the doubt concerning the scope of the application of the rules has been removed. The administration is now obliged to apply the rules of natural justice at any stage before a decision that affects rights, interests or legitimate expectations is made.[18]

Before 27 April 1994 the question was why a person should be heard before a decision is made. As the 1996 constitutional dispensation caters for participation by the nation in government, the question is now why a person should not be heard. The effect of this is that a person is entitled to a hearing in all cases of decisions determining or affecting rights. The nature of the particular right, freedom or expectation does not affect a person's right to be heard.[19]

21.3.3.3 Justifiable administrative action

Where any of a person's rights are affected or threatened, he/she has the right to administrative action which is justifiable in relation to the reasons given for it. The problem with this clause is that the courts will have to interpret the meaning of "justifiable in relation to the reasons given". This will be a difficult task. In the 1996 Constitution no mention is made of the justifiability of an administrative action. The requirement of justifiability in the 1993 Constitution has been substituted with the requirement of reasonableness in the 1996 Constitution; that is, apart from being lawful and procedurally fair, administrative actions must also be reasonable.

The reason for this could possibly be that reasonableness is a much wider term than justifiability. An administrative action which may be justifiable in the light of the reasons furnished therefor may still unreasonably affect rights, freedoms and legitimate expectations.

The inclusion of reasonableness as a requirement for administrative justice is related to two doctrines which have held sway in South Africa.[20] The first is whether reasonableness is an independent requirement for an administrative action; that is, whether unreasonableness in itself can give rise to review. Traditionally the courts adopted a narrow approach on the question of reasonableness as a requirement for administrative action. This meant that unreasonableness is only of material importance if it is an indication of some other deficiency in the administrative action. This "other deficiency" could be either *mala fides*, ulterior motive or that the person making the decision did not apply his/her mind to the matter.[21] The second doctrine, which is actually a corollary of the first, is that only a certain degree of unreasonableness will be taken into account. The degree required is that an action must be "grossly unreasonable to so striking a degree"[22] that it warrants intervention. The effect of this approach, known as the symptomatic approach, is that an administrative action may not be declared invalid simply because of its unreasonable effect. There must be something additional, namely, *mala fides*, ulterior motive, or not applying one's mind to the matter.

The minority decision in *Theron v Ring van Wellington van die NG Sendingkerk in Suid-Afrika*[23] took the view that unreasonable administrative action may be subject to judicial review on the grounds of the common-law presumption against unreasonableness. This would have meant that the courts would have been compelled to apply the common-law rule against unreasonableness, with the effect that unreasonable administrative action would be invalid, save for those cases specifically provided for by statute. In later cases[24] the courts stuck to the narrow approach to unreasonableness.

Justifiable administrative action is action that is based on reason. This means that all the jurisdictional facts must have been considered before a decision is reached; that is:[25]

- relevant factors must be considered;
- irrelevant factors must be discarded;
- the weight attached to a specific factor must not be disproportionate.

Due to the particular expertise and/or qualifications of the person or body making the decision, provision is made for a subjective element. The person or body making the decision must, however, be able to substantiate the decision objectively. In *Minister of Law and Order v Hurley*[26] it was held that the words "he has reason to believe" in section 29 of the Internal Security Act of 1982 did not leave the question whether to arrest or not to the subjective judgement of the arresting officer. The officer had to have objective grounds for holding the belief. It would not be sufficient if such arresting officer thought that he had reason to believe that there were reasonable grounds.

21.3.4 Administrative justice and the police official

Because of their nature and effect, police actions can be categorised as a specific type of administrative action.[27] Police actions normally have immediate effect and are more often than not exercised in an emergency situation. Police actions like arrest, detention, interrogation and the ascertainment of bodily features are serious infringements of personal freedom as well as of personality rights. In terms of section 205(3) of the 1996 Constitution the objects of the police service are:

- the prevention, combating and investigation of crime;
- the maintenance of public order;
- protecting and securing the inhabitants of the Republic and their property;
- upholding the law.

These obligations must always be balanced against the rights and freedoms of the individual. It is important to remember that the Constitution has created a material constitutional state where the state authority is inherently bound to higher values. The main aim of a material constitutional state is the protection of the freedom of the individual. This means that the freedom of the individual is one of the higher values which inherently binds the state authority. The practical implication of this is that the rights entrenched in the Bill of Rights may only be infringed in the exceptional and limited situations prescribed by the limitation clause.[28]

A police official is part of the state authority and all official actions are administrative actions that must be reconciled with the requirements of the Constitution regarding administrative justice. This means that, before a police official acts, he or she will have to consider all the relevant requirements for the administrative action. In the past, innumerable police actions were not strictly prescribed in the enabling Act. As an example, although section 38 of the Criminal Procedure Act of 1977 prescribes four methods of securing the attendance of an accused person at the trial, there was no obligation on the police official to use the least severe of these methods. The situation will now be completely different. If a police official arrests an accused, he or she will have to be able to justify objectively his or her decision to use the most severe method (namely arrest) and not one of the less serious methods. The same goes for search. Where, in the past, most searches were conducted without a search warrant, searches can now only be conducted without a search warrant in exceptional circumstances.

The administrative justice clause will not only have an influence on the external functioning of the police service but also on its internal functioning. The administrative justice clause will become increasingly more important for the manager in managing his or her station, branch or division. Gone are the days when decisions could be made at the whim of the commander and subordinates could be expected to execute decisions without question. Before a manager reaches a decision about anything that could have an influence on the rights of a subordinate, he or she will have to consider the requirements of the administrative justice clause. The most important principle to be taken into account when dealing with subordinates is the *audi alteram partem* principle. It is imperative that this principle be adhered to in all actions involving staff, be it leave, promotion, transfers or suspension.

21.4   SUGGESTED READING AND SOURCES

Baxter, L. 1984. *Administrative Law,* 2 ed. Cape Town: Juta.

Burns, Y. 1994. Administrative justice. *SA Public Law.*

Cachalia, A, *et al.* 1994. *Fundamental Rights in the New Constitution.* Cape Town: Juta.

Hoexter & Boulle. 1989. *Constitutional and Administrative Law: Basic Principles.* Cape Town: Juta.

Mureinik, E. 1994. A bridge to where? Introducing the Interim Bill of Rights. 1994(10) *SAJHR.*

Van Wyk, DH. 1980. Suid-Afrika en die regstaatidee. *TSAR.*

Wiechers, M. 1984. *Administratiefreg,* 2 ed. Durban: Butterworths.

Wiechers, M. The fundamental laws behind our Constitution. Reflections on the judgement of Schreiner JA in the Senate case. *Fiat Iustitia. Essays in memory of Olivier Deneys Schreiner.*

··························

ENDNOTES

1   Wiechers *Administratiefreg 2.*

2   Baxter 2.

3   Section 4 of the 1993 Constitution.

4   Preamble of the 1993 Constitution.

5   Van Wyk 152.

6   Wiechers *The Fundamental Laws behind our Constitution* 382–394.

7   Cachalia *et al* 72.

8   Mureinik 31.

9   Burns 347.

10   Mureinik 38.

11   Wiechers *Administratiefreg* (n 15) 176.

12   Burns 352.

13   Ibid.

14   See the preamble and section 2 of the 1996 Constitution.

15   Section 36 of the 1996 Constitution (the limitation clause).

16   Mureinik 39.

17   *Administrator Transvaal v Traub* 1989 (4) SA 731 (A).

18   Burns 352.

19   Burns 353.

20   Mureinik 39.

21   *Union Government (Minister of Mines and Industries) v Union Steel Corporation SA Ltd* 1928 AD 220. *National Transport Commission v Chetty's Motor Transport* 1972 (3) SA 727 (A).

22   *National Transport Commission v Chetty's Motor Transport*, supra.

23   1976 (2) SA 1 (A).

24   *Goldberg v Minister of Prisons* 1979 (1) SA 14 (A) and *Castel NO v Metal and Allied Workers Union* 1987 (4) SA 795 (A).

25   Burns 356.

26   1986 (3) SA 568 (A).

27   Wiechers *Administratiefreg* 158 and 377.

28   Section 36 of the 1996 Constitution and section 33 of the 1993 Constitution.

Chapter 22

The Right to Assembly, Demonstration, Picket and Petition

Dalene Clark

SUMMARY

SECTION 17 of the 1996 Constitution makes provision for the right to assembly, demonstration, picket and petition.

Regulation of the right to demonstrate is found in the Regulation of Gatherings Act 205 of 1993. Regulation is necessary for the simple reason that, despite the embodiment of this right in the Constitution, demonstrations demand management, even if only to control the impact which any large demonstration will naturally have on normal commerce.

The process of notification prior to a demonstration illustrates clearly that this right does not depend on the discretion of local authorities. Notification is necessary to enable all stakeholders, namely those organising demonstrations, the local or state authorities and the police, to prepare for the event, thus ensuring maximum participation in the demonstration, as well as maximum protection of the rights of those who are not participating.

The limitation of this right is to be found within the section itself, in terms of laws of general application and, more specifically, within the framework of the 1996 Constitution. The point is made that, although this right is embodied in the Constitution, it is not an absolute right.

22.1 INTRODUCTION

Protests, assemblies, and mass demonstrations have played a central role in the political struggles of the past forty years. The majority of South Africans had but one mode of political participation available to them: at the right time and place they could "vote with their feet", they could toyi-toyi, they could demonstrate.[1] This chapter attempts to define the right to assembly as well as the necessary procedures for the effective management of large gatherings. A number of Acts of general application and the relevant limitations are addressed in an attempt to enable the reader to set the constitutional boundaries of these rights.

22.2 KEY OBJECTIVES

The key objectives of this chapter are to enable students to:
* recognise the relevance of this right in view of South Africa's past;
* understand the application of the Regulation of Gatherings Act and the concomitant responsibility of managing such gatherings;
* identify who the main stakeholders in the process are;
* understand the relevance of notification;.
* understand the powers of the police in terms of section 9 of the Regulation of Gatherings Act;
* give an overview of the internal and external limitations of section 17 of the 1996 Constitution.

22.3 APPLICABLE LAW

The 1996 Constitution, sections 17, 33 and 36

The Regulation of Gatherings Act 205 of 1993, sections 2, 3 and 9

The Police Service Act 68 of 1995, section 13

Government Gazette 17065 GN 509 (22 March 1996)

The Criminal Procedure Act 51 of 1977, sections 20 and 22

The Arms and Ammunition Act 75 of 1969, section 41

The Prohibition of Disguises Act 16 of 1969

The Internal Security Act 74 of 1982

22.4 INTERPRETATION AND DISCUSSION

22.4.1 Section 17 of the 1996 Constitution

Section 17 of the 1996 Constitution makes provision for the right to assembly, demonstration, picket and petition as follows:

> "Everyone has the right, peacefully and unarmed, to assemble, to demonstrate, to picket, and to present petitions."

The right to demonstrate is as fundamental a right of democratic citizenship as the right to take part in political campaigns. Where the purpose of the demonstration is protest, the demonstration is at the core of free expression in a democracy.

Section 17 of the 1996 Constitution protects the rights of citizens to gather and to manifest their opposition to or support for any legitimate demand and to present demands to the authorities.

The rights protected by section 17 are not limited to gatherings, demonstrations, picketing and petitions directed at the authorities or at the government, but can relate to opposition to any agency or policy or person, whether in the government or not. It is, however, incumbent on the government to respect this right and to ensure that its own activities, and the law, allow the proper exercise of the right.

In the United States of America the right of assembly is afforded the greatest protection in what are known as public forums. The Supreme Court has held that streets, parks and sidewalks are public property. For example, in the case of *Brown v Louisiana*,[2] the court struck down the breach of peace convictions of African-American students who had peaceably assembled in a public library to protest silently against whites-only policy. In contrast, in *Greer v Spock*,[3] two regulations barring political activities on a military base were upheld by the court. In justifying its conclusion the court wrote that the purpose of a military base is "to train soldiers, not to provide a public forum". Whether or not a venue can be defined as public or private will therefore inevitably have an impact on the exercise of this right in South Africa.

22.4.2 Management of demonstrations

Regulation of the right to demonstrate is found in the Regulation of Gatherings Act of 1993, which was signed by the President in January 1994. This Act embodies the notion of "demonstration as of right": the notion that the ability to hold a public gathering, assembly, picket, or demonstration is not necessarily contingent upon a local or state authority's approval.[4]

Despite the embodiment of this right in the Constitution, this Act was necessary because demonstrations demand management, even if only to control the impact which any large demonstration will inevitably have on normal commerce.

Important matters which must be addressed include: the procedures which should be followed before a demonstration takes place; the ways in which the authorities should be made aware of the plans for a demonstration; what powers the government should have to regulate those plans; and — most importantly — how the process should be designed to facilitate negotiations for an agreed-upon demonstration between the organisers and the appropriate authorities.

22.4.2.1 Processes prior to a demonstration/notification

Section 2 of the Regulation of Gatherings Act (hereinafter referred to as the Act) makes provision for the appointment of three parties who are essential to the management of a proposed demonstration. They are:

- those organising demonstrations;
- the local or state authorities; and
- the police.

Section 2(1)(*a*) of the Act provides that "an organization or any branch of an organization intending to hold a gathering shall appoint a person to be responsible for the arrangements for that gathering and to be present thereat"; this person is the convenor. Section 2(2)(*a*) provides that "the Commissioner or a person authorized thereto by him shall authorize a suitably qualified and experienced member of the Police … to represent the Police at consultations and negotiations …". Section 2(4) provides that "a local authority within whose area of jurisdiction a gathering is to take place … shall appoint a suitable person … to perform the functions, exercise the powers and discharge the duties of a responsible officer …".

22.4.2.2 Notification

The Goldstone Commission of 1992 strongly recommended that demonstrators simply be required to give timely notice to the appropriate authorities before a demonstration, thus abandoning the procedures provided for by the Internal Security Act of 1982 in this respect. It was suggested that the content of the notice should be simple, useful, and specified by law. Similarly, in the Netherlands and Germany, notice need only be given to local authorities prior to a demonstration and no formal permission need be obtained in Great Britain.

The "notice only" system makes it quite clear that the right to demonstrate peacefully does not depend upon the discretion of local authorities. It requires the authorities to initiate restrictive action, thus reinforcing the right to demonstrate and emphasising a crucial point which has been problematic in South Africa: that failure to comply with the legal requirements preceding a demonstration does not necessarily require forceful action. Finally, it encourages both parties to negotiate, making it clear that authorities will have to justify any restriction before a neutral body of review.

According to Heymann, notice of a proposed demonstration or other similar gathering should be given as soon as the organisers begin issuing invitations to the occasion.[5]

Section 3 of the Regulation of Gatherings Act of 1993 regulates the notice of gatherings. In section 3(2) it is stipulated that "the convenor shall not later than seven days before the date on which the gathering is to be held, give notice of the gathering to the responsible officer" (of the local authority). Two important provisos are contained in section 3(2): firstly, that "if it is not reasonably possible for the convenor to give such notice earlier than seven days before such date, he shall give such notice at the earliest opportunity" and, secondly, that "if such notice is given less than 48 hours before the commencement of the gathering, the responsible officer may by notice to the convenor prohibit the gathering".

Once a notice has been received by the local authority, that authority will normally be responsible for convening a meeting between representatives of the local authority, the police, the organisers and any other interested parties to consider the arrangements for the demonstrations. Local authorities should develop and publish their procedures.

22.4.3   The powers of the police

To prevent unnecessary intervention by police officials and to provide for intervention when necessary, the powers of the police are set out fairly comprehensively in section 9 of the Regulation of Gatherings Act of 1993. This section gives full efficacy to the fundamental rights as set out in section 17 of the 1996 Constitution, while effectively balancing the interests of the wider community.

Section 9 of this Act reads as follows:

"(1)   If a gathering or demonstration is to take place, whether or not in compliance with the provisions of this Act, a member of the Police —

(*a*)   may, if he has *reasonable grounds* to believe that the Police will not be able to provide adequate protection for the people participating in such a gathering or demonstration, notify the convenor and such people accordingly;

(*b*)   may prevent people participating in a gathering from proceeding to a different place or deviating from the route specified in the relevant notice or any amendment thereof or from disobeying any condition to which the holding of the gathering is subject in terms of this Act;

(c) may, in the case of a responsible officer not receiving a notice in terms of section 3(2) more than 48 hours before the gathering, restrict the gathering to a place, or guide the participants along a route, to ensure —

    (i) that vehicular or pedestrian traffic, especially during traffic rush hours, is least impeded; or

    (ii) an appropriate distance between participants in the gathering and rival gatherings; or

    (iii) access to property and workplaces; or

    (iv) the prevention of injury to persons or damage to property;

(d) may order any person or group of persons interfering or attempting to interfere with a gathering or demonstration to cease such conduct and to remain at a distance from such gathering or demonstration specified by him;

(e) may, when an incident, whether or not it results from the gathering or demonstration, causes or may cause persons to gather at any public place, by notice in a manner contemplated in section 4(5)(a) specify an area considered by him to be necessary for —

    (i) the movement and operation of emergency personnel and vehicles; or

    (ii) the passage of a gathering or demonstration; or

    (iii) the movement of traffic; or

    (iv) the exclusion of the public from the vicinity; or

    (v) the protection of property;

(f) shall take such steps, including negotiations with the relevant persons, as are in the circumstances reasonable and appropriate to protect persons and property, whether or not they are participating in the gathering or demonstration.

(2) (a) In the circumstances contemplated in section 6(6) or if a member of the Police of or above the rank of warrant officer has reasonable grounds to believe that danger to persons and property, as a result of the gathering or demonstration, cannot be averted by the steps referred to in subsection (1) if the gathering or demonstration proceeds, the Police or such member, as the case may be, may and only then, take the following steps:

    (i) Call upon the persons participating in the gathering or demonstration to disperse, and for that purpose he shall endeavour to obtain the attention of those persons by such lawful means as he deems most suitable, and then,

(ii) in a loud voice order them in at least two of the official languages and, if possible, in a language understood by the majority of the persons present, to disperse and to depart from the place of the gathering or demonstration within a time specified by him, which shall be reasonable.

(b) If within the time so specified the persons gathered have not so dispersed or have made no preparations to disperse, such a member of the Police may order the members of the Police under his command to disperse the persons concerned and may for that purpose order the use of force, excluding the use of weapons likely to cause serious bodily injury or death.

(c) The degree of force which may be so used shall not be greater than is necessary for dispersing the persons gathered and shall be proportionate to the circumstances of the case and the object to be attained.

(d) If any person who participates in a gathering or demonstration or any person who hinders, obstructs or interferes with persons who participate in a gathering or demonstration —

(i) kills or seriously injures, or attempts to kill or seriously injure, or shows a manifest intention of killing or seriously injuring, any person; or

(ii) destroys or does serious damage to, or attempts to destroy or to do serious damage to, or shows a manifest intention of destroying or doing serious damage to, any immovable property or movable property considered to be valuable, such a member of the Police of or above the rank of warrant officer may order the members of the Police under his command to take the necessary steps to prevent the action contemplated in subparagraphs (i) and (ii) and may for that purpose, if he finds other methods to be ineffective or inappropriate, order the use of force, including the use of firearms and other weapons.

(e) The degree of force which may be so used shall not be greater than is necessary for the prevention of the actions contemplated in subparagraphs (d)(i) and (ii), and the force shall be moderated and be proportionate to the circumstances of the case and the object to be attained.

(3) No common law principles regarding self-defence, necessity and protection of property shall be affected by the provisions of this Act."

Woolman and De Waal voice their concern on the possible use of deadly force as follows:[6]

> "Section 9(2)(*e*) provides that the force necessary to prevent the killing or serious injury of persons or the destruction or serious damage to immovable property must be 'necessary', 'moderated', and 'proportionate to the circumstances'. It thereby places some 'philosophical' limits on deadly force. However, section 9(2)(*d*) expressly allows the use of 'firearms and other weapons' for crowd control. Sections 9(3) and 13(1)(*b*) insulate the common-law defences of self-defence, necessity, and protection of property from the effect of section 9(2)(*e*). Section 9(2)(*d*) also permits the use of force where there are apparently 'manifest intentions' to kill or seriously to injure persons or to destroy or seriously damage property. Read together, these provisions create innumerable opportunities for the police to use deadly force to curb 'potentially violent' or 'potentially destructive' demonstrations. While these conditions do not quite swallow the commitment to 'moderated' and 'proportionate' force, they do permit the police to keep their licence to kill."

To allay these fears, the following should be borne in mind in a situation where the use of force to effect an arrest becomes necessary. The police official must act in accordance with section 13(3)(*b*) of the South African Police Service Act of 1995 which states that:

> "Where a member who performs an official duty is authorised by law to use force, he or she may use only the minimum force which is reasonable in the circumstances."

The intent of the police official will therefore not be to use deadly force but, if necessitated to do so, the official will have to act in accordance with a special service order issued on 14 August 1996 which embodies specific instructions on the use of force when effecting an arrest.

Most importantly, in cases where a demonstration is triggered suddenly by a dramatic event (where the demonstration is likely to lack clearly identifiable organisers and the demonstrators are likely to fail to give the required notice) and where the police or local authority find it necessary to change conditions in what are legitimately emergency situations, section 33 of the 1996 Constitution must be adhered to. The response of the authorities in these situations should be to attempt, even at that late stage, to facilitate the demonstration and reasonably to accommodate its needs to those of other members of the public. As the demonstrators' rights are affected or threatened (see section 33(*a*)), reasons must be furnished in writing, unless the reasons for the administrative action have been public (that is, to the demonstrators). (See section 33(*c*)). In accordance with section 33(*d*), the administrative action must be justifiable in relation to the reasons given for it. (For the purposes of this discussion, it should be noted that pending the legislation envisaged in section 33, Schedule 6: Transitional Arrangements specifies under article 23 that this section remains essentially the same as section 24 of the 1993 Constitution.)

24.4.4 Limitation of section 17

A democratic public can properly insist upon demonstrations and protests being carried out peacefully and without violence. To this end the rights embodied in section 17 of the 1996 Constitution are specifically limited (in addition to the general limitation provided for in section 36 of the Constitution) within the section itself. Section 17 only constitutionally entrenches the exercise of these rights if they are exercised peacefully and unarmed. One of the central responsibilities of the police is to facilitate the qualified right to demonstrate.

With regard to the prerequisite of being unarmed it should be noted that the possession of dangerous weapons is prohibited in terms of *Government Gazette* 17065 GN509, dated 22 March 1996. The possession of firearms at any gathering at or in public places has also recently been prohibited in terms of the provisions of a notice in the *Government Gazette*. This prohibition applies from 16 September 1996. Where applicable, the police may utilise sections 20 and 22 of the Criminal Procedure Act of 1977 to seize firearms suspected to have been used in the commission of an offence or which can on reasonable grounds be believed to be intended to be used in the commission of an offence. In terms of section 41(1)(*a*) of the Arms and Ammunition Act of 1969, firearms which are not completely covered or carried in holders as specified may also be seized by the police. In anticipation of the presence of firearms, mobile safekeeping facilities should be present as well as a proper record-keeping mechanism. If a mobile facility is unavailable, the person should be referred to the nearest police station, in order to relinquish the weapon for the duration of the demonstration.

In order to facilitate the possible institution of criminal proceedings against demonstrators, it is necessary for the police to keep the Prohibition of Disguises Act of 1969 in mind. This Act makes it an offence for any person to be found disguised in any manner whatsoever in circumstances from which it may reasonably be inferred that such a person has the intention of committing or inciting, encouraging or aiding any other person to commit some offence or other.

As section 17 of the 1996 Constitution does not include the right to carry arms, the removal of such arms will not be deemed to infringe the constitutional right to demonstrate.

Section 17 of the 1996 Constitution expressly states that every person has the *right* to assemble and demonstrate. If existing legislation limits this right, it will be necessary to invoke section 36 of the 1996 Constitution to test the constitutionality of such limitation. Subsection 36(1) provides that:

"(1) The rights in the Bill of Rights may be limited only in terms of law of general application to the extent that the limitation is reasonable and justifiable in an open and democratic society based on human dignity, equality and freedom, taking into account all relevant factors including —

(*a*) the nature of the right;

(*b*) the importance of the purpose of the limitation;

(*c*) the nature and extent of the limitation;

(*d*) the relation between the limitation and its purpose; and

(*e*) less restrictive means to achieve the purpose."

Bearing the above-mentioned limitation clause in mind, a hypothetical example will be used to test the constitutionality of the exercise of the right embodied in section 17 of the 1996 Constitution.

Two thousand prospective adoptive parents gather at Church Square to march to the Union Buildings in protest against a proposed Bill advocating abortion up to the second trimester. Speeches are made, petitions are passed around and the crowd intends embarking on a march in peak-hour traffic, following a route mapped out the day prior to the march. There is no violence nor threat of violence and no one is armed. The police arrive and in terms of section 9(1)(*c*) of the Regulation of Gatherings Act notify the convenor and proceed to restrict the marchers to Church Square. The marchers are unable to proceed on their route or to hand over their petition.

Firstly, one needs to ask whether the conduct of the marchers falls within the activity protected by the right to assemble, demonstrate, picket and petition. This can be answered affirmatively, as the crowd have assembled to exercise the rights embodied in section 17. One must also note that section 17 limits itself internally in the same way as German Basic Law,[7] where assemblies or demonstrations which are not peaceful or which involve armed participants remain unprotected. As this assembly is not violent and the participants are unarmed, it can safely be said that they are exercising their rights within the parameters of this constitutionally protected right.

Secondly, one needs to ask whether governmental action infringes, breaches or denies the right to assembly. The action by the police clearly infringes the right to assembly. The next step is therefore to apply the limitation clause to determine whether the action taken passes constitutional muster; in other words, whether the restriction is saved by the limitation provisions. Section 9 of the Regulation of Gatherings Act of 1993 forms part of "law of general application". Due to the fact that the march was planned less than forty-eight hours in advance and was scheduled to take place in peak-hour traffic, the restriction of the persons to the square is deemed to be reasonable and justifiable — an obligation rests on the police to minimise obstructions to vehicular or pedestrian traffic and to ensure the safety of the persons taking part.

On the other hand, if any existing legislation totally negates this right, it must be seen to be inconsistent with the provisions of the Constitution and therefore of no force and effect to the extent of the inconsistency when brought before a court of law. This does not mean that the whole Act or statute will be of no force and effect, but only the stipulation which is inconsistent.

Although section 17 of the 1996 Constitution concerns a "right" and no one can be expected to ask for permission to do what they are already entitled to do, for practical reasons and in public interest local authorities should define how notice should be given and what is considered to be timely notice. This does not mean that this right is an unrestricted right. The local authority may in the public interest take note of the intended demonstration subject to certain limitations. These limitations would have to be in line with the limitation clause.

It should be noted that at present section 46(3) of the Internal Security Act of 1982 regulates the position regarding riotous and prohibited gatherings. In terms of this section of the Act, the Minister of Law and Order (now known as the Minister of Safety and Security) may, if he deems it necessary or expedient in the interests of state security, the maintenance of public order or peace in the country, prohibit:

(*a*) any gathering in any area; or

(*b*) a specific gathering or any gathering of a specific nature, class or kind at a specific place or in a specific area or anywhere in the Republic,

during any period or on any day or during specific times or periods within any period.

Although no specific restriction is placed on the timing of a ministerial injunction (as is the case with an injunction by a magistrate), it may not remain effective for an unlimited period. An example of a section 46(3) injunction is found in *Government Gazette* 9141 RK 579/84 of 30 March 1984, which reads in Afrikaans as follows:

> "Aangesien ek, Louis le Grange, Minister van Wet en Orde, dit dienstig ag vir die handhawing van die openbare rus, verbied ek hierby ingevolge artikel 46(3) van die Wet op Binnelandse Veiligheid, 1982 (Wet 74 van 1982) enige byeenkoms in die Republiek van Suid-Afrika van 1 April 1984 tot en met 31 Maart 1985, behalwe in die gevalle van byeenkomste — (1) van 'n bona fide-sportaangeleentheid; of (2) wat geheel en al en vir solank as wat hulle duur binne die mure van 'n gebou plaasvind; of (3) wat ek of die landdros van die betrokke distrik te eniger tyd uitdruklik magtig."

The Minister may exempt certain gatherings from his injunction. He or a magistrate authorised by him may also be approached at a later stage — after an injunction has been issued for exemption. In terms of section 72(*b*) of the Internal Security Act of 1982, if an injunction is issued in terms of section 46, the Minister must table a report in Parliament within fourteen days if Parliament is in session. As many of the sections of the Internal Security Act have already been repealed, it will be interesting to see if the above-mentioned sections will be found to be constitutional.

Lastly, it should be noted that demonstrators who cause damage and those who urge them on presently remain civilly responsible for that damage, if they can be identified and proven to have been at fault. Participation in a demonstration provides no special immunity. Woolman and De Waal state that "each member of the demonstration is jointly and severally liable for the damage caused. Joint and several liability for riot damage creates the potential for huge personal liability."[8]

Due to the fact that the rights in section 17 of the 1996 Constitution are exercised in groups in public areas, it must be borne in mind that a continuous balance between the exercise of the demonstrators' rights and the rights of those not participating will continuously have to take place. As long as the police act under the umbrella of generally applicable legislation and meet the requirements set down in the limitation clause they will be justified in their actions.

22.5   SUGGESTED READING AND SOURCES

Chaskalson, M. 1996. *Constitutional Law of South Africa*. Cape Town: Juta.

Heymann, 1992. *Towards peaceful protest in South Africa*. Testimony of a multinational panel regarding the lawful control of demonstrations in the Republic of South Africa before the Commission of Inquiry regarding the Prevention of Public Violence and Intimidation. Pretoria, 1992.

Woolman, S & De Waal, J. 1994. Freedom of assembly: Voting with your feet. In *Rights and Constitutionalism*. Cape Town: Juta.

ENDNOTES

1   Woolman & De Waal 292.

2   383 US 131 (1966).

3   424 US 828 (1976).

4   Woolman & De Waal 295.

5   There is no reason why the police or the municipality should not take the initiative and contact the organiser to initiate negotiations as soon as they hear of the event. It is not necessary for them to wait until six days before to begin preparations just because the sponsors wait until the last moment. In Australia, Britain and Holland the police initiate contact and get negotiations going as soon as they are aware that an event is being planned. Vide Heymann 64.

6   At 298–299.

7   Woolman & De Waal 328.

8   Woolman & De Waal 298.

Chapter 23
The Right to a Fair Trial

Gordon Hollamby

SUMMARY

*T*HE constitutional right to a fair trial is not an entirely new development in South African criminal procedure. The presumption of innocence, the right to remain silent and the proscription of compelled confessions have for many years been recognised as basic principles of our law, although all of them have, to a greater or lesser degree been eroded in the past.

The right to a fair trial is accorded to an accused person. A person who is not accused is not entitled to the protection afforded in section 35(3) of the 1996 Constitution.

As a minimum, the right to a fair trial includes the basic rights set out in sections 35(3)(*a*) to (*o*) of the 1996 Constitution. However, a fair trial does not only relate to fundamental justice and fairness in criminal procedure and the proceedings at the trial of the accused person. It also includes the right to be treated fairly, constitutionally and lawfully by policing authorities and state organs prior to the trial.

23.1   INTRODUCTION

This chapter deals with the right to a fair trial. It is the right of an accused person. While it is appreciated that when a criminal matter reaches the trial stage, the matter is mostly out of the hands of the police and in the realm of the courts, it still remains extremely important for members of the Police Service to know what the right to a fair trial entails. This right should therefore not be seen in isolation, but should rather be seen as the final hurdle to be crossed in order to secure a conviction.

23.2   KEY OBJECTIVES

The key objectives of this chapter are to enable students to:
- define what is meant by a "fair trial";
- know the manifestations of the right to a fair trial as set out in paragraphs (*a*) to (*o*) of section 35(3) of the 1996 Constitution;
- handle requests for access to the contents of the police docket.

23.3   APPLICABLE LAW AND INTERNATIONAL INSTRUMENTS

The 1996 Constitution, section 35(3)

The 1993 Constitution, section 25(3)

The Criminal Procedure Act 51 of 1977, sections 73(2), 75, 80, 84, 85, 87, 106(1)(*c*) and (*d*), 144, 158, 159(1) and (2), 170A, 178(2), 203, 217(1)(*b*), 309(1) and (3), 316(1)

The Drugs and Drug Trafficking Act 140 of 1992, section 21(1)(*a*)

The Law of Evidence Amendment Act 45 of 1988, section 3

The Magistrates' Courts Act 32 of 1944, section 6(2)

The Canadian Charter of Human Rights, section 11

23.4   INTEPERPRETATION AND DISCUSSION

23.4.1   Section 35 of the 1996 Constitution

Section 35 of the 1996 Constitution outlines in broad and basic terms the fundamental constitutional rights of arrested, detained and accused persons. The section is divided into three subsections. The first deals with the rights of persons arrested for the alleged commission of an offence. The second deals with the rights of detained persons, including sentenced prisoners. The third is concerned with the right of an accused person to a fair trial. The section is not an all-inclusive list of rights, but contains an important set of guidelines to the rights of arrested, detained and accused persons. This chapter will deal mainly with the last of these subsections, the right to a fair trial.

23.4.2   The right to a fair trial

Section 35(3) of the 1996 Constitution reads as follows:

"(3)   Every accused has a right to a fair trial, which includes the right —

(*a*)   to be informed of the charge with sufficient details to answer it;

(*b*)   to have adequate time and facilities to prepare a defence;

(*c*)   to a public trial in an ordinary court;

(*d*)   to have their trial begin and conclude without unreasonable delay;

(*e*)   to be present when being tried;

(*f*)   to choose, and be represented by, a legal practitioner, and to be informed of this right;

(*g*)   to have a legal practitioner assigned to the accused by the state, and at state expense, if substantial injustice would otherwise result, and to be informed of this right;

(*h*)   to be presumed innocent, to remain silent, and not to testify during the proceedings;

(*i*)   to adduce and challenge evidence;

(*j*)   not to be compelled to give self-incriminating evidence;

(*k*)   to be tried in a language that the accused person understands or, if that is not practicable, to have the proceedings interpreted in that language;

(*l*)   not to be convicted for an act or omission that was not an offence under either national or international law at the time it was committed or omitted;

(*m*)   not to be tried for an offence in respect of an act or omission for which that person has previously been either acquitted or convicted;

(*n*)   to the benefit of the least severe of the prescribed punishments if the prescribed punishment for the offence

has been changed between the time that the offence was committed and the time of sentencing; and
   (*o*)   of appeal to, or review by, a higher court."
Also relevant are sections 35(4) and (5). They read as follows:
   "(4)   Whenever this section requires information to be given to a person, that information must be given in a language that the person understands.
   (5)   Evidence obtained in a manner that violates any right in the Bill of Rights must be excluded if the admission of that evidence would render the trial unfair or otherwise be detrimental to the administration of justice."

The concepts embodied in these provisions are by no means an entirely new departure in South African criminal procedure. The presumption of innocence, the right of silence and the proscription of compelled confessions have for 150 years or more been recognised as basic principles of our law, although all of them have to a greater or lesser degree been eroded by statute and in some cases by judicial decision.[1] The resulting body of common law and statute law forms part of the background to this section.

The only difference is that these concepts are now constitutionally entrenched. As formulated in section 35(3), the right to a fair trial is but a modified restatement of section 25(3) of the 1993 Constitution.[2] Judicial pronouncements on this subsection can still therefore serve a useful purpose and will be relied upon. In line with the rest of the 1996 Constitution, "user friendly" or "plain language" was used, which is an improvement. Some new clauses were added and these will also be dealt with below.

23.4.3   Limitations on the right to a fair trial

The right to a fair trial is not an absolute right.[3] It may be limited in terms of law of general application to the extent that the limitation is reasonable and justifiable in an open and democratic society based on human dignity, equality and freedom, and taking into account all relevant factors.[4] Also, derogation from some subsections[5] of the right to a fair trial is possible once a state of emergency has been declared.[6]

23.4.4   What is a fair trial?

Under section 35(3) every accused person shall have the right to a fair trial, which shall include the basic rights set out in subsections (*a*) to (*o*). It is clear, therefore, that the minimum and basic rights are set out in the section, but that it is not an exhaustive list of rights enjoyed by an arrested person in respect of a fair trial. A "fair trial" will obviously also entail the right to be tried by an independent, impartial and unbiased court or tribunal or presiding officer and to make full answer and make full defence.[7] A fair trial does not only mean fairness in respect of the procedure during the trial.[8] In *S v Zuma*[9] the Constitutional Court held that the right to a fair trial conferred by section 25(3) of the 1993 Constitution "is broader than the list of specific rights set out in paras (*a*)–(*j*) of the subsection. It embraces a concept of a substantive fairness which is not to be equated with what might have passed muster in our criminal courts before the Constitution came into force."

There is therefore no doubt that the constitutional right of an accused person to a fair trial does not only relate to fundamental justice and fairness in the procedure and the proceedings at his or her trial. It also includes the right to be treated fairly, constitutionally and lawfully by policing authorities and state organs prior to the trial.

> "It may very well happen that conduct on the part of investigating or law enforcement authorities is so inherently unconstitutional, so fundamentally unfair, that future due process becomes virtually impossible and that a constitutionally guaranteed fair trial also becomes an impossibility. Under these circumstances the courts will also find, and should find, that a fair trial is not possible; or if the unconstitutional conduct comes to the knowledge of the court only at the trial, that the accused is entitled to an acquittal under appropriate circumstances."[10]

It is important to realise that the right is that of an *accused* person. The *Oxford English Dictionary*[11] defines "accused" as the person "who is accused in a court of justice, the prisoner at the bar". A person who has not yet been accused is not entitled to the protection offered. Section 25(3) of the 1993 Constitution is therefore clearly concerned only with persons who are accused of offences in a court of law and has no application to domestic disciplinary tribunals.[12]

The specific rights set out in section 35(3) of the 1996 Constitution are dealt with individually in the sections which follow.

23.4.4.1 The right to be informed of the charge with sufficient details to answer it [13]

The right to be informed with sufficient details of a charge affects the right to a fair trial in the sense that an accused person necessarily suffers prejudice in preparing for trial where the case to be met is not made clear. Clearly, an accused person who is not informed of his or her rights is not in a position to defend himself or herself properly or at all. Sufficient detail must mean detail necessary to prepare a full and proper answer or defence; to be able fully to challenge evidence presented by the state in cross-examination and generally to present evidence and argument as defence to the charges.[14]

Under the Criminal Procedure Act of 1977, an accused person is entitled to be provided with a charge sheet describing the relevant offence in detail and containing such particulars as the time and place at which the offence is alleged to have been committed, the person (if any) against whom and the property (if any) in respect of which the offence is alleged to have been committed, so that the accused can be fully informed of the nature of the charge.[15] The accused person is entitled to examine the charge at any stage of the criminal proceedings[16] and in the Supreme Court the accused person is entitled to be served with a copy of the indictment, accompanied by a notice of trial.[17] An accused person can object to the charge on the grounds that the charge does not contain sufficient particulars of any matter alleged in the charge.[18] The court may then order the state to deliver particulars[19] and, where the prosecution fails to comply with such an order, the court may quash the charge.[20]

Before 27 April 1994 and the advent of constitutionalism, an accused person was not entitled to have access to the contents of the police docket or to the results of the police investigation. The attitude was that a privilege attaches itself to the statements of witnesses and to information contained within the police docket.[21] This approach came under severe constitutional attack[22] and the matter was resolved by the Constitutional Court in *Shabalala v Attorney-General, Transvaal*.[23] Although the Constitutional Court held that the "blanket docket privilege" expressed by the rule in *R v Steyn*[24] is inconsistent with the 1993 Constitution to the extent that it protects from disclosure all the documents in a police docket, in all circumstances, regardless of whether or not such disclosure is justified for the purpose of enabling the accused properly to exercise his or her right to a fair trial, the court nevertheless held that the state is entitled to resist a claim by the accused for access to any particular document in the police docket. The basis for such refusal could be that:

- such access is not justified for the purposes of enabling the accused properly to exercise his or her right to a fair trial;
- there is reason to believe that there is a reasonable risk that access to the relevant document would lead to the disclosure of state secrets or the identity of an informer;
- there is a reasonable risk that such disclosure might lead to the intimidation of witnesses or otherwise prejudice the proper ends of justice.[25]

Members of the Police Service should therefore carefully consider each request for access to information contained in the police docket. As a general guideline, it should be remembered that just as there is no justification for a "blanket docket privilege", there is equally no blanket entitlement to access to all the information held by the police.

23.4.4.2   The right to have adequate time and facilities to prepare a defence[26]

This right was not entrenched in the 1993 Constitution.[27] However, it is now clear that the right to a fair trial includes the right to have adequate time and facilities available in order to prepare a proper defence. What constitutes adequate time and facilities must be assessed on a different basis at the various stages of the proceedings, having regard also to the question whether the accused defends himself or herself in person, or through legal representation.[28]

The right to have adequate time and facilities available to prepare a defence is limited by the right of every accused to have his or her trial begin and conclude without unreasonable delay.[29] Although section 75 of the Criminal Procedure Act of 1977 provides that an accused person shall be tried at a summary trial, a balance must be struck between an "instant trial",[30] the proper preparation of a defence, and the interests of the community at large.

23.4.4.3 The right to a public trial in an ordinary court[31]

Criminal proceedings are to be conducted in open court. The right to a public trial is fundamental to the principle of an open and democratic society based on freedom and equality in general, and to a fair criminal justice system in particular.[32] A secret trial or a trial behind closed doors with no public access is in principle unconstitutional.[33] However, it stands to reason that under certain exceptional circumstances criminal proceedings may be conducted behind closed doors, for example in order to protect children and certain classes of witnesses.[34] If any person, other than the accused, disturbs the peace or order of the court, the court may order that such person be removed from the court and that he or she be detained in custody until the rising of the court.[35]

The right of members of the media to attend a criminal trial is also of great importance in order to ensure that justice is not only done but is manifestly seen to be done.[36]

There is also the right of a trial before an ordinary court of law. The state will therefore not be constitutionally entitled to constitute a special court of law to hear a specific matter. It is in this context that Chaskalson *et al*[37] submit that the provisions of section 148 of the Criminal Procedure Act of 1977 are unconstitutional and that the Minister of Justice and the State President are no longer legally entitled to constitute a special superior court to conduct a trial relating to a charge which relates to the security of the state or to the maintenance of the public order.

23.4.4.4 The right of an accused person to have his or her trial begin and conclude without unreasonable delay[38]

Under this section every accused person has the right to have his or her trial begin and conclude without unreasonable delay.[39] What constitutes an unreasonable delay is obviously a matter of degree objectively to be determined according to the facts. It will have to be answered with reference to factors such as the nature of the charges, whether serious or not, whether complicated or not, the personal circumstances of the accused, whether the accused person is under arrest or on bail or warning pending trial, the availability of a court and presiding officer, the diligence with which the investigation was done, and so on.[40]

The period will start running from the time that the accused person is charged; a withdrawal of the charges before the plea does not interrupt the running of that period where the accused is later again brought before court. In *In re Mlambo*[41] the accused was charged with theft in 1986 and appeared in court twelve times in 1987 without the trial date ever being set. The charge was then withdrawn by the state and the accused was again charged in 1990 and the trial date set. The Zimbabwe Supreme Court held that in the absence of an explanation by the state for the extraordinary delay, such delay was not reasonable. A permanent stay of proceedings was granted.

What is the appropriate remedy for the infringement of the right to be tried without unreasonable delay? In *Berg v Prokureur-Generaal van Gauteng*[42] the Supreme Court held that a permanent stay of criminal proceedings[43] should only be granted in exceptional circumstances where the applicant has established that he or she has been improperly prejudiced by the long delay and that all lesser remedies have been exhausted. The lesser remedies include the formal objection by the state for a postponement and the seeking of a mandamus to compel the state to proceed with the prosecution.

Investigating officers and state witnesses have as much right to the speedy disposition of a criminal case as has the accused. They should therefore follow the same strategy and object to any unwarranted request for a postponement from the accused (or the state prosecutor). At the very least, the state prosecutor should be informed that the state witnesses are available and that the matter can proceed.

23.4.4.5 The right to be present when being tried[44]

In terms of section 158 of the Criminal Procedure Act of 1977 all criminal proceedings shall take place in the presence of the accused. The Appeal Court has held that the provisions of this section are peremptory and cannot be waived.[45] However, section 159(1) of the Criminal Procedure Act of 1977 provides that the court may direct that an accused be removed and that the proceedings continue in his or her absence if the accused conducts himself or herself in a manner which makes the continuance of the proceedings in his or her presence impracticable.[46] This provision in the Criminal Procedure Act of 1977 therefore appears to be unconstitutional.[47]

23.4.4.6 The right to choose, and be represented by, a legal practitioner, and to be informed of this right[48]

The broad right to legal representation created by this provision encompasses the following attendant rights: to choose a legal practitioner, to be represented by a legal practitioner, and to be informed of these rights. It is clear that the presiding officer at the trial is now obliged[49] to inform the accused person of his or her rights and then to afford the accused person a reasonable opportunity to exercise these rights and to obtain legal representation or to apply for legal representation at state expense.[50] This section fortifies the provision in the Criminal Procedure Act of 1977 to the effect that an accused person is entitled to be represented by his or her legal representative at criminal proceedings.[51]

In *S v Solo*,[52] heard in the Eastern Cape Division of the Supreme Court, the accused was initially represented in the regional court by an attorney chosen by the accused himself. However, the attorney was unable to continue his defence as the accused lacked the necessary funds. The regional court then ordered that the attorney be paid at state expense. The accused then requested a postponement in order to secure a more senior and more experienced legal representative. The trial court refused the request for a postponement. On appeal it was held that such a refusal constituted a denial of the accused's rights to be represented by a legal practitioner of his choice and the conviction and sentence were set aside.

However, the Constitutional Court has held that section 25(3)(*e*) of the 1993 Constitution does not confer a right to legal representation at state expense by a legal practitioner of the accused's personal choice.[53] It is only where the accused person makes his or her own arrangements for legal representation that the right caters for the personal choice of legal practitioner.

23.4.4.7 The right to have a legal practitioner assigned to the accused by the state, and at state expense, if substantial injustice would otherwise result, and to be informed of this right[54]

The Constitutional Court has as yet not had an opportunity to decide in what circumstances the state would be constitutionally compelled to provide a legal practitioner for an indigent accused.[55] In *S v Vermaas; S v Du Plessis*[56] the Constitutional Court did, however, point out that the decision whether an accused person is entitled on the strength of section 25(3)(*e*) of the 1993 Constitution to obtain legal representation is

> "pre-eminently one for the Judge trying the case, a Judge much better placed than we are by and large to appraise, usually in advance, its ramifications and their complexity or simplicity, the accused person's aptitude or ineptitude to fend for himself or herself in a manner of those dimensions, how grave the consequences of a conviction may look, and any other factor that needs to be evaluated in the determination of the likelihood or unlikelihood that, if the trial were to proceed without a lawyer for the defence, the result would be 'substantial justice' ".

23.4.4.8 The right to be presumed innocent, to remain silent, and not to testify during the proceedings[57]

Under this section every accused person has the right to be presumed innocent. The state has to prove the guilt of the accused beyond a reasonable doubt and must show beyond a reasonable doubt that the accused committed the offences charged. Pretrial treatment of the accused should proceed from the assumption that the accused person is innocent and his or her fundamental rights are not to be disturbed or ignored on an unconstitutional assumption of guilt before it is proved by the state in a fair and public hearing.[58]

The presumption of innocence was, of course, recognised in our common law.[59] However, this right was much eroded by statutory provisions and especially by the use of reverse onus clauses. Reverse onus clauses, in which the burden of proof in respect of some matters is cast upon the accused, may be unconstitutional and in breach of this subsection. Whether the reverse onus clause is unconstitutional will, of course, depend on many aspects, as will be highlighted by some examples from our case law.

In *S v Zuma*[60] the issue for determination was the constitutionality of section 217(1)(*b*)(ii) of the Criminal Procedure Act of 1977, the provisions of which presume, unless the contrary is proved, that a confession made by an accused has been made freely and voluntarily, if it appears from the document containing the confession that such confession was indeed made freely and voluntarily. The court found the reverse onus to be unconstitutional, as it could occur that, given proof aliunde of the crime itself, a conviction could follow from an admissible confession notwithstanding the court's reasonable doubt that it was freely and voluntarily made. The practical effect would be that the accused is required to prove a fact in order to avoid conviction.

However, the Constitutional Court did emphasise that this finding does not mean that:[61]

- all statutory provisions creating presumptions in criminal cases are invalid, or that
- every legal presumption reversing the onus of proof is invalid.

Another example will serve to illustrate this point.[62] The presumption contained in section 21(1)(*a*)(i) of the Drugs and Drug Trafficking Act of 1992[63] was declared to be invalid and of no force and effect in *S v Bhulwana; S v Gwadiso*.[64] The section provided that if it is proved that the accused was found in possession of dagga exceeding 115 grams "it shall be presumed, until the contrary is proved, that the accused dealt in such dagga". The Constitutional Court held that the presumption of innocence in section 25(3)(*c*) of the 1993 Constitution required that the prosecution bear the burden of proving all the elements of a criminal charge. A presumption which relieved the prosecution of a part of that burden so that a conviction could ensue despite the existence of reasonable doubt, amounted to a breach of the constitutional right. This is not to say that the amount of dagga is an insignificant factor. If the accused is found to have been in possession of a large quantity, it might, depending on all the circumstances and in the absence of an explanation giving rise to a reasonable doubt, be "sufficient circumstantial evidence of dealing and a justification for the imposition of a higher penalty".[65]

23.4.4.9 The right to adduce and challenge evidence[66]

The accused has the right to adduce and challenge evidence. The complete exercise of this right is, however, hindered by the use of the intermediary,[67] the rule against the cross-examination of one's own witnesses unless they are declared hostile[68] and the admission of hearsay evidence.[69]

The right to cross-examination forms the essence of the right to challenge or confront a state witness. It would appear that the outright denial of both direct examination and direct cross-examination in section 170A of the Criminal Procedure Act of 1977 constitutes a prima facie infringement of this constitutional right. The crucial question, however, is whether cross-examination through an intermediary is nevertheless reasonable and justifiable in an open and democratic society based on human dignity, equality and freedom.[70] It is submitted that it is.[71]

Hearsay evidence is, in principle, inadmissible. However, section 3 of the Law of Evidence Amendment Act of 1988 makes provision for the admission of certain categories of hearsay evidence at both criminal and civil proceedings, including judicial discretion. The admission of hearsay evidence bears directly upon the accused's right to challenge evidence.[72] The application of section 3 of the Law of Evidence Amendment Act of 1988 has therefore become a constitutional issue, with regard to which De Vos and Van der Merwe[73] reach the following conclusion after an investigation of comparable American jurisprudence:

> "[O]ur discretionary admission of hearsay is not *per se* unconstitutional. The final test will be whether in the particular circumstances of the case, the trial court has exercised its discretion with proper regard to the fact that an accused should not be denied his constitutionally guaranteed right to enjoy due process of law. A haphazard exercise of the discretion will yield an unconstitutional result."

23.4.4.10 The right not to be compelled to give self-incriminating evidence[74]

Every accused person has the constitutional right not to be a compellable witness against himself or herself. The trial court therefore cannot call the accused to give evidence in a criminal trial, nor can the state. Obviously, if an accused person does decide to testify, he or she cannot refuse to answer questions in respect of the charges on the ground that the answer may incriminate him or her. Under the Criminal Procedure Act of 1977[75] the accused, *as a witness*, cannot be compelled to answer any question which does not relate to the charges brought against him or her and which may tend to incriminate him or her in respect of criminal offences other than the ones with which he or she is charged.

The right against self-incrimination is closely connected to the right to remain silent and not to testify during the proceedings which is entrenched in subsection 35(3)(*b*). Similar provisions are found in the Fifth Amendment to the United States constitution, article 12(1)(*f*) of the Namibian constitution and section 11(*d*) of the Canadian Charter of Rights and Freedoms.

It is standard practice in criminal trials at the close of the state's case for the trial magistrate to advise the unrepresented accused that he or she is not obliged to give evidence but has the right to remain silent. It is further practice to warn such accused that if he or she elects to remain silent, as he or she is entitled to do, the court can possibly draw an adverse inference from the silence. The way the warning is couched virtually compels an accused person to enter the witness box.[76] The question is then posed whether "an adverse inference from silence (or the 'threat' of an adverse inference from silence) [is] constitutionally permissible where an accused must decide whether or not to rely on his constitutional passive defence right?"[77]

23.4.4.11 The right to be tried in a language that the accused person understands or, if that is not practicable, to have the proceedings interpreted in that language[78]

This section affords every accused person the right to be tried in a language which he or she understands or, failing this, to have the proceedings interpreted to him or her. This is a fundamental and basic right since an accused person who is unable to follow the proceedings and the language in which it is conducted will be unable to instruct a legal representative, will generally be unable to make a proper defence, and will certainly be unable to exercise the rights guaranteed in the Constitution as well as in the common law and elsewhere.[79]

If evidence is given in a language with which the accused is not, in the opinion of the court, sufficiently conversant, a competent interpreter must be called by the court in order to translate such evidence into a language with which the accused professes to be or appears to the court to be sufficiently conversant.[80] In *S v Ngubane*[81] the proceedings had been interpreted to the accused, who was Zulu speaking, in Tswana, by an interpreter who could not speak Zulu. The Supreme Court (Transvaal Provincial Division) adopted a rather restricted approach and construed section 25(3)(i) of the 1993 Constitution as meaning that interpretation should take place simultaneously with the testimony being given.[82] The Court held that the accused had been deprived of his fundamental right to be tried in a language which he understands, or to have the proceedings interpreted to him.[83]

23.4.4.12 The right not to be convicted for an act or omission that was not an offence under either national or international law at the time it was committed or omitted[84]

Under this section an accused person has the right not to be convicted of an offence in respect of any act or omission which was not an offence under either national[85] or international law at the time that it was committed. The right is wider in scope than its predecessor,[86] as it also covers crimes under international law.[87] The constitutional right not to be convicted of a retroactive crime is important because it is based on the principle of legal certainty and fairness against citizens who know the law as it stands and not as it will stand in future.

23.4.4.13 The right not to be tried for an offence in respect of an act or omission for which that person has previously been either acquitted or convicted[88]

This section affords every accused person the right to *autrefois convict* and *autrefois acquit.* This is constitutional recognition of the general principle that no accused person should either be tried or sentenced twice for the same offence.[89] In terms of the Criminal Procedure Act of 1977, an accused person is entitled to plead that he or she has already been convicted or acquitted of the offence charged.[90]

23.4.4.14 The right to the benefit of the least severe of the prescribed punishments if the prescribed punishment for the offence has been changed between the time that the offence was committed and the time of sentencing[91]

Penal provisions are usually interpreted in favour of the accused person, not only where they are subject to more than one interpretation, but generally.[92] This approach is also recognised at common law[93] and is now fortified by the constitutional right against retrospectivity. The accused's liability in respect of punishment is thus determined in accordance with the law as it stood at the time of the commission of the offence. Any subsequent increased punishment for the specific offence cannot be imposed upon the accused.[94]

This does not mean that the Supreme Court cannot increase a sentence on appeal at its own instance. Although in general the court of appeal would be slow to reduce a sentence that was properly imposed, section 309(3) of the Criminal Procedure Act of 1977[95] specifically entitles a court of appeal to increase any sentence imposed upon the appellant or to impose any other form of sentence, in lieu of or in addition to the original sentence.[96]

The same cannot be said of a subsequent decrease in the sentence or the provision of an additional option of punishment promulgated subsequent to the commission of the offence or act in question.[97] The accused person will no doubt be entitled to enjoy the benefit of such a reduction in punishment.[98]

The 1993 Constitution has already had an impact on sentencing[99] and no less is expected of the 1996 Constitution.

23.4.4.15 The right of appeal to, or review by, a higher court[100]

Parties dissatisfied with the outcome of a criminal trial can bring the matter before a higher court than the court of first instance, either by way of review or by way of appeal. Review and appeal are not the same thing. Where the complaint is about conviction or sentence, the convicted person should approach the higher court by way of an appeal. If the complaint is about the methods of the trial or any irregularity involved in arriving at the conviction, the best procedure is to bring the complaint by way of review.[101]

Under this subsection every accused person has the right to have recourse by way of appeal or review to a higher court than the court of first instance. Presently, under the Criminal Procedure Act of 1977, as far as appeal is concerned, any person convicted of any offence by a lower court may appeal against such conviction and against any resultant sentence or order to the division of the Supreme Court having jurisdiction.[102] No leave to appeal is necessary and there is an automatic right to appeal. An accused person convicted of any offence before a superior court, however, may within a period of fourteen days of the passing of any sentence as a result of such conviction or within such extended period as may on application on good cause be shown, apply for leave from the judge convicting and sentencing such person.[103] There is no automatic appeal and leave to appeal is necessary. The appeal lies to a Full Bench of the Supreme Court, unless leave is given to appeal to the Appellate Division.[104] The requirement for leave to appeal is that the trial court should be satisfied that there are reasonable prospects of success on appeal.

The question has been raised whether this requirement for leave to appeal is constitutional in the light of section 25(3)(*b*) of the 1993 Constitution. On the one hand it is argued that the right in question provides for an unqualified right of appeal making leave to appeal unnecessary.[105] On the other hand, it has been held that the section does not confer an absolute right of appeal but merely a right to an appeal where the procedural requirements for an appeal are otherwise met.[106] In yet another instance, it was held that the reasonable prospects test is a permissible limitation on the right of appeal in terms of the limitation clause.[107]

23.5   SUGGESTED READING AND SOURCES

Chaskalson, M, Kentridge, J, Klaaren, J, Marcus, G, Spitz, D & Woolman, S. 1996. *Constitutional Law of South Africa*. Cape Town: Juta.

De Vos, W le R & Van der Merwe, SE. 1993. Hoorsê: Verlede, hede en 'n handves. *Stellenbosch Law Review*, 1993 (4), 7–40.

Du Toit, E *et al*. *1993. Commentary on the Criminal Procedure Act*. Cape Town: Juta.

Fennell, P, Harding, C, Jörg, N & Swart, B (eds). 1995. *Criminal Justice in Europe: A Comparative Study*. Oxford: Clarendon Press.

Gutto, SBO. 1996. The Constitutional Court's opening salvo in confronting the fundamental "mischief" of the past and sowing the seeds for the new South African jurisprudence: *S v Zuma. South African Journal on Human Rights*, 1996 (12), 47–55.

Israel, JH, Kamisar, Y, & LaFave, WR (eds). 1989. *Criminal Procedure and the Constitution*. St. Paul, Minnesota: West Publishing.

Kriegler, JC. 1993. *Hiemstra. Suid-Afrikaanse Strafproses*, 5 ed. Durban: Butterworths.

Hogg, PW. 1992. *Constitutional Law of Canada*, 3 ed. Toronto: Carswell.

Nel, F and Bezuidenhout, J (compilers). 1995. *Human Rights for the Police*. Cape Town: Juta.

Mosikatsana, T. 1996. The presumption of innocence and reverse onus: Due process under the South African bill of rights: *S v Bhulwana; S v Gwadiso. South African Journal on Human Rights*, 1996 (12), 125–131.

Platto, C (ed). 1991. *Trial and Court Procedure Worldwide*. London: Graham & Trotman.

Sarkin, J. 1996. The Constitutional Court's decision and legal representation: *S v Vermaas; S v Du Plessis. South African Journal on Human Rights*, 1996 (12), 55–61.

Sieghart, P. 1983. *The International Law of Human Rights*. Oxford: Clarendon Press.

South African Law Commission. 1994. Final Report on Group and Human Rights. Pretoria: Government Printer.

Steyn, LC. 1981. *Uitleg van Wette*, 5 ed. Cape Town: Juta.

Van der Merwe, SE. 1994. The constitutional passive defence right of an accused *versus* prosecutorial and judicial comment on silence: Must we follow *Griffin v California? Obiter* 1994 (15), 1–21.

Van Wyk, D, Dugard, J, De Villiers, B & Davis, D (eds). 1994. *Rights and Constitutionalism*. Cape Town: Juta.

....

ENDNOTES

1   *S v Zuma* 1995 (2) SA 642 (CC) para 12. See also *Klein v Attorney-General, Witwatersrand Local Division* 1995 (3) SA 848 (WLD) at 862A–B where Van Schalkwyk J held that, apart from the right to legal representation at state expense, the common-law principles were not broadened or accentuated by the codification of the right to a fair trial in the 1993 Constitution.

2   See Chapter 7 of Nel & Bezuidenhout for an exposition of section 25(3) of the 1993 Constitution.

3   *Berg v Prokureur-Generaal van Gauteng* 1995 (11) BCLR 1441 (T) at 1450F–G.

4   Section 36(1) of the 1996 Constitution.

5   Subsection 35(5) and paragraphs (*d*) and (*n*) of subsection 35(3) of the 1996 Constitution.

6   Section 37(5)(*c*) of the 1996 Constitution.

7   The "trial" envisaged by section 11(1) of the 1993 Constitution does not in all circumstances require a procedure duplicating all the requirements and safeguards embodied in section 25(3): *Nel v Le Roux NO* 1996 (4) BCLR 592 (CC). See also Hogg 44–34.

8   Chaskalson *et al* 27–18.

9   1995 (2) SA 642 (CC); 1995 (4) BCLR 401 (CC) para 16. For a commentary on this case, see Gutto 47 et seq.

10 Chaskalson *et al* 27–18 to 27–19.

11 Second edition, Oxford: Clarendon Press 1989, 94.

12 *Cuppan v Cape Display Supply Chain Services* 1995 (4) SA 175(D) at 179H–I.

13 Section 35(3)(*a*) of the 1996 Constitution.

14 Chaskalson *et al* 27–21.

15 Section 84 of the Criminal Procedure Act of 1977. See also *S v Hugo* 1976 (4) SA 536 (A) at 540E; *S v Ismail & others* 1993 (1) SACR 33 (D) at 40c–d. See further Du Toit *et al* 14ff; Hiemstra 224ff.

16 Section 80 of the Criminal Procedure Act of 1977.

17 Section 144 of the Criminal Procedure Act of 1977.

18 Section 85(1)(*d*) of the Criminal Procedure Act of 1977.

19 Section 87 of the Criminal Procedure Act of 1977.

20 Section 85(2)(*b*) of the Criminal Procedure Act of 1977.

21 *R v Steyn* 1954 (1) SA 324 (A).

22 See *S v Sefadi* 1994 (2) BCLR 23 (D); *S v Majavu* 1994 (2) BCLR 56 (CkGD); *Khala v Minister of Safety and Security* 1994 (2) BCLR 89 (W); *S v Botha en andere* 1994 (4) SA 799 (W); *S v Fani* 1994 (1) BCLR 43 (E); *S v James* 1994 (1) BCLR 57 (E); *S v Smith* 1994 (1) BCLR 63 (SE); *Qozoleni v Minister of Law and Order* 1994 (1) BCLR 74 (E); *S v Nassar* 1994 (5) BCLR 60 (NmHC); *Phato v Attorney-General, Eastern Cape* 1994 (5) BCLR 99 (E); *Nortje v Attorney-General of the Cape* 1995 (2) BCLR 236 (C); *S v Dontas* 1995 (3) BCLR 292 (T); *S v Mtyuda* 1995 (5) BCLR 646 (E).

23 1995 (12) BCLR 1593 (CC) at 1621G–H.

24 1954 (1) SA 324 (A).

25 *Shabalala v Attorney-General, Transvaal* 1995 (12) BCLR 1593 (CC) at 1622C–D.

26   Section 35(3)(*b*) of the 1996 Constitution.

27   South African Law Commission *Final report on Group and Human Rights* para 4.202.

28   Sieghart 113.

29   Subsection 35(3)(d) of the 1996 Constitution. This subsection is discussed below.

30   Chaskalson *et al* 27–26. See also *S v Yantolo* 1977 (2) SA 146 (E); *S v Khumbusa* 1977 (1) SA 394 (N); *Siqodolo v Attorney-General* 1985 (2) SA 172 (E); *S v Seheri en andere* 1964 (1) SA 29 (A); *S v Baloyi* 1978 (3) SA 290 (T).

31   Section 35(3)(*c*) of the 1996 Constitution.

32   See *Botha v Minister van Wet en Orde* 1990 (3) SA 937 (W) in the context of *in camera* trials.

33   Chaskalson *et al* 27–19.

34   Section 153 of the Criminal Procedure Act of 1977. See also *Needham v British Columbia* (1993) 95 DLR (4th) 754 (BCCA).

35   Section 178(2) of the Criminal Procedure Act of 1977.

36   *R v Sussex Justices; Ex parte McCarthy* [1924] 1 KB 256 at 259.

37   At 27–19.

38   Section 35(3)(*d*) of the 1996 Constitution.

39   This is not the same as the right to a speedy trial. See also *S v Strowitzki* 1995 (1) BCLR 12 (NmHC).

40   The right to have adequate time and facilities to prepare a defence can obviously impact on the right to have a trial begin and end without unreasonable delay. See also Chaskalson *et al* 27–20.

41   1992 (2) SACR 245 (ZS).

42   1995 (11) BCLR 1441 (T) at 1450D–G. See also *S v Strowitzki* 1995 (1) BCLR 12 (NmHC).

43   On a stay of criminal proceedings pending the implementation of the Truth and Reconciliation Commission, see *Pollock v Weitz NO* 1995 (3) BCLR 342 (D).

44   Section 35(3)(*e*) of the 1996 Constitution.

45   *S v Roman* 1994 (1) SACR 436 (A).

46   See also section 159(2) of the Criminal Procedure Act of 1977 which defines the circumstances under which a court may grant an accused leave of absence. See also Hiemstra 410–411.

47   Compare, however, *Illinois v Allen* 397 US 337, 90 S.Ct 1057, 25 L.Ed 2d 353 (1970).

48   Section 35(3)(*f*) of the 1996 Constitution.

49   See also *S v Radebe, S v Mbonani* 1988 (1) SA 191 (T) per Goldstone J at 196F–I; *S v Khanyile* 1988 (3) SA 795 (N) per Didcott J; *S v Rudman, S v Mtwana* 1992 (1) SACR 70 (A). But see *S v Mkhize* 1990 (1) SACR 620 (N); *S v Morrison* 1988 (4) SA 164 (T); *S v Rudman, S v Johnson, S v Xaso, Xaso v Van Wyk* 1989 (3) SA 368 (E).

50   See the discussion on section 35(3)(*f*) of the 1996 Constitution below.

51   Section 73(2) of the Criminal Procedure Act of 1977.

52   1995 (5) BCLR 587 (E).

53   *S v Vermaas; S v Du Plessis* 1995 (7) BCLR 851 (CC) at 859F–G. The US Supreme Court has noted in this regard that the Sixth Amendment guarantees only competent represen-

54   Section 35(3)(g) of the 1996 Constitution.

55   Du Toit *et al* 11–6C.

56   1995 (2) SACR 125 (CC) para 15. See also Sarkin 55 et seq.

57   Section 35(3)(*h*) of the 1996 Constitution.

58   Chaskalson *et al* 27–23.

59   See the remarks of Mahomed J in *S v Acheson* 1991 (2) SA 805 (NmHC) at 822A–B.

60   1995 (4) BCLR 401 (CC).

61   At para 41.

62   See also *Freiremar SA v Prosecutor-General of Namibia* 1994 (6) BCLR 73 (NmHC); *S v Coetzee* 1994 (4) BCLR 58 (W); *S v Titus* 1995 (3) BCLR 263 (NmHC); *S v Van den Berg* 1995 (4) BCLR 479 (NmHC); *S v Strauss* 1995 (5) BCLR 623 (O); *S v Frames (Cape Town) (Pty) Ltd* 1995 (8) BCLR 981 (C).

63   The Constitutional Court also found the presumption of dealing arising from proof that the accused was found in possession of any undesirable dependence-producing substance in section 21(1)(*a*)(i) of the Drugs and Drug Trafficking Act of 1992 unconstitutional: *S v Julies* 1996 (7) BCLR 899 (CC).

64   1995 (12) BCLR 1579 (CC). See also Mosikatsana 125 et seq.

65   At para 21.

66   Section 35(3)(i) of the 1996 Constitution.

67   Section 170A of the Criminal Procedure Act of 1977.

68   Section 190 of the Criminal Procedure Act of 1977.

69   Section 3 of the Law of Evidence Amendment Act 45 of 1988.

70   Section 36(1) of the Constitution, 1996.

71   See also *Coy v Iowa* 487 US 1012 (1988) with regard to the use of a one-way screen during the testimony of a child witness.

72   See *Ohio v Roberts* 448 US 566 (1980).

73   At 40.

74   Section 35(3)(i) of the 1996 Constitution.

75   Section 203 of the Criminal Procedure Act of 1977.

76   *S v Hlongwane* 1992 (2) SACR 484 (N) at 487i.

77   Van der Merwe 7.

78   Section 35(3)(*k*) of the 1996 Constitution.

79   Kriegler 414: "Dit is allerweë wenslik vir 'n voorsittende beampte in 'n veeltalige land soos Suid-Afrika om op sy hoede te wees vir taalprobleme. Dit is klaarblyklik noodsaaklik vir geregtigheid dat die beskuldigde alles moet verstaan ...". See also Chaskalson *et al* 27–28.

80   Section 6(2) of the Magistrates' Courts Act of 1944. See also rule 61(1) of the Supreme Court Rules for a similar provision regarding the Supreme Court.

81   1995 (1) BCLR 121 (T).

82   Per Kirk-Cohen J at 122H.

83 See also section 170A of the Criminal Procedure Act of 1977 on the use of the intermediary where children are to give evidence.

84 Section 35(3)(1) of the 1996 Constitution.

85 This refers to an offence as recognised by South African law, ie common law and statutory law.

86 Section 25(3)(f) of the 1993 Constitution.

87 Cf section 11(g) of the Canadian Charter of Rights. See also Hogg 48–22 Iff.

88 Section 35(3)(m) of the 1996 Constitution.

89 Chaskalson et al 27–27.

90 Sections 106(1)(c) and (d) of the Criminal Procedure Act of 1977.

91 Section 35(3)(n) of the 1996 Constitution.

92 Steyn 96; *R v Milne & Erleigh* (7) 1951 (1) SA 791 (A) at 823D–F.

93 *R v Mazibuko* 1958 (4) SA 353 (A); *R v Sillas* 1959 (4) SA 305(A).

94 Chaskalson *et al* 27–27.

95 See further Du Toit *et al* 30–31. See also section 309A of the Criminal Procedure Act of 1977 for the position regarding appeals against conviction and sentence of chiefs and headmen.

96 See also *S v Sonday* 1994 (5) BCLR 138 (C) where the Supreme Court (Cape of Good Hope Provincial Division) held that the power conferred in terms of this section is not in conflict with the constitutional right to a fair trial or to a fair appeal.

97 Chaskalson *et al* 27–27.

98 Chaskalson *et al* 27–27. See also *S v Gininda en 'n ander* 1978 (4) SA 466 (E); *S v Ndlovu* 1978 (3) SA 829 (T).

99 In terms of the "postamble" of the 1993 Constitution, there is "a need for reparation but not for retaliation, a need for abuthu but not for victimisation". See also *S v Makwanyane* 1995 (3) SA 391 (CC); *S v Williams* 1995 (3) SA 632 (CC); *S v Blank* 1995 (1) SACR 62 (A).

100 Section 35(3)(o) of the 1996 Constitution.

101 On the grounds for review, see *Standard Bank of Bophuthatswana Ltd v Reynolds NO* 1995 (3) BCLR 305 (B).

102 Section 309(1)(a) of the Criminal Procedure Act of 1977.

103 Section 316(1) of the Criminal Procedure Act of 1977.

104 Section 316 of the Criminal Procedure Act of 1977. See also Du Toit *et al* 31–6ff; Hiemstra 846ff.

105 This argument was raised, but not decided, in *S v Van Schoor* 1995 (8) BCLR 927 (E).

106 *S v Bhenga* 1995 (3) BCLR 394 (D).

107 *S v Nocuse* 1995 (5) BCLR 607 (Tk).

Chapter 24
Alternative Techniques of Investigation

Tertius Geldenhuys

SUMMARY

*I*N this chapter the law relating to the use of traps, undercover operations and the interception of communications and postal articles as alternative techniques of investigation will be analysed.

24.1   INTRODUCTION

By far the majority of criminal offences are investigated by the police by means of overt methods of investigation. These include sealing off the scene of the crime, observing the scene with the object of finding clues which may give an indication as to who may have committed the offence, lifting finger-prints from objects at the scene of the crime, questioning persons who may possibly have information relating to the commission of the offence, questioning suspects, conducting forensic tests, compiling identikits of suspects, etc. These investigation techniques may be termed *overt investigation techniques* since a member who employs such techniques normally identifies himself or herself or is clearly identifiable as a member of the Service and normally explains that he or she is investigating the offence. Especially where a member deals with a suspect while employing these techniques, the suspect is fully aware that he or she is dealing with a member of the Service because the member must inform the suspect that he or she has a right to remain silent and that anything he or she says may be used as evidence in court against him or her and, furthermore, that he or she is entitled to consult with a legal practitioner.

Sometimes, however, especially in the case of organised crime and so-called "victimless crimes", where the victim of the offence is a willing partner in the commission of the offence (such as dealing in dangerous drugs or illicit dealing in diamonds, where the "victim" or buyer co-operates with the seller and does not feel that he or she is a victim of an offence), these overt investigation techniques are ineffective. If the buyer is approached by a member of the Police Service, he or she will simply deny that the offence was committed. The same applies to organised crime where the accomplices in the commission of the offence will simply deny that an offence has been committed out of fear that they too will be prosecuted or will be killed if they disclose information. In these cases it becomes necessary to consider utilising different investigation techniques. These techniques include the sending of undercover agents to join the crime syndicate and gather information which would enable the police to act against all members of the syndicate in one swoop; the setting up of traps where the dealer in contraband is unaware that the "buyer" with whom he is dealing, is actually a member of the Service; and the interception of communications (such as wiretapping) where the suspect is unaware that his or her conversations are being recorded and listened to by the police.

24.2   KEY OBJECTIVES

The key objectives of this chapter are to enable students to:

- discuss the general legal principles regarding the use of covert investigation techniques by members of the South African Police Service;
- relate these general principles to specific covert investigation techniques such as the use of traps, undercover operations, and the interception of postal articles and communications;
- understand when a member of the Police Service may or may not use the different covert investigation techniques;
- understand the legal pitfalls and procedural requirements which must be addressed in each case.

24.3   APPLICABLE LAW

The 1996 Constitution, sections 14, 35 and 205(3)

The Criminal Procedure Act 51 of 1977, section 252A

The Interception and Monitoring Prohibition Act 127 of 1992, sections 2, 3, 4, 7 and 8

24.4   INTERPRETATION AND DISCUSSION

24.4.1   General

In terms of section 35(1) of the 1996 Constitution, every arrested person has the right to remain silent, to be informed of the consequences of making a statement and not to be compelled to make any confession or admission that could be used in evidence against him or her. In terms of section 35(3)(*h*) and (*i*) of the 1996 Constitution, every accused has the right to a fair trial, which includes the right to remain silent and not to testify during the proceedings. It should be clear from this that a member of the Police Service who utilises *overt investigation techniques* and keeps the suspect informed of his or her rights in terms of the Constitution will be complying with the duties imposed upon him or her by the Constitution. Where such techniques are employed, the suspect will have no reason to complain that his or her rights were infringed during the investigation. In those cases where *covert investigation techniques* are applied, the position is not that simple. When an undercover agent is sent to infiltrate a crime syndicate, that agent must endeavour to gain the trust of the other members of the syndicate, which often means turning a blind eye when crimes are committed in his or her presence. In extreme cases, the agent may even have to take part in the commission of an offence in order to gain the trust of the syndicate and, in so doing, obtain more information concerning the syndicate so that all of its members and accomplices can be identified and be connected by means of evidence to the offences committed. Furthermore, by secretly listening to the private conversations of persons suspected of being involved in the commission of offences, the listeners will inevitably also overhear private conversations which will have nothing to do with the commission or planning of crimes. In this way the privacy of these persons is seriously infringed. Apart from this, a member of the Service who poses, for example, as a buyer of drugs and who approaches a suspected drug dealer to buy drugs, actually encourages the dealer to sell the drugs and then arrests him or her for having done so. The difficulty worsens when the member poses as a drug dealer and then arrests the buyer for buying drugs from him or her. The question is whether this can be reconciled with the functions of the police to prevent and combat crime, as set out in section 205(3) of the 1996 Constitution. The answer to this question will depend on a number of factors that will be discussed in more detail below. However, it should be obvious that the utilisation of *covert investigation techniques* will only be justifiable if the evil that one seeks to combat is a greater evil than the use of such techniques. To determine this, the court will have to weigh the interests of the community in combating the crimes involved against the interests of the community in the protection of its members against the infringement of their constitutional rights.

Each of these investigating techniques will now be discussed in more detail.

24.4.2 The setting of police traps and other undercover operations

In terms of section 252A(1) of the Criminal Procedure Act of 1977, a member of the Service or his or her agent may make use of a trap or engage in an undercover operation in order to detect, investigate or uncover the commission of an offence, and the evidence thus obtained shall be admissible in court if the conduct of the member does not go beyond providing an opportunity to commit an offence.

This section authorises members of the Service to make use of traps and to engage in undercover operations only in certain limited circumstances. The section further clearly indicates that it is the intention of the legislature that evidence obtained by means of a trap or during an undercover operation which does not fall within these limited circumstances may be *excluded* by the court. If persons who are authorised by this section to make use of traps or to engage in undercover operations employ these investigation techniques in circumstances other than those specifically authorised by this section, the evidence thus obtained will not be taken into consideration by the court in deciding whether the accused is guilty or not. As such evidence is normally vital for a conviction, the exclusion thereof will normally lead to the acquittal of the accused. The legislature is therefore saying to members that it will be futile to make use of these techniques in circumstances not authorised by this section, since the evidence obtained in this way will be disregarded by the court. The reason for the exclusion of such evidence is made clear in section 252A(3)(*a*). In terms of this section a court may exclude the evidence if it was obtained *in an improper or unfair manner in that the admission of the evidence would render the trial unfair or would otherwise be detrimental to the administration of justice.* The admission of evidence obtained through the unauthorised use of these investigation techniques would therefore infringe upon the accused's right to a fair trial which is protected in section 35(3) of the 1996 Constitution.

The use of these investigation techniques is authorised only when the *conduct of the member does not go beyond providing an opportunity to commit an offence.* If the conduct of the member amounts to inciting the suspect to commit the offence or includes a threat that, if the suspect does not commit the offence, he or she or his or her family will be harmed, such conduct will be viewed as going beyond providing an opportunity to commit the offence. On the other hand, if the police receive information on oath that a person is a drug dealer and this information seems to be confirmed by their own observations, it would not go beyond providing the opportunity to commit an offence to send a trap to him or her or to buy drugs from him or her. In determining whether or not the conduct of a member went beyond providing an opportunity to commit the offence, a court will have to consider whether the accused was an innocent person who would not have committed the offence had it not been for the persuasion, incitement, inducement, threats or instigation of the police official, or whether the accused would have committed the offence in any event even if the police did not make use of this investigation technique, but, would, in such a case, probably not have been apprehended.

In terms of section 252A(2), a court, in considering whether the conduct of the member went beyond providing an opportunity to commit an offence, has to take into account —

> (*a*) whether, prior to the setting of the trap or the use of an undercover operation, approval, if so required, was obtained from the Attorney-General to use this method of investigation and the extent to which the instructions or guidelines issued by the Attorney-General were adhered to;
>
> (*b*) the type of offence that was under investigation, including —
>> (i) whether the security of the state, the safety of the public, the maintenance of public order or the national economy is seriously threatened thereby;
>> (ii) the prevalence of the offence in the area concerned; or
>> (iii) the seriousness of such offence;
>
> (*c*) the availability of other techniques for the detection, investigation or uncovering of its commission or the prevention thereof in the particular circumstances of the case and in the area concerned;
>
> (*d*) whether the average person in the position of the accused would have been induced into the commission of an offence by the kind of conduct employed by the member or his or her agent;

    (*e*)   the degree of persistence and number of attempts made by the official or his or her agent before the accused agreed to the commission of the offence;

    (*f*)   the type of inducement used, including the degree of deceit, trickery, misrepresentation or reward;

    (*g*)   the timing of the conduct, in particular whether the official or his or her agent instigated the commission of the offence or became involved in an existing unlawful activity;

    (*h*)   whether the conduct involved an exploitation of human characteristics such as emotions, sympathy or friendship or an exploitation of the accused's personal, professional or economic circumstances in order to increase the probability of the commission of the offence;

    (*i*)   whether the official or his or her agent has exploited a particular vulnerability of the accused such as a mental handicap or a substance addiction;

    (*j*)   the proportionality between the involvement of the official or his or her agent as compared to that of the accused, including an assessment of the degree of harm caused or risked by the official or his or her agent as compared to the accused and the commission of any illegal acts by the official or his or her agent;

    (*k*)   any threats, implied or expressed, made to the accused by the official or his or her agent;

    (*l*)   whether, prior to the setting of the trap or the use of an undercover operation, there existed any suspicion, entertained upon reasonable grounds, that the accused had committed an offence similar to that to which the charge relates;

    (*m*)   whether the official or his or her agent acted *bona fide* or *mala fide;* or

    (*n*)   any other factor which in the opinion of the court has a bearing on the question.

Since a court will take the above-mentioned factors into account when considering whether conduct goes beyond providing an opportunity to commit an offence, a police official must also take these factors into account when considering whether or not to use this investigation technique.

In considering the above-mentioned factors, the following should be taken into account.

- The issuing of *instructions or guidelines by the Attorney-General*, referred to in paragraph (*a*) above, is provided for in subsection (4). The South African Police Service is presently engaged in discussions with the Attorneys-General on the contents of these guidelines.
- The reference in paragraph (*c*) above to the availability of other investigation techniques should be interpreted to refer to other techniques which would be effective to detect, investigate or uncover the offence.

- The reference to *an average person in the position of the accused* in paragraph (*d*) above should be interpreted to mean an average *innocent* person.
- The more persistent a member is and the more attempts that are made to get the suspect to commit the offence, the less likely it is that evidence concerning the commission of the offence will be regarded as admissible.
- The reference to *reward* in paragraph (*f*) refers to a reward offered to a member of the public to act as agent of the police in trapping the suspect or to undertake an undercover operation. By offering a reward to such a person for the successful conclusion of the operation, such a person is given a reason to ensure that the operation will be successful and therefore has a reason to lie concerning the degree of pressure he or she exerted on the suspect to get him or her to commit the offence. The higher the reward offered, the more likely it is that he or she would exert undue pressure on the suspect to commit the offence.

Section 252A(3)(*b*) provides that a court shall, in deciding on the admissibility of evidence obtained by means of a trap or undercover operation, weigh the public interest against the personal interest of the accused and shall have regard to a number of factors, including —

- the nature and seriousness of the offence or its consequences, the difficulty of detecting it in another manner, its prevalence in the area and the degree of repugnance towards it;
- the effect of the operation on the interests of the accused, including the extent to which his or her rights were disregarded; whether these rights could have been complied with and the prejudice suffered by the accused;
- the nature and seriousness of the infringement of the accused's constitutional rights; and
- whether the investigation technique which was used was proportional to the seriousness of the offence.

In terms of section 252A(6) of the Criminal Procedure Act 1977, the burden to prove on a balance of probabilities that the evidence should be admitted rests on the prosecution.

In terms of section 252A(5)(*a*) of the Criminal Procedure Act 1977, a member or his or her agent who commits an offence in the course of setting up a trap or an undercover operation shall not be liable for such offence if —

(*a*)   the offence relates to the trap or undercover operation; and

(*b*)   the member or his or her agent acted in good faith.

In terms of section 252A(5)(*b*), a prosecution for such an offence must be authorised in writing by the Attorney-General.

The term "undercover operation" is not defined in the Act. The meaning of this term will therefore have to be interpreted by the courts. It is suggested that any operation in which a member of the Police Service or his or her agent intentionally keeps secret the fact that he or she is a member or agent of a member and pretends not to be a member or the agent of a member, would qualify as an undercover operation, provided that such operation is undertaken to detect, investigate or uncover the commission of an offence.

24.4.3   Interception of communications and postal articles

Postal and telecommunication services are regarded as part of the essential infrastructure of a country. Without these services, no modern economy can survive. People rely on these services to communicate with one another and do so only because they believe in the commitment of the corporations that are responsible for rendering these services to ensure the privacy of telephonic conversations and the contents of postal articles. If people should lose faith in the confidentiality of communications by telephone line or in the integrity of the postal services not to open their postal articles, the economy and the government will slowly grind to a halt.

Section 14 of the 1996 Constitution entrenches the right to privacy of every person and specifically mentions that this right shall include the right not to have the privacy of their communications infringed.

Section 2(1) of the Interception and Monitoring Prohibition Act of 1992, takes this one step further by prohibiting any person from —

(*a*)   intentionally and without the knowledge or permission of the dispatcher intercepting a communication which has been or is being or is intended to be transmitted by telephone or in any other manner over a telecommunications line; or

(*b*)   intentionally monitoring a conversation by means of a monitoring device so as to gather confidential information concerning any person, body or organisation.

In terms of section 8(1) of that Act, a contravention of section 2(1) constitutes an offence.

It is, however, unfortunately also true that people involved in the commission of offences also make use of telephones to arrange their criminal activities and also send postal articles to one another in the course of these activities. If the police were unable to intercept these communications and postal articles, it would seriously hamper their investigations into organised crime. This has always been recognised and provision for such interceptions is therefore made in the Interception and Monitoring Prohibition Act of 1992, for the police to make such interceptions where this is necessary and justified. In view of the seriousness of the infringement of privacy by such an interception, strict rules are laid down which must be complied with before such an interception may take place.

In terms of the said Act, such an interception may only take place in terms of a directive issued by a High Court judge designated for this purpose by the Minister of Justice.[1]

In order to obtain such a directive, an application must be submitted to the judge. Such an application must be made by a commissioned officer of the South African Police Service with the approval of an Assistant Commissioner who has been designated in writing for this purpose by the National Commissioner and must convince the judge on grounds mentioned in the written application —

(i)   that the offence that has been or is being or will probably be committed, is a serious offence that cannot be properly investigated in any other manner and of which the investigation in terms of the said Act is necessary;

(ii)   that the security of the Republic is threatened or that the gathering of information concerning a threat to the security of the Republic is necessary;[2] or

(iii) an investigation in terms of the said Act may disclose information that may contribute to preventing the perpetration of a serious offence.[3]

If the judge is thus convinced as set out above, he or she may direct that —

(*a*)   a particular postal article or a particular communication which has been or is being or is intended to be transmitted by telephone or in any other manner over a telecommunications line be intercepted;

(*b*)   all postal articles to or from a person, body or organisations or all communications which have been or are being or are intended to be transmitted by telephone or in any other manner over a telecommunications line, to or from a person, body or organisation be intercepted; or

(*c*)   conversations by or with a person, body or organisation, whether a telecommunications line is being used in conducting those conversations or not, be monitored in any manner by means of a monitoring device.[4]

Such a directive shall be issued by the judge concerned for a period not exceeding three months at a time, and the period for which it has been issued shall be mentioned in the directive.[5] Such a directive may be extended for periods not exceeding three months at a time if the judge is convinced that the extension is necessary.[6]

A member who executes a directive or assists with the execution of a directive may —

(*a*)   take possession of and examine any postal article or telegram to which the directive applies, or, as the case may be, listen in to or make a recording of any communication to which the directive applies;

(*b*)   return a postal article or telegram that was taken into possession in terms of paragraph (*a*) or cause it to be returned to the person or organisation responsible for the transmission of the postal article or telegram, for transmission to the addressee concerned if such postal article or telegram, in the opinion of an Assistant Commissioner, may be returned without prejudice to the maintenance of law and order in the Republic or without prejudice to the security of the Republic, as the case may be;

(c) on the instructions of the officer or member who made the application, dispose of the postal article or telegram that was taken into possession in terms of paragraph (a) in such manner as the maintenance of law and order in the Republic or the security of the Republic requires, if such officer or member, as the case may be, is of the opinion that the postal article or telegram concerned cannot be returned in terms of paragraph (b) without prejudice to the maintenance of law and order in the Republic; or without prejudice to the security of the Republic, as the case may be.[7]

A member who executes a directive or assists with the execution of a directive may, for the purposes of the Act, at any time enter upon any premises in order to instal, maintain or remove a monitoring device, or to intercept or take into possession a postal article, or to intercept any communication, or to instal, maintain or remove a device by means of which any communication can be intercepted.[8]

Any person who is or was concerned in the performance of any function in terms of the said Act shall not disclose any information which he or she obtained in the performance of such a function, except —

(a) to any person who of necessity requires it for the performance of his or her functions in terms of the said Act;

(b) if he or she is a person who of necessity supplies it in the performance of his or her functions in terms of the said Act;

(c) such information which is required in terms of any law or as evidence in any court of law; or

(d) to any competent authority which requires it for the institution of an investigation with a view to the institution of any criminal prosecution.[9]

24.5 SUGGESTED READING

Colman, H. 1954. The judicial approach to trapping cases. *SALJ*, 71, 120.

Crofton, MJ. 1977. Problems in the use of police traps. In *Law Review*, 12, 12.

ENDNOTES

1 Section 3(1)(*a*) of the Act.

2 Section 3(1)(*b*)(i) read with section 3(2)(*a*) of the Act.

3 Section 3(6) of the Act.

4   Section 2(2) of the Act.
5   Section 3(3) of the Act.
6   Section 3(4) of the Act.
7   Section 4(2) of the Act.
8   Section 4(4) of the Act.
9   Section 7(1) of the Act.

Chapter 25
The Exclusion of Unconstitutionally Obtained Evidence

Dalene Clark

SUMMARY

S OUTH AFRICA has followed the English common-law approach to the admissibility of relevant evidence obtained in an unlawful manner. This means that there was principally no bar to the admission of evidence obtained in this way. This inclusionary approach is incompatible with a Bill of Fundamental Rights. Entrenched rights are not worth more than the paper they are written on if a court is principally still bound to admit evidence which has been obtained in an unlawful, that is, an unconstitutional manner. The so-called exclusionary rule has been developed by the United States Supreme Court. The initial, rigid approach excluded all evidence found in an unlawful way, but has been tempered to serve the interests of society. This means that in certain circumstances unlawfully obtained evidence will be admitted. The Canadian Charter expressly includes a qualified exclusionary rule. The Canadian courts are therefore left with a discretion as to the exclusion or admission of evidence. Section 35(5) of the 1996 Constitution embodies a constitutionally entrenched qualified exclusionary rule. This means that there is a clean break with the common-law inclusionary rule of the past and clearly illustrates that there will also not be a strict application of this rule. The South African provision is based on the Canadian approach and to this end a golden midway has been chosen between the two extremes of absolute exclusion and absolute admission of evidence.

25.1   INTRODUCTION

The 1996 Constitution provides in section 35(5) that: "evidence obtained in a manner that violates any right in the Bill of Rights must be excluded if the admission of that evidence would render the trial unfair or otherwise be detrimental to the administration of justice". As the exclusionary rule is entrenched in the Bill of Rights, questions arise such as why an exclusionary rule is necessary and whether this rule should be applied rigidly or in a qualified manner.

But, first of all, one needs to know what the term "exclusionary rule" means and where it comes from before the application of this rule can be understood.

Basically, the exclusionary rule is a rule which excludes real, documentary and oral evidence which has been unconstitutionally obtained.

25.2   KEY OBJECTIVES

The key objectives of this chapter are to enable students to:
* understand what the exclusionary rule is;
* be able to explain the common-law approach to the admissibility of unlawfully obtained evidence;
* be able to describe the argument in favour of an exclusionary rule and the practical effect of not applying this rule;
* understand the constitutional impact of the exclusionary rule;

- be able to identify areas in which this rule is applied in the United States, as well as areas in which the rigidity of the exclusionary rule has relaxed in cases of good faith;
- explain the role of this rule in Canada.

25.3   APPLICABLE LAW

The 1996 Constitution, section 35(5)
The Criminal Procedure Act 51 of 1977, sections 29 and 252
The Canadian Charter of Human Rights, section 24

25.4   INTERPRETATION AND DISCUSSION

25.4.1   The South African position prior to the 1996 Constitution

The position in South Africa regarding the admissibility of evidence is partially governed by statute and partially by common law.[1] According to section 252 of the Criminal Procedure Act of 1977, "the law as to the admissibility of evidence ... shall apply in any case not expressly provided for in the Criminal Procedure Act or any other law". In terms of the English common-law approach, there is in principle no bar to the admissibility of relevant evidence obtained in an unlawful manner.

The common-law rule governing the admissibility of evidence gleaned in an unlawful manner embodies a strict "inclusionary approach"[2] (this means including evidence obtained in an unconstitutional manner).

In the case *Kuruma, Son of Kainu v R*[3] it was decided that, if the evidence was relevant, the court should not be concerned as to how the evidence was obtained. In *R v Mabuya*[4] evidence obtained as a result of an alleged unlawful police search of a private dwelling was admitted. In *R v Uys and Uys*[5] documents discovered as a result of an alleged illegal search were found to be admissible. In the case *S v Nel*[6] the basis of the inclusionary rule was explained as follows: evidence obtained in an unlawful manner could only be excluded where, firstly, the accused had been *compelled* to provide evidence against himself and, secondly, where the evidence had been obtained by *force* from an accused.[7]

Now that the South African position has been explained, it is necessary to look at the basis of both the inclusionary and the exclusionary rules.

25.4.2   The inclusionary approach

The inclusionary rule is based on the philosophy of crime control. From this viewpoint the most important aim of the criminal process is the suppression of criminal activity. This means that the goal of fighting crime is so important that no matter how evidence is obtained, it will be admitted if it can be used to prosecute. A few of the arguments used by Van der Merwe[8] to endorse this approach are as follows:

- the end justifies the means — in other words, at the end of the day a criminal is prosecuted;
- the probative value of evidence is not impaired by the unlawful method employed in acquiring such evidence; and the relevance of such evidence cannot be affected by the mere fact that it was unlawfully procured;
- the police should not be "handcuffed" in their detection and investigation of crime — in other words, the police should be able to use any and all means in their fight against crime;
- criminals do not impose restrictions upon themselves in their choice of weapons; why should the police?

25.4.3   The exclusionary approach

In contrast to the inclusionary rule, the exclusionary rule is based on the philosophy of due process. The primary function, it is argued, of the criminal trial is not to convict the accused, but to ensure that the conviction takes place in terms of a procedure which duly and properly acknowledges the rights of the accused at every critical stage during the pretrial, trial, and post-trial procedures.

This argument gathers momentum when presented with a bill or rights which guarantees due process and places important constitutional limitations upon official power. If there is no due process and no exclusionary rule, the rights in the Bill of Rights are stripped of their status as constitutional guarantees.

In *Mapp v Ohio*[9] the importance of the exclusionary rule is explained as follows:

> "Having once recognized … that the right to be secured against rude invasions of privacy by state officers is … constitutional in origin, we can no longer permit that right to be an empty promise. Because it is enforceable in the same manner and to like effect as other basic rights secured by the due process clause, we can no longer permit it to be revocable at the whim of any police officer who, in the name of law enforcement itself, chooses to suspend its enjoyment. Therefore the individual gets what the constitution guarantees him, the police officer gets that to which honest law enforcement entitles; courts get the judicial integrity so necessary in the true administration of justice."

Judicial "remote control" is created by the exclusionary rule over police in the field.

The argument in favour of the exclusionary rule is based on the belief that the truth need not and should not be established at all cost because there are higher values in the best interests of which illegally obtained evidence should in principle not be admitted. The exclusionary rule can, unfortunately, produce the acquittal of someone who had in all probability engaged in criminal activity. As explained in *S v Lwane*,[10] where the accused (witness) had not been warned that he was not obliged to give evidence exposing himself to a criminal court, "if the criminal goes free in order to serve a larger and more important end, then social justice is done, even if individual justice is not".

The exclusionary rule is not primarily aimed at discouraging unconstitutional official conduct. Its true purpose is to serve as an effective internal tool for maintaining and protecting the value system as a whole; but if officials are as a result of the exclusionary rule deterred from infringing fundamental rights, then so much the better.[11]

Van Rooyen[12] argues as follows:

> "Upon close analysis it is clear that the policy decision that certain relevant and credible evidence may not be obtained — has already been taken by the rules regulating pre-trial police powers (called 'primary rules') and is not newly imposed by the exclusionary rule 'the secondary rule'. The secondary rule merely 'enforces' the primary rules."

For example, section 29 of the Criminal Procedure Act of 1977 does not allow a male police official to search a female accused/suspect. This is the primary rule which regulates police conduct. Society accepts that in certain circumstances evidence will be lost, for example if a female arrestee flushes evidence down the toilet before she is searched. If the male officer searches and finds evidence, the evidence will be excluded as a result of the secondary rule (being the exclusionary rule). To sum up: the primary rule can cause evidence to be lost. But, if the primary rule is ignored, the secondary rule (the exclusionary rule) excludes the evidence.

As the 1996 Constitution expressly includes a provision under the right to fair trial which precludes evidence obtained in a manner that violates a right in the Bill of Rights, the debate as to whether we should have an exclusionary rule is moot. The question which remains is whether this exclusionary rule should be applied strictly — that is, excluding all evidence unconstitutionally obtained, or in a qualified manner — that is, taking all the circumstances into consideration. To expound the exclusionary rule as found in section 35(5) of the 1996 Constitution one must of necessity consider international law. To this end the American, Canadian and German approach will be examined briefly.

25.4.4   The American approach

The exclusionary rule has been developed by the courts in the United States and is not found expressly in the constitution. According to Van der Merwe,[13] the exclusionary rule generally works well in the United States, most notably in the following areas.

- *Illegal searches and seizures.*[14]
- *Questioning by the police.* For example, in the case *Miranda v Arizona*,[15] a suspect in a rape case was arrested, picked out in a line-up and subse-

quently confessed to the crime. However, the suspect was at no stage warned of his constitutional rights and, as a result, the court held:

"Prior to any questioning, the person must be warned that he has a right to remain silent, that any statement he does make may be used as evidence against him, and that he has a right to the presence of an attorney, either retained or appointed. The defendant may waive effectuation of these rights, provided the waiver is made voluntarily, knowingly and intelligently. If, however, he indicates in any manner and at any stage of the process that he wishes to consult with an attorney before speaking there can be no questioning. Likewise, if the individual is alone and indicates in any manner that he does not wish to be interrogated, the police may not question him. The mere fact that he may have answered some questions or volunteered some statements on his own does not deprive him of the right to refrain from answering any further inquiries until he has consulted with an attorney and thereafter consents to be questioned."

Because of the failure to give the above-mentioned warning, no evidence obtained during that time could be admitted.[16]

- *Securing identification evidence in breach of the Fifth or Sixth Amendments*: In the case *Gilbert v California*[17] a man was convicted of armed robbery and of murder and was sentenced to death. The US Supreme Court reversed judgment on the basis that his right to have an attorney present at the police line-up was violated. In our law an irregularity at the parade merely affects the weight of the identification evidence.

- *Police methods that "shock the conscience"*: In the case *Rochin v California*[18] it was held that where police officials arranged for an involuntary stomach pump in order to obtain evidence, their conduct violated due process as it shocked the conscience and was therefore inadmissible.

Even though the application of this rule has proved successful, it has also shown that a rigid application of this rule can bring the criminal justice system into disfavour. The US Supreme Court has therefore relaxed the rigid application of the exclusionary rule in cases of good faith. Examples of the relaxation of this rule are the following:

- When an official has reasonably relied and acted upon a statute which was only later held to be a violation of a constitutionally entrenched right.

- Where the evidence would have eventually been discovered anyway, the so-called "inevitable discovery". For example, in the case *Nix v Williams,*[19] a man was found guilty on evidence (chemical tests on the body) of a body which he had pointed out to the police after an appeal by a police official to point out the body so that the parents of the girl would be able to give her a "Christian burial". The accused held that his Sixth Amendment right was violated as his lawyer was not present at the time of the appeal by the police official. The US Supreme Court held that the body would ultimately or inevitably have been discovered even if no violation had taken place. The court held further that challenged evidence which is in some sense the product of illegal activity is permissible if the prosecution establishes on a preponderance of probabilities that the evidence/information ultimately would have been discovered by lawful means. It was further held, that, to establish the admissibility of such evidence, the prosecution need not prove the absence of bad faith in originally securing such evidence.

- Unconstitutionally obtained evidence can be used in cross-examination to challenge an accused's testimony.
- The police practice of "stopping and frisking" a suspect in circumstances where a police official observes unusual conduct and suspects on less-than-normal probable cause that a crime may have been committed, does not violate the constitutional prohibition against unreasonable search and seizure.

It is therefore clear that public policy plays a role in the admission or exclusion of unconstitutionally obtained evidence. In other words, the courts look at whether the best interests of society are served by the admission or exclusion of evidence.

25.4.5   The Canadian and German approach

An exclusionary rule is expressly provided for in the Canadian Charter. Section 24(2) of the Canadian Charter states: "[I]f evidence was obtained in a manner which infringed or denied any rights or freedoms guaranteed by this Charter, the evidence shall be excluded if it is established that, having regard to all the circumstances, the admission of such evidence would bring the administration of justice into disrepute". According to *R v Collins*,[20] this section refers to disrepute in the eyes of concerned citizens and not of judges, lawyers and the police. Another way of saying this is that public policy must play a decisive role.

The Charter's position with respect to evidence obtained in violation of the Charter of Rights falls between two extremes. Section 24(2) rejects the USA approach that automatically excludes evidence obtained in violation of the Bill of Rights. It also shuns the position at common law that all relevant evidence is admissible, no matter how it was obtained.

In *R v Collins* Seaton JA was also careful to point out that nothing in section 24(2) of the Canadian Charter suggests a discretion. He ruled that once it has been established that admission of the evidence would bring the administration of justice into disrepute, the evidence shall be excluded. This does not mean that the court cannot consider *a wide variety of factors* in determining whether the admission of certain evidence would bring the administration of justice into disrepute. And, in this sense, the Canadian courts are left with a discretion.[21]

As the German approach basically corresponds with the Canadian approach, it is appropriate briefly to explain their approach to the exclusionary rule. The rule of law requires the exclusion of evidence, regardless of its weight or value, in cases of police brutality or other aggravated illegality. The principle of proportionality calls for the exclusion of probative evidence obtained by means which are excessively intrusive when compared with the triviality of the offence investigated and the sphere of privacy invaded. According to one fitting metaphor, the principle of proportionality means that one should not shoot sparrows with a canon.

25.5   CONCLUSION

The South African version of the exclusionary rule clearly does not follow the rigid approach originally followed in the United States or the inclusionary approach found at common law. Evidence is only excluded if it "would render the trial unfair or otherwise be detrimental to the administration of justice".[22] A qualified application of the exclusionary rule is based on the grounds that a rigid application deprives the court of a discretion and that the exclusion of all evidence will not serve the best interests of society. The infringement of any fundamental right of a suspect may be deliberate or cruel or may be trivial and accidental. Surely intentional and unintentional infringements cannot be treated in the same manner. The South African provision is clearly based on the Canadian approach and to this end a golden midway has been chosen between the two extremes of absolute exclusion and absolute admission of evidence.

It is suggested that when the admission or exclusion of evidence is considered by South African courts, the question to be asked should be whether public policy would demand the exclusion of evidence which is of high probative value but which was obtained as a result of a technical, minor and accidental infringement of a fundamental right. In an unreported judgment *Key v The Attorney General, Cape of Good Hope Provincial Division & another*,[23] delivered on 15 May 1996, Judge Kriegler found the following:

> "In any democratic criminal justice system there is a tension between, on the one hand, the public interest in bringing criminals to book and, on the other, the equally great public interest in ensuring that justice is manifestly done to all, even those suspected of conduct which would put them beyond the pale. To be sure, a prominent feature of that tension is the universal and unceasing endeavour by international human rights bodies, enlightened legislatures and courts to prevent or curtail excessive zeal by state agencies in the prevention, investigation or prosecution of crime. But none of that means sympathy for crime and its perpetrators. Nor does it mean a predilection for technical niceties and ingenious legal stratagems. What the Constitution demands is that the

accused be given a fair trial. Ultimately, as was held in *Ferreira v Levin*, fairness is an issue which has to be decided upon the facts of each case, and the trial judge is the person best placed to take that decision. At times fairness might require that evidence unconstitutionally obtained be excluded. But there will also be times when fairness will require that evidence, albeit obtained unconstitutionally, nevertheless be admitted."

The concluding opinion is held that the inclusion of section 35(5) in the 1996 Constitution will ensure that the criminal justice system, including the courts, will be held in high esteem by the public at large, irrespective of the fact whether in a particular case unconstitutionally obtained evidence has been excluded or admitted.

The responsibility resting on police officials to act within the parameters of the Constitution and in respect of individuals' constitutionally entrenched rights is explained by McQuoid-Mason[24] as follows:

"Should police officers fail to measure up to the requirements of the Constitution, and neglect the rights of individuals they have detained and arrested, they run the risk of allowing persons who might subsequently be convicted by a court of law for a criminal offence to escape on the technicality that the police officer concerned has failed to respect their constitutional rights. This could have tragic consequences bearing in mind the present tide of criminal conduct in this country. By respecting the rights preserved in the Constitution, and enforcing the provisions of the Constitution correctly, the police will not only be contributing to developing a human rights culture in South Africa, but will also ensure that potentially guilty criminals are not able to escape their just desserts on the basis that their constitutional rights have been violated."

25.6   SUGGESTED READING AND SOURCES

Nel, F & Bezuidenhout, J (compilers). 1995. *Human Rights for the Police.* Cape Town: Juta.

Skeen, Andrew. 1988. The admissibility of improperly obtained evidence in criminal trials. *SACJ* (1988), 389.

Van der Merwe, SE. 1993. Unconstitutionally obtained evidence. In *Stellenbosch Law Review* (1993), 173.

Van Rooyen, JH. 1975. Investigation and prosecution of crime. In *Acta Juridica*, 70.

ENDNOTES

1 Nel & Bezuidenhout 214.

2 Van der Merwe 178.

3 1955 AC 197 203.

4 1927 CPD 181.

5 1940 TPD 405.

6 1987 (4) SA 950 (W).

7 Van der Merwe 178.

8 At 180.

9 367 US (1961).

10 1966 (2) SA 433(A).

11 Van der Merwe 193.

12 At 70.

13 At 195.

14 *Mapp v Ohio* 367 US 643 (1961).

15 384 US 436 (1966).

16 Nel & Bezuidenhout 155.

17 388 US 263 (1967).

18 388 US 263 (1957).

19 467 US 431 (1984).

20 (1983) 5 CCC (3d) 141 (BCCA).

21 Van der Merwe 202.

22 Section 35(5) of the 1996 Constitution.

23 Case no CCT 21/94.

24 McQuoid-Mason as quoted in Nel & Bezuidenhout at 158.

Chapter 26
Freedom of Expression

Lene Johannessen

Tracey Cohen

SUMMARY

*T*HIS chapter will explain how the right to freedom of expression is provided for in the South African Constitution and what limitations or restrictions can permissibly be imposed on those who are exercising this right. It will explain how freedom of expression applies generally to people living in South Africa and will furthermore explain the legal framework for the exercise of the right in relation to members of the South African Police Service (SAPS). Examples will be given to illustrate how the right applies and what limitations can be imposed on it.

26.1 INTRODUCTION

Freedom of expression is recognised as one of the cornerstones of a democratic society. The commitment to freedom of expression is founded on the notion that expression is more deserving of protection from government regulation than are other forms of social practice. A number of arguments have been advanced to justify this commitment, the most influential of which may be summarised as follows:

- to seek and attain truth is an inherently good activity;[1]
- participation in social and political decision-making is to be fostered and encouraged;[2]
- the diversity in forms of individual self-fulfilment and human flourishing ought to be cultivated in an essentially tolerant, indeed welcoming environment, not only for the sake of those who convey a meaning but also for the sake of those to whom it is conveyed.[3]

Freedom of expression is a fundamental right protected by the South African Constitution. However, no right is absolute in operation and all rights may be limited under certain circumstances. Moreover, the existence of a Bill of Rights often places various fundamental rights in conflict with one another. For example, freedom of expression may conflict with the right to equality if, for example, freedom of expression is used to advocate racial, gender, or other forms of inequality. It is then through a process of "rights-balancing", that the role of the courts must determine which right should triumph in a given situation.

26.2 KEY OBJECTIVES

The key objectives of this chapter are to enable students to:

- understand what is meant by freedom of expression and to be conversant with the essential role it plays in a functioning democracy;
- be conversant with the particular form of protection granted to freedom of expression in the South African Constitution;
- be conversant with the conditions which limit this protection;
- understand the legal framework regulating freedom of expression, specifically in relation to members of the South African Police Service.

26.3   APPLICABLE LAW

The 1996 Constitution, sections 8, 16 and 36
The 1993 Constitution, section 15
The South African Police Service Act 68 of 1995
The Canadian Charter of Rights and Freedoms, article 19
The Universal Declaration of Human Rights, article 2(*b*)
The International Covenant on Civil and Political Rights, article 19
The African Charter on Human and Peoples' Rights, article 9(1)
The American Convention on Human Rights, article 13
The European Convention on Human Rights, article 10

26.4   INTERPRETATION AND DISCUSSION

26.4.1   Relevant section of the 1996 Constitution

Because freedom of expression is so important for the functioning of a democracy, it has been included in the Bill of Rights which is contained in the 1996 Constitution.[4]

Section 16 reads as follows:

"16 (1)   Everyone has the right to freedom of expression, which includes —
   (*a*)   freedom of the press and other media;
   (*b*)   freedom to receive and impart information and ideas;
   (*c*)   freedom of artistic creativity; and
   (*d*)   academic freedom and freedom of scientific research.

16 (2)   The right in subsection (1) does not extend to —
   (*a*)   propaganda for war;
   (*b*)   incitement of imminent violence; or
   (*c*)   advocacy of hatred that is based on race, ethnicity, gender or religion, and that constitutes incitement to cause harm."

It follows from the wording of this clause that the forms of expression specified in section 16(1) are not inclusive. In other words, the right to freedom of expression goes beyond those areas of expression and activity which are specifically listed. Freedom of expression goes beyond the mere freedom to speak and write words and would embrace, for example, symbolic acts intended to convey an idea such as flag burning or wearing a symbolic armband.[5]

Despite the broad areas of speech and expression which are protected by the Constitution, certain categories of speech are excluded. This means that one cannot rely on the right to freedom of expression to propagate war, to incite to imminent violence, or to advocate hate against other groups of society, which constitutes incitement to cause harm.

The 1993 Constitution came into force with the first democratic election in South Africa in April 1994. The 1993 Constitution (as well as the 1996 Constitution which now replaces the 1993 Constitution) bestows fundamental rights on all the citizens of the country, including all members of the South African Police Service, which encompasses the Reserve Police Service, the metropolitan police service, the municipal police service and the national public order policing units, all of which are established in terms of the South African Police Service Act.[6]

However, no right is absolute in operation and all the fundamental rights in the Constitution can be limited when there is an important reason to do so. In the past, the expression of opinions and ideas could be restricted simply because they conflicted with the policies of the authorities and the government. However, now a person's right to freedom of expression can only be limited under certain circumstances and when certain requirements are met.

Section 36 of the 1996 Constitution, the limitations clause, provides that a right may be limited only when it is done by way of a law of general application and only to the extent that the limitation is *reasonable and justifiable in an open and democratic society based on human dignity, equality and freedom*. Furthermore, in limiting the right one must take into account all relevant factors, including the nature of the right, the importance of the purpose of the limitation, the nature and extent of the limitation, the relation between the limitation and its purpose and whether any less restrictive means could be used to achieve the purpose.

This means that any limitation of the right imposed on someone must comply with these criteria. Thus, a limitation on the right to freedom of expression cannot be imposed simply because the state does not agree with someone's political or other viewpoints. Only when a limitation on the expression of such viewpoints can be justified according to the above-mentioned criteria is it a lawful limitation.

Examples of how this right can be limited in the context of the South African Police Service are provided below.

26.4.2 Comparison of the protection of freedom of expression in the 1993 Constitution with the provisions in the 1996 Constitution

The new freedom of expression clause in the 1996 Constitution differs in substantial ways from the corresponding clause in the 1993 Constitution. In some areas the new clause provides a more comprehensive protection of freedom of expression than did the 1993 Constitution, while in other areas it constitutes a serious denigration of the right.

The freedom of expression clause in the 1993 Constitution guarantees the right to freedom of speech and expression. As indicated above, section 16(1) of the 1996 Constitution only speaks of the right to freedom of expression. However, "expression" is considered to be a wider concept than "speech" and embraces far more than just the written or spoken word. Thus, the fact that the wording of the final clause has left out specific reference to "speech" does not mean that the ambit of the clause has been limited.

The clause in the 1996 Constitution includes the freedom to receive and impart information and ideas. This is an addition to the freedom of expression clause, as section 15 of the 1993 Constitution did not make clear whether "the right to gather information preparatory to its expression" was included. Without an explicit guarantee of the right to receive and impart information, the right to freedom of expression, and particularly the right of the media, can be restricted.

The inclusion of the right to receive and impart information and ideas in the right to freedom of expression brings the provision more in line with a number of international human rights provision, which include this aspect.[7]

The right to academic freedom has been strengthened by moving it from the freedom of opinion clause in the 1993 Constitution to the freedom of expression clause in the 1996 Constitution. Having the freedom to *express* academic findings implies greater academic freedom than simply *holding academic and scientific opinions.*

Apart from the general limitation clause in section 36, the right to freedom of expression in section 16 contains an internal limitation clause. In other words, the right to freedom of expression is not just subject to the general limitation clause like any other right, but is, in addition, subject to its own limitation clause, contained in section 16(2). This subsection provides that the right to freedom of expression does not extend *to propaganda for war; incitement of imminent violence; or advocacy of hatred based on race, ethnicity, gender or religion, and that constitutes incitement to cause harm.* The main limitation of the right to freedom of expression, compared with the protection of the right granted in the 1993 Constitution, is found in section 16(2).

If the Constitution did not include subsection 16(2), the state would be precluded from passing laws regulating incitement to hatred. It would mean that any such law would be susceptible to constitutional challenge and would only survive if the state were able to justify the law in terms of the requirements of limitation. Section 16(2), on the other hand, means that a law introducing excessive sanctions, for example a fine of R50 000,00 and/or up to five years' imprisonment for advocating hatred based on race, ethnicity, gender or religion, which constitutes incitement to cause harm, would essentially be immune from constitutional attack. In other words, if any person were to be prosecuted under a law with such excessive sanctions, it would not be open to him or her to raise as a defence the fact that the law was unconstitutional as it unjustifiably and unreasonably violated the guarantee of freedom of expression. All that would be open to the accused would be to argue that the words in question did not advocate hatred based on one or more of the listed grounds.

The effect of section 16(2) will probably be to insulate from constitutional attack any laws which facilitate the banning of publications and films that advocate hatred based on, for example, race.

Section 15(2) of the 1993 Constitution, which provided that all media financed by or under the control of the state should be regulated in a manner which ensured impartiality and the expression of a diversity of opinion, has been omitted from the final section on freedom of expression. This means that any law pertaining to media regulation by the state which does not reflect impartiality or the expression of a diversity of opinion is not directly subject to constitutional review, at least in so far as its impartiality is concerned. Even in section 15(2) of the 1993 Constitution, no provision was made to ensure the *independence* of media financed by or under the control of the state. The guarantee of impartiality and the expression of a diversity of opinion did not include an express constitutional guarantee against government interference with publications. The 1996 Constitution omits all these guarantees.

26.4.3   The Criminal Procedure Act 51 of 1977

The Criminal Procedure Act prescribes to a large extent the manner in which policing should be effected. However, there is nothing in the Criminal Procedure Act that has direct bearing on the right to freedom of expression and the police.

26.4.4   The South African Police Service Act 68 of 1995

The 1995 South African Police Service Act (the Act) repeals the Police Act of 1958 and supersedes the South African Police Service Rationalisation Proclamation of 1995.[8]

The Act provides for the establishment, composition, organisation, regulation and control of the South African Police Service. It sets out, amongst other things, the powers, duties and functions of all SAPS members; it provides for the issuing of regulations and regulates appointments, terms and conditions of service.

The Act takes cognisance of the attempt to establish and maintain a human rights culture in South Africa. Chapter 15 of the Act expressly recognises the need for the South African Police Service to "uphold and safeguard the fundamental rights of every person as guaranteed by Chapter 3 of the 1993 Constitution". Section 13 of the Act echoes this sentiment by stating that a member may exercise the powers and perform such duties and functions as are by law conferred on or assigned to a police official, subject to the Constitution and *with due regard to the fundamental rights of every person*. In other words, the Act recognises that effective and democratic policing must take place within the context of a human rights culture, where the fundamental rights of citizens are acknowledged and cannot be disregarded.

At present (October 1996) a new code of conduct is being drafted for the South African Police Service. The Code is not yet in operation, but when it comes into effect it will apply to all members of the service, at all levels. This Code yet again recognises the establishment of a new constitutional order promising to realise the commitment to creating a safe and secure environment for all people in South Africa "with the Constitution, the law and the needs of the community as the foundation of approach ... and by upholding and protecting the fundamental rights of all people".

The right to freedom of expression extends to all members of the SAPS, just as it does to any other citizen. However, due to the nature of their employment, it is generally recognised that certain reasonable and justifiable limitations can legitimately be imposed on the police in their capacity as members of the service. This is because of the particular role that they play as peace officers, attempting to combat crime and to maintain public order and security; it is the duty of the police to serve everyone and not be to seen or perceived to be giving any particular group preferential treatment.

For example, if a member of the service were to wear a badge showing support for a particular political party, members of the public who support an opposition party may feel reluctant to approach that police official for assistance. Preventing a member of the service from wearing such badge is a restriction on that member's right to freedom of expression. However, the limitation is not on a police official's right to *hold* political opinions but rather on the right to *express them during the course of his/her work* and would appear to be reasonable and justifiable in the circumstances.

Furthermore, because police personnel sometimes have access to classified and confidential material in the course of their work, certain restrictions can also be legitimately imposed on them as far as their right to speak publicly about such confidential information is concerned.

Of particular relevance to the issue of freedom of speech and the police is section 46 of the Act, which provides that:

"(1) No member shall

    (*a*)   publicly display or express support for or associate himself or herself with a political party, organisation, movement or body;

    (*b*)   hold any post or office in a political party, organisation, movement or body;

    (*c*)   wear any insignia or identification mark in respect of any political party, organisation, movement or body; or

    (*d*)   in any other manner further or prejudice party-political interests.

(2) Subsection (1) shall not be construed as prohibiting a member from (*a*) joining a political party, organisation, movement or body of his or her choice; (*b*) attending a meeting of a political party, organisation, movement or body: Provided that no member shall attend such a meeting in uniform; or (*c*) exercising his or her right to vote."

There is an overriding public interest in maintaining the impartial operation of the South African Police Service. For that reason it is important that
public service workers do not engage in explicit political activities, which
might give the impression that one political party's policies are favoured
within the Council.

It is clear from the above that the Act and Code do in fact impose some
limitations on the right to freedom of expression of SAPS personnel when
compared with the rights of ordinary citizens. However, it would seem that
these restrictions can be justified, owing to the particular role and responsibility of members of the service.

26.4.5   Law of defamation

The purpose of the law of defamation is to protect a person's right to an
untarnished reputation. In so doing it continually strives to strike a balance
between the competing interests of freedom of expression on the one hand,
and protection of reputation on the other.

At present the position regarding the law of defamation in South Africa
is unclear. This is due mainly to prevailing uncertainty about the extent to
which a person who has been sued for defamation may rely on the constitutional right to freedom of expression as laid down in the 1993 Constitution. The 1996 Constitution has clarified the position somewhat by allowing
private individuals in a defamation suit to rely directly on the freedom of
expression clause in their defence (so-called horizontal application).[9] However, a recent judgment in the Constitutional Court[10] ruled that, whilst the
1993 Constitution does not have horizontal application, in terms of section
35(3) courts are obliged, in the application and development of the common law, to have due regard to the "spirit, purport and objects" of Chapter
3, the Bill of Rights.[11]

Recently, in the case of *Holomisa v Argus Newspapers Ltd,*[12] the court
also found that, when the issue is of public interest, it is more difficult for
someone who is suing for defamation to prove his/her claim. However, yet
another court found that this was not the case, since the value of human
life and dignity is worthy of greater protection than matters of public
interest.[13]

It follows from this brief outline of recent decisions on defamation that the
exact position regarding the extent to which the common law of defamation
is to be informed by the value of freedom of speech under the 1993 Constitution is not entirely clear. One can, however, assume that with the enactment
of the 1996 Constitution, which makes express provision for individuals to
rely on the Bill of Rights in private disputes, the position will be clarified.

Apart from the constitutional implications on the law of defamation, there
remain the established common-law defences which can be relied on by a
police official who is sued for defamation in the course of his or her work. A

defence of qualified privilege applies for statements made in the discharge of a duty or in the furtherance or protection of an interest. The privilege against liability for defamation will be lost, however, if the defamer was actuated by an improper motive or express malice in uttering or publishing the statement. The law recognises legal, moral and social duties or interests. However, the test is an objective one and the court must judge the situation by the standard of the ordinary, reasonable man, having regard to the relationship between the parties and the surrounding circumstances.

Another defence against a defamation action is that of truth for the public benefit. The common law does not recognise truth in itself as a good defence: the element of public benefit must also be present. It is not necessary that the statement should be literally true in every detail; it is sufficient if it is substantially true as a whole in every material part.

The third defence under the common law is that the defamatory statement was made as a fair comment. This defence as been concisely summarised in an early Appellate Division case as follows:

> "... the defence rests upon a right of every person to express his real judgment or opinion honestly and truly upon matters of public interest."14

The requirements for this defence are: (*a*) it must be "fair", (*b*) the factual allegations on which the comment is made must be true, and (*c*) the comment must be on a matter of public interest.

A member of the SAPS has the same right to sue any individual who makes defamatory statements against him/her, but such an individual can to some extent also rely on his or her constitutional right to freedom of expression. However, the position is uncertain and depends on whether the public interest defence will be upheld by the Appellate Division. In certain circumstances someone sued for defamation by a member of the service will also be able to rely on the defence of qualified privilege if the disputed statements are published in the discharge of a duty, the exercise of a right or furtherance of a legitimate interest.

Members of the public can rely directly on the constitutional right to freedom of expression in their dealings with the police. As outlined above, a true democracy is characterised, amongst other things, by the extent to which private citizens can express their opinions freely about the government at all levels. Robust criticism, however unreasonable, must be tolerated and any limitation of this right must be shown by the government to be reasonable and justifiable in an open and democratic society.

The Police Service is furthermore not allowed to discriminate against certain individuals or groups of society simply because they are exercising their right to freedom of expression by way of harsh criticism.

The only risk a member of the public runs by exercising his or her freedom of expression is to be sued for defamation by a member of the SAPS in his/her individual capacity.

26.4.6   Case law

Courts around the world have entrenched the right to freedom of expression by interpreting it as deserving particular protection. In *Palko v Connecticut* [15] Cardozo J said:

> "(Freedom of thought and speech) is the matrix, the indispensable condition, of nearly every other form of freedom."

The European Court of Human Rights has repeatedly expressed similar views, namely that

> "(f)reedom of expression ... constitutes one of the essential foundations of a democratic society and one of the basic conditions for progress ... it is applicable not only to 'information' or 'ideas' that are favourably received or regarded as inoffensive or as a matter of indifference, but also to those that offend, shock or disturb. Such are the demands of pluralism, tolerance and broadmindedness without which there is no 'democratic society'." [16]

Following the introduction of the Bill of Rights in the 1993 Constitution, the importance and meaning of the right to freedom of expression has been described by South African courts as follows:

> "The history of liberty shows that the currency of every free society is to be found in the marketplace of ideas where, without restraint, individuals exchange the most sacred of all their commodities. If the market is sometimes corrupt or abused or appears to serve the interests of the wicked and unscrupulous, that is reason enough to accept that it operates in accordance with the rules of human nature.
>
> "In a free society all freedoms are important, but they are not all equally important. Political philosophers are agreed about the primacy of the freedom of speech. It is the freedom upon which all others depend; it is the freedom without which the others would not long endure." [17]

With particular reference to freedom of the press it has been said that

> "[t]he role of the press in a democratic society cannot be understated. The press is in the front line of the battle to maintain democracy. It is the function of the press to ferret out corruption, dishonesty and graft wherever it may occur and to expose the perpetrators. The press must reveal dishonest, mal- and inept administration. It must also contribute to the exchange of ideas already alluded to. It must advance communication between the governed and those who govern. The press must act as the watchdog of the governed." [18]

26.4.7   Relevant international instruments

The freedom of expression is enshrined in all major international human rights instruments as can be seen from the following examples.

Article 19 of the Universal Declaration of Human Rights provides that: "Everyone has the right to freedom of opinion and expression; this right includes freedom to hold opinions without interference and to seek, receive and impart information and ideas through any media and regardless of frontiers."

Article 19 of the International Covenant on Civil and Political Rights provides that

"1.   Everyone shall have the right to hold opinions without interference.

2.   Everyone shall have the right to freedom of expression; this right shall include freedom to seek, receive and impart information and ideas of all kinds, regardless of frontiers, either orally, in writing or in print, in the form of art, or through any other media of his choice.

3.   The exercise of the rights provided for in paragraph 2 of this article carries with it special duties and responsibilities. It may therefore be subject to certain restrictions, but these shall only be such as are provided by law and are necessary:

(*a*)   For respect of the rights or reputations of others;

(*b*)   For the protection of national security or of public order, or of public health or morals."

Article 10 of the European Convention on Human Rights states that

"(1)   Everyone has the right to freedom of expression. This right shall include freedom to hold opinions and receive and impart information and ideas without interference by public authority and regardless of frontiers. This Article shall not prevent states from requiring the licensing of broadcasting, television or cinema enterprises.

(2)   The exercise of these freedoms, since it carries with it duties and responsibilities, may be subject to such formalities, conditions, restrictions or penalties as are prescribed by law and are necessary in a democratic society, in the interests of national security, territorial integrity or public safety, for the prevention of disorder or crime, for the protection of health or morals, for the protection of the reputation or rights of others, for preventing the disclosure of information received in confidence, or for maintaining the authority and impartiality of the judiciary."

Article 9 of the African Charter on Human and Peoples' Rights provides that:

"(1)   Every individual shall have the right to receive information.

(2)   Every individual shall have the right to express and disseminate his opinions within the law."

26.5   CONCLUSION

One of the cornerstones of a well-functioning democracy is the right to freedom of expression. It means that everyone must be able to speak their minds freely, in public as well as in private, without fear, regardless of who they are or to which political party or population group they belong. Without a voice and the right to put forward views, the citizen cannot contribute to political and social change, and without such contribution from the citizen there would be no true democracy.

Freedom of expression is not the property of any political system or ideology. It is, as outlined above, a universal human right, defined and guaranteed in international law. Freedom of expression as a human right means that every individual has the right to hold opinions and to express them without fear and it includes the right of everyone to "receive and impart information and ideas". Freedom of expression therefore entails press freedom and freedom of all media as one of its principal guarantees. Censorship is any interference with the individual or with the means of communication that denies these basic rights and freedoms or arbitrarily encroaches upon them.[19]

Certain areas of law will be affected by the introduction of the constitutional right to freedom of expression.

26.5.1   Defamation

As outlined above, defamation cases which have been heard by the courts after the enactment of the 1993 Constitution have had vastly different outcomes, depending largely on whether or not the sitting judge believed in the so-called horizontal application of the Bill of Rights (that is, whether or not the Bill of Rights applies to disputes between private individuals in addition to its undisputed application between the state and a citizen), thus making the common law of defamation subject to direct constitutional scrutiny. This legal problem has been solved by way of extending the application to be binding on "all natural and juristic persons if applicable" (section 8(2)). This means that future defamation actions will be subject to constitutional scrutiny and that the development of the common law must directly take cognisance of the right to freedom of expression in section 16.

26.5.2   Hate speech regulation

With or without the hate speech clause in section 16(2), hate speech could be prohibited or curbed in a number of ways, including criminal sanctions to provide for the indictment, conviction and punishment of speakers or publishers, and censorship legislation in terms of which publications and films could be controlled or banned.

26.5.3   Censorship legislation

The existing Publications Act of 1974 fails to comply with the requirements of section 16.

The Film and Publications Bill, which is due to repeal the old Publications Act and to take over the regulation and, in some instances, the censoring of certain types of material, will probably be in accordance with section 16, if the Bill is passed in its most recent form. It remains to be seen, however, to what extent the intensive lobbying by various interest groups that want to limit access to pornographic material will be successful in limiting the provisions in the Bill any further, when it is finally tabled in Parliament.

26.6   SUGGESTED READING AND SOURCES

Boyle, K. 1988. Introduction in *Article 19, World Report 1988 — Information, Freedom and Censorship.*

Cachalia, A, *et al*. 1994. *Fundamental Rights in the New Constitution.* Cape Town: Juta.

Chaskalson, M, Kentridge, J, Klaaren, J, Marcus, G, Spitz, D & Wolmarans, S. 1996. *Constitutional Law of South Africa.* Cape Town: Juta.

Coliver, S (ed). 1992. *Striking a Balance: Hate Speech, Freedom of Expression and Non-Discrimination.* Article 19, Human Rights Centre, University of Essex, London.

Davis, D (ed). 1996. *Chapter 2 of the Republic of South Africa Constitution Bill: A Comparison with the Interim Constitution.* Occasional paper 25, Centre for Applied Legal Studies.

Johannessen, L. 1994. Freedom of expression and information in the new South African Constitution and its compatibility with international standards. *South African Journal of Human Rights*, 10.

Marcus, G. 1994. Freedom of expression under the Constitution. *South African Journal on Human Rights*, 10.

Meiklejohn, A. 1948. Free speech and its relation to self-government. *Supreme Court Review.*

Press Law and Practice: A Comparative Study of Press Freedom in European and other Democracies. Published by Article 19 for UNESCO, 1993.

Spitz, D. 1994. Freedom of expression and commercial speech. Unpublished paper for the Constitutional Law Course at the University of the Witwatersrand.

Stuart, K. 1990. *Newspaperman's Guide to the Law*, 5 ed. Durban: Butterworths.

ENDNOTES

1. This normative vision has a classical liberal pedigree in the work of John Milton *A Speech for the Liberty of Unlicensed Printing* (1644) and John Stuart Mill *On Liberty* (1859).

2. See Meiklejohn *Free Speech and its Relations to Self-government* (1948).

3. *Irwin Toy v Quebec* (A–G) (1989) 58 DLR (4th), 577, 612 (SCC). See Spitz at 1.

4. See also section 2(*b*) of the Canadian Charter on Fundamental Rights:

   "(2) Everyone has the following fundamental freedoms

   (*b*) freedom of thought, belief, opinion, and expression, including freedom of the press and other media of communication ..."

   and the First Amendment of the Constitution of the United States of America, which states that "Congress shall make no law ... abridging the freedom of speech, or of the press; or the right of people peaceably to assemble ...".

5. *Tinker v Des Moines Independent Community School District* 393 US 503 and *United States v O'Brien* 391 US 367; Cachalia *et al* 54.

6. 68 of 1995.

7. See, for example, Article 19 of the Universal Declaration of Human Rights, Article 19 of the International Covenant on Civil and Political Rights, Article 9(1) of the African Charter on Human and Peoples' Rights (which provides every individual with the right to receive information), Article 13 of the American Convention on Human Rights and Article 10 of the European Convention on Human Rights.

8. Published by Proclamation no 5, 1995, dated 27 January 1995.

9. Section 8 of the 1996 Constitution states that the Bill of Rights applies to all laws and binds the legislature, the executive, the judiciary and all organs of state. This means that the Constitution operates both horizontally between private individuals and vertically between the state and individuals.

10. *Du Plessis & others v De Klerk & others* 1995 (3) SA 850 (CC).

11. See also *Holomisa v Argus Newspapers Ltd* 1996 (2) SA 588 (W).

12. 1996 (2) SA 588 (W).

13. *Bogoshi v National Media Limited & others*, Witwatersrand Local Division, case no: 94/29433.

14. *Crawford v Albu* 1917 AD 102.

15. 302 US 326–7.

16. *Handyside v UK*, judgment of 7 December 1976, Series A no 24, para 49. See also, inter alia, *Lingens v Austria*, judgment of 8 July 1986, Series A no 103 para 41, and *Jersild v Denmark*, judgment of 23 September 1994, Series A no 298.

17. *Mandela v Falati* 1994 (4) BCLR 1 (W) at 8D–F.

18. *Government of the Republic of South Africa v 'Sunday Times' Newspaper & another* 1995 (2) SA 221 (T) at 2271.

19. Boyle ix.

Chapter 27

Common-law Labour Rights for the South African Police Service and its Members in the Workplace

Dirk Bouwer

27.1   SUMMARY AND INTRODUCTION

*T*HE employment relationship is a relationship between two persons in their respective capacities as "employer" and "employee". The aim of this chapter is to define this relationship by identifying its essential elements.

The identified elements will then be applied to the relationship between the South African Police Service[1] and its members in order to determine whether an employment relationship exists between these parties.

After identifying the employment relationship between members of the SAPS (in their capacities as "employees") and the SAPS (in its capacity as an "employer"), the common law-labour rights and freedoms will be identified and applied to this employment relationship.

It will be shown that this relationship is an administrative employment relationship.

The consequence of this special administrative employment relationship will be examined. The rules of natural justice must be applied by the SAPS before the liberty, rights (property or existing rights) or legitimate expectations of any of its members may be prejudicially affected.

27.2   KEY OBJECTIVES

The key objectives of this chapter are to enable students to:
* identify the employment relationship;
* determine whether an employment relationship exists between the South African Police Service and its members;
* identify the fundamental elements of the contract of employment between the South African Police Service and its members;
* identify the common-law rights and obligations that derive from the employment relationship;
* identify the internationally recognised basic labour principles;
* understand that the employment relationship between the South African Police Service and its members is an administrative employment relationship, which means that the principles of natural justice must be applied before the South African Police Service in its capacity as "employer" can infringe upon the existing rights or legitimate expectations of any of its employees;
* determine under what circumstances the rules of natural justice become applicable;
* identify the principles that underlie the rules of natural justice; and
* determine (in general) the content of the different rules of natural justice.

27.3   APPLICABLE LAW

The 1993 Constitution, sections 2, 8, 24, 212 and 237
The 1996 Constitution, sections 200 and 207

The South African Police Service Act of 1995, sections 2, 5, 24, 27, 28, 29, 40,
41, 48 and 72

The Police Act of 1958

The Public Service Act of 1994, section 2

The Government Service Pension Act of 1973

Bophuthatswana Police Act 7 of 1978

Transkei Police Act 16 of 1979

Gazankulu Police Act 5 of 1980

Qwaqwa Police Act 7 of 1980

KwaZulu Police Act 14 of 1980

Ciskei Police Act 32 of 1983

Venda Police Act 4 of 1985

Lebowa Police Act 6 of 1985

KwaNdebele Police Act 11 of 1986

KaNgwane Police Act 4 of 1988

27.4 INTERPRETATION AND DISCUSSION

27.4.1 The theoretical framework and content of labour rights and duties for members of the South African Police Service: The common-law position

27.4.1.1 Introduction

In order to determine the constitutional position regarding the regulation of labour rights within the SAPS, it is appropriate and expedient to identify the common-law principles regulating the employment relationship and the contract of employment.

Following this discussion, the relationship between the SAPS and its members will be investigated in order to determine whether an employment relationship exists between them. It is necessary to ascertain the existence of an employment relationship between members of the SAPS in their capacities as "employees"[2] and the SAPS in its capacity as "employer".[3]

If an employment relationship between the SAPS and its members exists, the common-law duties of an employee and employer, as well as the internationally recognised basic labour principles underlying the employment relationship, will apply.

27.4.1.2 Defining the employment relationship

The employment relationship is a relationship between two persons[4] in their respective capacities as "employee" and "employer". The basis of this relationship between the employee and the employer is an agreement. In terms of this agreement, the employee undertakes to place[5] his or her personal services at the disposal of the employer, while the employer undertakes to remunerate the employee for his or her services.[6] This agreement manifests itself in practice in the form of a contract of employment.[7] It is thus clear that the employment relationship is identified and regulated through the contract of employment.

The employment relationship can be one of any number of different types, each of which is characterised by a different combination of common law, statutory regulation and market forces (including collective bargaining).[8] It is therefore difficult to define the contract of employment. With this in mind, the contract of employment may be defined as follows:

> "A contract of employment is an agreement between two legal personae (parties) in terms of which one of the parties (the employee) undertakes to place his personal services at the disposal of the other party (the employer) for an indefinite or determined period in return for a fixed or ascertainable wage, and which entitles the employer to define the employee's duties and (usually) to control the manner in which the employee discharges them." [9]

The elements generally regarded as characteristic of the contract of employment (agreement) are the following:

- the agreement is a *voluntary agreement*;
- the agreement is between two *legal persons* in their respective capacities as "employee" and "employer";
- in terms of the agreement, the employee agrees *to make his or her personal services available for or to render his or her personal services* to[10] the employer;
- the agreement will be for an *indefinite or specified period*;
- in terms of the agreement, the employer agrees *to pay a fixed or ascertainable wage* to the employee for the availability or rendering of his or her services; and
- in terms of the agreement, the employee will make available or render his or her services in a *subordinate manner*[11] to the employer.

As indicated above, the contract of employment requires two parties: an "employee" and "employer". Although it has become common practice in larger establishments to define standard conditions of service for all, or for certain classes of employees, this in itself does not create a contractual relationship between one employer and the aggregate of employees concerned. There is a separate and distinct contractual relationship between each individual employee and the employer. [12]

27.4.1.3   Establishing the existence of a contract of employment

The following broad tests have generally been applied by our courts in an attempt to identify the contract of employment.

- **The supervision and control test**

  This test is based on the control exercised by the employer over the employee in terms of the agreement. The power (right) to control was previously regarded as one of the most important elements (*essentialia*) of the contract of employment. This power of control is based on the employer's right to control not only "what work has to be done" but also "the manner in which that work has to be done".[13] However, as a general test it is clearly no longer adequate because the extent of this right of control remains a matter for debate.[14]

- **The organisation or integration test**

Uncertainty regarding the extent of control required by the control test led to the establishment of the organisation test. In terms of this test, a contract of employment exists when a person is employed as part of the business, and his or her work is done as an integral part of the business.[15] However, this test was rejected as too imprecise in *Smit v Workmen's Compensation Commissioner*.[16]

- **The dominant impression or multiple test**

In terms of the dominant impression or multiple test, a court will not regard one criterion or factor as conclusive in determining the relationship between an alleged employer and employee: the court must examine the relationship as a whole. It will then assess which aspects of the relationship favour the view that the relationship is one of employment. The court will balance these aspects against those which tend to show the existence of another type of relationship, and then determine which side of the scales is heavier. If the dominant impression created by the facts is that of a contract of employment (service), then the court will rule accordingly.[17]

In assessing the nature of the relationship, the following factors (*indicia*) could be regarded as relevant.

- The fact that the employer has the right of supervision and control over the employee is still regarded as an important *indicium* of a contract of service. The greater the degree of supervision and control an employer exercises, the stronger the possibility that the contract is one of service.
- The intention of the parties with regard to the alleged employee's capacity to perform services for persons other than the alleged employer will also be taken into account. The greater the number of restrictions on the "employee's" capacity to perform services for persons other than the "employer", the stronger the possibility that the contract is one of service.
- Another important *indicium* is the intention of the parties regarding the "employer's" responsibility to provide the tools or equipment with which the "employee" works. The greater the degree of responsibility to provide such tools or equipment, the stronger the possibility that the contract is one of service.
- Whether the parties intend the alleged payment to be for time worked or for work completed is another important fact to be considered. The greater the indication that payment is for time worked, the stronger the possibility that the contract is one of service.

- The courts will also consider whether it was the intention of the parties that the "employee" should have a personal obligation to perform the work or whether he or she could nominate another person to carry out his or her tasks. The greater the indication that there is a personal obligation on the "employee" to do the work, the stronger the possibility that the contract is one of service.

- Whether the parties intended that the "employee" should be entitled to membership of the employer's pension and other funds will also be relevant. The greater the indication that the alleged employee is entitled to membership of the employer's pension and other funds, the stronger the possibility that the contract is one of service.

Despite the valid criticisms which have been levelled against it, this test is the one which enjoys the support of the courts and has been utilised in many recent decisions.[18]

27.4.1.4 Establishing the existence of a contract of employment between the South African Police Service and its members

27.4.1.4.1 The composition of the South African Police Service

The South African Police Service Act of 1995[19] determines that the South African Police Service shall consist of —

"(*a*) all persons who immediately before the commencement of this Act were members —

    (i) of a force which, by virtue of section 236(7)(*a*) of the Constitution, is deemed to constitute part of the Service;

    (ii) appointed under the Rationalisation Proclamation;

    (iii) of the Reserve by virtue of section 28(2) of this Act;

(*b*) members appointed in terms of section 28(2) of this Act; and

(*c*) persons who become members of the Reserve under section 48(2) of this Act."

Thus, in terms of the South African Police Service Act of 1995, the South African Police Service consists of the following persons:

- persons who immediately before 15 October 1995 were members in terms of the Police Act of 1958;[20] Bophuthatswana Police Act of 1978;[21] Transkei Police Act of 1979;[22] Gazankulu Police Act of 1980;[23] Qwaqwa Police Act of 1980;[24] KwaZulu Police Act of 1980;[25] Ciskei Police Act of 1983;[26] Venda Police Act of 1985;[27] Lebowa Police Act of 1985;[28] KwaNdebele Police Act of 1986;[29] and KaNgwane Police Act of 1988;[30, 31]

- persons who immediately before 15 October 1995 were members appointed under the Rationalisation Proclamation;[32]

- persons who immediately before 15 October 1995 were members of the Reserve Police Service referred to in section 48 of the South African Police Service Act of 1995, by virtue of the Rationalisation Proclamation;[33]

- persons who are appointed as members of the SAPS in terms of the South African Police Service Act of 1995;[34] and
- persons who become members of the Reserve Police Service under the South African Police Service Act of 1995.[35]

In essence, the South African Police Service consists of those persons who are employed in terms of the South African Police Service Act of 1995, in the capacity of members of the South African Police Service.[36]

A "member" of the SAPS[37] refers to the following person —

- any member of the Reserve Police Service while such member is on duty in the SAPS;[38]
- any temporary member while employed in the SAPS;
- any person appointed in terms of any other law to serve in the SAPS and in respect of whom the Minister of Safety and Security has prescribed that he or she is deemed to be a member of the SAPS for the purposes of this Act; and
- any person designated by the Minister of Safety and Security in terms of a notice in the *Government Gazette* as a member of the SAPS.[39]

In the light of the above discussion regarding the employment relationship and contract of employment,[40] it is absolutely clear that an employment relationship exists between members of the SAPS and the SAPS itself, for the following reasons.

- The SAPS has the right of supervision and control over its members; this is clearly illustrated by the provisions of section 207 of the 1996 Constitution, section 24 of the South African Police Service Act of 1995, as well as by the provisions regulating discipline, legal procedure and offences in sections 24 and 40 of the South African Police Service Act of 1995.
- The rendering of services by members of the Service to persons (or organisations) other than the SAPS is restricted.[41]
- It is common knowledge that the SAPS provides its members with the necessary clothing, tools and equipment to perform their duties.
- It is further common knowledge that the SAPS remunerates its members for time worked on a monthly basis.
- Members are under an obligation to render their services in their personal capacity.
- Members are members of the Government Service Pension Fund in terms of the Government Service Pension Act of 1973.[42]
- The intention of the SAPS when appointing people as members is to appoint such persons in an employment relationship and in their capacity as employees of the SAPS with certain labour rights. This is abundantly clear in terms of section 24 and Chapter 9 of the South African Police Service Act of 1995.

In addition, it is clear that the content of the contract of employment between the SAPS and its members is regulated statutorily in terms of the provisions of the South African Police Service Act of 1995 and the Public Service Act of 1994.

In terms of the Public Service Act of 1994, "public service" is interpreted as meaning the public service as contemplated in section 8 of the Act.[43] The Act[44] determines that the public service shall consist, *inter alia,* of persons who:

"(*a*) hold posts on the fixed establishment —
    (ii) in the services;"

Thus, in terms of the Public Service Act of 1994, the public service shall consist, *inter alia*, of persons who hold posts in the SAPS.[45]

The provisions of the Public Service Act of 1994 apply to (or in respect of) officers and employees who are employed in terms of the Act, whether they are employed within or outside the Republic of South Africa, and in respect of persons who were employed in the public service or who are to be employed in the public service.[46]

As indicated above, persons employed in terms of the provisions of the South African Police Service Act of 1995 are also regarded as public servants. Thus, the Public Service Act of 1994 is also applicable to persons who are employed in terms of the South African Police Service Act of 1995, except in so far as the Act provides otherwise.[47]

The Public Service Act of 1994 provides further that, where persons employed in terms of the South African Police Service Act of 1995 are not excluded from the provisions of the Public Service Act of 1994, the provisions of the Public Service Act of 1994 shall apply only in so far as they are not contrary to the law governing the employment of persons who are employed in terms of the provisions of the South African Police Service Act of 1995.[48]

However, the provisions of the South African Police Service Act of 1995 do not exclude the provisions of the Public Service Act of 1994.

Thus, the provisions of the South African Police Service Act of 1995 will be the source of first instance[49] regulating the employment conditions of persons who are employed in terms of the South African Police Service Act of 1995. The Public Service Act of 1994 will apply whenever there is a lacuna in the provisions of the South African Police Service Act of 1995 regulating the employment conditions of persons who are employed in terms of the Act.[50] Technically, the provisions of the Public Service Act of 1994 will also apply in so far as they are not contrary to the provisions of the South African Police Service Act of 1995.

27.4.1.5 The common-law duties of the employee

The common-law rights and obligations of the employer (SAPS) and the employees (members of the SAPS) derive from a number of sources,[51] namely:

- the provisions of the South African Police Service Act of 1995 and the Public Service Act of 1994;
- the regulations issued in terms of the South African Police Service Act of 1995 and the Public Service Act of 1994;

- the provisions of the common law; and
- custom and practice.

In most cases the parties to the service agreement do not define the entire content of their relationship. For instance, the parties expressly agree on matters such as wages, holidays and hours of work, but seldom specify the extent of the employee's duties of obedience, care and fidelity, or the content of the employer's duty of care towards the employee. The latter form part of the "standard" terms of the common law contract of employment. The main provisions of the contract of employment between the SAPS and its members are regulated by the provisions of the South African Police Service Act of 1995 and the Public Service Act of 1994, as well as by those provisions issued in terms of these Acts.

The common-law duties of the employee are the following.

- Since the principal obligation of the employee in terms of the service contract is to place his or her personal services at the disposal of the employer,[52] it follows that the rendering of services by the employee to the employer from the agreed date and for the duration of the contract is a prerequisite to his or her right to claim payment of wages.[53]
- The courts have held that it is implied in every service contract that employees must generally exercise "due diligence and skill" in the fulfilment of their duties.[54]
- The employee is under a positive duty to harness his or her energies and skills in order to further the employer's interests. He or she must devote all his or her normal working hours to the employer's interest and may not without the employer's permission simultaneously work for another employer during these hours. This implies that there is an obligation on the employee to serve the employer honestly and faithfully.[55]
- Subordination is an additional implied duty of the employee and, in terms of our common law, all employees are required to show a reasonable degree of respectfulness and courtesy towards their employers.[56]
- A further implied duty of the employee is to refrain from conduct (misconduct) that adversely affects the employment relationship, contrary to the spirit of the contract of employment.[57]

27.4.1.6 The common-law duties of the employer

The common-law duties of the employer include the following.

- The employer is under an obligation to receive the employee into service, that is, to appoint the employee. This obligation is the corollary of the employee's duty to enter and remain in service. However, this right is not absolute: the employer is only obliged to receive the employee into service and to remunerate the employee from the date agreed upon.[58]
- The payment of wages by the employer in return for the duties performed by the employee is essential and fundamental to the contract of employment. Where there has been no agreement on wages, either the contract is

not a contract of employment or it is implied that payment should be in accordance with prevailing custom and practice in the industry and locality concerned.[59]

- In terms of the common law, there is a duty on the employer to take reasonable care to ensure the safety of his or her employees.[60] This includes the provision of safe premises, safe machinery and tools, as well as a safe system of work.[61] This obligation, however, is not an absolute one.[62]

- In terms of the common law, the employer and employee will agree on the employee's working hours. If their agreement makes no provision for maximum hours of work, the hours of work will be regulated by custom.[63]

- At common law the employer is not obliged to grant an employee vacation, sick or occasional leave, unless expressly or tacitly agreed otherwise. Even then, the employee had no right to payment for the period of absence, unless expressly or tacitly agreed otherwise.[64]

- Certain duties are imposed on an employer in terms of various employment statutes, for example to make contributions to pension funds, to keep certain prescribed records, to provide the employee with a certificate of service.[65]

- At common law the employer is not obliged to provide medical services or accommodation for employees.[66]

- An employer may (under certain circumstances) be held civilly liable (and in certain circumstances, even criminally liable) for the unlawful acts of employees.[67]

27.4.1.7 Introduction to basic labour rights

Although the powers and functions [68] of the SAPS are of an essential nature and of national importance, members of the SAPS are still "employees" or "workers" and in that capacity are entitled to be accorded the internationally recognised basic labour principles that underlie industrial democracy. The internationally recognised rights underlying the employment relationship are the following:

- the right to work;
- the right to associate;
- the right to collective bargaining;
- the right to withhold labour, as manifested in strikes and lockouts;
- the right to protection; and
- the right to development.

These rights are often referred to as "freedoms" or "abilities". However, every right accorded to one party implies a corresponding duty on the other party.

27.4.1.8 Conclusion

In the light of the above discussion, the following conclusions can be drawn.

- Employment relationships exist between members of the SAPS (in their capacities as "employees") and the SAPS itself (in its capacity as "employer").
- The contract of employment between the SAPS and its members is statutorily regulated in terms of the provisions of the South African Police Service Act of 1995 and the Public Service Act of 1994.
- The employer (SAPS) and the employees (members of the SAPS) have certain rights and obligations that derive from the provisions of the South African Police Service Act of 1995 and the Public Service Act of 1994, and from regulations issued in terms of these Acts, from the common law, and custom and practice.
- Although the powers and functions of the SAPS are of an essential nature and of national importance, members of the SAPS are still "employees" or "workers" and in that capacity are entitled to be accorded the internationally recognised basic labour rights (or freedoms) to work; to associate; to collective bargaining; to withhold labour; to protection; and to development.

27.4.2 The influence of administrative law on the employment relationship between the South African Police Service and its members

27.4.2.1 Introduction

The employment relationship between the SAPS (employer) and its members (employees) does not involve a simple contract of service between two private individuals, but a form of employment which invests the employees with a particular status protected by law.[69]

In this instance the employer is a public authority whose decisions[70] regarding the employment relationship involve the exercise of an administrative (public) power authorised and described in terms of the South African Police Service Act of 1995 and the Public Service Act of 1994. This employment relationship between the SAPS and its members is thus a special employment relationship subject to the principles of administrative law. The employment relationship between the members (employees) and the SAPS (employer) is thus a special administrative employment relationship. The employment contracts of members of the SAPS can therefore be referred to as administrative contracts of employment, which are in principle status agreements, on account of the peculiar status which administrative law accords such employees.[71]

Because the powers vested in the employer (SAPS) in terms of the above-mentioned statutes could result in an infringement of the existing (common-law) rights or expectations of the employees (members of the SAPS), the rules of natural justice must be applied before such infringements can take place.[72]

27.4.2.2 The application of the rules of natural justice

The traditional approach is that, when a statute empowers a public official or body to make a decision prejudicially affecting an individual's liberty or his or her property rights[73] or existing rights,[74] the latter has a right to be heard before the decision is taken.[75]

As far as the timing of the opportunity is concerned, a hearing *prior* to the taking of the decision is usually required. There may, however, be exceptional circumstances where it is necessary to act with expedition and to allow the individual to make representation afterwards. The individual thus obtains the opportunity of persuading the official to change his or her mind.[76]

The rules of natural justice will, however, only apply where they are not expressly or by necessary implication excluded by statute.[77] In the *Zenzile* case, however, the Appellate Division found that the precarious nature of temporary employment and an Act's silence regarding the position of temporary employees do not necessarily warrant an inference that it was the legislature's intention to divest such employees of their common-law right to a hearing before their (summary) dismissal.[78] The court found that the employees who had been employed temporarily in a full-time capacity should have been heard before their dismissal.

In the *Traub* case, the Appellate Division expanded the applicability of the rules of natural justice to include an individual's legitimate expectation that a decision taken by the public authority will be favourable, or at least that before an adverse decision is taken he or she will be given a fair hearing.[79]

The legitimate expectation doctrine can be interpreted in two ways. Sometimes it is expressed in terms of some substantive benefit, advantage or privilege which the individual concerned can reasonably expect to acquire or retain and which it would be unfair to deny such person without prior consultation or a prior hearing. At other times, it refers to a legitimate expectation to be accorded a hearing before some decision adverse to the interests of the person concerned is taken.[80]

A legitimate expectation may arise either from an express promise given on behalf of a public authority, or from the existence of a regular practice which the claimant can reasonably expect to continue.[81]

Thus, the rules of natural justice will only apply to members of the SAPS in the following circumstances.

- The member of the SAPS must prove that he or she *is possessed of a specific liberty, property right,*[82] *existing right,*[83] *or a legitimate expectation.*[84]
- The member of the SAPS must prove that the SAPS has *infringed or prejudicially affected* his or her liberty, property rights, existing rights or legitimate expectations.
- The member of the SAPS must prove that the SAPS has *public power* to act (to infringe or prejudicially affect the liberty, property, existing rights or legitimate expectations of a member of the SAPS),[85] as is authorised in terms of a statute.[86]

27.4.2.3 The content of the rules of natural justice

The rules of natural justice are common-law rules that are also applicable to administrative enquiries and hearings flowing from the administrative employment relationship between the SAPS (employer) and its members (employees). Their aim is to ensure that public authorities (in this case, the SAPS) do not act arbitrarily and that they make fair decisions which are in the public interest.[87] The rules require that a fair procedure be followed and not that the same standard of proceedings as that adopted by a court of law should apply. The rules are therefore a manifestation of those fundamental principles of fairness which underlie the administrative employment relationship between the SAPS (employer) and its members (employees).[88]

The rules of natural justice, which vary in content, may conveniently be divided into two sets of principles:

- *Audi alteram partem* principle. This principle provides that the prejudicially affected member (employee), whose liberty, property right, other existing right, or legitimate expectation has been infringed by the SAPS (employer), should (as a rule) be afforded an opportunity to state his or her case before the intended action is taken.

This principle entails the following.[89]

  - Sufficient and timeous notice of the intended action and of any charges that may be brought against a member should be given by the SAPS.
  - The affected member should be given a reasonable time to prepare a defence.
  - The affected member should personally be present at his or her hearing (although not necessarily always).[90]
  - The affected member should be given the opportunity of a hearing (to present his or her case) before the decision prejudicially affecting his or her liberty, existing right or legitimate expectation is taken. It is not always required that oral representations by the member concerned be heard. Applicable regulations may require that nothing more than the opportunity to make written representations be given. For example, if members strike, the national or provincial commissioner concerned may, without a hearing, summarily discharge such members from the SAPS. In such a case, the members concerned are allowed to make representations only after their discharge.[91]
  - In the absence of a prescribed procedure, a proper opportunity to make representations (whether verbal or written) should be afforded.[92]
  - There is a duty on the SAPS to disclose any charges and prejudicial allegations against the affected member before and during the hearing.
  - In those cases where a member has the right to a personal audience, he or she should be given the opportunity to call and controvert evidence, to cross-examine and, under certain specific circumstances, to have legal representation.

- The affected member should be given a proper opportunity to prepare for the hearing to enable him or her to rebut the charges against him or her.

- *Nemo iudex in sua causa* principle. The purpose of this principle is to ensure the absence of bias and of any interest, whether pecuniary or personal, on the part of the decision-making institution (in this case, the SAPS in its capacity as "employer").

As indicated above, these principles will apply, except when they are excluded by statute either expressly or by necessary implication. Relevant legislation may not expressly grant security of employment to temporary or probationary employees due to the precarious nature of their employment.93 In the *Zenzile* case, however, the Appellate Division found that this does not necessarily warrant an inference that it was the legislature's intention to divest such employees of their common-law right to a hearing before their (summary) dismissal.94 The court found that employees who had been employed temporarily in a full-time capacity should have been heard before their dismissal.

Finally, it should be mentioned that an individual can waive his or her right to make verbal or written representations.95

27.5   SUGGESTED READING AND SOURCES

Basson, AC. 1994. *South Africa's Interim Constitution*. Cape Town: Juta.

Baxter, L. 1994. *Administrative Law*. Cape Town: Juta.

Beatty, D. 1993. Constitutional labour rights: Pros and cons. *ILJ* 1.

Ben-Israel, R. 1988. *International Labour Standards: The Case of Freedom to Strike*. New York: Kluwer.

Bouwer, D. 1995. *The Right to Strike — An International Perspective*. LLM thesis, Rand Afrikaans University, 1995.

Cachalia, *et al.* 1994. *Fundamental Rights in the New Constitution*. Cape Town: Juta.

Davies, M & Freedland, P. 1984. *Labour Law: Text and Material*. London: Stevens & Sons.

Grogan, J. 1993. *Riekert's Basic Employment Law*, 2 ed. Johannesburg: Juta.

IFCOL. 1989. *Development Law Strategies*. Pretoria: IFCOL.

ILO. 1994. *Freedom of Association and Collective Bargaining*. Geneva: ILO.

Le Roux, P & Van Niekerk, A. 1994. *The South African Law of Unfair Dismissal*. Johannesburg: Juta.

Olivier, MP. 1991. Legitimate expectation and the protection of employment. *TSAR*, 483.

Olivier, MP. 1994. Proposed legislation for the Police Service: A constitutional fiasco and labour relations nightmare? *TSAR*, 803.

Potgieter, O. 1992. *Die Reg op Arbeid — 'n Regsvergelykende Perspektief.* LLD thesis, University of Potchefstroom, 1992.

Rautenbach, IM. 1994. Grondwetlike bepalings ter beskerming van die wese van menseregte. *TSAR*, 403.

Rose-Innes, LA. 1963. *Judicial Review of Administrative Tribunals in South Africa.* Cape Town: Juta.

Rycroft, A & Jordaan, B. 1992. *A Guide to South African Labour Law*, 2 ed. Johannesburg: Juta.

Wiehahn, NJ. 1981. *Die Volledige Wiehahn Verslag: Dele 1–6 en die Witskrif op elke Deel.* Johannesburg: Lex Patria.

Woolman, S. 1994. Riding the push-me pull-you: Constructing a test that reconciles the conflicting interests which animate the limitation clause. 1994 *SAJHR* 60.

· ·

ENDNOTES

1 Hereafter referred to as "the SAPS".

2 Hereafter referred to as "the members".

3 Hereafter referred to as "the SAPS".

4 In their respective capacities as a legal person.

5 To make available or render his or her personal services.

6 Grogan 18.

7 See discussion in Rycroft & Jordaan 1–32.

8 Davies & Freedland 110–111.

9 Grogan 17.

10 To perform certain specified and/or implied duties.

11 Under the command and control of the employer or his or her representative.

12 Grogan 19.

13 *Colonial Mutual v MacDonald* 1931 AD 412 at 436.

14 *Rodriquess v Alves* 1978 (4) SA 834 (A) at 842A.

15 *Stevenson, Jordan E Harrison Ltd v Macdonald Evans* [1952] 1 TLR 101 at 111.

16 1979 (1) SA 51 (A) at 63.

17 See *Smit* for the application of this test.

18   Le Roux & Van Niekerk 58–59.

19   Act 68 of 1995, section 5.

20   Act 7 of 1958.

21   Act 7 of 1978.

22   Act 16 of 1979.

23   Act 5 of 1980.

24   Act 7 of 1980.

25   Act 14 of 1980.

26   Act 32 of 1983.

27   Act 4 of 1985.

28   Act 6 of 1985.

29   Act 11 of 1986.

30   Act 4 of 1988.

31   See s 5(2)(*a*)(i) of the South African Police Service Act of 1995, as well as s 236(7)(*a*) of the 1993 Constitution, read together with item 2 of Schedule 6 of the Constitution.

32   See s 5(2)(*a*)(ii) of the South African Police Service Act of 1995, as well as sections 12 and 13 of Proclamation no R5, 1995, issued ito s 237(3) of the 1993 Constitution, read together with s 72 of the South African Police Service Act of 1995, read together with items 2 and 24(3) of the Constitution.

33   See s 5(2)(*a*)(iii) of the South African Police Service Act of 1995, as well as section 12(2)(*k*)of Proclamation No R5, 1995, issued ito s 237(3) of the 1993 Constitution, read together with items 2 and 24(3) of the Constitution.

34   See sections 5(2)(*b*), 27 and 28(2) of the South African Police Service Act of 1995, as well as sections 8 and 212 of the 1993 Constitution, read together with item 2 of the Constitution.

35   See sections 5(2)(*c*), and 48(2) of the South African Police Service Act of 1995, read together with item 2 of the Constitution.

36   See the definition of "member" as contemplated in s 1(x) of the Act.

37   See s 1(vi) of the South African Police Service Act of 1995.

38   Except for the purposes of any provision of the Act in respect of which the national commissioner may otherwise prescribe; see s 1(vi)(*a*) of the Act.

39   Section 29 of the Act.

40   See paragraphs 27.4.1.2 and 27.4.1.3 above.

41   See the relevant regulation issued in terms of s 24 of the Act.

42   See s 5(2)(*a*) of Act 57 of 1973.

43   See the interpretation of "public service" in s 8 of the Act.

44   See s 8 of the Public Service Act of 1994.

45   See the interpretation of "services" in s 1 of the Act.

46   Provided that the Act shall only apply to (or in respect of) officers and employees, except in so far as s 2(1) of the Act provides otherwise and except where it is inconsistent with the context or clearly inappropriate.

47   See s 2(1) of the Act.

48 See s 2(2) of the Public Service Act of 1994.

49 The main source.

50 Thus, the Public Service Act of 1994, will be the source of second instance, when determining the employment conditions of persons who are employed in terms of the South African Police Service Act of 1995.

51 Rycroft & Jordaan 50.

52 See *Smit* supra at 61C.

53 Grogan 30.

54 *Wallace v Rand Daily Mails Ltd* 1917 AD 479 at 482 and *Friedlander v Hodes* 1944 CPD 169.

55 Grogan 40 and *Coolair Ventilator v Liebenberg* 1967 (1) SA 686 WLD at 690.

56 Rycroft & Jordaan 62.

57 Grogan 46.

58 Grogan 60 and Rycroft & Jordaan 65.

59 Grogan 62 and Rycroft & Jordaan 67.

60 *Van Deventer v WCC* 1962 (4) SA 28 (T).

61 *Van Deventer* supra at 31.

62 *SAR&H v Cruywagen* 1938 CPD 219 at 229.

63 Grogan 64.

64 Rycroft & Jordaan 82.

65 See the applicable provisions of the South African Police Service Act of 1995 and the Public Service Act of 1994.

66 Grogan 73–4.

67 Rycroft & Jordaan 85–6.

68 Section 205(3)of the 1996 Constitution.

69 *Administrator, Transvaal ao v Zenzile* 1991 (1) SA 21 (A) at 22F–H and *Administrator, Transvaal ao v Traub* 1989 (4) SA 731 (A); (1989) 10 *ILJ* 823 (A).

70 For example, dismissals, disciplinary enquiries, transfers, promotions. In exceptional circumstances, such as in the *Traub* case, such decisions can involve reappointments affecting a particular member's advancement in his or her professional career and/or in the hierarchical structure of the SAPS, especially where there has been a specific past practice in this regard.

71 *Zenzile* 22F–H.

72 Olivier *Legitimate Expectation and the Protection of Employment* at 487.

73 In *Sibiya aa v Administrator, Natal aa* 1991 (2) SA 591 (D) at 539A–B, the court held that the *audi* principle came into play not only when existing rights were affected but also when the property of the individual was affected. According to the court, the concept of property to which the *audi* rule related was wide enough to include economic loss consequent upon the dismissal of a public sector employee.

74 In *Sibiya* at 538F–I, the court held that the rules of natural justice do not require that the decision of the public body should, when viewed from the angle of the law of contract, involve actual legal infraction of the individual's existing rights. It requires simply that the decision should adversely affect such a right. No more has to be demonstrated than that an existing right is, as a matter of fact, impaired or injuriously affected.

75   *Traub* case 748G–H.

76   *Traub* case 750C–F and Baxter 587.

77   *Traub* case 748G–I and Olivier *Legitimate Expectation and the Protection of Employment* at 488.

78   *Zenzile* case 37F–38I.

79   *Traub* case 733B–D.

80   *Traub* case 758D–E.

81   *Traub* case 756I–J.

82   In *Sibiya aa v Administrator, Natal aa* 1991 (2) SA 591 (D) at 539A–B, the court held that the *audi* principle came into play not only when existing rights were affected but also when the property of the individual was affected. According to the court, the concept of property to which the *audi* rule related was wide enough to include economic loss consequent upon the dismissal of a public sector employee.

83   In *Sibiya* at 538F–I, the court held that the rules of natural justice do not require that the decision of the public body should, when viewed from the angle of the law of contract, involve actual legal infraction of the individual's existing rights. It requires simply that the decision should adversely affect such a right. No more has to be demonstrated than that an existing right is, as a matter of fact, impaired or injuriously affected.

84   For example, dismissals, disciplinary enquiries, transfers, promotions. In exceptional circumstances, such as in the *Traub* case, such decisions can involve reappointments affecting a particular member's advancement in his or her professional career and/or in the hierarchical structure of the SAPS, especially where there has been a specific past practice in this regard.

85   For example, the authority to dismiss, to discipline, to transfer, to withhold promotion or to demote.

86   For example, the South African Police Service Act of 1995 and the Public Service Act of 1994.

87   Olivier *Legitimate Expectation and the Protection of Employment* at 487.

88   Olivier *Legitimate Expectation and the Protection of Employment* at 487 and Baxter 540.

89   Baxter 541; Rose-Innes, chapters 11 and 12; Olivier *Legitimate Expectation and the Protection of Employment* 487–9.

90   Traub 75G–J.

91   Section 41 of the South African Police Service Act of 1995.

92   Olivier *Legitimate Expectation and the Protection of Employment* at 488 and *Lunt v University of Cape Town* 1989 (2) SA 438 (C) at 446H–J; 449D, I–J en 450C–D. See also the *Zenzile* case at 40A–G en *Administrator, Transvaal aa v Theletsane aa* 1991 (2) SA 192 (A) at 206C–G.

93   *Moodley aa v Minister of Education* 1989 (3) SA 221 (A) 235C–236C.

94   *Zenzile* case at 37F–38I.

95   Olivier *Legitimate Expectation and the Protection of Employment* at 489; *Moyo v Administrator of Transvaal* 1988 (9) *ILJ* 372 (W) at 386C–D; *Gwala v Director of Education, Natal* 1988 (9) *ILJ* 789 (W) at 799B–C.

Chapter 28

Constitutional Labour Law Rights for the South African Police Service and its Members in the Workplace

Dirk Bouwer

28.1   SUMMARY AND INTRODUCTION

*T*HE Constitution of the Republic of South Africa, 1996 is the supreme law of the Republic. Any law or conduct inconsistent with the Constitution is invalid. The duties imposed by its provisions must be performed.

The 1996 Constitution makes provision for a Bill of Rights. This Bill of Rights is the cornerstone of democracy in South Africa. The state (including the South African Police Service) must respect, protect and fulfil the rights contained in the Bill of Rights.

The Bill of Rights makes provision, *inter alia,* for labour rights to regulate labour relations between the following parties to the employment relationship:

- employees (including members of the South African Police Service);
- trade unions (including trade unions that represent the interests of members of the South African Police Service) and federations of trade unions;
- employers (including the South African Police Service in its capacity as an employer); and
- employers' organisations (of which the South African Police Service in its capacity as an employer is a member) and federations of employers' organisations.

The rights contained in the Bill of Rights (including the constitutionally recognised and protected labour rights) are subject to the limitations contained or referred to in Chapter 2 of the 1996 Constitution.

The aim of this chapter is to identify and determine the content of the constitutionally recognised and protected labour rights that apply to the employment relationship within the South African Police Service.

28.2   KEY OBJECTIVES

The key objectives of this chapter are to enable students to:

- identify the labour rights that are recognised and protected in terms of section 23 of the 1996 Constitution;
- identify the labour rights that serve to protect "workers" (employees) in terms of sections 23(1) and (2) of the 1996 Constitution;
- identify the labour rights that serve to protect the employer in terms of sections 23(1) and (3) of the 1996 Constitution;
- identify the labour rights and freedoms embodied in sections 23(1), (4) and (5) of the 1996 Constitution which serve to protect all trade unions and employers' organisations;
- identify the constitutional principles embodied in sections 36 and 39 of the 1996 Constitution which prescribe how constitutional rights may be limited and what requirements they must fulfil in order to be constitutionally valid and enforceable;
- determine the content and meaning of the constitutional principles that are prescribed by sections 36 and 39 of the 1996 Constitution;
- determine the distinction between a "right" and a "freedom" or "liberty";

- determine the content of the constitutional right to fair labour practices, with specific reference to the meaning of "fairness" and the right not to be unfairly dismissed;
- determine the content of the constitutional labour rights of members of the SAPS in their capacity as "employees";
- determine the content of the constitutional labour rights of the SAPS in its capacity as "employer";
- determine the content of the constitutional labour rights of the trade unions representing the members of the SAPS and of the employers' organisations of which the SAPS is a member; and
- determine the content of the "freedom" of a trade union representing the interests of members of the SAPS, which serves to protect its interests by means of security arrangements contained in collective agreements.

28.3   APPLICABLE LAW AND INTERNATIONAL INSTRUMENTS

The 1996 Constitution, sections 2, 7, 8, 23, 33, 35, 36, 39 and 205

The Labour Relations Act of 1995, sections 5, 7, 8, 19, 25–30, 65, 95–97, 185, 187, 188 and 213

The South African Police Service Act of 1995, sections 24 and 41

The Public Service Act of 1994

Canadian Charter of Rights and Freedoms, 1982

European Convention for the Protection of Human Rights and Fundamental Freedoms, 1952

German Constitution, 23 May 1949

ILO Convention no 158 of 1982, article 4

28.4   INTERPRETATION AND DISCUSSION

28.4.1   The constitutional rights regulating labour relations

28.4.1.1   Constitutional labour rights: Section 23 of the 1996 Constitution

In Chapter 2 of the 1996 Constitution,[1] the Bill of Rights recognises the following rights with regard to labour relations:

"(1)   Everyone has the right to fair labour practices.

(2)   Every worker has the right —

(a)   to form and join a trade union;

(b)   to participate in the activities and programmes of a trade union; and

(c)   to strike.

(3)   Every employer has the right —

(a)   to form and join an employers' organisation; and

(b)   to participate in the activities and programmes of an employers' organisation.

(4) Every trade union and every employers' organisation has the right —

    (*a*) to determine its own administration, programmes and activities;

    (*b*) to organise; and

    (*c*) to form and join a federation.

(5) Every trade union, employers' organisation and employer has the right to engage in collective bargaining. National legislation may be enacted to regulate collective bargaining. To the extent that the legislation may limit a right in this Chapter, the limitation must comply with section 36(1).

(6) National legislation may recognise union security arrangements contained in collective agreements. To the extent that the legislation may limit a right in this Chapter, the limitation must comply with section 36(1)."

28.4.1.2 Content of the constitutionally recognised and protected labour rights

Section 23 of the 1996 Constitution confers constitutional status on labour rights in three categories, namely:

- those labour rights pertaining to a "worker";
- those labour rights pertaining to an "employer"; and
- those labour rights pertaining to a "trade union" and "employers' organisation".

The following labour rights are constitutionally protected for a "worker":

- the right to form and join a trade union;[2]
- the right to participate in the activities and programmes of a trade union;[3] and
- the right to strike.[4]

The following labour rights are constitutionally protected for an "employer":

- the right to fair labour practices;[5]
- the right to form and join an employers' organisation;[6] and
- the right to participate in the activities and programmes of an employers' organisation.[7]

The following labour rights and *freedom* are constitutionally protected for a "trade union" and an "employers' organisation":

- the right to fair labour practices;[8]
- the right to determine its own administration, programmes and activities;[9]
- the right to organise;[10]
- the right to bargain collectively;[11]
- the right to form and join a federation;[12] and
- the *freedom* of a union to protect its interests by means of security arrangements contained in collective agreements.[13]

28.4.2 The constitutional limitation of labour rights

28.4.2.1 Introduction

It is clear that the 1996 Constitution, in general terms, recognises and protects the fundamental labour rights of *all workers* — including members of the South African Police Service in their capacity as employees or workers.[14]

The 1996 Constitution is the supreme law of the Republic of South Africa. Any law or conduct inconsistent with its provisions shall be invalid and any duties imposed by it must be performed.[15]

The state must respect and is responsible for protecting, promoting and fulfilling the rights contained in the Bill of Rights.[16, 17]

Thus, in principle, members[18] of the South African Police Service[19] are possessed of those constitutionally recognised and protected labour rights accorded to workers and the state (including the SAPS)[20] must respect, protect, promote and fulfil these labour rights.[21, 22]

28.4.2.2 The limitation of labour rights for members of the South African Police Service

(a) Introduction: Sections 36 and 39 of the 1996 Constitution

It is trite that no right, whether entrenched or not, has absolute protection.[23] The Constitution makes express provision for this by stating that the rights[24] in the Bill of Rights are subject to the limitations contained or referred to in section 36 and elsewhere in the Bill.[25] Thus, the constitutionally recognised fundamental labour rights of workers in South Africa[26] may in fact be limited.

Section 36 of the 1996 Constitution provides as follows:

"(1) The rights in the Bill of Rights may be limited only in terms of law of general application to the extent that the limitation is reasonable and justifiable in an open and democratic society based on human dignity, equality and freedom, taking into account all relevant factors including —

(*a*) the nature of the right;

(*b*) the importance of the purpose of the limitation;

(*c*) the nature and extent of the limitation;

(*d*) the relation between the limitation and its purpose; and

(*e*) less restrictive means to achieve the purpose.

(2) Except as provided in subsection (1) or in any other provision of the Constitution, no law may limit any right entrenched in the Bill of Rights."

Section 39 of the 1996 Constitution regulates the interpretation of the rights (including labour rights) contained in the Bill of Rights as follows:

"(1) When interpreting the Bill of Rights, a court, tribunal or forum —

> (*a*)   must promote the values that underlie an open and
> democratic society based on human dignity, equality
> and freedom;
> (*b*)   must consider international law; and
> (*c*)   may consider foreign law."

As discussed above, the 1996 Constitution recognises and protects the labour rights of workers (including members of the SAPS in their capacities as "workers") in general terms.[27] However, the recognition and protection of these labour rights are subject to certain constitutional limitations.[28]

The constitutional limitations that shall or may have an effect on these rights are the following.

(1)   In terms of section 36(1) of the 1996 Constitution —

- labour rights *may* be limited by law of general application;[29]
- this limitation must, however, be reasonable and justifiable in an open and democratic society based on —
  - human rights;
  - equality; and
  - freedom;[30]
- this limitation must further take all relevant factors into account, including —
  - the nature of the right;
  - the importance of the purpose of the limitation;
  - the nature and extent of the limitation;
  - the relation between the limitation and its purpose; and
  - less restrictive means to achieve the purpose.

(2)   In terms of section 39(1) of the 1996 Constitution, a court, tribunal or forum when interpreting the Bill of Rights —

- must promote the values that underlie an open and democratic society based on human dignity, equality and freedom;
- must consider international law; and
- may consider foreign law.

The entrenchment of the above-mentioned fundamental labour rights shall not be construed as denying the existence of any other rights or freedoms recognised or conferred by common law, customary law or legislation to the extent that they are consistent with Chapter 2 of the 1996 Constitution.[31]

(b)   *The content and meaning of the limitation clause*

The South African courts with constitutional jurisdiction will be called upon to give content and meaning to the limitation clause. As our limitation clause contains provisions which are similar to those in other jurisdictions,[32] it is important to investigate these foreign sources.[33]

- The first and most important source, both textually and structurally, is the general limitation clause in section 1 of the *Canadian Charter of Rights and Freedoms,* 1982, which guarantees all the rights and freedoms which it embodies, subject to such *reasonable* limits prescribed by law as can be *demonstrably justified in a free and democratic society*.[34] Although by no means identical, our Constitution provides that a fundamental right may be limited by law of general application, provided that such limitation is *reasonable* and *justifiable in an open and democratic society* based on freedom and equality.[35]

- The second source is the *European Convention for the Protection of Human Rights and Fundamental Freedoms,* 1952, which limits various rights in the same way as the limitation clause of our Constitution. For example, article nine provides that the limitation on the right to freedom of thought shall be *subject only to such limitations as are prescribed by law and are necessary in a democratic society in the interests of public safety, for the protection of public order*.[36]

- The third source is article 19.2 of the *German Constitution,*[37] which mirrors section 33(1)(*b*) of our 1993 Constitution, in that it provides that a limitation shall also *not negate the essential content of the right in question*.[38]

A two-stage approach can be followed to determine the constitutional validity of the limitations of the labour rights of members of the SAPS.

The first stage of enquiry

The first stage of enquiry involves determining whether or not a specific right has been infringed. That is, the first step is to establish whether the labour rights of members of the SAPS have been infringed by the instruments that regulate their conditions of service.

Accordingly, the fundamental labour rights accorded to employees will have to be defined in order to determine whether these rights also apply to members of the SAPS.[39] The sources that determine the scope and extent of these rights are the 1996 Constitution, relevant legislation prescribing the conditions of service of members of the SAPS[40] and international instruments.

If the answer is in the affirmative, the second stage comes into operation: that is, determining whether the restriction is saved by the provisions of the limitation clause.[41]

It is therefore necessary to progress to the second stage of the enquiry in order to determine whether the restrictions are validated by the limitation clause of our Constitution.

The second stage of enquiry

The second stage of enquiry involves determining whether the limitations or restrictions imposed on the constitutionally recognised and protected labour rights of members of the SAPS are validated by the limitation and interpretation clauses of the 1996 Constitution.

In order for such limitation or restriction to be constitutional and therefore valid, it must comply with the following constitutional tests.[42]

- **The first test:** Any labour right conferred on members of the SAPS can only be limited by law and that law must be of general application.
- **The second test:** This test supposes that the limitation ought to be reasonable. In this regard, the leading case in Canadian jurisprudence is undoubtedly *R v Oakes*.[43] It was held in this case that a limitation will pass the test of reasonableness[44] only under the circumstances listed below.

(1) If the limitation is of *sufficient importance* to *outweigh* the constitutionally protected right (weight issue)

In order to be of "sufficient importance" (and therefore "reasonable" in outweighing the fundamental labour rights of members of the SAPS), the limitation must be directed at the realisation of collective goals of fundamental importance and must be motivated by concerns which are "pressing and substantial"[45] in a "democratic society".

The following arguments are put forward to overcome the weight issue.

- The prevention, combatting and investigation of crime; the maintenance of public order; the protection and securing of the inhabitants of the Republic of South Africa and their property; and the upholding and enforcement of the law are fundamental tasks of the SAPS.[46]
- Continued perseverance in the rendering of the above-mentioned essential (policing) services to this country on a continuous and unhindered basis is of vital and fundamental importance for every citizen and for the whole of South Africa.
- The objective and collective goals of the relevant limitation are of pressing and substantial concern, in that chaos and instability would result in South Africa if the SAPS were to be hindered in any way in its rendering of essential services. The limitation is further justified by the fact that it gives substantive effect to other constitutional guarantees.[47]

(2) If the *means* are *proportional* to the object of the limitation (means issue)

The principle of proportionality or alternative means requires that, before labour rights can be curtailed,[48] it must first be determined whether or not an effective alternative way of dispute resolution exists. This principle requires that the limitation —

- must be "rationally connected to its objective";
- must infringe "as little as possible" on members' fundamental right to strike; and
- must make provision for alternative means to be afforded to affected members of the SAPS so that there is "proportionality" between its effects and the objectives of the limitation.

- **The third test:** The limitation of SAPS members' labour rights must be justifiable in an open and democratic society based on the values of freedom and equality. According to Cheadle,[49] this test has been interpreted to require the court to have regard to similar legislation in other democratic societies in order to see how the balance between fundamental rights and society's broader interests is maintained.[50] In the *Oakes* case,[51] the court adopted a value-based analysis when interpreting this test: "... guided by the values and principles essential to a free and democratic society which ... embody, to name a few, respect for the inherent dignity of the human person, commitment to social justice and equality, accommodation of a wide variety of beliefs, respect for cultural and group identity, and faith in social and political institutions which enhance the participation of individuals and groups in society ... ."

It is clear from those international documents that do in fact recognise the labour rights of members of the Police Service, that such recognition is subject to the laws of the particular country. These international instruments do not, however, prevent lawful restrictions on these rights of members of the SAPS. This limitation is based upon, and has as its collective goal, the prevention, combating and investigation of crime; the maintenance of public order; the protection and securing of the inhabitants of the Republic of South Africa and their property; and the upholding and enforcement of the law.[52]

These values are recognised as being of sufficient importance in an open and democratic South African society based on freedom and equality.[53] Furthermore, if the above-mentioned objectives which the limitation aims to achieve are taken into account, the labour rights of members of the SAPS will of necessity have to be limited in order to respect the sensibilities of others or to achieve "the greater good of the majority".[54]

- **The fourth test:** The limitation of the labour rights of members of the SAPS must not "negate the essential content of the right". This requirement gives explicit recognition to the fact that what is at stake in this test is the legitimate *circumscription* of the labour rights of members of the SAPS and *not the visceration* or absolute prohibition of these rights.[55] According to Rautenbach, when determining whether the essential content of a right is negated, specific reference must be made "... na die besondere reg wat ter sprake is en die besondere omstandighede waaronder die reg aangetas is. ... Daar behoort dus altyd ook gevra te word watter betekenis 'n bepaalde reg nòg die beperking daarvan *vir die betrokke individu* het ... ."[56] (... to the particular right and the specific conditions under which the right may be affected. ... The question should also always be what does a particular right and the restriction thereof mean to the individual concerned...)

  In the light of the above discussion, the following conclusions can be drawn.

- In principle, members of the SAPS are accorded the internationally accepted labour rights[57] that underlie the employment relationship; these rights are constitutionally recognised and protected in terms of section 23 of the 1996 Constitution.

- However, these constitutionally recognised fundamental labour rights may be constitutionally limited, but only by law of general application. Furthermore, such limitation will be permissible only to the extent that it is reasonable and justifiable in an open and democratic society based on freedom and equality and to the extent that it does not negate the essential content of the right in question. In terms of the Constitution, the exercise of these fundamental labour rights shall or may, in certain circumstances, be curtailed. Section 39 determines that when interpreting such a right, a court of law *must* promote the values which underlie an open and democratic society based on freedom and equality, *must* consider international law, and *may* consider foreign law.

- In principle, the *absolute* infringement of the labour rights of members of the SAPS is *prima facie* unconstitutional, as these rights are constitutionally recognised and protected.
- Section 36 of the 1996 Constitution requires that, before a fundamental right can be limited, the limitation must fulfil the relevant constitutional requirements in order to be constitutionally valid and enforceable.
- The 1996 Constitution places no constitutional limitations on the applicability of these labour rights. These labour rights therefore also apply to members of the SAPS in their capacities as "employees"/"workers".

28.4.2.3 The distinction between a "right" and a "freedom" or "liberty"

With reference to the freedom of a union to protect its interests by means of security arrangements contained in collective agreements,[58] it is important to distinguish between a "right" and a "freedom" or "liberty". This distinction is necessary because there is a marked difference in the legal consequences flowing from a "right" and a "freedom" respectively.

If a person has a "right" to do something, not only is he/she legally able to do so, but others are under an obligation not to interfere with his/her actions. Recognition by the state of the labour rights of workers (including members of the SAPS) implies a correlative duty on the state to protect these constitutionally recognised and protected rights.

If a person has only a "freedom" or "liberty" to do something, then all it means is that such a person is not under a legal duty to refrain from such action. A freedom is an aspect of a person's power to participate in legal intercourse — and not a right as such — and can only be seen as a capacity based on a person's legal personality. However, this does not mean that other people are necessarily wrong when attempting to prevent him/her from exercising his/her "freedom", because they have no legal duty to let such a person behave in such a way.

Such a freedom cannot, however, be equated with a right, as any attempt to exercise this "freedom" puts the worker in an unprotected and even perilous position. Thus a freedom is more precarious than a right would be.

A "freedom" can become a basic human right when such a freedom is expressly provided for as a right and is guaranteed as such either constitutionally or by statute. The freedom can be transformed into a full legal obligation with universal scope if it is recognised by the material sources of international law.[59]

28.4.3 The constitutional right to fair labour practices

28.4.3.1 Introduction

The *Concise Oxford Dictionary* [60] defines "fair" also as "... in a fair manner ...". In Afrikaans the corresponding word is "billik" which, according to the *Groot Woordeboek,*[61] may also be translated as "reasonable; ... fair, just, equitable, fair minded ...".

These definitions of "fair" are far from precise.

In order to determine what is actually meant by the term "fair", it is necessary to understand what "unfair" means.

In *SADWU v The Master Diamond Cutters' Association of SA,*[62] the industrial (labour) court says the following with regard to the word "unfair":

> "It is apparent that one has to establish the meaning of that word from subparas (i) to (iv) of para (*a*) of the definition and also from para (*b*) thereof ... The *Shorter Oxford English Dictionary* at 2297 defines 'unfair' *inter alia* as 'not fair or equitable, unjust', 'unfavourable'. In the Afrikaans text the corresponding word is 'onregverdig', which according to Kritzinger, Schoonees & Cronje *Groot Woordeboek* (11 ed 1972) at 425, may also be translated as 'unjust, inequitable'... For the purpose of this analysis, one could probably accept that the word 'unfairly' in the context used in the definition, could mean, subject to the meaning further attributed thereto in the examination of the remainder of the definition, 'inequitable' or 'unjustified'." [63]

28.4.3.2 The determination of the content of fairness

According to Brassey,[64] fairness must be judged in the context of the facts of each case. In *UAMAWU v Fodens SA,* the industrial (labour) court decided that "fairness" —

> "... [i]s the righteousness of the particular case; it can therefore only become exclusively relevant in specific situations ... In so far as fairness is applicable all relevant matters surrounding the specific case in the framework that reasonably belongs to the actual supposition are to be taken into account and the deciding criteria are to be uncovered, evaluated and weighed."

In the *SADWU* case it was decided that the determination of what is fair or unfair is an exercise in statutory interpretation, and not a matter of personal inclination.[65] In this case the court sought to construe the nature of fairness by looking at the *definition* of an "unfair labour practice" (as defined in the Labour Relations Act of 1995), as a whole.

"Unfair labour practice", is defined in the Labour Relations Act of 1995 as —

"… any unfair act or omission that arises between an employer and an employee, involving —

(*a*) the unfair discrimination, either directly or indirectly, against an employee on any arbitrary ground, including, but not limited to race, gender, sex, ethnic or social origin, colour, sexual orientation, age, disability, religion, conscience, belief, political opinion, culture, language, marital status or family responsibility;

(*b*) the unfair conduct of the employer relating to the promotion, demotion or training of an employee or relating to the provision of benefits to an employee;

(*c*) the unfair suspension of an employee or any other disciplinary action short of dismissal in respect of an employee;

(*d*) the failure or refusal of an employer to reinstate or re-employ a former employee in terms of any agreement."

The reason for the labour court's search for a true definition of fairness is to be found in the fact that fairness (equity) is the touchstone of the labour court's jurisdiction.66

According to Brassey, the definition of an "unfair labour practice" is not the *only* interpretative source, and, when this definition fails as a guide (as it invariably will, because it is so open textured), it is necessary to look at the Labour Relations Act of 1995 as a whole.67

Whatever the content of the concept of fairness, it is clear that the Labour Relations Act of 1995 positions itself neutrally between the interests of the employer and employee.68 It does not expressly attempt to advance the interests of either party at the expense of the other.69 The interests of both employer and employee will always be of concern to the court whenever it has to consider the fairness or otherwise of particular conduct.70

Secondly, as far as the content of the concept of fairness is concerned, Rycroft and Jordaan point out that both the unfair labour practice definition and the court's discretion are creatures of statutes.71 Both were introduced to further the objects of the Labour Relations Act.72 The content of "fairness" must therefore always be measured against the objects of the Act itself.73

The objects of the Labour Relations Act of 1995 are, *inter alia,* to give effect to the constitutionally recognised and protected labour rights and to provide procedures for the resolution of labour disputes and, in this way, to prevent industrial unrest.74

It is the duty of the labour court to determine any dispute that has been referred to it in terms of item 3 of Schedule 7 of the Labour Relations Act of 1995.

These disputes can be divided into disputes of rights and disputes of interests. However, the distinction between disputes of right and interest is not absolutely clear.75

- Broadly speaking, disputes of right 76 concern the infringement, application or interpretation of existing rights embodied in a contract of employment, collective agreement or statute.77

- On the other hand, disputes of interest (or "economic" disputes) concern the creation of fresh rights, such as higher wages, the modification of existing collective agreements and improved service conditions.[78]

28.4.3.3 The right not to be unfairly dismissed

In terms of section 185 of the Labour Relations Act of 1995, every employee (including members of the SAPS in their capacities as employees) has the right not to be unfairly dismissed.[79]

The dismissal of an employee is automatically unfair[80] if the employer's reason for the dismissal is —

- the fact that the employee belongs to a trade union or has participated in (or supported) legal strike or protest action;
- the fact that the employee refused to do any work normally done by an employee who at the time was taking part in a strike or was locked out;
- an attempt to compel the employee to accept a demand in respect of any matter of mutual interest between the employer and employee;
- the fact that employee is pregnant; and
- unfair discrimination, either directly or indirectly, against an employee on any arbitrary ground, including, but not limited to, race, gender, sex, ethnic or social origin, colour, sexual orientation, age, disability, religion, conscience, belief, political opinion, culture, language, marital status or family responsibility.

A dismissal that is not automatically unfair, will be unfair if the employer fails to prove[81] the following.

- *The employer must prove that the reason for the dismissal is a fair reason —*
    - related to the employee's conduct or capacity; or
    - based on the employer's operational requirements.[82]

The employer's reason for dismissing an employee must be both valid and fair.[83] *Validity* "goes to proof and to the applicability to the particular employee of the reason for the dismissal".[84] The enquiry is whether the facts on which the employer relied to justify the dismissal actually existed and whether the employer has established the facts by evidence.[85] The *fairness* of the reason for a dismissal relates to the gravity of the infraction and whether the sanction imposed, was warranted.[86]

- *The employer must prove that the dismissal was effected in accordance with a fair procedure.*[87]

The industrial (labour) court has consistently required that an employee who faces dismissal for alleged misconduct should be given the opportunity to state his or her case concerning the charges brought against him or her, and to bring mitigating circumstances to the employer's notice.[88] According to the *NAAWU* case, the question is always whether the procedure followed by the employer was fair. In *Administrator of Transvaal v Theletsane* the Appeal Court decided that no specific test can be laid down for determining whether or not a hearing is fair — everything will depend upon the circumstances of the particular case. There are, however, at least two fundamental principles that must be satisfied before a hearing can be said to be fair: there must be notice of the contemplated action and a proper opportunity to be heard.[89] In *Mhlangu v CIM Deltak* (1986) 7 *ILJ* 346 (IC) the court held that the employer should also:

(*a*)   inform the employee of the complaint against him or her;

(*b*)   arrange for a prompt hearing and give the employee adequate notice of it;

(*c*)   allow the employee to be represented by a workmate and allow him or her to call witnesses;

(*d*)   ensure that the evidence is interpreted into his or her home language and inform him or her of the decision on the issue of culpability;

(*e*)   take the employee's service record into account when deciding on the disciplinary sanction;

(*f*)   tell him or her what penalty is being imposed; and

(*g*)   give him or her the right to appeal to another level of management.
       In determining whether or not

- the reason for dismissal is a fair reason, or
- the dismissal was effected in accordance with a fair procedure,

the relevant principles contained in Schedule 8 of the Labour Relations Act of 1995 must be taken into account.[90]

28.4.4   The constitutional labour rights of members of the South African Police Service in their capacity as workers

28.4.4.1   Introduction

The constitutionally recognised and protected labour rights can collectively be referred to as the right to freedom of association.[91]

The employee's (including a member of the SAPS in his or her capacity as an "employee") right to freedom of association is an inclusive right. This concept embodies several individual rights, namely:

- the right of every employee to form and join trade unions;
- the right of every employee to protect his/her economic and social interest by participating in the activities and programmes of a trade union;
- the right of employees to promote their interests through a process of collective bargaining; and
- the right of employees in the final instance to strike.[92]

According to Potgieter,[93] the right to freedom of association includes the following:

   "• the right of all employees and employers to form and join organisations of their own choice;
   - the right of such organisation to draw up its own constitution and rules;
   - the right to appoint their own representatives;

- the right to organise the activities and administration of the organisation, as well as to formulate programmes, without the interference of public authorities;
- the right to protection against dissolution and suspension;
- the right to form federations and confederations of unions and to affiliate with international organisations;
- the right to incorporation, independent of conditions which limit the right to freedom of association." (translation)

Potgieter [94] continues by stating that —

"... [T]he right to freedom of association contains two elements: the right to associate and the right to organise. Important criteria to assess the recognition of this right are the equality of the various trade unions (as a guarantee for exercising freedom of association at individual level) and the independence of unions from the state ..." (translation)

It is further clear that, not only are the rights to freedom of association (including the right to form and join trade unions and the right to participate in the activities and programmes of a trade union),[95] collective bargaining and strike action complementary to each other, but they also follow one another sequentially. The right to freedom of association is thus a *conditio sine qua non* (requirement) for the realisation of the rights of collective bargaining and strike action. It follows that recognition of the right to freedom of association implies simultaneous recognition of the complementary right to conduct collective bargaining.

Only once workers are organised can they use their ultimate trump card in the collective bargaining process — the threat of the collective withholding of labour. Workers' organisations cannot exist if workers are not free to join them, to work for them and to remain in them. The freedom to organise is a well-founded fundamental human right in both international and national law. It is, however, also complementary to and a *conditio sine qua non* (requirement) of collective bargaining.

According to Kaburise, one can confidently state that the right to organise incorporates collective bargaining. Kaburise submits that, if the right to organise incorporates collective bargaining, it also incorporates a right to strike.[96] The right to strike is a complementary right of the right to organise, since both are meant to help achieve equality in the workplace.[97]

Thus, the right to freedom of association is a *conditio sine qua non* (requirement) for the realisation of the rights of collective bargaining and strike action. It follows that absolute restriction and prohibition of the right to freedom of association and of the right to strike have the effect that the rights to organise and to bargain collectively are also severely restricted.

28.4.4.2 The content of the South African Police Service employees' right to freedom of association in terms of the Labour Relations Act of 1995

The purpose of the Labour Relations Act of 1995 [98] is, *inter alia,* to give effect to the labour rights of employees (including members of the SAPS in this capacity), which are recognised and protected by the provisions of the 1996 Constitution. [99]

Chapter II of the Labour Relations Act of 1995, as well as the South African Police Service Labour Regulations, [100] regulate the right to freedom of association of members of the SAPS. In terms of the Labour Relations Act of 1995, every member of the SAPS [101] has the right —

- to participate in forming a trade union or federation of trade unions, and
- to join a trade union, subject to its constitution.

Every member of the SAPS who is a member of a trade union has the right — [102]

- to participate in the lawful activities of the trade union of which he or she is a member, with the proviso that members are absolutely prohibited from striking, inducing any other member to strike or conspiring with another person to strike; [103] it is important to remember that the SAPS is, in terms of section 213 of the Labour Relations Act of 1995, considered an essential service and therefore prohibited in terms of section 65 of the Act to strike;
- to participate in the election of any of its office bearers, officials or trade union representatives;
- to stand for election and be eligible for appointment as an office bearer or official and, if elected or appointed, to hold office; and
- to stand for election and be eligible for appointment as a trade union representative and, if elected or appointed, to hold office.

However, members of the SAPS at the management level, as well as those members who participate in policy-making, are not permitted to represent or assist trade unions in their lawful activities. [104]

Every member of the SAPS who is a member of a trade union, which is a member of a federation of trade unions, has the right — [105]

- to participate in its lawful activities;
- to participate in the election of any of its office bearers or officials; and
- to stand for election and be eligible for appointment as an office bearer or official and, if elected or appointed, to hold office.

Further, the Labour Relations Act of 1995 and the South African Police Service's Labour Regulations [106] protect the right to freedom of association of members of the SAPS by regulating that no person (including the SAPS in its capacity as an "employer") may — [107]

- discriminate against a member for exercising or not exercising any of the above-mentioned rights;

- deprive a member of employment for exercising or not exercising any of the above-mentioned rights; and
- act prejudicially against a member for exercising or not exercising any of the above-mentioned rights.

A provision in any contract that contradicts or limits the above-mentioned protection is invalid.[108]

28.4.5 The constitutional labour rights of the South African Police Service in its capacity as employer

28.4.5.1 Introduction

See discussion in paragraph 28.4.4.1 above.

28.4.5.2 The content of the right to freedom of association accorded to the SAPS as employer in terms of the Labour Relations Act of 1995

The purpose of the Labour Relations Act of 1995[109] is, *inter alia,* to give effect to the labour rights of employers (including the SAPS in this capacity), which are constitutionally recognised and protected by the provisions of the 1996 Constitution.[110]

Chapter II of the Labour Relations Act of 1995 regulates the SAPS's right to freedom of association (in its capacity as an "employer"). In terms of the Labour Relations Act of 1995, the SAPS[111] has the right —

- to participate in forming an employers' organisation or a federation of employers' organisations, and
- to join an employers' organisation, subject to its constitution.

The SAPS, in its capacity as an employer and a member of an employers' organisation, has the right —[112]

- to participate in its lawful activities;
- to participate in the election of any of its office bearers, officials or trade union representatives;
- to stand for election and be eligible for appointment as an office bearer or official and, if elected or appointed, to hold office; and
- if a natural person, to stand for election and be eligible for appointment as a trade union representative and, if elected or appointed, to hold office and, if a juristic person, to have a representative to stand for election and be eligible for appointment as a trade union representative and, if elected or appointed, to hold office.

The SAPS as a member of an employers' organisation, which is a member of a federation of employers' organisations, has the right —[113]

- to participate in its lawful activities;
- to participate in the election of any of its office bearers or officials; and
- if a natural person, to stand for election and be eligible for appointment as a trade union representative and, if elected or appointed, to hold office

and, if a juristic person, to have a representative to stand for election and be eligible for appointment as a trade union representative and, if elected or appointed, to hold office.

Further, the Labour Relations Act of 1995, protects the SAPS's right to freedom of association, by regulating that no person (including any trade union) may —[114]

- discriminate against the SAPS in its capacity as an employer for exercising or not exercising any of the above-mentioned rights;
- prevent the SAPS from exercising any of the above-mentioned rights; and
- prejudice the SAPS for exercising or not exercising any of the above-mentioned rights.

A provision in any contract that contradicts or limits the above-mentioned protection, is invalid.[115]

The SAPS shall, in its capacity as an employer, exercise its managerial responsibilities and prerogatives subject to the provisions of the SAPS Labour Regulations and any other law (including the 1996 Constitution and the Labour Relations Act of 1995), including collective agreements concluded in terms of and according to the provisions of the above-mentioned regulations.[116]

28.4.6 The constitutional labour rights of trade unions representing members of the SAPS and employers' organisations of which the SAPS is a member

28.4.6.1 Introduction

See the discussion in paragraph 28.4.4.1 above.

The *Concise Oxford Dictionary* defines[117] a trade union as —

"an organised association of workers in a trade or group of allied trades or a profession, formed for protection and promotion of their common interests".

"Trade union" is defined in the Labour Relations Act of 1995[118] as —

"an association of employees whose principal purpose is to regulate relations between employees and employers, including any employers' organisation".

An "employee organisation" is defined in the SAPS Labour Regulations[119] as follows —

"An organisation consisting of employees formally associated together and organised in a staff association, trade association or trade union, for the purpose of regulating relations between themselves or some of them and the employer."

On the other hand, an "employers' organisation" is defined in the Labour Relations Act of 1995[120] as —

"Any number of employers associated together for the purpose, whether by itself or with other purposes, of regulating relations between employers and employees or trade unions."

A trade union or an employers' organisation may apply for registration according to the procedures laid down by the Labour Relations Act of 1995.[121]

However, if a trade union or employers' organisation does not register as such, it cannot take part in the establishment or proceedings of a bargaining council for the SAPS.[122]

If a trade union or an employers' organisation intends to apply for registration in terms of the Act, its constitution must comply with the requirements laid down by the Act.[123]

The effect of registration[124] is the following:

- it is proof that a registered trade union or an employers' organisation is a body corporate;
- the registration does not make a member of a registered trade union or an employers' organisation liable for any of its obligations or liabilities;
- a member or office bearer of a registered trade union or an employers' organisation is not personally liable for any loss suffered by any person as a result of an act performed or omitted in good faith by the member or office bearer while performing their functions for or on the behalf of the union or organisation; and
- service of any document directed to a registered trade union or an employers' organisation at the address most recently provided to the Registrar of Labour Relations will be for all purposes service of that document on that union or organisation.

In terms of the SAPS Labour Regulations, a trade union that represents members of the SAPS must be registered in accordance with the prescriptions prescribed by the National Commissioner of the SAPS as an employee organisation, notwithstanding the fact that such a trade union is registered in terms of the Labour Relations Act of 1995.[125] Such a trade union shall, after it has been registered in terms of regulation 6, be recognised by the SAPS.[126]

28.4.6.2 The content of the labour rights of trade unions representing members of the SAPS and employers' organisations of which the SAPS is a member in terms of the Labour Relations Act of 1995

The purpose of the Labour Relations Act 1995[127] is, *inter alia,* to give effect to the labour rights of trade unions and employers' organisations, which are constitutionally recognised and protected by the provisions of the 1996 Constitution.[128]

Every registered and recognised trade union representing members of the SAPS and every employers' organisation of which the SAPS (in its capacity as an employer) is a member, has the right — [129]

- to determine its own constitution and rules and to hold elections for its office bearers, officials and representatives;[130]

- to plan and organise its administration and lawful activities;
- to bargain collectively within the National Negotiating Forum.[131] The National Negotiating Forum will be deemed to be a bargaining council that has been established in terms of section 37(3)(*b*) of the Labour Relations Act of 1995.[132] The provisions of the SAPS Labour Regulations will have the effect and status of a collective agreement binding on the state (including the SAPS), the parties to the National Negotiating Forum and all the members of the SAPS;[133]
- to participate in forming a federation of trade unions or a federation of employers' organisations;
- to join a federation of trade unions or a federation of employers' organisations, subject to its constitution, and to participate in its lawful activities; and
- to affiliate with, and participate in the affairs of any international workers' organisation or international employers' organisation or the International Labour Organisation, and contribute to, or receive financial assistance from, these organisations.

28.4.7 Security arrangements contained in collective agreements for trade unions representing members of the SAPS

28.4.7.1 Introduction

See the discussion in paragraph 28.4.2.3 above.

28.4.7.2 The content of the freedom of a trade union representing members of the SAPS to protect its interests by means of security arrangements contained in collective agreements in terms of the Labour Relations Act of 1995

It is important to remember that neither a trade union (representing members of the SAPS) nor an employers' organisation has an enforceable, constitutionally recognised and protected right to the provision of security arrangements within a collective agreement. The provision of security arrangements within a collective agreement is simply a freedom accorded to a trade union or employers' organisation, which freedom the SAPS (in its capacity as an "employer") is not obliged to recognise. The provision of such security arrangements for trade unions or employers' organisations is dependent on negotiations undertaken and binding and enforceable collective agreements between the parties within the Negotiating Forum (Bargaining Council).

The Labour Relations Act of 1995 makes provision, *inter alia,* for the following security arrangements for a trade union or an employers' organisation.

- *Agency shop agreements:* A representative trade union and an employers' organisation may conclude a collective agreement, to be known as an agency shop agreement, requiring the SAPS to deduct an agreed agency fee from the wages of the members of the SAPS who are identified in the agreement and who are not members of the trade union. For these purposes, a "representative trade union" means a registered trade union in terms of the Labour Relations Act of 1995, or two or more registered trade unions acting jointly, whose members form a majority of the members of the SAPS employed — [134]

- by the SAPS in a sector of the SAPS;[135] or
- by the members of an employers' organisation (whereof the SAPS is a member), in a sector and area in respect of which the agency shop agreement applies.

This agency shop agreement must be concluded in a collective agreement and in accordance with the provisions of section 25 of the Labour Relations Act of 1995.

- *Closed shop agreements:* A representative trade union and an employers' organisation may conclude a collective agreement, to be known as a closed shop agreement, requiring all the members of the SAPS covered by the agreement to be members of the trade union. For these purposes, a "representative trade union" means a registered trade union in terms of the Labour Relations Act of 1995, or two or more registered trade unions acting jointly, whose members form a majority of the members of the SAPS employed — [136]
  - by the SAPS in a sector of the SAPS;[137] or
  - by the members of an employers' organisation (of which the SAPS is a member), in a sector and area in respect of which the closed shop agreement applies.

This closed shop agreement must be concluded in a collective agreement and in accordance with the provisions of section 26 of the Labour Relations Act of 1995.

28.5 SUGGESTED READING AND SOURCES

Basson, AC. 1994. *South Africa's Interim Constitution*. Cape Town: Juta.

Baxter, L. 1994. *Administrative Law*. Cape Town: Juta.

Beatty, D. 1993. Constitutional labour rights: Pros and cons. 1993 *ILJ* 1.

Ben-Israel, R. 1988. *International Labour Standards: The Case of Freedom to Strike*. New York: Kluwer.

Bouwer, D. 1995. *The Right to Strike — An International Perspective*. LLM thesis, Rand Afrikaans University, 1995.

Brassey, MSM. 1988. *The New Labour Law*. Cape Town: Juta.

Cachalia, *et al.* 1994. *Fundamental Rights in the New Constitution*. Cape Town: Juta.

Davies, M & Freedland, P. 1984. *Labour Law: Text and Material.* London: Stevens & Sons.

Grogan, J. 1993. *Riekert's Basic Employment Law*, 2 ed. Johannesburg: Juta.

IFCOL. 1989. *Development Law Strategies.* Pretoria: IFCOL.

ILO. 1994. *Freedom of Association and Collective Bargaining.* Geneva: ILO.

Kritzinger. 1986. *Groot Woordeboek*, 13 ed. Pretoria: Van Schaik.

Le Roux, P & Van Niekerk, A. 1994. *The South African Law of Unfair Dismissal.* Johannesburg: Juta.

Olivier, MP. 1991. Legitimate expectation and the protection of employment. 1991 *TSAR* 483.

Olivier, MP. 1994. Proposed legislation for the Police Service: A constitutional fiasco and labour relations nightmare? 1994 *TSAR* 803.

Potgieter, O. 1992. *Die Reg op Arbeid — 'n Regsvergelykende Perspektief.* LLD thesis, University of Potchefstroom.

Rautenbach, IM. 1994. Grondwetlike bepalings ter beskerming van die wese van menseregte. 1994 *TSAR* 403.

Reichman, PJ & Mureinik, E. 1980 Unfair labour practices. 1980 *ILJ* 1.

Rycroft, A & Jordaan, B. 1992. *A Guide to South African Labour Law*, 2 ed. Johannesburg: Juta.

The Concise Oxford Dictionary. 1984. 7 ed. Oxford: Clarendon Press.

Wiehahn, NJ. 1981. *Die Volledige Wiehahn Verslag: Dele 1–6 en die Witskrif op elke Deel.* Johannesburg: Lex Patria.

Woolman, PJ. 1994. Riding the push-me pull you: Constructing a test that reconciles the conflicting interests which animate the limitation clause. *SAJHR*, 60.

....

ENDNOTES

1 Section 23.
2 Section 23(2) of the 1996 Constitution.
3 Section 23(2) of the 1996 Constitution.
4 Section 23(2) of the 1996 Constitution.
5 Section 23(1) of the 1996 Constitution.
6 Section 23(3) of the 1996 Constitution.
7 Section 23(3) of the 1996 Constitution.
8 Sections 23(1); 8(2) and 8(4) of the 1996 Constitution.

9 Section 23(4) of the 1996 Constitution.

10 Section 23(4) of the 1996 Constitution.

11 Section 23(5) of the 1996 Constitution.

12 Section 23(4) of the 1996 Constitution.

13 Section 23(6) of the 1996 Constitution.

14 Sections 23(1) and 23(2) of the 1996 Constitution.

15 Section 2 of the 1996 Constitution.

16 Chapter 2 of the 1996 Constitution.

17 Section 7(2) of the 1996 Constitution.

18 In the members' capacity as "employees" or "workers".

19 Hereafter referred to as "the SAPS".

20 Including the SAPS in its capacity as an organ of the state — see s 8(1) of the 1996 Constitution — and in its capacity as an "employer".

21 Section 23 of the 1996 Constitution.

22 Bouwer chapter 3, paragraph 3.2.

23 See discussion in Bouwer chapter 3, paragraph 3.3; Basson 49; Cachalia 106.

24 Including the above-mentioned labour rights and freedoms — see paragraph 28.4.2.1 above.

25 See s 8(3) of the Constitution.

26 Including members of the SAPS in their capacities as employees.

27 Section 23.

28 Sections 36 and 39 of the 1996 Constitution.

29 Section 36(1) of the 1996 Constitution.

30 Section 36(1) of the 1996 Constitution.

31 Section 39(3) of the Constitution.

32 Basson 49 and Cachalia 107.

33 See section 39(1) of the 1996 Constitution. However, Cachalia utters a word of caution with regard to the use of comparative studies as our Constitution contains a stricter limitation for certain rights (must also be "necessary") before the limitation will be valid — something which is unknown in the Canadian jurisdiction.

34 Our emphasis.

35 Our emphasis.

36 Our emphasis.

37 Of 23 May 1949, as amended.

38 Our emphasis.

39 See discussion in paragraph 28.4.1.2 above.

40 The South African Police Service Act 68 of 1995 and the Public Service Act of 1994 (Proclamation 104 of 1994). See paragraph 27.4 of previous chapter dealing with the common-law labour rights of members of the SAPS in the workplace.

41 Cachalia suggests that this two-stage approach which the Canadian courts have developed to determine the constitutional validity of any law ought to be adopted in respect

of our Constitution. Cachalia's reasons are that our Constitution's limitation clause follows that of the Canadian Charter, on the one hand, and provides a sensible and logical framework for analysing and employing comparative authority in developing our own jurisprudence on the other (at 107)

42 Section 36(1) of the 1996 Constitution; Bouwer chapter 3, paragraph 3.3; Cheadle 101; Basson 50 and Cachalia 106.

43 26 DLR (4th) 200.

44 See *R v Edward Brooks & Art Ltd* 35 DLR (4th) 41.

45 See the commentary in the *Brooks* case at 41 regarding how our limitation clause will work in practice.

46 Section 205(3) of the 1996 Constitution.

47 See Woolman 60, 86.

48 Section 36 of the 1996 Constitution; Olivier (1994) 805 and Beatty 9.

49 At 102.

50 Section 39 of the 1996 Constitution.

51 At 212–214.

52 Section 205(3) of the 1996 Constitution.

53 Woolman 64.

54 See European Commission in *Handyside v UK* 1 EHRR 737, 93; Cachalia 115.

55 *AG, Quebec v Quebec Association of Protestant School Boards* 10 DLR (4th) 321; Cachalia 115.

56 Rautenbach 403, 406.

57 See paragraph 27.4.1.7 of previous chapter dealing with the common-law labour rights of members of the SAPS in the workplace.

58 See paragraph 28.4.2.1 above and section 23(5) of the 1996 Constitution.

59 International treaties, international custom and general principles of law; see Ben-Israel 4 & 5.

60 At 347.

61 At 76.

62 (1982) 3 *ILJ* 87 (ic).

63 At 116F–H.

64 Brassey 60.

65 Brassey 61.

66 Section 193 and items 2, 3 and 4 of Schedule 7 of the Labour Relations Act 66 of 1995.

67 At 61.

68 Brassey 63.

69 *Sasol Industries (Pty) Ltd v SACWU* (1990) 11 *ILJ* 1010 (LAC).

70 *Consolidated Frame Cotton Corporation v The President, IC* (1986) 7 *ILJ* 489 (A).

71 Rycroft & Jordaan 167.

72 Brassey 63.

73 Rycroft & Jordaan 168.

74 See preamble of Act.

75 See *Metal & Electrical Workers Union of SA v National Panasonic Co* (1991) 12 *ILJ* 533 (C) at 537E–F.

76 Including unfair labour practices; Reichman & Mureinik (1980) *ILJ* 1 at 21.

77 Rycroft & Jordaan 168–175.

78 Rycroft & Jordaan 169.

79 The meaning of dismissal is defined in s 186 of the Labour Relations Act of 1995.

80 See s 187 of the Labour Relations Act of 1995.

81 Section 188 of the Labour Relations Act of 1995.

82 See article 4 of the ILO Convention No 158 of 1982: "The employment of a worker shall not be terminated unless there is a valid reason for such termination connected with the capacity or conduct of the worker or based on the operational requirements of the undertaking, establishment or service."

83 *Kompecha v Bite My Sausage CC* (1988) 9 *ILJ* 1077 IC at 1081A–B.

84 Rycroft & Jordaan 196 and *Govender v SASKO (Pty)* (1990) 11 *ILJ* 1282 (IC) at 1285F–G.

85 *Changula v Bell Equipment* (1992) 13 *ILJ* 101 (LAC).

86 *Govender* case at 1285F–G.

87 See article 7 of the ILO Convention No 158 of 1982: "[T]he employment of a worker shall not be terminated for reasons related to the worker's conduct or performance before he is provided with an opportunity to defend himself against the allegations made, unless the employer cannot reasonably be expected to provide this opportunity."

88 According to Rycroft & Jordaan 203–4 and *NAAWU v PPC* (1985) 6 *ILJ* 369 (IC) at 378E–F.

89 1991 (2) SA 192 (A) at 206C–E.

90 Section 188 of the Labour Relations Act of 1995.

91 Section 23 of the 1996 Constitution.

92 Ben-Israel 27.

93 At 32.

94 At 32.

95 Including freedom of organisation (right to organise).

96 In IFCOL at 4.

97 Ben-Israel 27; Kahn-Fruend 201 and Potgieter 31.

98 See preamble and section 1 of the Act.

99 Section 23 of the Constitution.

100 Issued in terms of section 24 of the South African Police Service Act of 1995 (see regulation 2(1)) and accepted in terms of s 19 of the Labour Relations Act of 1995.

101 Section 4(1) of the Act. In terms of s 213 of the Act, the definition of "employee" includes any person who works for the state. This includes members of the SAPS.

102 Subject to the constitution of that trade union. See s 4(2) of the Act.

103 See s 41 of the South African Police Service Act of 1995, read together with sections 65(1)((*d*)(i) and 213 (definition of "essential service") of the Labour Relations Act of 1995. The absolute prohibition of strike action by members may be unconstitutional — see chapter 3 of Bouwer.

104 See regulation 2(2).

105 Subject to the constitution of that trade union. See s 4(3) of the Act.

106 See regulation 2(3) and (4).

107 Section 5 of the Act.

108 Unless the contractual provision is permitted in the Labour Relations Act of 1995 — see s 5(4) of the Act.

109 See preamble and s 1 of the Act.

110 Section 23 of the Constitution.

111 Section 6(1) of the Act. In terms of s 2 of the Act, the SAPS is included in the application of this Act.

112 Subject to the constitution of that trade union. See s 6(2) of the Act.

113 Subject to the constitution of that trade union. See s 4(3) of the Act.

114 Section 7 of the Act.

115 Unless the contractual provision is permitted in the Labour Relations Act of 1995; see s 7(4) of the Act.

116 See regulation 2(11).

117 At 1134.

118 Section 213 of the Act.

119 Regulation 1(1).

120 Section 213 of the Act.

121 Sections 95 and 96 of the Act.

122 Sections 27–30 (30(1)(*o*)) of the Labour Relations Act of 1995.

123 Section 95(5) of the Act.

124 Section 97 of the Labour Relations Act of 1995.

125 Regulation 6.

126 Regulation 7 of the SAPS Labour Regulations.

127 See preamble and s 1 of the Act.

128 Section 23 of the Constitution.

129 Section 8 of the Labour Relations Act of 1995.

130 Subject to the provisions of Chapter VI and s 30, as well as item 18(4) of Schedule 7 of the Labour Relations Act of 1995.

131 In accordance with the collective bargaining procedures laid down by the provisions of the SAPS Labour Regulations, issued in terms of s 24 of the South African Police Service Act of 1995. See also sections 31 and 32, and items 18 and 19 of Schedule 7 of the Labour Relations Act of 1995.

132 See item 20(*d*) of Schedule 7 of the Labour Relations Act of 1995.

133 See item 19 of Schedule 7 of the Labour Relations Act of 1995.

134 Section 25 of the Act.

135 Section 25 and the definition of "workplace" in section 213 of the Act.

136 Section 26 of the Act.

137 Section 26 and the definition of "workplace" in section 213 of the Act.

Chapter 29
State of Emergency

Marius Pansegrouw

SUMMARY

*A*S it is clear that human rights are not absolute and may be infringed upon, this chapter will show that curtailment of fundamental rights during a state of emergency is both historically and internationally acceptable. It is also clearly shown that the provisions in the Constitution of the Republic of South Africa, 1996, authorising the declaration of a state of emergency are in line with international norms and standards in this regard, in that there is adherence to the so-called Syracuse Principles. The Constitution provides for the circumstances under which an emergency can be declared, parliamentary oversight, judicial supervision, a list of non-derogable rights and limits on detention without trial.

29.1   INTRODUCTION

It is a familiar concept that human rights are not absolute and may be infringed upon in various ways, for example by declaring a state of emergency. In this regard Van Wyk, Dugard, De Villiers and Davis[1] state as follows:

> "Fundamental or human rights are exercised within the context of a specific society. They are as a rule not absolute and are limited by the rights of others and by the legitimate needs of society. Public order, safety, health, morals, and democratic values are generally recognized as justifying the imposition of limitations on the exercise of various fundamental rights. The enforcement of human rights is to be matched by 'accommodations in favour of the reasonable needs of the State to perform its public duties for the common good'. The organs of state have to balance conflicting demands and rights. Such limitations are as a rule of a permanent nature and are normally contained in a special 'limitation clause' in a constitution or international human rights instrument.

> "A different type of 'limitation' applies in times of public emergency threatening the 'life of the nation'. Special measures may be required to protect the state and society during such periods. It may then be necessary for the state to suspend temporarily its obligation to protect fundamental rights. The conditions under which this may happen are usually found in a special 'suspension' or 'derogation' clause."

The purpose of this chapter is, however, to give a brief outline of the historical basis for such a form of limitation, as well as the legal boundaries within which such a state of emergency operates.

29.2   KEY OBJECTIVES

The key objectives of this chapter are to enable students to discuss:
- the historical background relating to states of emergency;
- the basis on which a state of emergency can be declared;

- the possible level of derogation of certain fundamental rights;
- the role of the courts during such an emergency;
- applicable international human rights instruments.

29.3   APPLICABLE LAW AND INTERNATIONAL INSTRUMENTS

The 1996 Constitution, section 37
The State of Emergency Act of 1995, section 2
International instruments:
> The International Covenant of Civil and Political Rights (ICCPR) of 1966
> The Standard Minimum Rules for Prisoners

29.4   INTERPRETATION AND DISCUSSION

29.4.1   HIstorical background

It is generally accepted that in times of war or internal revolt a state may encroach upon the rights of the individual, in terms of the principle *salus rei publicae suprema lex* contained in Roman law. According to Carpenter,[2] this limitation is also based on the principles of self-defence and necessity, while martial law also forms part of the prerogative powers derived from English law.[3] The principles relating to the authority to declare a state of emergency are well settled as part of the South African common law and moved the Constitutional Court to declare the following regarding section 37:[4]

> "K.   NT37: STATES OF EMERGENCY
> [91]   NT 37 envisages national legislation authorising the temporary and partial curtailment of the Bill of Rights in limited circumstances and subject to detailed conditions. In principle there can be no objection to such authorisation. Partial curtailment of a bill of rights during a genuine national emergency is not inherently inconsistent with 'universally accepted fundamental human rights, freedoms and civil liberties'."[5]

At this point it should, however, be noted that a state of emergency declared in terms of the Constitution[6] will differ to a large degree from previous states of emergency such as those declared from 1984 onwards. In this regard Van Wyk *et al*[7] state as follows:

> "This particular clause and the powers contained therein cannot be interpreted as if they are continuations of the pre-1993 dispensation. They are based on a completely new legal footing and are to be construed as forming part of a new and original legal and constitutional order. Emergency powers are now to be exercised in terms of a system which aims at the *protection* of fundamental rights."

This comment will be discussed in detail later.

29.4.2   Declaration of a state of emergency

It should be noted that section 37 of the 1996 Constitution (see endnote 4) provides that a state of emergency must be declared in terms of an Act of Parliament. This section should be read with Schedule 6, section 2, which provides that:

"Continuation of existing law

2. (1)   All law that was in force when the new Constitution took effect, continues in force, subject to —

(*a*)   any amendment or repeal; and

(*b*)   consistency with the new Constitution.

(2)   Old order legislation that continues in force in terms of subitem (1) —

(*a*)   does not have a wider application, territorially or otherwise, than it had before the previous Constitution took effect unless subsequently amended to have a wider application; and

(*b*)   continues to be administered by the authorities that administered it when the new Constitution took effect, subject to the new Constitution."

The result of the above-mentioned sections is that the State of Emergency Act[8] will continue to exist and will be the Act in terms of which a state of emergency can be declared by the President. The said Act also makes provision for the President to promulgate emergency regulations in terms of which officials may issue orders, rules and by-laws to administrate the said state of emergency.[9]

It is, however, most important to note that section 37[10] clearly stipulates that a state of emergency may only be declared when the *life of the nation* is threatened by certain actions; therefore it is vital to interpret the meaning of this phrase. The following quotation clearly sets out the meaning of the phrase and the circumstances under which such a declaration will be possible:

"(*a*)   The emergency must be actual or imminent. There must be a real threat of war, invasion, general insurrection or disorder, or a national disaster must already exist. A 'preventive emergency' will be unlawful. Convincing proof of the existence of an imminent threat will be required. This requires a factual judgment of the evidence available.

(*b*)   The emergency must be of exceptional magnitude. This usually requires a threat to the whole of the population. An emergency experienced in one part of the country only but affecting the whole nation will satisfy this requirement. A localized emergency affecting only the local population may be problematic, although some commentators find it acceptable. Chowdhury provides the following useful discussion:

'Relying upon the decision of the European Court in *Ireland v UK*, Buergenthal points out that a public emergency need not engulf or threaten to engulf the entire nation before it can be said to "threaten the life of the nation". One must distinguish between the seriousness of a threat and the geographical boundaries in which the threat appears or from which it emanates. A public emergency which threatens the life of a nation "could presumably exist even if the emergency appeared to be confined to one part of the country — for example one of its provinces, states or cantons — and did not threaten to spill over to other parts of the country". A contrary interpretation, argues Buergenthal, would be unreasonable since it would prevent a state party from declaring a public emergency in one of its remote provinces where a large scale armed insurrection was in progress because it appeared that the conflict would not spread to other provinces.'

(*c*) The life of the nation must be threatened. This requirement is found in both the European Convention and the ICCPR. This has been interpreted by the European Court in the *Lawless* case to refer to an exceptional situation of crisis or emergency which affects the whole population and constitutes a threat to the organized life of the community of which the state is composed ... Another commentator interprets this requirement to mean a crisis situation affecting the population as a whole and constituting a threat to the organized existence of the community which forms the basis of the State.

(*d*) A state of emergency must be a measure of last resort. If the ordinary law of the land can deal with the needs of a situation, a state of emergency is not permissible. The normal provisions of the law should first be exhausted. They include the limitation clause providing for everyday constitutionally acceptable limits to the exercise of human rights.

(*e*) A state of emergency must be a temporary measure. This flows from its very nature. Suspension of rights must therefore end when the threat has disappeared. Permanent states of emergency are unlawful."[11]

29.4.3   Derogation of fundamental rights

Section 37(5)[12] sets out the extent to which fundamental rights can be infringed during a declared[13] state of emergency. The following important rights[14] are, however, regarded as non-derogable, namely:[15]

(*a*) The right to life (section 11);

(*b*) The right to remain silent and to be informed of such right (section 35(1)(*a*)(*b*));

(*c*) the right to be informed of the charge (section 35(3)(*a*));

(*d*) the right to a public trial before an ordinary court (section 35(3)(*c*));

(*e*) the right to choose and be represented by a legal practitioner (section 35(3)(*f*));

(*f*) the right to be presumed innocent (section 35(3)(*h*));

(*g*) the right to of appeal to, or review by a higher court (section 35(3)(*o*)).

Section 35(5) also clearly states that even during a state of emergency evidence will be excluded if the admission of such evidence would render the trial unfair.

Apart from the rights discussed above, section 37(6) and (7) provides for important safeguards to prevent the abuse of authority by the state and its organs by stipulating that:

"(6) Whenever anyone is detained without trial in consequence of a derogation of rights resulting from a declaration of a state of emergency, the following conditions must be observed:

(*a*) An adult family member or friend of the detainee must be contacted as soon as reasonably possible, and informed that the person has been detained.

(*b*) A notice must be published in the national *Government Gazette* within five days of the person being detained, stating the detainee's name and place of detention and referring to the emergency measure in terms of which that person has been detained.

(*c*) The detainee must be allowed to choose and be visited at any reasonable time by a medical practitioner.

(*d*) The detainee must be allowed to choose and be visited at any reasonable time by a legal representative.

(*e*) A court must review the detention as soon as reasonably possible, but no later than 10 days after the date the person was detained, and the court must release the detainee unless it is necessary to continue the detention to restore peace and order.

(*f*) A detainee who is not released in terms of a review under paragraph (*e*), or who is not released in terms of a review under this paragraph, may apply to a court for a further review of the detention at any time after 10 days have passed since the previous review, and the court must release the detainee unless it is still necessary to continue the detention to restore peace and order.

(g)   The detainee must be allowed to appear in person before any court considering the detention, to be represented by a legal practitioner at those hearings, and to make representations against continued detention.

(h)   The state must present written reasons to the court to justify the continued detention of the detainee, and must give a copy of those reasons to the detainee at least two days before the court reviews the detention.

(7)   If a court releases a detainee, that person may not be detained again on the same grounds unless the state first shows a court good cause for re-detaining that person."

29.4.4   Role of the courts

Apart from the limitations set out above, the single most important safeguard contained in the 1996 Constitution is the authority of the courts as set out in section 37(3):

"(3)   Any competent court may decide on the validity of —

(a)   a declaration of a state of emergency;

(b)   any extension of a declaration of a state of emergency; or

(c)   any legislation enacted, or other action taken, in consequence of a declaration of a state of emergency."

The involvement of the judiciary as watchdog complies with international norms[16] and with the guiding principles set out in South African case law.

In *Ganyile v Minister of Justice* De Villiers JP stated:

"In Plato's Republic where one has the *res politica* the judiciary often has to state that action taken by the executive is justified on the principle *salus reipublicae suprema lex est.* On the other hand the Supreme Court is the protector of the rights of the individual citizen, and will protect him against unlawful action by the executive in all its branches in the same way as in England the Supreme Court will protect the British even from the Crown."[17]

In similar vein, Lord De Villiers stated in *In re Kok and Balie*:

"The disturbed state of the country ought not, in my opinion, to influence the Court, for its first and sacred duty is to administer justice to those who seek it and not to preserve the peace of the country. The civil courts of the country have but one duty to perform and that is to administer the laws of the country without fear, favour and prejudice independently of the consequences which ensue."[18]

The fact that the courts will be able to exercise extensive jurisdiction over all actions taken during a state of emergency and also over all legislation enacted at such times will play a major role in preventing the kind of abuses which occurred during previous states of emergency, namely:

"(1) When the courts decided that 'reason to believe' implied that the arresting officer must base this belief upon objective jurisdictional facts justiciable in a court of law, arrest and detention based upon the subjective opinion of the arresting officer were introduced. It is, of course, much more difficult to prove the absence of an honestly held opinion than it is to prove the absence of objective grounds for the infringement. To make matters worse, the onus of proof was expressly shifted from the arresting officer to the arrestee;

(2) When it became clear that the courts would insist on compliance with the *audi alteram partem* rule before an order for continued detention was issued, the operation of this rule was expressly excluded. This left the judiciary with only the power to insist that this rule be complied with after the order to further detain had been issued;

(3) When the courts found that some measures were invalid on the basis of an improper delegation of powers, the regulations were amended to provide for the necessary delegation thereof;

(4) The authorities have sought to exclude judicial control of executive action by means of so-called ouster clauses. Fortunately, the courts have not allowed these clauses completely to oust their jurisdication to examine the validity of executive action."[19]

29.4.5 Applicable human rights instruments during a state of emergency

Apart from the safeguards set out above, section 37(4) provides that:

"(4) *Any legislation enacted in consequence of a declaration of a state of emergency may derogate from the Bill of Rights only to the extent that —*

(*a*) the derogation is strictly required by the emergency; and

(*b*) the legislation —

(i) *is consistent with the Republic's obligations under international law applicable to states of emergency;*

(ii) conforms to subsection (5); and

(iii) is published in the national *Government Gazette* as soon as reasonably possible after being enacted (own emphasis)."

As far as international law is concerned, it is clear from the following that our courts have taken note of the relevant principles and their application as seen:

"The South African courts have already indicated their preparedness to adhere to other international standards, such as the

'Standard Minimum Rules' on the treatment of prisoners. In *S v Daniel* this was done without any detailed analysis of their legal status. The Supreme Court simply accepted them as 'riglyne vir die behandeling van gevangenes wat deur talle lande as 'n bloudruk vir hulle gevangenisstelsels beskou word'. It also took judicial notice of the fact that prison authorities in South Africa already follow a policy of adhering to these guidelines. This seems to suggest that international state practice and standards are acceptable as a yardstick for executive action." [20]

The Standard Minimum Rules for Prisoners[21] makes provisions for minimum standards by providing, *inter alia*, for:[22]

(*a*)   Separation of categories
(*b*)   Accommodation
(*c*)   Personal hygiene
(*d*)   Clothing and bedding
(*e*)   Food
(*f*)   Exercise and sport
(*g*)   Medical services
(*h*)   Discipline and punishment
(*i*)   Contact with the outside world
(*j*)   Religion

South Africa is also a signatory of the International Covenant of Civil and Political Rights (ICCPR),[23] which was signed by President Nelson Mandela on 3 October 1994.[24] This Convenant contains a set of principles which should guide the application and extent of emergency powers. These principles are also referred to as the Syracuse Principles and have been incorporated to a large degree in section 37[25] by making provision for:[26, 27]

(*a*)   the circumstances under which an emergency can be declared;
(*b*)   parliamentary oversight;
(*c*)   judicial supervision;
(*d*)   non-derogable rights;
(*e*)   limits on detention without trial.

29.5   SUGGESTED READING AND SOURCES

Basson, D. 1987. Judicial activism in a state of emergency: An examination of recent decisions of the South African courts. *SAJHR*, 3 (1).

Cachalia, *et al.* 1994. *Fundamental Rights in the New Constitution*. Cape Town: Juta.

Chowdhury. 1989. *Rule of Law in a State of Emergency*. Pinter Publishers.

Frankowski & Shelton. 1992. *Preventative Detention*. Martinus Nijhoff Publishers.

Liebenberg. 1995. The International Covenant on Economic, Social and Cultural Rights and its implications for South Africa. *SAJHR*, 11 (3).

Oraa. 1992. *Human Rights in States of Emergency in International Law.* Oxford University Press.

Patel & Watters. 1994. *Human Rights, Fundamental Instruments and Documents.* Butterworths.

Van Wyk, D, Dugard, J, De Villiers, B & Davis, D (eds). 1994. *Rights and Constitutionalism: The New South African Legal Order.* Cape Town: Juta.

. . . .

ENDNOTES

1 Van Wyk, D, Dugard, J, De Villiers, B & Davis, D (eds) 629.

2 Carpenter 105.

3 Carpenter at 106.

4 The Constitution of 1996, which reads as follows:

"States of emergency

37. (1) A state of emergency may be declared only in terms of an Act of Parliament, and only when —

(*a*) the life of the nation is threatened by war, invasion, general insurrection, disorder, natural disaster or other public emergency; and

(*b*) the declaration is necessary to restore peace and order."

5 Certification of the Constitution of the Republic of South Africa, 1996: Case CCT 23/96.

6 The 1996 Constitution.

7 Van Wyk *et al* 631.

8 Act 86 of 1995.

9 Section 2 of Act 86 of 1995.

10 See endnote 4.

11 Van Wyk *et al* 653 and 655.

12 The 1996 Constitution.

13 In terms of Act 86 of 1995.

14 This is not an exhaustive list and section 37(5) should be consulted for the full extent of the limitations.

15 The rights refer to are the rights contained in the 1996 Constitution.

16 Chowdhury 55, 58; Oraa 40–2.

17 1962 (1) SA 847 (E) at 653.

18 1879 Buch 45 at 66.

19 Basson 42–43.

20 Van Wyk *et al* 652.

21   The Standard Minimum Rules were adopted by the First United Nations Congress on the Prevention of Crime and Treatment of Offenders in 1955 at Geneva and were approved by the Economic and Social Council of the United Nations by Resolutions 663 (XXIV) of 31 July 1957 and 2076 (LXII) of 13 May 1977.

22   Patel & Watters 342–351.

23   ICCPR, 1966, 999 United Nations Treaty Series, 171.

24   Liebenberg 359.

25   The 1996 Constitution.

26   Cachalia, A, Cheadle, H, Davis, D Haysom, N, Maduna, P & Marcus, G at 118.

27   Frankowski & Shelton 1 et seq.

Chapter 30
Sentence and Sentencing

Basil King

SUMMARY

SENTENCING is the final stage in most criminal proceedings. "Straftoemeting", the Afrikaans equivalent, sounds far more ominous. The imposition of punishment, the nearest translation, although invoking ideas of something foreboding, hardly does justice to the process which only begins after an offender has been convicted. In this chapter the various sentence options available to the courts and the manner in which the correct punishment ought to be decided upon are discussed.

30.1 INTRODUCTION

Some thirty years ago a judge in the United States passed the following remark:

> "What happens to the offender after conviction is the least understood, the most fraught with irrational discrepancies, and the most in need of improvement of any phase in our criminal justice system."[1]

This statement is also relevant to the South African criminal process. Very little, if any, training is given at tertiary level in the art of sentencing. Magistrates aspiring for appointment in the district and regional criminal courts are required to undergo a course at the Department of Justice's training centre, Justice College, and during this course these candidates receive lectures covering the principles of punishment and aspects relating to specific sentence options. The lack of adequate formal training in the art of sentencing, together with the lack of established and generally accepted standards, often lead to a disparity in sentencing.

30.2 KEY OBJECTIVE

The key objective of this chapter is to enable students to:
- discuss the various sentence options provided for in the Criminal Procedure Act of 1977[2] and the considerations applicable at this stage of criminal proceedings.

30.3 APPLICABLE LAW

Adjustment of Fines Act 101 of 1991
Child Care Act 74 of 1983, section 14
Correctional Services Act 8 of 1959
Criminal Procedure Act 51 of 1977
Magistrates' Court Act 32 of 1944
Prevention and Treatment of Drug Dependency Act 20 of 1992
The 1993 Constitution
The 1996 Constitution

When dealing with sentencing and the various sentence options available, reference must be made to chapter 28 of the Criminal Procedure Act of 1977 which deals not only with the various sentence options but also with the procedure prior to and after sentencing. Chapter 27 of the same Act deals with previous convictions. This is highly relevant to the sentence process, and the pertinent sections therein will also be discussed.

→ The first section under chapter 28 of the Criminal Procedure Act of 1977, section 274, deals with evidence on sentence and the rights of the parties to address the court on the matter of sentence.

Section 275 of the Criminal Procedure Act of 1977 merely provides that another judicial officer, in the absence of the judicial officer who convicted the accused, may deal with the matter of sentence.

→ Section 276 of the Criminal Procedure Act of 1977 sets out the nature of punishments that a court may impose. Subsection (1) thereof reads:

"(1) Subject to the provisions of this Act and any other law and of the common law, the following sentences may be passed upon a person convicted of an offence, namely —

(*a*) the sentence of death;

(*b*) imprisonment, including imprisonment for life or imprisonment for an indefinite period as referred to in section 286B(1);

(*c*) periodical imprisonment;

(*d*) declaration as an habitual criminal;

(*e*) committal to an institution established by law;

(*f*) a fine;

(*g*) a whipping;

(*h*) correctional supervision;

(*i*) imprisonment from which such a person may be placed under correctional supervision in his discretion by the Commissioner."

Subsections (2) and (3) of section 276 contain supplementary provisions relating to the imposition of the provided-for sentences.

Section 276A deals with the imposition of correctional supervision and will be discussed in more detail later on.

Sections 277 to 279 deal with aspects relating to the sentence of death; because this sentence option no longer exists due to the Constitutional Court's having declared such sentence unconstitutional,[3] these sections will not be discussed.

Section 280 contains provisions relating to cumulative sentences and orders for the concurrent running of sentences.

→ Section 281 deals with the interpretation of certain provisions in other Acts relating to imprisonment and fines.

Section 282 provides for the antedating of a sentence in certain circumstances.

→ Section 283 deals with the discretionary powers a court has in regard to sentences.

→ Section 284 provides that the minimum period of imprisonment that may be imposed is four days unless the offender is sentenced to be detained until the rising of the court.

Section 285 governs the imposition of periodical imprisonment.

→ Section 286 deals with the declaration of an offender as a habitual criminal.

→ Section 286A deals with the declaration of an offender as a dangerous criminal and section 286B provides for the imposition of imprisonment for an indefinite period.

Section 287 provides for the imposition of imprisonment in default of payment of a fine.

Section 288 sets out the procedure or the steps to be taken for the recovery of a fine.

Section 289 provides for the procedure to be followed by a court to enforce payment of a fine.

Section 290 provides for the manner of dealing with juvenile offenders, whilst section 291 stipulates the duration of orders made in terms of the section.

Sections 292 to 295 deal with the imposition of whipping of adult and juvenile offenders.[4]

Section 296 provides for the committal of an offender to a treatment centre.

Section 297 provides for the conditional or unconditional postponement of the passing of sentence and for the conditional suspension of sentence, as well as for the discharge of an accused with a caution.

→ Section 298 provides for the correction of a wrong sentence and section 299 deals with the issue of a warrant for the execution of a sentence.

Section 92 of the Magistrates' Court Act of 1944[5] provides for the criminal jurisdiction of the magistrates' courts, district and regional courts.

→ Section 25 of the 1993 Constitution[6] (section 35 of the 1996 Constitution) sets out the fundamental rights of detained, arrested and accused persons, including sentenced prisoners.

Chapter 27 of the Criminal Procedure Act of 1977 is entitled "Previous Convictions" and contains four sections, sections 271, 271A, 272 and 273, relating to proving previous convictions, certain previous convictions falling away, what constitutes proof of such convictions and further particulars of same.

30.4   INTERPRETATION AND DISCUSSION

Sentencing is not easy to classify into a particular area of law for, although (as can be seen from the above-mentioned sections) the procedural rules are defined, the decision in respect of the actual sentence is left up to the individual sentencing officer. However, in terms of our system of precedent, the Supreme Courts have provided guidelines regarding the factors which must

be considered at this stage of the proceedings. In S v *Rabie*[7] the Appellate
Division stated clearly that:

> "Punishment should fit the criminal as well as the crime, be fair to
> society, and be blended with a measure of mercy according to the
> circumstances."

The process by which this is applied in our courts brings the personalisa-
tion (or individualisation) of punishment to the fore. The theories of punishment, namely retribution, deterrence, prevention and rehabilitation, will not
be discussed in any detail here.

Included in an accused's right to a fair trial (see section 25 of the 1993
Constitution and section 35 of the 1996 Constitution) is his or her right to be
sentenced within a reasonable time after conviction (section 25(3)(*j*) of the
1993 Constitution and section 35(3)(*d*) of the 1996 Constitution). The procedure followed in practice in our courts in regard to sentence can be divided
into the following: the presentence investigation phase (which includes hearing evidence), the address phase and the imposition of sentence phase.

30.4.1   The presentence phase

Once the accused has been convicted, the state will indicate whether or not
he or she has previous convictions. As mentioned above, chapter 27 of the
Criminal Procedure Act of 1977 regulates this process.

No definition of a previous conviction is given in the Criminal Procedure
Act of 1977. Our courts have, however, on occasion indicated that "previous
conviction" must be understood to be a finding of guilty to some or other
offence in a court of law.[8]

Section 271(4) of the Criminal Procedure Act of 1977 provides that the
court must, once previous convictions have been properly proven, take such
conviction into account when assessing sentence. It is obvious that where an
offender continually commits crimes he or she is a danger to the community
and that it is the court's duty to protect society by imposing a preventive and
deterrent sentence.

Despite an offender's having a number of previous convictions, should he
or she have a lengthy "clean" period prior to the latest transgression, this
ought to be taken into account when assessing sentence.

A previous conviction which is the subject of a pending appeal is not
regarded as a previous conviction — S v *Mazwi*.[9] Previous convictions, compiled from records held by the South African Police Criminal Record Centre,
are usually listed on form SAP 69. This form must be signed by the designated officer (commanding officer) at the Centre and when tendered it is
prima facie proof of the facts contained therein. In this regard see sections
271(1) and 272 of the Criminal Procedure Act of 1977.

The court must then ask the accused whether he or she admits or denies
the listed previous convictions. Should any be denied, the prosecutor must

decide whether or not to call evidence to prove the conviction so denied and the court will then decide the matter on evidence.

Although the importance of previous convictions declines with time, section 271A of the Criminal Procedure Act of 1977 provides that certain convictions fall away as previous convictions after a period of ten years if the accused has not been convicted of an offence for which he or she may receive a sentence of more than six months' imprisonment within the period of ten years following the last conviction. The convictions that fall away, however, are only those for which the passing of sentence was postponed and for which the accused was subsequently discharged with a caution (section 297(1)(*a*)(i) read with section 297(2)), or was deemed to have been discharged with a caution (section 297(1)(*a*)(ii) read with section 297(3)), or was actually discharged with a caution in terms of section 297(1)(*c*), and also any conviction for a less serious offence (that is, an offence for which the accused could not have received a sentence of more than six months' imprisonment).

Following this process, the court then proceeds either to hear any evidence that it considers necessary for sentence or any evidence that the parties may wish to present. The legislature stipulates in no less than three sections that evidence can be presented to the court with regard to sentence.

Where an accused pleads guilty and is convicted without evidence having been tendered, there is often very little information regarding the accused or other essentials upon which to determine sentence. Sections 112(3) and 140(4) of the Criminal Procedure Act of 1977 are identical and provide as follows:

✔ "Nothing in this section shall prevent the prosecutor from presenting evidence on any aspect of the charge, or the court from hearing evidence, including evidence or a statement by or on behalf of the accused, with regard to sentence, or from questioning the accused on any aspect of the case for the purposes of determining an appropriate sentence."

(These two sections, however, appear in chapters 17 and 20 respectively.)

The third section (and the first section under chapter 28) regarding evidence prior to sentence is section 274 of the Criminal Procedure Act of 1977, which reads as follows:

✔ "(1) A court may, before passing sentence, receive such evidence as it thinks fit in order to inform itself as to the proper sentence to be passed.

✔ (2) The accused may address the court on any evidence received under subsection (1), as well as on the matter of the sentence, and thereafter the prosecution may likewise address the court."

It is in terms of these provisions that aggravating factors and mitigating circumstances or factors are presented to the court. Although "mitigating circumstances" have not been defined, the legislature has statutorily defined the term "aggravating circumstances". In section 1 of the Criminal Procedure Act

448

of 1977 the following definition occurs:

" 'aggravating circumstances', in relation to

(b)   robbery or attempted robbery, means

(i)   the wielding of a firearm or any other dangerous weapon;

(ii)   the infliction of grievous bodily harm; or

(iii) a threat to inflict grievous bodily harm, by the offender or an accomplice on the occasion when the offence is committed, whether before or during or after the commission of the offence."

The legislature states emphatically that a perpetrator ("offender") or an accomplice is affected when aggravating circumstances are found to exist in regard to a robbery or an attempted robbery. The legislature requires some *nexus* with the crime (robbery or attempted robbery). The circumstances can arise before, during or after the commission of the offence.

Aggravating factors are not defined by the legislature. Aggravating factors are also not restricted to any single type of offence but they form part of the considerations relevant at sentencing stage in respect of any offence. Aggravating factors form part of the material considered at sentencing stage and which normally gives rise to a harsher sentence.

The effect of aggravating factors can give rise to:

- an increase in the moral blameworthiness of the accused in the eyes of the community;
- an increase in the reprehensibility of the accused's crime.

Contrary to the case of aggravating circumstances, the applicability of aggravating factors is not restricted to before, during or after the offence. For example, previous convictions are in certain circumstances an aggravating factor.

The accused and/or his or her legal representative can present mitigating factors to the court. The state (prosecutor) can do likewise. The court can, of its own accord, take note of mitigating factors. Mitigating factors can be presented via evidence and/or ex parte statements.

In practice it often happens that mitigating factors are outlined by way of unsworn ex parte statements by the accused and/or his or her legal representative. The state is asked whether it accepts such statements as correct and, if so, they are taken into account without further proof. Should the court feel that it cannot accept any particular fact placed before it in this manner, the accused and/or his or her legal representative should be informed of this to enable him or her to decide whether to lead evidence to establish the fact. In the latter case the state will have the opportunity of cross-examining any witnesses called. The state can also lead evidence in rebuttal.

Rabie and Strauss[10] list a number of generally accepted mitigating and aggravating factors gleaned from courts' judgments over the years.

Mention was made above to the fact that during this presentence phase evidence may also be heard; such evidence is, however, not restricted to the presentation of aggravating or mitigating factors, but includes evidence of probation officers or correctional officers tendered with the purpose of helping the court to arrive at a proper and just sentence.

30.4.2 The address phase

It is clear from section 274(2) of the Criminal Procedure Act of 1977 (quoted above) that after tendering of the "evidence", the accused (or his or her legal representative) and the prosecutor each have the right to address the court on the evidence as well on as the matter of sentence.

In practice, the accused or his or her legal representative will make use of this opportunity to request the most lenient sentence possible and could even go so far as to make suggestions regarding the nature and type of sentence that the court should impose. On the other hand, the prosecutor, on behalf of the state and as representative of the community, will call for a sentence that will demonstrate the court's outrage at the accused's behaviour, and will request almost the opposite of that requested by or on behalf of the accused, unless circumstances dictate otherwise. It must be borne in mind that it is required of a prosecutor to act fairly at all times and that his or her role does not now suddenly change to that of persecutor.

30.4.3 The imposition of sentence phase

Section 276, set out above, lists the sentences that may be passed by a court.

30.4.3.1 The death penalty

Although this sentence option has been declared unconstitutional, it is still listed under section 276(1) of the Criminal Procedure Act of 1977.[11] It will not be discussed as a sentence option here.

30.4.3.2 Imprisonment

The first option, following the now unconstitutional death penalty, is that of imprisonment (section 276(1)(*b*)). The court must, in the first instance, determine whether to remove the accused from society or whether to punish him or her within the community. Generally it is accepted that imprisonment is not to be lightly imposed. A careful and balanced decision regarding the offender's personal circumstances, the nature and extent of the offence and the interests of the community must be made when considering the imposition of imprisonment. The sentencer must continually be aware of not overemphasising or underemphasising any of these elements. The purpose of imprisonment is threefold.

The prime purpose of imprisonment is by its very nature retribution. The offender is punished for his or her misdeed. The offender's freedom is taken from him or her. He or she is cut off from family and friends. He or she is subject to the rules and regulations of the particular prison. The community (the victims) are satisfied that the offender's misdeeds have been avenged and that justice has been done.

Imprisonment is also imposed with the object of deterring the offender from committing similar (and other) offences (individual deterrence). In addition, imprisonment serves as a general deterrent. Others are, as a result of the imposition of imprisonment on the offender, deterred when it is shown that crime is not worth the gamble. At the same time society is protected by the imposition of imprisonment — firstly, by preventing a repetition of the crime and, secondly, by removing the offender from the community.

Incarceration of an offender provides an opportunity to reform or rehabilitate him or her. Rehabilitation is to the benefit of the offender and of the community. Section 2(2)(*b*) of the Correctional Services Act of 1959[12] provides that the function of the Department of Correctional Services is, as far as practicable, to apply such treatment to convicted prisoners and probationers as may lead to their reformation and rehabilitation and to train them in habits of industry and labour.

Section 92(1)(*a*) of the Magistrates' Court Act of 1944[13] reads as follows:

"Limits of jurisdiction in the matter of punishments. — (1) Save as otherwise in this Act or in any other law specially provided, the court, whenever it may punish a person for an offence —

(*a*) by imprisonment, may impose a sentence of imprisonment for a period not exceeding twelve months, where the court is not the court of a regional division, or not exceeding ten years, where the court is the court of a regional division;"

There are no hard and fast rules for imposing long-term imprisonment. In practice such imprisonment is generally reserved for cases where the offence is serious and/or the accused's character is such that the community must be protected against him or her.

Short-term imprisonment should not be resorted to too readily. There is little opportunity for rehabilitation of the offender in the short term and it can also lead to imprisonment losing its deterrent effect. The negative results of short-term imprisonment often nullify the appropriateness of imprisonment. This again emphasises the need for the trial court to exercise its discretion properly in regard to an appropriate sentence. Normally alternative forms of punishment, for example fines, suspended sentences, etc, ought to be considered. In the absence of a suitable alternative, short-term imprisonment can be imposed.

Section 284 of the Criminal Procedure Act of 1977 provides that the minimum period of imprisonment that may be imposed is four days, unless the offender is sentenced to be detained until the rising of the court.

Section 285 of the Criminal Procedure Act of 1977 deals with the imposition of periodical imprisonment, in lieu of any other punishment. Imprisonment thus cannot be imposed together with periodical imprisonment as punishment for a single offence.

Section 286(1) of the Criminal Procedure Act of 1977 provides that a superior court or a regional court may, if satisfied that an offender habitually commits offences and that the community should be protected against him or her and in lieu of any other punishment, declare such person a habitual criminal who will then be dealt with in accordance with the laws relating to prisons.

Section 286A of the Criminal Procedure Act of 1977 provides that a superior court or a regional court may, if satisfied that an offender represents a danger to the physical or mental wellbeing of other persons and that the community should be protected against such person, declare him or her a dangerous criminal.

In both cases the sentence is one of imprisonment, the length of which is not determined by the court. Section 65(4)(*b*)(iv) of the Correctional Services Act of 1959[14] states that a person who has been declared a habitual criminal is to be detained in prison for a period of at least seven years before he or she is placed on parole.

Section 286B(1) of the Criminal Procedure Act of 1977 provides that if a court has, in terms of section 286A, declared the person concerned to be a dangerous criminal, it shall sentence such a person to undergo imprisonment for an indefinite period. In addition, the court must direct that such person be brought before the court on the expiration of a period which may not exceed the jurisdiction of the court (for example, in the regional court, ten years). Note, the court determines this period and it commences from the date on which the person was sentenced to undergo imprisonment for an indefinite period.

In the case of a juvenile under the age of 21 years the court may deal with him or her in terms of section 290 of the Criminal Procedure Act of 1977 instead of imposing punishment.

Section 296(1) of the Criminal Procedure Act of 1977 provides that a person may, in addition to or in lieu of any sentence which may be imposed upon him or her, be ordered to be detained in a treatment centre established under the Prevention and Treatment of Drug Dependency Act of 1992,[15] provided that such order shall not be made in addition to any sentence of imprisonment (whether such imprisonment is direct or as an alternative to a fine), unless the whole of the sentence is suspended.

Section 332(2)(*c*) of the Criminal Procedure Act of 1977 provides that a person representing a corporate body, if convicted, shall not be given any punishment other than a fine.

A sentence of imprisonment terminates upon the last day of the period imposed, unless the prisoner is otherwise legally released.

Section 285(1) of the Criminal Procedure Act of 1977 provides that the imposition of periodical imprisonment is admissible in respect of all offences, other than those offences for which a minimum punishment is prescribed. Periodical imprisonment is imposed "in lieu of any other punishment", and it may therefore not be coupled with any other punishment.

Mention was made above of section 280; subsection 1 thereof stipulates that sentences are to be served cumulatively, that is, the one following the expiration, setting aside, or remission of the other. However, section 280(2) of the Criminal Procedure Act of 1977 authorises the court to order that two or more sentences of imprisonment be served concurrently — that is, that the periods will run together.

Although the Criminal Procedure Act of 1977 does not specifically provide therefor, the courts on occasion take counts together for the purposes of sentencing, thereby imposing one global sentence.

Section 282 of the Criminal Procedure Act of 1977 provides that, if a court of appeal or review sets aside any sentence of imprisonment and thereafter any sentence of imprisonment is again imposed, the court imposing such sentence may, if it is satisfied that the sentenced person served any part of the original sentence, order that the subsequently imposed sentence be antedated to a specified date (usually the date of the imposition of the original sentence), but not earlier than the date that the original sentence was imposed.

Section 276A(3) of the Criminal Procedure Act of 1977 provides for the conversion of certain sentences of imprisonment into correctional supervision, an aspect that will be discussed later.

30.4.3.3 Periodical imprisonment

Section 276(1)(*c*) refers to periodical imprisonment; this was commented on briefly above where reference was made to section 285 which governs the imposition of this form of imprisonment. Periodical imprisonment is normally imposed when the court is of the opinion that the offence warrants incarceration, but not on a full-time basis, and the accused has fixed employment which the court would not wish to interfere with. In such instances the accused is sentenced to a number of hours of periodical imprisonment, not exceeding 2000 hours and not less than 200 hours. The accused normally serves these hours over weekends. Again various factors, such as locality, determine the suitability of this punishment, as it can only be served at a prison and not in police cells.

30.4.3.4 Declaration of person as habitual criminal

Section 276(1)(*d*) provides for the declaration of a person as a habitual criminal as a sentence option; this too was referred to above, as it effectively amounts to imprisonment.

30.4.3.5 Committal to an institution

In terms of section 276(1)(*e*) the court may commit an accused to an institution established by law. Section 296 of the Criminal Procedure Act of 1977 governs the procedure in this regard. This type of sentence is usually imposed on persons requiring rehabilitation or treatment as a result of substance abuse. It will normally be considered if the addiction problem was the cause of the commission of the offence.

30.4.3.6 Fine

Section 276(1)(*f*) allows for the imposition of a fine as punishment.

Section 92(1)(*b*) of the Magistrates' Courts Act of 1944 determines the fine limit/jurisdiction of lower courts:

magistrates' court (district court): maximum R20 000;
regional court: maximum R200 000.

Section 283(1) of the Criminal Procedure Act of 1977 authorises a court to impose a lesser fine on someone who is punishable with a fine of any amount.

Section 287(1) of the Criminal Procedure Act of 1977 provides that, should a court impose a fine upon an accused, the court may impose imprisonment as an alternative sentence. The court is not obliged to impose alternative imprisonment. Should the accused not pay the fine which was imposed, and the court did not stipulate an alternative sentence of imprisonment, the court may order that the accused be brought before the court again and an alternative sentence of imprisonment may then be imposed (section 287(2)).

Section 288 of the Criminal Procedure Act of 1977 provides for the seizure and sale of a convicted person's movable property to enforce payment of a fine and, in the case of the Supreme Court, movable or immovable property in certain cases, even though an alternative term of imprisonment was imposed. The Supreme Court may authorise a lower court to issue a warrant of seizure for the convicted person's immovable property.

Section 289 of the Criminal Procedure Act of 1977 empowers a court to exact payment of the fine (the whole or any part) by seizure of money on the accused's person; or by recovering from his or her employer by means of a garnishee order any monies due, or to be due in future to him or her as salary or wages.

Section 297(5) of the Criminal Procedure Act of 1977, empowers a court to suspend the payment of an imposed fine until the expiration of a period not exceeding five years or on condition that the fine is paid over a period not exceeding five years in instalments and at intervals determined by the court. Section 297(6) of the Criminal Procedure Act of 1977 also allows a prisoner to be brought back to court so that the court can consider suspending the sentence on condition that the fine is paid in instalments.

Section 332(2)(*c*) of the Criminal Procedure Act of 1977 authorizes a court to impose only a fine upon the representative of a corporate body.

Various factors have to be considered by a court when deciding on the imposition of a fine as punishment. The court must decide firstly whether the offence justifies the imposition of a fine.

The sentencing officer must determine, against the background of all the circumstances of the case, whether the fine is an appropriate sentence.

Should the sentencing officer decide that a fine is in actual fact a suitable punishment for the offence, he or she must then determine what the amount of the fine must be in relation to the means of the accused.

An investigation must be conducted into the financial affairs of the accused, particularly into his or her ability to pay the fine either in a lump sum or over a period. Such period may not exceed five years (see section 297(5)). The Adjustment of Fines Act of 1991[16] stipulates that where any Act provides for a fine and/or imprisonment, and irrespective of whether the amount of the fine is specified in that Act or not, every twelve months' imprisonment provided for in such Act is equivalent to a fine of R20 000. The Act replaces, with certain specified exceptions, all existing penal provisions by using the maximum term of imprisonment prescribed for a particular offence as the basis for calculating the maximum amount of the fine that may be imposed. The Act stipulates that the ratio between the fine and the imprisonment is the same as the standard jurisdiction of a magistrate's court as contained in section 92(1) of the Magistrates' Court Act of 1944,[17] which is currently R20 000 per twelve months' imprisonment.

30.4.3.7 Correctional supervision

Subsections (*h*) and (*i*) of section 276(1) of the Criminal Procedure Act of 1977 provide for the imposition of correctional supervision and for imprisonment from which a person may be placed under correctional supervision. Although, in the latter instance, the sentence is strictly one of imprisonment, the procedure to be followed before the imposition of such imprisonment is prescribed in section 276A of the Criminal Procedure Act of 1977, which section also governs the imposition of correctional supervision and will thus be discussed here.

Section 276 A(1) of the Criminal Procedure Act of 1977 contains two requirements regarding the imposition of correctional supervision in terms of section 276(1)(*h*):

- a report from a probation officer or correctional officer regarding the accused must be presented to court;
- the period of correctional supervision must not exceed three years.

In practice the court must determine the period of correctional supervision, as well as the applicable conditions. Sight must not be lost of the practical implications of these conditions. According to case law, the passing of an appropriate sentence (including the conditions attached thereto) is the responsibility of the judicial officer and it may not, even with the imposition of correctional supervision, be abdicated to other instances or persons. In terms of section 276(3)(*b*) of the Criminal Procedure Act of 1977, this form of correctional supervision may be imposed for any offence. It is theoretically possible to impose correctional supervision with any other form of punishment mentioned in section 276(1) of the Criminal Procedure Act of 1977. Note that the provisions of section 280(2) of the Act provide that punishment of correctional supervision imposed in terms of section 276(1)(*b*) shall commence the one after the expiration, setting aside or remission of the other, in such order as the court may direct, unless the court orders that the correctional supervision periods run concurrently. An added proviso is that should the period of such punishments, on aggregate, exceed three years, a period of not more than three years shall be served, commencing from the date on which the first of the said periods commences, unless the court directs otherwise when imposing sentence.

In terms of section 276(1)(i) of the Criminal Procedure Act of 1977, the court may impose imprisonment from which the convicted person may be placed under correctional supervision at the discretion of the Commissioner of Correctional Services. Section 276 A (2) of the Criminal Procedure Act of 1977 again contains two requirements regarding the imposition of this sentence:

- the court must be of opinion that the offence justifies the imposition of imprisonment (with or without the option of a fine);
- such imprisonment must not exceed five years.

The Commissioner of Correctional Services may in terms of section 276A(3) of the Criminal Procedure Act of 1977 refer specific prisoners back to the court *a quo* for reconsideration of their sentences. Such an application (accompanied by a motivated recommendation) may only be submitted in respect of a prisoner whose effective remaining sentence (taking cognisance of the Department of Correctional Services release policy) is, on the date of application, five years' imprisonment or less. The procedure to be followed in such an application is detailed in section 276A(3) of the Criminal Procedure Act of 1977. After the court *a quo* has reconsidered a sentence under this section, the court may:

- confirm the existing sentence or order;
- convert the sentence to one of correctional supervision on such conditions as it may deem necessary;
- impose any other proper sentence — on condition that the latter sentence, if imprisonment, shall not exceed the period of the unexpired portion of imprisonment still to be served at that stage.

A court which has sentenced a person in terms of section 276(1)(*b*) or section 276(1)(*i*), or converted his or her sentence under section 276 A(3)(*e*)(ii) of the Criminal Procedure Act of 1977, whether constituted differently or not, may, on the basis of a motivated recommendation by a probation officer or the Commissioner of Correctional Services, find that the person is not fit to be subject to correctional supervision. The court concerned may in this instance, in terms of section 276A(4), reconsider that punishment and impose another appropriate punishment. The procedure under section 276A(3) of the Criminal Procedure Act of 1977 applies *mutatis mutandis.*

Section 287(4) of the Criminal Procedure Act of 1977 makes provision for the conversion of imprisonment (which has been imposed as an alternative to a fine) to correctional supervision. The section contains two requirements for the conversion of imprisonment to correctional supervision:

- the alternative imprisonment must not exceed five years;.
- the court imposing the sentence must not have directed otherwise.

The Commissioner of Correctional Services may, firstly, act in terms of section 287(4) of the Criminal Procedure Act of 1977, as if the convicted person has been sentenced to imprisonment as referred to in section 276(1)(*i*) of the Act. This means that the Commissioner of Correctional Services may at his discretion (without the court's intervention) convert the imprisonment to correctional supervision. Secondly, the Commissioner of Correctional Services may apply under section 287(4)(*b*) of the Criminal Procedure Act of 1977 for a reconsideration of such sentence by the court *a quo*. This may possibly only occur if a long period of alternative imprisonment had been imposed and uncertainty exists as to whether conversion is appropriate. Note that the prisoner's period of correctional supervision is reduced in proportion to any amount paid as a fine.

Section 290(1)(*a*) and 290(3) of the Criminal Procedure Act of 1977 enable a court to place any accused who is under the age of 18 years and between 18 and 21 years, respectively (instead of imposing punishment upon him or her or imposing any of the sentences which are specifically provided), under the supervision of a correctional official. In practice this will be tantamount to a monitoring of the supervisional case by a correctional officer.

Section 291(5) of the Criminal Procedure Act of 1977 provides for the reconsideration of any of the orders issued in terms of sections 290(1) or (3) of the Act. These orders may only be reconsidered if it appears that the offender, during such supervision or stay at the reform school, is not fit for such supervision or stay. This consideration has to be preceded by a motivated report from a probation or correctional officer or the person in charge of the reform school or his or her assignee. In such case the provisions of section 276A(4) of the Criminal Procedure Act of 1977 are applicable *mutatis mutandis*.

The standard conditions attached to a sentence of correctional supervision normally include house arrest, monitoring, community service and attendance of certain stipulated programmes.

Section 84B of the Correctional Services Act of 1959[18] contains a comprehensive exposition of what the relevant authorities may do should the person under supervision fail to comply with the conditions of his or her correctional supervision.

30.4.3.8 Postponement of the passing of sentence and suspension of sentence

Finally, under the sentence phase, mention must be made of section 297(1) of the Criminal Procedure Act of 1977, dealing with the postponement of the passing of sentence and the suspension of an imposed sentence, as well as providing for an order discharging an accused person with a caution (section 297(1)(*c*)). The period of postponement or suspension may not exceed five years.

Whenever the legislature prescribes a minimum sentence, the option of postponing the passing of sentence may not be used and only part of such sentence may be suspended (section 297(1) and 297(4)). Any part may be suspended, even the whole sentence, as long as the accused is ordered in such a case to be detained until the rising of the court.

The passing of a sentence can be conditionally postponed subject to any of the conditions listed under section 297(1)(*aa*) to (*hh*), or the accused can be released unconditionally but yet warned to appear if called upon so to do within the period of postponement. A sentence may not be unconditionally suspended.

The same conditions listed under section 297(1) apply in regard to suspended sentences. Various factors must be taken into account when considering whether to suspend a portion or the whole of the sentence and under what conditions.

The general rules here are the following:

- there must be some relationship between the nature of the offence and the condition imposed;
- the condition(s) must be stated clearly and unambiguously; and
- the condition(s) must be fair and reasonable.

Sections 297(7), 297(8) and 297(9) set out the procedure to be followed in the case of non-compliance with any stipulated condition.

30.4.3.9 Juvenile offenders

Two sections, namely sections 254 and 290, of the Criminal Procedure Act of 1977 deal with options available to the courts in respect of juvenile offenders. A juvenile can, of course, be dealt with under any of the above-mentioned sentence options.

Section 254 of the Criminal Procedure Act of 1977 reads as follows:

"Court may refer juvenile accused to children's court

(1) If it appears to the court at the trial upon any charge of any accused under the age of eighteen years that he is a child as referred to in section 14(4) of the Child Care Act, 1983 (Act 74 of 1983), and that it is desirable to deal with him in terms of sections 13, 14 and 15 of that Act, it may stop the trial and order that the accused be brought before a children's court mentioned in section 5 of that Act and that he be dealt with under the said sections 13, 14 and 15.

(2) If the order under subsection (1) is made after conviction, the verdict shall be of no force in relation to the person in respect of whom the order is made and shall be deemed not to have been returned."

This section deals with the category of juveniles under the age of 18 years facing any charge. As a starting point the juvenile accused's age will have to be determined even before considering the provisions of section 14(4) of the Child Care Act of 1983. Once it has been determined that the accused is under the age of 18 years, the court will then have to determine whether this juvenile falls within the ambit of section 14(4) of the Child Care Act of 1983.[19]

Various factors must be considered before invoking the provisions of this section. Stopping the trial in terms of section 254 of the Criminal Procedure Act of 1977 means just that; once it has ordered that the accused be taken before a children's court, the criminal proceedings cease.

The other section dealing with the convicted juvenile is section 290 of the Criminal Procedure Act of 1977, which reads:

"**290 Manner of dealing with convicted juvenile**

(1)   Any court in which a person under the age of eighteen years is convicted of any offence may, instead of imposing punishment upon him for that offence —

(*a*)   order that he be placed under the supervision of a probation officer or a correctional official; or

(*b*)   order that he be placed in the custody of any suitable person designated in the order; or

(*c*)   deal with him both in terms of paragraphs *(a)* and *(b)*; or

(*d*)   order that he be sent to a reform school as defined in section 1 of the Child Care Act, 1983 (Act 74 of 1983).

(2)   Any court which sentences a person under the age of eighteen years to a fine *or a whipping*[20] may, in addition to imposing such punishment, deal with him in terms of paragraph *(a)*, *(b)*, *(c)* or *(d)* of subsection (1)." [Our emphasis]

Section 290 creates three different situations or categories:

(i)   juveniles under the age of 18 years who can be dealt with *instead* of punishment being imposed;

(ii)   juveniles under the age of 18 years who are fined; and

(iii)   juveniles of or over the age of 18 years but under the age of 21 years who can be dealt with *instead* of punishment being imposed.

Section 291 of the Criminal Procedure Act of 1977 provides for the duration of section 290 orders, emphasising again the necessity of an accurate and proper age determination. The period is set at two years unless the court, at the time of making the order, determines a shorter period.

30.4.4   Conclusion

The 1993 Constitution and the 1996 Constitution have not affected the sentence phase of criminal proceedings, except where mention is made of the two types of punishment regarded as cruel and inhumane, namely the death penalty and whipping. The accused's right to be sentenced within a reasonable time is no innovation but a practice, albeit unwritten, which existed in the past. The fact that it is now a written right will obviously avail an accused of a remedy should any court allow proceedings, particularly at sentence stage, to drag on unnecessarily.

It was mentioned above that the task of the prosecutor does not end after conviction but that he or she is required to play a far more active role in regard to sentence. The same applies here to police officials, particularly investigators, as their close working with the offender(s) at time of arrest, as well as the evidence that they uncover during their investigations, can often be of assistance not only to the prosecutor but to the court as well. An aspect that comes to mind in this regard, and that is not dealt with in this chapter, is that of victim compensation, either by way of a separate order in terms of section 300 of the Criminal Procedure Act of 1977, or as a condition of suspension of a sentence (see section 297(1)(*b*) read with subsection (*a*)(i)(*aa*)). An investigator's knowledge in this regard might prove invaluable to the court when deciding on sentence, which could also result in victim compensation being utilised as it ought to be.

30.5   SUGGESTED READING AND SOURCES

Du Toit, E, De Jager, F, Paizes, A, Skeen, A & Van der Merwe, S. 1996. *Commentary on the Criminal Procedure Act*. Cape Town: Juta.

Ferreira, JC. 1979. *Strafproses in die Laer Howe*, 2 ed. Cape Town: Juta.

Geldenhuys, T & Joubert, JJ. *Criminal Procedure Handbook*, 2 ed.

Kriegler, J. 1993. *Hiemstra Suid-Afrikaanse Strafproses*, 5 ed. Durban: Butterworths.

Rabie, MA & Mare, MC. 1994. *Punishment. An Introduction to Principles*, 5 ed. Cape Town: Lex Patria.

·····················

ENDNOTES

1   *United States v Waters* 437F 2d 722 723 DC Civ 1970.

2   Act 51 of 1977.

3   *S v Makwanyane* 1995 (2) SACR 1 (CC).

4   In *S v Williams* 1995 (2) SACR 251 (CC) the question whether whipping imposed on juvenile male offenders is cruel and inhuman was decided and as such whipping was indeed declared unconstitutional; this will not be discussed here.

5   Act 32 of 1944.

6   Act 200 of 1993.

   1975 (4) SA 855 (A).

8   See *Weller* 1961 (2) SA 743 (A); *Rantsho* 1974 (4) SA 418 (T) and *Greveling* 1976 (2) SA 103 (O). In *Sullivan* 1977 (3) SA 1001 (RA) the court held that it was also required that the accused be sentenced.

9   *S v Mazwi* 1982 (2) SA 344 (T).

10   Rabie & Strauss.

11   See *S v Makwanyane* 1995 (2) SACR 1 (CC) for the court's reasons for declaring it unconstitutional.

12   Act 8 of 1959 as amended.

13   Act 32 of 1944.

14   Act 8 of 1959.

15   Act 20 of 1992.

16   Act 101 of 1991.

17   Act 32 of 1944.

18   Act 8 of 1959.

19   Section 14(4) in turn reads as follows:

"(4) At such inquiry the children's court shall determine whether —

     (*a*)   the child has no parent or guardian; or

     (*aA*) the child has a parent or guardian who cannot be traced; or

     (*b*)   the child has a parent or a guardian or is in the custody of a person who is unable or unfit to have the custody of the child, in that he —

        (i)   is mentally ill to such a degree that he is unable to provide for the physical, mental or social well-being of the child;

        (ii)   has assaulted or ill-treated the child or allowed him to be assaulted or ill-treated;

        (iii)   has caused or conducted to the seduction, abduction or prostitution of the child or the commission by the child of immoral acts;

        (iv)   displays habits and behaviour which may seriously injure the physical, mental or social well-being of the child;

        (v)   fails to maintain the child adequately;

        (vi)   maintains the child in contravention of section 10;

        (vii) neglects the child or allows him to be neglected;

        (viii) cannot control the child properly so as to ensure proper behaviour such as regular school attendance;

        (ix)   has abandoned the child; or

        (x)   has no visible means of support."

20   In view of the decision by the Constitutional Court in *S v Williams* 1995 (2) SACR 251 (CC) that the words "or a whipping" (italicised in section 290(2) supra) are unconstitutional and thus invalid and of no force and effect, the section must be read as if the words no longer appear therein.